The Underground Church

Studies in Critical Social Sciences Book Series

Haymarket Books is proud to be working with Brill Academic Publishers (www.brill.nl) to republish the *Studies in Critical Social Sciences* book series in paperback editions. This peer-reviewed book series offers insights into our current reality by exploring the content and consequences of power relationships under capitalism, and by considering the spaces of opposition and resistance to these changes that have been defining our new age. Our full catalog of *SCSS* volumes can be viewed at www.haymarketbooks.org/category/scss-series.

Series Editor
David Fasenfest, Wayne State University

Editorial Board
Chris Chase-Dunn, University of California–Riverside
G. William Domhoff, University of California–Santa Cruz
Colette Fagan, Manchester University
Martha Gimenez, University of Colorado, Boulder
Heidi Gottfried, Wayne State University
Karin Gottschall, University of Bremen
Bob Jessop, Lancaster University
Rhonda Levine, Colgate University
Jacqueline O'Reilly, University of Brighton
Mary Romero, Arizona State University
Chizuko Ueno, University of Tokyo

The Underground Church

Nonviolent Resistance to the Vatican Empire

Kathleen Kautzer

Haymarket Books
Chicago, IL

First published in 2012 by Brill Academic Publishers, The Netherlands
© 2012 Koninklijke Brill NV, Leiden, The Netherlands

Published in paperback in 2013 by
Haymarket Books
P.O. Box 180165
Chicago, IL 60618
773-583-7884
www.haymarketbooks.org

ISBN: 978-1-60846-281-0

Trade distribution:
In the U.S. through Consortium Book Sales, www.cbsd.com
In the UK, Turnaround Publisher Services, www.turnaround-psl.com
In Australia, Palgrave Macmillan, www.palgravemacmillan.com.au
In all other countries by Publishers Group Worldwide, www.pgw.com

Cover design by Ragina Johnson.

This book was published with the generous support of the Lannan Foundation and the Wallace Global Fund.

Printed in the United States.

10 9 8 7 6 5 4 3 2 1

Library of Congress Cataloging-in-Publication Data is available.

For Lily and Curran Chunn, my source of inspiration and hope for the future

CONTENTS

Series Editor's Preface ix
Foreword xi
Preface xv
Abbreviations of Catholic Reform Groups xvii

Introduction 1

PART ONE

BURNED OUT, BUMMED OUT, AND THROWN OUT:
PROGRESSIVE REFORMERS BEGIN THEIR WILDERNESS JOURNEY

1. Sower of Mustard Seeds: Call to Action 41
2. Rebuilding the Temple: Voice of the Faithful 55
3. Leaving Egypt: DignityUSA, Corps of Reserve Priests United
   for Service, Catholic Organizations for Renewal 85
4. Catholic Feminists Confront Goliath: Women's
   Ordination Conference, Women's Ordination Worldwide,
   Women-Church Convergence, Women's Alliance for
   Theology, Ethics and Ritual, Catholics for Choice 111
5. Toward a New City of God 135

PART TWO

TESTING THE WATERS AND PUSHING THE BOUNDARIES

6. Prophets without Honor: Vatican II Pastors are
   Disappearing 149
7. What Therefore Belongs to Caesar? Marginal
   Communities 169

PART THREE

NOTES FROM THE UNDERGROUND

8. The Catacombs Revisited: Underground Catholic
   Faith Communities 201
9. Something New Under the Sun? Underground Parishes 225

Conclusion 269

APPENDICES

Appendix A: Comparative Data on Vatican II Reform
   Organizations 307
Appendix B: Field Research 311

Bibliography 317
Index 335

SERIES EDITOR'S PREFACE

Vatican II not only initiated a process of reform in the Roman Catholic Church, but gave birth to the Reform Movement which has sought to continue this process. With the elections of Popes John Paul II and Benedict XVI, the Vatican moved back in a more traditional and conservative direction. The reform movement is a democratic religious movement composed of religious movement organizations. Its primary concerns are equality based on gender and sexual orientation as well as challenging abuses that have taken place within the church. Initially, it pursued insider strategies but frustrated by the Vatican's resistance to change, many involved in it have chosen an exit strategy and established independent Catholic churches. Unlike sects as understood by Ernst Troeltsch or Rodney Stark, these churches are not composed of the less affluent and less educated, but rather of the educated middle class who are in lower tension with this world. The Reform Movement is a movement of religious rationalization which exists in an ongoing dialectical tension with the traditional conservative Catholic hierarchy. This book *The Underground Church: Nonviolent Resistance to the Vatican Empire* by Kathleen Kautzer describes not only the organizations and churches of the reform movement, but the dynamic between it and the ossified patriarchal structure it seeks to reform. Thus understood, it not only employs a critical framework but the movement and countermovement it describes fits well with the mission of this series.

Warren S. Goldstein
Center for Critical Research on Religion
and Harvard University
Massachusetts USA

FOREWORD

I had the pleasure of teaching with sociologist Dr. Kathleen Kautzer at Regis College near Boston. It was a women's Catholic College at the time. Feminism permeated its culture and academics. As Religious Studies Ethics Professor, I led student discussions of challenges facing women in business, nursing, and religion. Dr. Kautzer, with her keen sociologist's eye, examined similar issues, but, I felt, often in a more holistic and experiential way than I.

I became very intrigued when I learned of her research into what was happening with Roman Catholic Womenpriests. This topic was strictly taboo in the eyes of church authorities, who later tried to enforce a ban on even discussing it. But forging ahead, Dr. Kautzer proposed to expand this research to include a comprehensive study of the Catholic Reform Movement as a whole.

This was a subject of great interest to me, growing up as I had in a pre-Vatican II world of the 1940s and '50s. I confess to being a true believer in those days, taking immense comfort in the enduring unchangeability of the Roman Catholic Church, with its absolute certitudes and clear-cut laws mapping out the path to salvation. Yes, the rules were often harsh, and hellfire loomed ever menacing, but the clarity and certitude seemed to make it all worthwhile.

This all changed in the 1960s. The Second Vatican Council shook up an institutional church that had become complacent and moribund. The fresh air let in by the reforms of the Council freed Catholics up to respond to the changing world. Dialogue with other religions was opened up; church authority was to become more collegial and shared; freedom for all religions in civil society was affirmed.

These freedoms newly enjoyed by Catholics coincided with a cultural revolution occurring in the wider society affecting politics, morality, and religion. Religious and political authority could no longer command unquestioning obedience. Sexual freedom replaced sexual repression. A kind of religious anarchy sprang up on Catholic college campuses. There was the spectacle of many nuns abandoning their religious garb and priests their roman collars. Others questioned their vocations, and left to join the laity. Small groups of Catholics experimented with the Eucharist, holding services in dormitory rooms using leavened rather than unleavened bread for Eucharist, and in rarer cases Coca-Cola and cookies replaced wine and bread.

Such initial giddy experiments had no staying power. But soon Catholics set out in earnest to implement and institutionalize Vatican II's reforms. They welcomed vernacular liturgy and increased lay participation. But reformers felt that these baby steps did not address systemic injustices such as the unequal treatment of women and the lack of redress for abuses of clerical power. The equal treatment and respect for human dignity that Catholics expected in their civic life was sorely lacking in their religious life.

Sociologists of knowledge like Peter Berger and Thomas Luckmann explained how worldviews are created by the societies in which people move. "We choose our beliefs by choosing our playmates," Peter Berger would say. Abuses of authority were quick to be challenged. The taken-for-granted view that women in the church could not be priests was called into question. Moral absolutes became relativized, as alternative belief systems entered the everyday consciousness of Catholics. Reformers began to selectively shape their communities around beliefs like these.

Particularly upsetting to hierarchs was a new resistance to the clerical caste system. Reformers were no longer content to accept a church divided into the powerful priest-Christians and the disempowered lay-Christians, into a clerical caste and outcastes, into pastors and sheep, into authorities who command and the rest who obey, into men who could aspire to a full priestly Christianity and women who were to be excluded.

The Vatican began in earnest to back away from the freedoms unleashed by Vatican II. Gone was its absolute grip on power. The top-down governing style no longer worked. The church entrusted to them appeared to be dissolving before their very eyes. So the hierarchs pushed back. And in doing so they began to drive the reform groups underground. The account of these tensions is the story that Dr. Kautzer recounts in this amazing book on the underground church.

Reports about parishes and groups that seemed to exist mysteriously in the shadows began to pop up in the press. People, myself included, began to wonder. Who belong to these communities? What is their relation to the Roman Catholic Church? Are their members loyal Catholics, or schismatic Catholics, or have they broken all ties? How do they view authority, or women's roles, or the creeds that define a Roman Catholic believer? Such communities were springing up everywhere, mostly as independent experiments in how to live as Vatican II Catholics in the face of Vatican disapproval. How was a person like me, vitally interested in reform, to get a hold on what was going on? Nobody had done a comprehensive systematic study of this complex and mostly invisible movement that was coming to be known as "the underground church."

Dr. Kautzer has undertaken the daunting task of first of all describing who these groups are, and then analyzing them using sociology, political science, anthropology, and theology. She uncovers the forces that pushed them to evolve in different ways and to engage in different strategies. She learned that these communities, while operating with little publicity at the margins of the mainline church, had no intention of subverting the church and every intention of being authentically loyal to the essentials of Catholic tradition.

Dr. Kautzer's study is experience based, drawing on interviews she conducted in the field with representatives of the full gamut of reform communities. She is right to claim her study to be "the only critical comprehensive study of the Catholic Reform Movement" (p. · · ·). She brings these communities out of the shadows and into the light. She gives them a face and a voice. She establishes their place and illumines the vital roles they play within the larger religious world, and in society at large. No one else has done this. We owe her a great debt of thanks for this invaluable research.

How will all this play out? Dr. Kautzer points out some cracks in the Movement. First, the implacable opposition of Rome is causing increasing ambivalence among reformers about what loyalty means in such a church. Second, Eucharist is central to the Catholic faith. Where will the priests come from? Will they be clerics, women and men ordained by schismatic bishops? Or lay priests, exercising "the priesthood of the faithful" conferred by Baptism? Recall that Jesus did not ordain any priests. Finally, the structures of these communities are unstable. This makes accountability and continuity difficult to maintain.

But there is hope. There are "rumors of angels," as Peter Berger might say. The "spiritual but not religious" mantra invoked by Catholic Christians is enlivened by

- a faith not in dogmas or condemnations but in a relation to a loving God, more present to me than I am to myself;
- hints of the divine discovered in science, philosophy, literature, and the arts;
- interreligious dialogue that reveals God speaking to us in many voices;
- and most of all, in the divine encountered through service to the poor and disenfranchised.

In the light of the unforeseeable outcomes presented us by Dr. Kautzer, a modest spiritual stance recommends itself:

1. Start here where you are.
2. Breathe as you go—eyes open, stay attentive.
3. Let go of expectations —The Spirit blows where it will.
4. Wait for the surprise.

Ed Stevens, Ph.D

PREFACE

Almost from the beginning of my research, I recognized that the Reform Movement of Vatican II Catholics highlighted in this study was fading in the face of increasingly hostile responses from American bishops and the rightward drift of recent papacies. The emergence of Voice of the Faithful (VOTF) in 2002 revitalized hope among some reformers when a broad range of Catholics mobilized in response to the deceit and malfeasance revealed by the clergy abuse crisis. Although VOTF drew widespread media attention, I quickly became convinced that VOTF's strategy of seeking concessions from staunchly conservative church hierarchs was doomed, particularly since the abuse crisis revealed deeply entrenched and far-reaching systemic problems in church governance. Vatican officials believed, perhaps correctly, that they could protect their own authority only by warding off any efforts at dialogue or reconciliation with reform groups, even ones as deferential as VOTF.

Although I recognized the formidable odds facing the Reform Movement, I remained convinced that it was a worthy focus for research. Even unsuccessful movements offer valuable insights for scholars in terms of documenting distinctive religious movements and analyzing reasons for their demise. Moreover, this movement can claim a few modest achievements. By focusing negative media attention on church authorities and by supporting lawsuits of clergy abuse victims, reformers did succeed in convincing church officials to adopt new policies regarding abuse and finances. The movement's advocacy for a range of liberal reforms also won support from broad sectors of the American Catholic laity.

More important, although many reform groups did experience massive defections, the movement has retained a vital core of activists, who have redirected their focus toward the creation of independent worship communities that give shape and substance to their vision of a renewed Catholicism. Although these emerging communities are fragile, they have generated hope and constructive efforts among reformers, who are no longer constrained by Vatican decrees. These communities exhibit a vibrant and forward-looking spirit, and a conviction that their vision is more viable and authentic than the backward-looking focus of the Vatican.

According to Catholic theologian O'Murchu (2010), the course pursued by reformers in my study reflects the appropriate response to a deeply entrenched power structure like the Roman Catholic Church; it cannot be reformed from within because resistance to reform is "too deeply rooted" (p. 26). O'Murchu advises, "What needs to happen for a religion like Roman Catholicism is for the people to withdraw their projections and give their energy instead to creative alternatives" (p. 36). Reformers arrived at this strategy by default, after decades of losing ground in their efforts at insider reform. As O'Murchu states, this stance by reformers "evokes and invites a whole different sense of what it means to be a religious believer and what it means to a participant in a credible faith community" (p. 37).

It remains to be seen whether these independent communities will attract the numbers and resources necessary to sustain themselves. By their very nature, religious movements are diffuse and their goals are often diverse and far-reaching. Thus, the long-term significance and accomplishments of this movement may not be obvious for many decades.

I am indebted to many persons for support during this research process. First, I would like to acknowledge the support of my husband, Clifton Chunn, and my children, Lily and Curran Chunn, who provided invaluable moral support, technical assistance, and a range of advice and dialogue. I am indebted to many of my colleagues at Regis College, including Deans Sarah Barrett, Paula Harbecke, and Pam Menke; faculty colleagues Ann Grady, Deb Cohan, Jan Leary, Ed Stevens, and Lauress Wilkins; and many members of the library and ITS staff, especially Eleanor Deady and Cecilia Roberts. These colleagues provided encouragement, advice, and a range of professional assistance. I was fortunate to receive a grant from Virginia Kaneb, an alumnus of Regis College, who has provided generous funding of research by Regis College faculty. I was also awarded several faculty development grants and a sabbatical from Regis College. These funds provided course releases and travel funds that were invaluable in completing my research. I owe a special debt of gratitude to Warren Goldstein, editor of the book series Studies in Critical Research on Religion, who provided patient, in-depth, and invaluable guidance in designing and expanding my theoretical framework and in preparing my manuscript for publication. My copy editor, Andrea Lee, has proven to be not just a superb copy editor but also a friend and advisor who played a significant role in shaping the manuscript. Finally, I would like to express gratitude to the numerous audiences (at academic conferences and reform group gatherings) who responded enthusiastically to my presentations and offered suggestions and new information, as well as to the many reformers whom I interviewed and who invited me to their gatherings and engaged in extensive correspondence.

ABBREVIATIONS OF CATHOLIC REFORM GROUPS*

ARCC	Association for the Rights of Catholics in the Church seeks to reform governance structures in the Roman Catholic Church.
CTA	Call to Action USA is a clearinghouse for reform groups.
CFC	Catholics for Choice promotes reproductive rights.
CITI	Celibacy Is the Issue provides certification and an online directory for married priests.
COR	Catholic Organizations for Renewal is a network of reform groups.
CORPUS	Corps of Reserve Priests United for Service is an association of married priests.
DignityUSA	DignityUSA promotes the rights of GLBT Catholics.
ECC	Ecumenical Catholic Communion is a network of independent Catholic communities.
FutureChurch	FutureChurch is a parish-based coalition that promotes women's equality and preserving parishes.
RCWP	Roman Catholic Womenpriests provides noncanonical training and ordination for women and men.
VOTF	Voice of the Faithful is an insider reform group that seeks to end clergy abuse and give laity a voice in policy making.
WATER	Women's Alliance for Theology, Ethics and Ritual is a think tank involved in feminist education and advocacy.
W-CC	Women-Church Convergence is a grassroots coalition of feminist reform groups.
WOC	Women's Ordination Conference is a feminist advocacy organization in the United States.
WOW	Women's Ordination Worldwide is an international feminist advocacy organization.

---

* More extensive data about these groups is provided in a chart in the Appendix A.

INTRODUCTION

Resurrecting the Spirit and Legacy of Vatican II

Since the 1970s, liberal American Catholics have sustained a Reform Movement to counteract the conservative drift of the Vatican and to preserve and expand on the vision and reforms of Vatican II. The Reform Movement, composed of highly educated, middle-class Catholics, is intent on creating an alternative model of church that exemplifies Vatican II's open, receptive attitude toward the modern world. In response to reformers' demands, church hierarchs have censured outspoken reformers and codified their conservative beliefs in formal church dogma and policy. This backlash from church officials has pushed liberal reformers in a sectarian direction, whereby they take positions and form worship communities outside Vatican control. By distancing themselves from the Vatican, reformers hope to resolve the tension inherent in their status as Catholics who cannot live with the restrictions imposed by reactionary church leaders, but cannot live without some connection to their Catholic roots.

Many observers of Vatican II reformers have decried their efforts by citing the mantra "No one takes on the Vatican and wins." Contrary to this mantra, the Reform Movement can claim modest but significant achievements that did not require approval of church hierarchs but do weaken Vatican authority. This Reform Movement, which represents as many as one hundred thousand Catholics and several hundred reform groups, can cite achievements in three areas:

1. Scholars credit the movement with influencing the views of American Catholics, a majority of whom now express liberal views on contraception, divorce, homosexuality, and equal roles for women.
2. The movement has effectively used pressure tactics, especially negative media attention and lawsuits by victims of clergy abuse, to achieve reforms in church policy regarding clergy abuse, financial accountability, and parish closures.
3. Many reform groups have attained autonomy from the Vatican by establishing worship communities outside Vatican control.

By creating *underground* worship communities, reformers hope to preserve essential features of their Catholic tradition while embracing new liturgical and governance systems that embody a more inclusive, democratic, and (in their view) authentic community engaged in the spiritual challenges of the modern and postmodern world. Corps of Reserve Priests United for Service (CORPUS) leader Anthony Padovano (2007a), among the most eloquent spokespersons for the Reform Movement, uses biblical imagery to capture their vision of "a new city of God on a distant mountain in an alien land" (p. 20). Thus, reformers aim not merely to restore Vatican II principles but also to redesign the entire structure from the bottom up, creating a church capable of meeting the challenges of the twenty-first century and beyond.

Liberal reform groups are likely to remain ineffectual in the short term. Nonetheless, reformers hope to lay the groundwork for future reform with ongoing efforts to educate and mobilize lay Catholics regarding reformers' key issues and the deeply entrenched flaws in current church structure. These structural flaws were exposed in 2002 when the clergy abuse crisis revealed widespread cover-ups and malfeasance on the part of many church hierarchs. In 2006 a study of Catholic dioceses in the United States revealed widespread financial mismanagement, whereby 85 percent of seventy-eight dioceses that responded to the survey reported embezzlement over the last five years (P. Feuerherd, 2006b, p. 18).

Although reformers continue to press for reform on key issues, privately they often acknowledge that the contemporary wave of the Reform Movement may fade in a decade or less, given the graying of the movement and the widespread apathy regarding church reform among most sectors of the laity, especially young Catholics. Scholars with expertise on Catholic issues have also predicted the demise of the Reform Movement, particularly since Pope Benedict XVI eased public concerns over the clergy abuse during his May 2008 visit to the United States when he pledged to end the crisis and engaged in an unprecedented meeting with abuse victims (Van Biema, 2008).[1]

---

[1] Public dismay over the clergy abuse crisis was reignited in 2010 with revelations of cover-ups and mishandling of clergy abuse by clerics in many European countries, including Pope Benedict during his tenure as Prefect for the Congregation for the Doctrine of the Faith (CDF). However, protests over these new revelations have surfaced primarily in Europe. Chapter 2 cites a range of studies indicating that many American Catholics have moved past the initial shock and outrage over the abuse crisis and are relatively complacent, as evidenced by more or less positive evaluations of American bishops.

Liberal Catholics: An Endangered Species?

I chose to undertake this study for the following reasons. First, I have a long-term interest and fascination with the Roman Catholic Reform Movement, in part as a result of participating for almost a decade in a spirituality group of women who were long-term activists in this movement. I wonder how these women sustain their activism and hope for reform in the face of continual stonewalling or setbacks. Does their activism undermine or enhance their spiritual development? To what extent does their spirituality serve as a source of motivation and inspiration for their efforts?

Second, I question whether the Reform Movement is merely a quixotic movement that appeals primarily to long-term Catholics who are unwilling to sever their ties with the institutional church. Does the movement offer any realistic hope of achieving structural reforms in the Roman Catholic Church in the near or long term? Does the movement command sufficient resources and are its strategies capable of achieving concrete concessions and structural reform?

Third, I am interested in documenting and analyzing the paths pursued by Roman Catholics who have given up on reform efforts yet sustain their loyalty to the Catholic tradition by creating worship communities that the Vatican has not authorized or approved. In this regard, I explore the structure, leadership, and viability of marginal and independent communities, since these issues take center stage and remain controversial within the Reform Movement.

Assessing the Movement: Is the Vatican Invincible?

Findings of the study center on several points. First, the Reform Movement sustains and enriches the spiritual search of reformers by providing them with a community of like-minded seekers who share their ambivalent relationship with Roman Catholicism and their enthusiasm for issues pertaining to religion and spirituality. Reform groups also sponsor a vast of array of workshops, lectures, and retreats by leading theologians, social scientists, and activists.

At a time when many Americans have chosen to abandon or weaken their ties to religious institutions, many of the reformers described in this study remain intensely religious and devote a considerable amount of their time and resources to reform activities or religious education and spiritual practice. Long-term reformers acknowledge that during this period their spiritual search has resulted in unexpected and life-changing reformulations of their theological beliefs and spiritual practice. However, unlike many of their cohorts, they remain deeply devoted to their religious heritage. Although there is considerable diversity in the religious beliefs and spiritual practices of reformers, most of them develop a more critical, less dogmatic understanding of Catholicism as a result of participating in reform activities.

Second, this study documents declines in membership and resources for most of the reform groups in the study. Many reformers have grown weary of their fruitless battle with church hierarchs, who increasingly respond to reformers with harsh rhetoric and punitive measures. Far from granting even token concessions to reformers, church hierarchs have imposed policies that stifle rather than advance the rights and status of feminists, gays and lesbians, and married priests who have been at the forefront of the movement.[2] Many reformers acknowledge that they have made few discernable inroads in promoting their reform agenda as a result of *insider strategies* (which are aimed at winning the hearts and minds of the Vatican and American bishops through various forms of advocacy, education, and lobbying). Vatican officials have little incentive to respond to Vatican II reformers given that their numbers are small and their demands challenge the conservative orientation of the two most recent popes.

As reformers abandon *insider strategies,* they become more willing to publicly criticize Roman Catholic hierarchs and the flaws of the institution. As they distance themselves from the Vatican, reformers increasingly adopt *outsider strategies* (which impose external pressure, including negative media attention, legal maneuvers, and the creation of alternative worship communities that force the hand of institutional leaders). Although reform groups have not become full-fledged sects, the decision to adopt outsider strategies is sect-like because these groups break off and form new institutions. Outsider strategies succeed at times because they force church officials to defend the reputation and viability of the church, which are threatened by negative publicity, lawsuits, and declining membership.

This study documents several policy-level changes at the diocesan and national levels achieved through *outsider strategies*. These reforms

---

[2] In the study the term *married priests* refers to men who were ordained as Roman Catholic priests but left the priesthood to marry.

include policies adopted by the United States Conference of Catholic Bishops (USCCB) to address clergy sexual abuse and to establish tighter financial controls for dioceses, as well as the Boston Archdiocese's decisions to fully disclose its annual budgets and to establish a review board, which resulted in the reversal of roughly 25 percent of planned parish closures. Hence, these victories confirm Gene Sharp's (1973) contention that even authoritarian organizations can be persuaded to enact reforms when their reputations and finances are threatened.

Third, this study documents small but growing networks of independent worship communities, both at the margin and outside the boundaries of the institutional church, that potentially could attract significant numbers of progressive Catholics who are disaffected by the institutional church. These communities exemplify both advantages and tradeoffs inherent in the decision to move in a sectarian direction. The autonomous nature of these communities enables reformers to create decentralized and participatory structures and innovative liturgies that embody liberal values. Conversely, by loosening or severing their ties to the Vatican, these communities forfeit the stability and legitimacy that their association with the institutional church confers. Therefore, these newly emerging sectarian groups have a tenuous status, as evidenced by their small, aging memberships, limited visibility, and meager resources. By engaging in activity considered schismatic by church officials, reformers also risk excommunication and other penalties and remain isolated from the larger Catholic community.

Although reformers as a whole share preferences for a church that, in the words of theologian Mary Hunt (2010), is "flatter, rounder, and more inclusive" (p. 3) than Vatican structures, reformers remain uncertain and divided about the type of structures they would design for the church of the future. Hence, my findings suggest that these independent communities face a precarious future because they have not as yet generated structures and resources necessary to sustain themselves.

ROOTS AND EVOLUTION OF THE CATHOLIC REFORM MOVEMENT

Reformist or Revolutionary?

The Reform Movement is primarily reformist in terms of its goals for church and societal reform, in that it favors incremental reform alongside preservation of many aspects of the institutional Roman Catholic Church.

The movement includes some revolutionary members who favor a nonviolent transformation of both church and societal structures designed to create more humane, egalitarian, peaceful, and environmentally sustainable models. Radicals within the movement include representatives from Pax Christi and the Catholic Worker Movement,[3] and theologians and adherents of radical feminism, Christian socialism, and liberation theology.

Notable Features of the Movement

The Reform Movement is noteworthy for its distinctiveness (that attracts and sustains liberal Catholics whose own spiritual search runs totally counter to that of the institutional Roman Catholic Church), its diversity of reform organizations (that have maintained ongoing communication and collaboration for four decades), and its alternative worship communities (that represent new types of liberal "parishes" or "Eucharistic communities" for those who no longer find conventional religion attractive or palatable).

Major Catalyst of the Movement

The major catalyst for the first wave of the Reform Movement was the 1976 Conference entitled "Call to Action: Liberty and Justice for All," a gathering of clerics and lay Catholics organized by the USCCB to solicit lay input. American bishops endorsed some conference resolutions regarding peace and justice but were dismayed by resolutions favoring changes in church teachings on contraceptives, expanded roles for women, support for homosexuals, and a bill of rights for lay members (*After Detroit*, 1977). American bishops ignored these objectionable recommendations and refused calls for a follow-up conference, realizing that this exercise in lay participation had become too explosive and confrontational (Gibson, 2003). In 1977, several conference delegates formed a lay organization for progressive Catholics entitled Call to Action (CTA) to promote the liberal reforms approved at the 1976 USCCB conference. Currently CTA serves as

---

[3] Pax Christi is a Catholic organization that "strives to create a world that reflects the Peace of Church by exploring, articulating, and witnessing to the Christian call to nonviolence" (www.paxchristiusa.org). The Catholic Worker Movement encompasses more than 185 communities that remain committed to "nonviolence, prayer, voluntary poverty, and hospitality to the homeless, hungry, and forsaken" (www.catholicworker.org).

a clearinghouse for several hundred reform groups that have emerged since 1976.

Roots of the Movement in the Vatican II and Sixties Era

The first liberal Catholic reform groups emerged during the late sixties and early seventies, a historical period in which liberal social movements were gaining strength and visibility. These movements in turn engendered the formation of several of the earliest Catholic reform groups as follows:

> DignityUSA, founded in 1969, is an advocacy organization for gay, lesbian, bisexual, and transgender (GLBT) Catholics.
>
> The Corps of Reserve Priests United for Service (CORPUS), founded in 1974, is an organization composed primarily of married priests who oppose mandatory celibacy.
>
> Women's Ordination Conference (WOC), founded in 1975, is a feminist advocacy organization that favors ordination of women to the priesthood.

Founders of these reform groups acknowledge that the optimistic and heady spirit of the 1960s era inspired them to believe that even an organization as tradition-bound as the Roman Catholic Church could and would succumb to reform and renewal. These reformers also came of age during the Vatican II era when many Catholic parishes were introducing Vatican II reforms. The movement includes many resigned nuns and priests who took their religious vows when religious orders were undergoing dramatic transformations ushered in by Vatican II. Some activists were members of underground-type ecumenical house churches in the 1960s or had participated in the antiwar, civil rights, and feminist and gay liberation movements. Even now this group of early reformers represents the left wing of the progressive Reform Movement, whose ranks now include a more diverse and less liberal variety of Catholics.

The second wave of the Reform Movement attracted Catholics who acknowledge their roots in Vatican II but make no reference to the 1960s. The two most prominent second-wave reform groups include FutureChurch and Voice of the Faithful (VOTF), both of which represent moderate and conservative Catholics and express support for the teachings of the Magisterium.[4] Founded in 1990, FutureChurch describes itself

---

[4] The Magisterium refers to "the teaching office of the Church. It consists of the Pope and the Bishops" (Most, 1990). Although VOTF and FutureChurch accept the teachings

as "a national coalition of parish-based Catholics who seek the participation of all baptized Catholics in the life of the Church" (FutureChurch, *About Us,* 2004). FutureChurch has focused on reforms aimed at alleviating the priest shortage, expanding the role of women in the church, and assisting parishes facing closure. VOTF emerged in Boston in 2002 and describes itself as an insider reform group intent on organizing a broad membership of conservative, moderate, and liberal Catholics. Long-term movement activists describe VOTF members as a "second layer of Catholics" who ignored the first wave of reform activity but were spurred to action primarily by the clergy abuse crisis.[5]

Losing the Culture Wars within Catholicism

The growing polarization between conservative and liberal Roman Catholics over the past four decades reflects the analysis of Hunter (1991), who points to the increasing significance of culture wars between liberals and conservatives in American society. Wuthnow (1988) emphasizes the growing "conflict between liberals and conservatives within religious denominations." My study reveals how these culture wars surface not only in struggles between liberal reformers and conservative church hierarchs but also in conflicts among the more conservative and liberal members within each reform group and, to a lesser degree, among different reform groups.

My content analysis of geographic distribution of chapters in three reform groups, DignityUSA, VOTF, and CTA,[6] revealed that reformers are clearly concentrated in the those states coded blue (liberal) in the 2008 U.S. presidential election:

---

of the Magisterium, individual members within both groups often do reject some Church teachings. Unlike VOTF, FutureChurch qualifies its loyalty to the Magisterium by favoring opening ordination to "all baptized Catholics," but it also "works with an attitude of respect for church teachings" and avoids expressions of support for "gay marriage" or "pro-choice" positions (*FutureChurch- Separating fact,* 2010).

[5] At the early VOTF conferences, some VOTF activists admitted that, before the abuse crisis, they were relatively complacent Catholics who befriended like-minded Catholics in their parish and paid little attention to Vatican pronouncements. Consequently, some were shocked to discover at VOTF conferences that Vatican II had been rolled back by recent popes and that liberals and conservatives were deeply divided over Church teachings.

[6] These are the only three reform groups in the study that list chapters on their websites.

	Number of Chapters in Blue States	Number of Chapters in Red States
CTA	56	20
VOTF	22	2
DignityUSA	23	5

Although these figures demonstrate that reform groups reflect the red state-blue state divide, they should be interpreted with caution, as there is no data available on number of members within each chapter.[7]

Culture wars are most obvious in VOTF because it is the only reform group that describes itself as a centrist organization. Since its founding in 2002, VOTF's efforts to find common ground between liberal and conservative Catholics have evoked considerable tension and discord. VOTF's conservative members resist any association with liberal reform groups, while liberals push VOTF to support reforms strongly opposed by conservatives, such as an end to mandatory celibacy, equal roles for women, and gay rights. Some form of the culture wars has surfaced even in reform groups that are, in varying degrees, uniformly liberal, such as groups representing feminists and GLBT persons. Within these liberal groups, the least liberal members favor strategies that are deferential to church hierarchs while the more left-leaning members favor confrontational strategies.

Controversy over one's loyalty to the Catholic tradition and the institutional church emerged in every reform group in the study, especially when discussing independent ordinations and worship communities. Even some of the most liberal Catholics hold some combination of liberal and conservative beliefs, for example by opposing "abortion on demand" or expressing reservations about stem cell research. As the faction least favored by the last two papacies, liberal reformers have strong incentives to rethink their relationship with the institutional church or explore the range of alternative worship communities.

Losing the Battle over Vatican II

Leaders of reform groups confess that "this is a difficult period for the Reform Movement" (referring to the years following the selection of

---

[7] Some chapters were in the pink/purple category, as follows: CTA: 19, VOTF: 7, and DignityUSA: 14.

Cardinal Ratzinger as Pope Benedict XVI). Most reform groups[8] have suffered losses in membership and contributions as their members are increasingly disgruntled at the prospects for reform under a reactionary papacy and with an aging network of activists whose outreach to young Catholics has largely failed. Almost four decades after the movement began, many activists are reeling at their church's abandonment of Vatican II and what they perceive as the punitive "Inquisition-like"[9] treatment of liberal theologians and activists.

Some activists describe Vatican II as "dead" since recent papacies seem intent on restoring a pre-Vatican II church. This study documents many conservative moves of Pope John Paul II and Pope Benedict XVI that include punishing liberal dissidents, imposing more rigid and conservative dogma, lifting restrictions on the Latin Mass, and reversing many liberal Vatican II reforms regarding liturgy and the role of laypersons in church governance.

Although Vatican II documents have a liberal bent, they represent a compromise between liberal and conservative factions. Since Vatican II documents are official church policy, conservative hierarchs do not criticize them directly, but rather emphasize those conservative principles affirmed by Vatican II. VOTF cofounder James Muller explains:

> Today both traditional and progressive Catholics urge greater adherence to the principles of Vatican II, although different teachings are emphasized. Traditionalists stress the recognition of papal primacy expressed by the council, while progressives seek an increased role of the rank-and-file faithful in church affairs. (Muller & Kenney, 2004, p. 219)[10]

Vatican II principles favored by the reformers are the ones least favored by the Vatican, which has the authority to cherry-pick its preferred options.

The sense of near despair one encounters among reformers becomes clear as one considers the mindset of the Vatican and the theological

---

[8] One notable exception is Catholics for Choice (CFC) whose budget was more than three million U.S. dollars in 2006. However, CFC is not a membership organization and functions primarily as a think tank rather than a reform organization.

[9] The term *inquisition* is occasionally used by reformers to describe punitive treatment of some activists. Paul Collins's (2002) book entitled *The Modern Inquisition* describes the Vatican's Congregation for the Doctrine of the Faith (CDF)'s decision to censure seven prominent Catholics, many of whom are featured speakers at meetings of reform groups.

[10] Muller and Kenney (2004) note that this debate over Vatican II affected even interpretations of the clergy abuse crisis as "traditionalists have blamed a lack of discipline for the crimes, while progressives believe that secrecy and resistance by the hierarchy to lay influence contributed to the problem" (p. 219).

premises of Pope John Paul II and his successor Benedict XVI. In his book *All the Pope's Men: The Inside Story of How the Vatican Really Thinks* (2004), John Allen Jr., Vatican correspondent for the *National Catholic Reporter*, explains that Vatican officials believe a strong papacy is critical to safeguarding the Catholic tradition, given that the pope is regarded as the successor to Peter to whom Christ entrusted the faith. Thus Allen explains, "His responsibility weighs heavily in the consciousness of Vatican officials and implies first of all a duty to integrity in the transmission and presentation of the doctrine of the Roman Catholic faith" (p. 194). This belief in papal responsibility for safeguarding the faith underlies the reaction of John Paul II and Benedict XVI to the advocacy efforts of reform groups. Given their staunchly conservative beliefs, these popes define their role as protecting the integrity and sanctity of the tradition from demands of reformers, whose reform agendas they regard as the misguided and relativistic convictions of postmodern society. For Benedict, in particular, relativism is the "central crisis of modern culture," which he intends to halt by "reinvigorating the faith and reconstituting the very idea of holding a firm belief in a divine, unchanging and uncompromising truth" (Benedict as cited in Gibson, 2006, p. 271).[11]

Despite the bleak prospects facing reformers, CORPUS leader Anthony Padovano exhibits an uncanny ability to pull treasures from the ruins by emphasizing a range of Vatican II principles that survive and even thrive despite conservative counterattacks. Padovano (2010) claims that of the sixteen Vatican II documents, the seven most pivotal ones still stand. Affirming the vision of reformers he exclaims:

> There is no future in reactionary Catholicism. The Council has held; young people find it in the zeitgeist and in the world they inhabit; the essence of the Council is embedded in the truth and wisdom and life of the human family and the sign of our times. It is all inescapable now. When the world fails, authentic Catholics will speak out; when the Church fails, the world will correct it. This is what the incarnation and the gift of the Spirit mean for our age. (p. 18)[12]

---

[11] Benedict expresses his criticism of relativism as follows: "Absolutizing what is not absolute but relative is called totalitarianism. It does not liberate man, but takes away his dignity and enslaves him" (Pope Benedict XVI, as cited in Gibson, 2006, p. 271).

[12] Padovano's (2010) rhetoric would no doubt offend many moderate and conservative Catholics, particularly when he states: "Today there is a sense that no healthy person would choose to preside over, live and work, in such an unstable and unreal environment" (p. 19).

Thus Padovano urges reformers to persist in the struggle and "survive retrenchment" by relying on conscience, friendship, and vision to sustain their "creative resistance" (p. 21) because the "institutional Church is worth it" (p. 21).

Padovano's upbeat tone is echoed by Sister Chris Schenk, executive director of FutureChurch (2010), who is heartened by Pope Benedict's beatification of Cardinal John Henry Newman on September 19, 2010. Schenk notes that Newman's writings were "foundational to Vatican II teachings on the dignity of the laity" (p. 1) and "the primacy of conscience." Schenk also cites many recent actions by reformers that would have been inconceivable twenty years ago, including the protests against parish closings, petitions to include women in the 2003 Vatican Synod on the Eucharist, and open discussions by bishops, priests, and laypersons regarding celibacy and women's ordination.

Research Relevant to this Study

My study is the only critical, comprehensive study of the Catholic Reform Movement. The most recent books on the Reform Movement include two on feminist Catholic reform groups. *Good Catholic Girls: How Women Are Leading the Fight to Change the Church* by Angela Bonavoglia (2005) is an entertaining and well-documented but uncritical overview of Catholic feminists. It predicts a hopeful future for the Reform Movement but ignores its lack of progress on reform issues as well as the declines in membership and morale documented in my study. *Catholic and Feminist: The Surprising History of the American Catholic Feminist Movement* by Mary Henold (2008) is a historical study of the Catholic feminist movement from the 1960s through the 1980s that analyzes the "nature and significance of Catholic feminism as a distinct branch of American feminism" (p. 3).

Three books are focused exclusively on the newest reform group, VOTF. *Faithful Revolution: How Voice of the Faithful Is Changing the Church* by Tricia Colleen Bruce (2011) examines VOTF as an intra-institutional social movement and how its insider status "shape[s] the form, strategies, and collective identity" of this movement (p. 5). *Voices of the Faithful: Loyal Catholics Striving for Change* by William D'Antonio and Anthony Pogorelc (2007) and *Keep the Faith, Change the Church* by James E. Muller and Charles Kenney (2004) contain primarily descriptive data about VOTF's history and membership, although the former does include a series of essays evaluating VOTF's strategies.

Catholic Identity: Balancing Reason, Faith, and Power by Michelle Dillon (1999) is a sophisticated analysis of how her sample of primarily "pro-change Catholics" maintains their allegiance to the Roman Catholicism while embracing liberal beliefs that contradict Vatican positions. Dillon's study has limited applicability to my research because it was published in 1999.

The research with the clearest correspondence to my study is John P. Plummer's (2004) published doctoral dissertation that examines the "independent sacramental movement," a term Plummer coined to describe the growth of worship communities rooted in but not formally affiliated with their host denomination.[13] Although Plummer's research includes both conservative and liberal groups, the generalizations he drew about communities in his sample resemble the liberal independent communities cited in this study as follows:

a. Communities attract persons excluded from mainstream liturgical churches due to "gender, sexuality, race, culture, style of worship, ... theology" (p. 66).
b. Members of these groups demonstrate "a high degree of individual commitment and liturgical involvement" (p. 66).
c. Ordination is open to a "larger percentage of the membership than in mainstream churches" (p. 66).
d. Liturgies in these communities demonstrate a "wild creativity" in their "intermingling of old and new" (p. 67). Many independents claim some connection to early Christian communities (p. 70).

Plummer's description of members of independent communities as "a glorious procession of beloved misfits into the divine kingdom" (p. 68) is an apt description for progressive Catholics in my study as well.[14] Those drawn to independent communities are more likely to be women,

---

[13] Plummer's (2004) study includes independent groups with roots in Catholic, Unitarian, Quaker, Episcopalian, Anglican, Lutheran, Methodist and Gnostic denominations as well as Buddhism and other esoteric traditions. His book includes very little numerical data, but he does state that "most independent sacrament churches in North America are first and foremost the descendants of the western liturgical churches, especially the European Old Catholic Churches" (p. 15). My study describes a number of communities formed by Catholic reformers that are affiliated with Old Catholic churches.

[14] Although some may interpret *misfits* as a pejorative term, Plummer clearly does not imply a negative judgment, given that he describes these persons as "beloved," and he himself is an independent Catholic bishop. The term *misfit* obviously refers to the fact that participants in the independent movement do not fit neatly into the qualifications for ministry, liturgical practices, and theological beliefs of conventional denominations.

married persons, and GLBT persons who are excluded from ordination in many denominations. Founders of these communities design structures and liturgies to embody their newly emerging perceptions regarding the form and shape of the beloved community envisioned by Jesus and other great religious figures.

Plummer's research also confirms my conclusion that independent worship communities are fluid and unstable in character due to their rebellious spirit and lack of uniform structure. He describes the movement as "widely scattered, anarchic, and sometimes difficult to locate" (p. 3), as clergy and laity move "with relative ease" (p. 3) among different jurisdictions and communities themselves emerge and fold at a rapid pace.[15]

THEORETICAL FRAMEWORK

This study draws on a range of theories from sociology, political science, anthropology, and theology to interpret and analyze the various dimensions of the movement, including its emergence and evolution; its structure, tactics, and strategies; its long- and short-term goals; and its range of organizations that represent diverse memberships and theological orientations.

The Dialectics of Church and Sect

Sociologists Max Weber and Ernst Troeltsch's church-sect theory provides a useful framework for interpreting the dialectical interaction between the institutional Roman Catholic Church and the Reform Movement. This theory identifies churches as characterized by (in abbreviated form): (1) membership based on birth, (2) formalized hierarchy and dogma, (3) inclusive of social structure, (4) oriented toward universal conversion, and (5) adjusted to social order. Sects are characterized by (in abbreviated form): (1) separation from general society, (2) exclusivity in attitude and social structure, (3) emphasis on prior conversion, (4) voluntary membership, (5) "spirit of regeneration," and (6) "attitude of ethical austerity" (O'Dea as cited in Stark & Bainbridge, 1985, p. 21).

---

[15] Echoing Plummer's study, Peter F. Anson's (2006) study of independent bishops in the United States revealed many schisms within independent dioceses that were often unable to resolve disputes over leadership or theology or both.

My study traces the Catholic Reform Movement's gradual tendency to become more sect-like in response to the rightward shift of the Vatican. The Reform Movement has many characteristics of sects, including its small, faithful membership, its disapproval of clericalism and openness to nonordained presiders, its emphasis on creative, spontaneous forms of worship and charismatic forms of leadership, and its rhetoric claiming its resemblance to early Christian communities. The independent worship communities created by reformers obviously resemble sects by crafting their own theology, liturgies, and governance structures. Reformers also exhibit a type of "prior conversion" in that most reformers were originally fairly conservative Catholics who gradually adopted liberal views. These independent communities also exhibit some tendency toward reverting to a church-like model as they attract members who are less liberal and less interested in church reform than reformers who founded these communities. Niebuhr (1929) predicted this tendency of sects to revert to churches as they become institutionalized.

The Reform Movement is also sect-like in its rejection of some features of the status quo, as most of its members oppose the wars in Iraq and Afghanistan and policies that maximize the growing inequality between rich and poor. In contrast to the Vatican, however, a majority of reformers favor liberal laws and court rulings regarding reproductive rights, equal roles for women, and acceptance of divorce and homosexuality. So, in many respects, the Catholic Reform Movement is more accepting of the status quo (especially liberal public polices) than church hierarchs whose ultraconservative views are outside the mainstream of the beliefs of most Americans, especially Vatican teachings that prohibit married priests, contraceptives, and remarriage for divorced persons.

The membership of the Reform Movement is primarily well-educated, middle-class Catholics rather than lower-class persons who historically are involved in sects.[16] Further, the Reform Movement's theology is the counter opposite of sects that emphasize exclusive membership and fundamentalist theology. Instead, the Catholic Reform Movement challenges what it regards as an increasingly fundamentalist-leaning theology of Roman Catholic hierarchs who seem intent on restoring pre-Vatican II theology and practices. Reformers renounce the growing tendency of church hierarchs to impose various forms of penalties, including denial of

---

[16] Consistent with my study, Glock and Stark (1965) present research confirming that sects are not exclusively lower class.

sacraments and excommunication, on both lay members and clerics who challenge their restrictive pronouncements.

In many respects, the Roman Catholic Church can be classified as a church *par excellence* in that it has a diverse international membership, is a large bureaucratic organization with a professional, trained clergy, emphasizes sacraments and church teaching as significant in personal salvation, offers a formal, uniform liturgy, and exhibits some connections to status quo institutions. The tendency of church hierarchs toward increased conservatism reflects a trend favoring increased institutionalization, in which dogma and membership criteria become codified and explicit. Although the church has condoned or tolerated many aspects of contemporary culture, it embraces some ultraconservative positions that contradict even the views of most Roman Catholics.[17] By the same token, church officials are not universally conservative in that they take liberal stances on some peace and social justice issues, as evidenced by Pope John Paul II's public denunciation of the George W. Bush administration's invasion of Iraq and the support of American bishops for many social welfare programs.

My application of the church-sect typology reflects the analyses of Goldstein (2011), whose review of a range of research on religious conflict concludes that "religious conflict in the USA is shaped by dialectic of religious and secular movements and counter-movements" (p. 77). He critiques the interpretations of scholars of religious conflict between conservatives and liberals as competition in a religious marketplace. Goldstein's analysis points to a dialectic interaction between religious conservatives and religious liberals that moves in a progressive direction toward increased secularization.

Consistent with Goldstein (2011), my data exposes a dialectical pattern of movement and countermovement within Catholicism. The liberal reforms of Vatican II and liberal cultural trends in the United States and Europe evoked a countermovement by conservative church hierarchs to

---

[17] Reflecting on this trend, at the 2008 CTA conference two of the Reform Movement's most distinguished leaders, Anthony Padovano and Joan Chittister, described Vatican leaders as a "cult" due to their isolationist and authoritarian tendencies and their disconnect from contemporary culture. (See chapter 5 for a description of their remarks.) However, their characterizations do not match the sociological definitions of a cult that specify "a group without much internal discipline with a loose-knit structure" or a group that represents "the beginning phase of a new religion" (K. A. Roberts, 2004, p. 188). In sociological terms, Padovano and Chittister are describing a sect that has exclusive membership policies and fundamentalist theology.

reimpose traditional norms. This countermovement in turn evoked a Reform Movement in the 1970s among liberal Catholics intent on preserving and expanding on the reforms of Vatican II. Although the liberal Reform Movement never posed a serious threat to Vatican authority, it strengthened the resolve of church hierarchs to persist in their efforts to stamp out Vatican II reforms. In the face of the Vatican's staunch and unrelenting rejection of liberal reforms, many reformers are forming sect-like communities where they can practice Catholicism on their own terms. A second wave of reform groups emerged in 2002 in reaction to revelations of widespread clerical sexual abuse and policies of cover-up by church hierarchs. The long-term impact of this scandal on the credibility and stability of the institutional church have not yet been fully documented.

The relevance of the church-sect typology to my study is enhanced when interpreted as a measure of organizational precariousness as originally intended by Weber-Troeltsch and Niebuhr, J. Coleman (1968) asserts that "the concepts of church-sect have become imprecise and nonoperational" (p. 55) because they no longer have a consistent and universal meaning as they are applied to diverse forms of religious organizations and historical contexts. Consistent with Coleman's recommendations, I have applied the church-sect concept as a measure of precariousness. My data reveals the precariousness of the church type as revealed by the Roman Catholic Church's struggles to prevent and contain sectarian movements among both conservative and liberal Catholics, as well as defection by a diverse range of Catholics whose allegiance to Catholicism has waned. For its part, the Reform Movement faces types of uncertainty characteristic of sects, whose lack of resources and instability leads to defections by some members.

Demerath and Thiessen's (1966) study of the sect *Freie Gemeinde* in Wisconsin applied four measures of organizational precariousness, namely, social status, leadership stability, tangibility of goals, and membership recruitment. The Catholic Reform Movement would earn a fairly low score of precariousness according the Demerath and Thiessen's scale as follows:

1. Their members are primarily middle class rather than "low-status groups."
2. They have some formal leadership roles rather than relying on "spontaneous leadership."

3. Their goals are fairly tangible rather than unrealistic.[18]
4. They do not impose strict or "militant and totalitarian" commitments on members.

My application of this scale is obviously speculative, in part because the indices are vague. As Coleman points out, these indices need to become more precise to ensure accurate and consistent measurements. In the case of my study, liberal reform groups include a variety of different types and each group represents unique circumstances that require separate assessments.

Organizational Theories of Freeman and Turner

This study applies organizational theory of feminist political scientist Jo Freeman and anthropologist Victor Turner. Both of these theories bear some connection to Weber-Troeltsch's church-sect typology described above.

Freeman's (2009) theory regarding the "tyranny of structurelessness" challenges the tendency of reformers to avoid debates over structure due to their antibureaucratic preferences and their allegiance to the egalitarian models proposed by Catholic feminist theologians. Freeman's research on feminist consciousness-raising groups reveals that failure to establish workable and clearly defined structures and formal leadership roles undermines rather than bolsters democratic and egalitarian objectives. Paradoxically, the actual operations of these groups often violated and undermined the very principles they were designed to uphold. Although groups claimed to be leaderless, leaders did emerge but could not be held accountable because there were no formal measures of accountability. The lack of formal procedures for decision making and governance hampered rather than facilitated genuine power sharing among members.[19]

---

[18] The goals of liberal reformers may be unrealistic in terms of winning approval from Church hierarchs, but they are not unrealistic for sect-like groups that operate outside Vatican control.

[19] Turner (1969) describes *communitas* as by its very nature as "relatively undifferentiated" and as a "community of equals who submit together to the general authority of the ritual elders" (p. 96). Although he describes structure as a "differentiated and often hierarchical system of politic-legal-economic positions (p. 96), he does not rule out the possibility of egalitarian structures. It seems fair to conclude that Turner would share the criticisms of Freeman regarding the ineffectiveness and nonsustainable nature of structureless groups.

Hence Freeman's research is consistent with Weber-Troeltsch's emphasis on the instability of sect-like groups that have poorly defined structures.

Anthropologist Victor Turner (1969) provides a useful framework for analyzing religious organizations by identifying the dialectical tensions between structure and antistructure (or *communitas*). One might speculate that both the institutional Roman Catholic Church and the marginal and independent communities described in this study have failed to achieve the dialectic between structure and *communitas* that Turner claims "no society can function adequately without" (p. 129). Turner defines structure as a formal allocation of "positions and statuses" (p. 131), while *communitas* has a "spontaneous, immediate, concrete nature" (p. 127), and is the realm of "artists and prophets" who "enter into vital relations with other men in fact or imagination" (p. 128). Structure is essential for orderly functioning of a society, while *communitas* bolsters and complements structure by forging bonds of solidarity among members and providing an outlet for expressive tendencies.

Turner's dialectic between structure and *communitas* bears a close resemblance to the church-sect dialectic of Weber-Troeltsch.[20] Weber-Troeltsch's concept of "church" corresponds to Turner's concept of "structure" that describes well-defined systems of governance and belief, while the concept of "sect" corresponds to "*communitas*" with its emphasis on egalitarianism and revival. As predicted by Turner and Weber-Troeltsch, both types of structures contain their own inherent contradictions. Hence, liberal reformers point to the negative fallout from overemphasis on structure within the institutional church. They decry rigid rules, clericalist norms, and a tepid, formalistic type of worship experience. Consequently, reformers are forming sect-like groups that embody the spirit of *communitas* in their anticlericalism, intense religious expression, and strong communal bonding. However, these sect-like groups lose some members who return to churches that offer a more extensive range of services (especially religious education) and more attractive settings than these poorly funded groups can provide. Thus both types of organizations are inherently unstable, and excesses in either direction lead to oscillation to the opposite pole of the dialectic.[21]

---

[20] Although the theories of Weber-Troeltsch and Turner are similar, I have chosen to include both in my analysis because each contributes distinct insights. The goals of liberal Catholic reformers bear a closer resemblance to Turner's concept of *communitas* than to Weber-Troeltsch's concept of sect.

[21] It may be that conservative Catholics are in part attracted to independent conservative communities (such as those affiliated with the Society of St. Pius X) because they

A Revivalist Movement

The Reform Movement corresponds to Stark and Bainbridge's (1985) categorization of revivalist movements, which are sect-like in nature and which emerge to "protect and maintain deep attachments to the traditional religions rather than efforts to create religions" (p. 444). Consistent with a revivalist movement, the Reform Movement arose in areas where "traditional churches are still reasonably vigorous" (p. 444). Hence, the movement draws adherents primarily from former or disaffected Catholics who reside primarily in the Midwest and Northeast where there are high concentrations of Roman Catholics. The Reform Movement also confirms Stark and Bainbridge's prediction that revivalist sects emerge during early stages of secularization when traditional churches are just beginning to experience loss of members.[22] Although reformers initially hoped to revive Catholicism from within, they eventually retreated to and beyond the margins of the institutional church in order to escape Vatican repression.

The Reform Movement contradicts, to some degree, the pattern of sects described by Stark and Bainbridge that "reassert the general compensators of traditional faith because these have not been (and cannot be) invalidated by scientific discovery" (p. 435). Catholic reformers do hope to retain certain "compensators" they value from the Catholic tradition (including its elaborate rituals, music, prayers, religious artifacts, and sophisticated theology), as well as rewards (including its networks of hospitals, schools, social service agencies, and parishes). Nonetheless, reformers do not view their theology and philosophy as a bulwark against scientific findings that challenge and discredit many traditional Catholic teachings. On the contrary, reformers favor new forms of theology and worship that integrate and celebrate the contributions of science and liberal social policies. Hence, many reformers respond to trends favoring secularization and rationalization, not by retrenchment but rather by embracing feminist, liberation, and environmentalist theologies that incorporate new understandings of history and the human condition. These theologies are expansive and informed enough to address both the threats and the opportunities posed by the contemporary world.

---

offer a more communal atmosphere than is available in mainstream parishes. However, my study did not include conservative communities and, hence, has no basis for evaluating this possibility.

[22] Stark and Bainbridge (1985) hypothesize that cults form in "later stages of church weakness" when traditional churches are experiencing massive defections.

Far from defending the irreconcilable boundaries between the sacred and the profane, and science and religion, reformers identify with theologies that point to the dynamic and elaborate intersections between these dichotomies.

The movement's theological orientation favoring integration of science and an open attitude toward the modern world does, in large measure, match Max Weber's predictions regarding the trend toward increased rationalization of religion. However, Margaret Steinfels (2010), codirector of the Fordham Center on Religion and Culture, challenges the applicability of Weber's prediction regarding the "disenchantment of the world" that accompanies "the ascendancy of the rational and scientific sensibility not only on the grand scale of human events, but on the small ones of everyday life" (p. 12). Drawing on her own experience growing up in a "Chicago Catholic landscape," she asserts that, at least for many Catholics of her generation, "the world was of a piece—the inner and the outer, the sacred and the profane, the parish and the precinct, the Catholic and the Democratic Party, the family and the neighborhood" (p. 12).

Steinfels (2010) attributes the declining influence of Catholic culture following Vatican II to the shortcomings of church hierarchs who failed "to grasp that an adult faith depends on persuasion, and not on fiat" (p. 13). As more Catholics attended college during this period, often Catholic colleges, they were dismayed by the failure of church hierarchs to offer cogent and convincing explanations of church teachings. According to Steinfels, church hierarchs relied on a form of reasoning that was "not based on empirical evidence and human experience" and "came to be seen as more rationalizing than rational" (p. 12). Steinfels cites the failure of the hierarchy to win lay support for the papal encyclical *Humanae Vitae* prohibiting contraception and the autocratic and isolationist tendencies of Pope John Paul II as critical factors leading to the church's declining authority and the polarizing trends of sectarianism and factionalism that plague the contemporary church. Thus, Steinfels concludes, it was the flawed reasoning of church hierarchs rather than secularization per se that led to the "disenchantment" of many Catholics.

Furthermore, Weber's prediction regarding the tendency of religion to move from an emphasis on otherworldly to this-worldly goals does not adequately describe the views of liberal reformers. Most reformers view this type of dualism as reflecting the worldview of a bygone era. Although reformers devote much of their energy to reform of church and societal structures, they would reject any attempt to describe their goals as purely secular. On the contrary, they would insist that one finds God and the sacred in solitary prayer, in a community of fellow seekers, and in efforts to create a more just and sustainable society. Although many reformers believe in some sort of life after death, they interpret biblical language and church teachings about salvation and the Second Coming as symbolic and visionary rather than as a concrete or literal prediction of humanity's future. Speakers at reform group gatherings do not cite the rewards of salvation or the threat of damnation as incentives to motivate activism.

Culture Wars in Religious Denominations

The battles between religious conservatives and religious liberals involve many of the same hot-button issues that characterize societal-wide culture wars, including reproductive rights, equal rights for women, acceptance of homosexuality and divorce, and democratization of social institutions. Consistent with the analyses of Wuthnow (1988) and Hunter (1991) cited above, my study documents the growing polarization between liberals and conservatives within American Catholicism, whereby each side is pursuing strategies that widen the gap between each end of the spectrum, as conservatives move further to the right and liberals move further to the left. This deep culture-wars divide between Catholic liberals and conservatives is more significant than the church-sect theory in interpreting my data because it offers a convincing explanation as to why conservative Catholic hierarchs are so resistant to the demands of the Reform Movement and so punitive toward reformers.

Distinction between Religious Movement and Social Movement

My research centers on a religious movement, which Stark and Bainbridge (1985) define as "social movements that wish to cause or prevent change in a system of beliefs, values, symbols, and practices concerned with providing supernaturally based general compensators" (p. 23). While social movements are oriented toward supporting or opposing social change, religious groups hope to form religious organizations. Unlike a social movement, a religious movement cannot focus merely on secular strategies and goals. This difference is significant because the focus here is a religious movement that claims to represent the truths and values of the Roman Catholic tradition. Hence, this movement must design strategies, rationales, and goals that reflect Catholic principles and traditions. Although the Reform Movement aims to revive and transform this tradition, if it moves too far outside the boundaries and precedents of the tradition, its legitimacy is undermined. Despite these differences, social movement theory offers some useful insights in analyzing this movement.[23]

Confirmation of Resource Mobilization Theory

My research also supports the resource mobilization theory proposed by McCarthy and Zald (1977) that points to extensive range of resources and social networks that play a crucial role in forming and sustaining social movements. In many respects, my findings correspond to those of sociologist Aldon Morris who applied resource mobilization theory to his study of the American civil rights movement. Morris (1984) found little support for collective behavior theorists who discredit social movement participants by "characterizing their behavior as crude and elementary and as tension-releasing devices for pent-up frustration" (p. 276).[24] Morris concludes that "rational planning, well-developed preexisting communication networks and established leaders, institutions and organizations, rather than psychic strain, spontaneity, and emotionalism, were the driving force behind the [civil rights] movement" (p. 278).

Consistent with Morris, my study describes movement participants as highly rational and, generally speaking, remarkably restrained and deferential toward church hierarchs, despite their deeply felt frustration over the refusal of hierarchs to engage in dialogue over policy. My study also points to organizations and communications networks, which facilitated networking and membership outreach by reform groups.[25] Although the Reform Movement has relatively modest funding, it receives generous support from its most devoted members, a majority of whom are middle class and near or past retirement age, and consequently have discretionary income and leisure time to devote to movement activities. My study

---

[23] Both religious and social movements require resources and effective forms of leadership and structure.

[24] Morris (1984) did concur with collective behavior theorists that social movements aim to achieve social change and that "creativity and innovation are central to the efforts of people engaged in movement activities aimed at establishing a new social order" (p. 277).

[25] These networks include the USCCB Conference in 1976 cited above; CTA national conferences, which serve as a clearinghouse for reform groups; and personal and professional networks of resigned sisters and priests and liberal and radical Catholic theologians.

also documents the highly professional organizational skills of movement leaders whose conferences became "can't miss" events for many activists.

Although reform organizations are low-budget operations, the movement is strengthened by generous supporters and the availability of low-cost strategic choices. Numerous Catholic theologians and academics, who are often employed by the more liberal Catholic universities, serve as advisors for Catholic reform organizations and speak at their conferences, usually without any compensation. As noted throughout this book, the Reform Movement's major source of leverage vis-à-vis the Vatican and American bishops is media attention and lawsuits by clergy abuse victims that, with the exception of newspaper ads purchased by reform groups, entail little or no expenditures by reform groups.

Unlike the American civil rights movement, the Reform Movement never developed effective tactics and strategies capable of significantly disrupting the operations of the institutional church and reversing or even containing the conservative drift of Vatican policies. Despite its strategic failings, however, the Reform Movement retains many ardent supporters who, at least until recently, were unwilling to sever their ties to Catholicism. Although its achievements are modest, the movement has endured for more than four decades, a victory of sorts, particularly since several scholars credit movement groups with liberalizing the views of Catholic laypersons.

Although my study confirms resource mobilization theory, it also documents some examples of spontaneous behavior of the part of movement activists in response to events that shocked and enraged not only activists but also previously inactive Catholics. The most obvious example is the clergy abuse crisis, which aroused diverse categories of Catholics who candidly voiced their disgust at revelations of abuse and cover-up and flocked to demonstrations and conferences sponsored by reform groups. Similar spontaneous reactions emerged following the repression of Vatican II pastors and dramatic restructuring of dioceses by conservative bishops. These reactions are consistent with political scientist Freeman's (1999) premise that "it is the tension between spontaneity and structure that gives a social movement its peculiar flavor" (pp. 1–2).

Sharp's Model of Nonviolent Resistance

I use political scientist Gene Sharp's (1973, 2005) typology of nonviolent resistance to categorize and analyze the various forms of resistance strategies encompassed by the Reform Movement. By pointing to the fragility and fluidity of managerial power within even highly authoritarian organizations, Sharp's model is well suited to analyzing social change strategies where reformers have been shut out of formal decision-making processes. Sharp's typology presents parallel institutions as a last resort that brings external pressure to bear when internal reform mechanisms have failed. Consistent with Sharp's model, liberal Catholic reformers describe their experimentation with parallel institutions not as an exit route from the Catholic tradition but rather as an opportunity for redefining the terms and conditions of loyalty to their tradition.[26] This orientation of reformers is also consistent with their status as members of sectarian groups that claim to be purer, more authentic bearers of a religious tradition that has been corrupted or co-opted by church leaders. Theologian Terry Veling (1996) describes the types of marginal groups created by reformers as claiming a space safe from retribution and surveillance where members can probe the truths of their tradition and its applicability to the contemporary world.

A Nonviolent Movement: Turning the Other Cheek?

Although most reform groups have not been trained in theories of nonviolent resistance, many (especially CTA members) identify themselves as "peace and justice" types for whom violence is off-limits.[27] Further, the Reform Movement is comprised primarily of midlife and older Catholics raised in an era when priests were accorded a high degree of deference, even reverence. For this reason, as this study will document, reform

---

[26] Sharp's model poses an alternative perspective to the economist Albert Hirschman's (1970) classic model as outlined in his book *Exit, Voice and Loyalty: Responses to Declines in Firms, Organizations, and States*. According to Hirschman, disaffected members of organizations can choose exit (drop out) or voice (remain loyal but express dissent). Hirschman's theory has been widely cited by speakers at VOTF conferences to support VOTF's strategy of working for reform from within existing structures. Unlike Hirschman, Sharp poses a range of choices for reformers who might begin by voicing protest, but eventually adopt strategies that allow reformers some connection to their host organization, but also withdraw support from objectionable leaders and structures.

[27] New Testament scholar Walter Wink (1998) claims that Jesus's admonition to "turn the other check" has been misinterpreted as advocating passivity in the face of a hostile attack. According to Wink, "turning the other check" is a form of nonviolent resistance. Since Hebrew culture restricted the use of the left hand, a person who was struck on the right check would limit the blow of the assailant by exposing the other check because then the assailant would be forced to strike with the back off his or her right hand, and hence the blow would have less force. Drawing on his analysis of Hebrew culture, Wink interprets many of Jesus's teachings as advocating nonviolent resistance against injustice.

organizations as a whole have generally been very slow to challenge or confront priests or hierarchs and have continued to pursue insider strategies long after their ineffectiveness became obvious. My research did not uncover any incident of violent or even aggressive behavior at the demonstrations or other public events sponsored by reform groups.[28]

Even as many reform groups have finally abandoned the insider approach, Vatican II reformers emphasize their loyalty to the Catholic tradition by insisting they are motivated not by individual vindication or political correctness but rather by a movement of the Spirit seeking a more authentically Christian institution that will nurture the spiritual development of its members and command worldwide respect. If the Vatican wants to preserve the integrity and sanctity of tradition by warding off demands associated with Vatican II, liberal reformers want to revive Roman Catholicism as a vital, compassionate, and visionary institution.

Some reform groups do include workshops on nonviolent resistance strategies, especially CTA, but discussion of strategy at reform groups are limited primarily to protest and persuasion and do not consider the full range of strategies outlined by Sharp (1973). While reformers restrict themselves to nonviolent strategies, many regard their punitive and off-putting treatment by Vatican officials as a form of violence. CORPUS member George Clements (2007) laments that "all the scandals in the world are not going to force the boys in power to share their iron-fisted control over their institution" (p. 35). The metaphor of "iron-fisted control" clearly depicts a rather brutal image of Vatican officials. Mercy Sister Theresa Kane accuses "the male hierarchy" of "a dictatorial mindset and spiritual violence" when commenting on the investigation of U.S. religious women[29] initiated by the Vatican in December 2008 (Kane as cited in T. Fox, 2009c). Father Camilo Macisse (2003), former superior general of Discalced Carmelites, accuses the Roman Curia of violence based on its extreme centralism in governance, patriarchal authoritarianism that denies women any voice in policy making, its judicial system that does not grant accused persons basic rights of self-defense, and its policies of

---

[28] On several occasions, I observed clergy sexual abuse victims engage in heckling and jeering during demonstrations outside the Cathedral of the Holy Cross in Boston, particularly during the installation of Sean O'Malley as Cardinal of Boston in 2006. However, these victim-survivors were members of Survivors' Network of those Abused by Priests (SNAP) rather the reform groups named in this study.

[29] This Vatican investigation of religious sisters is described in chapter 7.

repression of progressive theologians and biblical scholarship. Macisse defines violence as "the application of physical, moral or psychological force to impose or coerce," which he claims "should be unthinkable in the community of believers founded by Jesus, the Prince of Peace."

While Roman Catholic officials do not engage in militaristic tactics toward church reformers, they do impose harsh penalties that correspond to Macisse's definition of violence. These penalties include excommunicating clergy and laypersons, denial of liturgical roles such as Eucharistic ministers, firing parish staff, and censoring liberal theologians. These penalties are considerably less severe and violent than the beheadings, burnings at the stake, and other forms of torture and murder imposed earlier in church history. Nonetheless, persons who consider Catholicism central to their identity, and who have developed strong bonds with members of their parishes and religious orders, often are devastated by excommunication or expulsion from their order or jobs. If they are excommunicated they lose the right to receive the sacraments. Several sisters whom I interviewed wept as they described their excruciating struggles over the choice of leaving the religious life that comprised most of their adult lives.[30] I also witnessed a prominent Catholic sister physically collapse at a podium as she wept and trembled in the midst of describing her struggle to endure the constant harassment of church hierarchs. My study records several examples of sisters and priests who returned to their orders after being excommunicated or resigning. Despite their ongoing dissent of church policies, they chose to return because they intensely missed their colleagues and the communal lifestyle of their religious order.

Gerald A. Arbuckle, S.M. (2004), analyzes the church's ambivalent relationship to violence[31] in *Violence, Society, and the Church: A Cultural Approach*. While Arbuckle credits Catholic Church officials for their efforts and statements favoring world peace, he notes the many types of violence evident in the church's autocratic form of government, including

---

[30] Many vowed religious persons who are expelled from their orders face dim employment prospects, especially those who are near retirement age. Some will lose not only their jobs but also their accrued pension, health care, and housing provided by their order.

[31] Arbuckle uses the term *violence* to refer not merely to physical force but also to violations of human rights and dignity. Hence the term *violence* can be applied to acts that involve intense psychological intimidation or demeaning behavior imposed on a victim who is often defenseless. Arbuckle's definition is consistent with the use of term *violence* adopted by many peace studies scholars. It is also consistent with Webster's definition of violence that includes "an injurious or destructive act" (*New International Webster's Collegiate Dictionary of the English Language*. (2002).

premodern types (gossip, shame, and ridicule), modern types (destructive envy, jealousy, and scapegoating), and bureaucratic types (resistance to change and authoritarian relationships). As Arbuckle documents, throughout history the Catholic Church has often aligned itself with violent, repressive regimes and has a shameful history that includes the Crusades, witch hunts, the Inquisition, and anti-Semitism. Arbuckle does credit Pope John Paul II for his public apologies regarding Christian indifference to the Holocaust, but he also critiques Vatican insistence that the institutional church bore no responsibility for the Holocaust. Church hierarchs also bear responsibility for the clergy abuse crisis, an egregious form of violence facilitated by hierarchs who imposed policies of secrecy, cover-up, and subservience.

Arbuckle (2004) adds his voice to the group of Catholic theologians favored by reform groups (such as Hans Küng and Joan Chittister) who insist that Catholic dissenters must struggle within both the church and society at large to create just structures capable of avoiding the whole range of violent relationships evident in every level of society. For their part, church hierarchs might term the action of reformers as a form of violence in that rejection of Vatican doctrine represents a violation of their obligations as church members and participation in "schismatic" communities represents a violation of church unity. Arbuckle insists, however, that the form of power exercised by the Vatican reflects violent characteristics in that it is unilateral, rejecting dialogue by "refusing to receive the influence of others" (p. xiii). Echoing the concerns of Catholic reformers, Arbuckle asserts that a number of Vatican officials have engaged in "theological and administrative violence" to thwart Vatican II reformers while favoring "restorationist and fundamentalist movements" (p. xviii).[32]

Thus, the struggle over how one defines and responds to violence is at the heart of the current impasse between liberal reformers and church hierarchs regarding the future direction and character of Catholicism. I share the perspective of Arbuckle and Macisse who describe the highly punitive, authoritarian, and patriarchal characteristics of the Vatican as violent in nature. Although church officials often champion the advancement of human rights and democracy in nation states, they fail to explain why these principles contradict the church's centralized authority and

---

[32] As part of this, 107 theologians were censured during the papacy of John Paul II (M. Fox, 2006, p. xviii).

church hierarchs' ever-accelerating demands for obedience and conformity. Church officials no longer resort to physical violence, but they wield what Macisse refers to as "moral and psychological force" by refusing to engage in dialogue with reformers, by penalizing and silencing liberal theologians and clerics, and by imposing clericalist norms that protect them from criticism and accountability. The cover-ups and lack of accountability revealed by the clergy abuse crisis provide shocking and revealing evidence of the dangers of unchecked power and groupthink that characterize Vatican officials.[33]

Scope of the Study—A Vast Terrain

This study intentionally adopts a broad scope that covers a wide range of reform groups and worship communities. It cannot provide as much in-depth coverage as a case study of one of the advocacy groups or worship communities in the Reform Movement. However, one attains a richer perspective on the liberal Catholic Reform Movement by examining the spectrum of religious movement organizations. Many reformers experiment with a range of choices, for example by moving from a Vatican II parish to a Eucharistic community and then to an underground parish. Often reformers learn of the existence of these options through their involvement in reform organizations, especially CTA, which has contact information for communities on its website.

The Catholic reform organizations in this study include first *advocacy groups* oriented toward achieving reforms within the current institutional structure of Roman Catholicism and, second, *parallel organizations* that are creating alternative structures within and outside the formal boundaries of Roman Catholicism, but define themselves as Catholic and retain many rituals and symbols from the Catholic tradition. (See Appendix A for charts that identify both types of groups.) The study focuses almost exclusively on the Catholic Reform Movement within the boundaries of the United States, although it does include brief references to similar activism in Europe and elsewhere. With the exception of VOTF,[34] all of the reform groups included in this study are liberal (albeit in

---

[33] VOTF spokespersons often emphasize that the church's cover-ups of abusive priests have enabled the violent behavior of abusive priests and resulted in many untold suicides among abuse victims.

[34] VOTF describes itself as a centrist reform organization that reaches out to conservative, moderate, and progressive Catholics, and, therefore, accepts the teachings of the

varying degrees) in that they favor full equality for women and gays and lesbians[35] in the church, an end to mandatory celibacy, approval of most forms of contraception, and a greater role for laity in decision making. Liberal reform groups ground their advocacy for their reform agendas in *theological liberalism* that interprets doctrine, scripture, and religious rules contextually in a manner that regards many religious teachings as metaphorical or in need of revision and expansion to include new historical understanding and contemporary realities. In contrast, Vatican officials and many American bishops embrace *theological conservatism* that applies a strict and often literal interpretation to doctrine, scripture, and religious rules of behavior.

Although this study is focused on liberal Catholic reformers, the progressive Catholic Reform Movement bears some similarities to conservative Catholic groups, whose independent worship communities are sometimes referred to as *underground*. Conservative Catholic reform groups, as described by Cuneo (1997) resemble liberal groups in that they include both advocacy and think-tank type organizations alongside independent worship communities, have limited access to church hierarchs, have small memberships and limited visibility within the United States, and evoke little interest from the larger Catholic community, especially younger Catholics. While the reform groups in this study are liberal, *The Underground Church* includes several references to conservative Catholic groups, including conservative attacks launched against VOTF during its early history and editorials directed at Benedict XVI urging him to extend to liberals the same types of outreach and reconciliation he extends to conservatives.

Why the Title *The Underground Church*?

The title of this book, *The Underground Church*, has proven somewhat controversial among the Vatican II reformers described in the book. On the negative side, some complain that the title has a subversive,

---

Roman Catholic Church on doctrinal issues, especially those raised by liberal reform groups.

[35] I am using the term *gays and lesbians* rather than *GLBT* because, with the exception of DignityUSA and Women-Church Convergence (W-CC), many reform groups have not formally taken positions in support of bisexual or transgender persons.

dismissive tone that suggests groups not sanctioned by the Vatican somehow lack legitimacy and authenticity. Conversely, those who like the title describe it as well suited to the largely invisible nature of the Reform Movement, which often attracts little publicity and operates at the margins of the institutional church, particularly since spokespersons for reform groups are increasingly denied access to Roman Catholic parishes and publications. I have chosen this title for several reasons.

First, the current Reform Movement described in this book has roots in a movement referred to as "the underground church" that surfaced during the 1960s and 1970s in which reform-minded Catholics held home masses and ecumenical gatherings in their search for a more authentic spirituality and form of community than was available in conventional parishes (Boyd, 1969).

Second, the term *underground church* has been used to describe Catholic communities that operate in secrecy under repressive governments such as the Roman Empire in early Christian history and, more recently, the Iron Curtain regimes in Eastern Europe that penalized Christians for practicing their faith. Like these historic underground churches, some members or groups within the Catholic Reform Movement meet secretly or take steps to escape the attention of church officials in order to avoid penalties imposed by church officials, including various forms of censure, prohibitions on use of church property, and even excommunication.

Third, the peace studies scholar Elise Boulding (1976) uses the term *underside of history* to describe subcultures and social movements of oppressed or marginalized persons who practice and promote cooperative, nonviolent values that contradict those of the dominant culture. In this regard, the Vatican II Reform Movement represents something of the "underside" or "underground" of the Roman Catholic Church during a period when its leadership is moving toward an increasingly authoritarian, repressive form of governance.

Fourth, notably, Dutch Dominicans use the term *underground church* to describe unauthorized lay-led communities in the Netherlands among Dutch Catholics that have emerged in response to the priest shortage (McClory, 2007b). Like American communities described in this study, these Dutch underground churches are experimenting with a range of liturgical innovations that include presiders who are not ordained clergy.

Who are Vatican II-Inspired Reformers?

Although there have been no formal studies on the demographic characteristics of persons in the Reform Movement as a whole, the evidence gathered in this study (primarily on the basis of interviews with activists) suggests that those who join are primarily Catholics who came of age during or shortly after Vatican II. They belonged to Catholic families and parishes, and many attended Catholic colleges and seminaries where the reforms of Vatican II were welcomed and put into practice in a variety of ways.

These reformers tend to be well educated. All of the reformers whom I interviewed had at least bachelor's degrees and the majority had master's degrees. Further evidence regarding the educational status of participants is indicated by the nature of reform group conferences that primarily feature speakers with academic credentials who give relatively sophisticated lectures on assigned topics. Reformers tend to be affluent (consistent with their high levels of education) because conference attendees are well dressed and capable of financing the fees and travel costs involved in these conferences. A consistent theme among all reformers in the study is that religion and spirituality were the central motivating force in their lives, and that Catholicism had been a significant influence on their *spiritual journey*, a term used by many respondents.

These generalizations about reformers mirror the findings of a study of VOTF members conducted by D'Antonio and Pogorelc (2007) detailed in the table 1.

Table 1. Demographic characteristics of VOTF members

Characteristic	Composition
Education	88% college degree
	60% graduate degree
Age	35% retired
	Only 11% born on or after 1961
Gender	59% female; 41% male
	Few differences in attitude or behavior
Ethnicity[36]	Predominately Caucasian
	2% Latino

---

[36] The study did not report a percentage of African American Catholics who are VOTF members.

Table 1. (*Cont.*)

Characteristic	Composition
Occupation	A majority professional and managerial
	35% earn $50,000–$100,000
	29% earn more than $100,000
Catholic schools	Majority attended Catholic schools
	57% attended Catholic colleges
Registered in a parish	85% registered
Attend mass weekly	66% (compared to 34% of all Catholics)
Church is "important or among the most important part of their life"	62% rank church as "important or among the most important"

These demographic characteristics match my observations of conference goers at all the reform group conferences I attended: members were predominately Caucasian, middle-aged or older, and (with the exception of gatherings of feminists[37] or married priests) usually included slightly more women than men.[38]

VOTF's centrist philosophy attracts more conservative and moderate members than the other more left-leaning reform groups described in the study. Nonetheless, there is a great deal of membership overlap, so one would expect some degree of similarity among members. It also seems probable that those persons with the deepest connection to the church (regardless of their theological persuasion) would be the ones most likely to become involved in reform groups on both the left and the right.

Given an increasingly hostile stance on the part of church officials, reformers face three choices: (1) Some choose to remain active in reform organizations by making annual pilgrimages to national conventions of their reform group and by supporting the modest reform initiatives

---

[37] Married priests' gatherings are predominately male, while feminist gatherings tended to be overwhelmingly female. The largest feminist advocacy organization in this study, WOC, conducted a survey of its members in 2007 which revealed 82 percent were female, only 14 percent were younger than fifty-five, 85 percent were Caucasian, 3 percent were other/mixed, and 11 percent did not respond (*Sneak Preview*, 2007, p. 7).

[38] All the conferences of reform groups I attended included some speakers or workshop leaders who were black or Hispanic. CTA and WOC have been particularly proactive in their efforts to attract minorities as officers and members. CTA has a special antiracism project and designed its 2007 national conference around the theme "From Racism to Reconciliation."

sponsored by these groups, such as petitions to church leaders. (2) Some drop out of the Reform Movement altogether. CORPUS leader Allen Moore (2007) explains that many are "tired of having bloody foreheads" (p. 24), referring to reformers' experience of repeatedly knocking their heads against Vatican resistance. Subsequently, these reformers often cease to participate in any form of institutionalized religion or they become members of a non-Catholic denomination, a small faith community, or an underground parish that conducts Catholic liturgies. (3) Some join with like-minded reformers to create, mentor, or promote the creation of an underground worship community. This study does include examples of reformers who pursued each of these options, but lacked sufficient data to estimate the size or percentage in each group.

Methodology of the Study

The methodology of this study is comprised primarily of the qualitative methods of field research (as detailed in Appendix B). and in-depth interviews. I conducted the study over a six-year period covering 2002–2008, although the most intensive research occurred during 2004–2006.

My study focuses primarily on the twelve largest and best-known liberal reform groups, but there are actually several hundred liberal groups listed on CTA's website. These include locally based groups such as the Fellowship of Southern Illinois Laity (FOSIL) and single issue groups, such as Save Our Sacrament (SOS), which opposes annulments for divorced persons. Over the course of my research, I attended almost one-hundred events, including conferences and meetings of reform groups and visits to Roman Catholic parishes, Eucharist communities, vigiling parishes, and independent parishes, as well as forums at academic institutions. In researching reform groups, I attended more than forty events sponsored by reform groups, including more than thirty events sponsored by nine of the twelve reform groups featured in part 1. I also conducted forty interviews with leaders and activists from eight of the twelve reform groups featured in part 1 and twenty pastors and members of marginal and underground communities in parts 2 and 3. My research included a content analysis of an extensive range of literature and newsletters published by reform groups and marginal and underground communities. I also maintained extensive files of local and national newspaper and magazine articles covering Catholic reform issues and underground worship communities.

I conducted most of my research in Boston where I live. My decision to attend many reform group meetings and worship services in Boston reflected considerations of expense and convenience. My sample is not a probability sample and hence I do not claim that my data is representative of all activists or reform organizations. Despite its limitations, my location in Boston was advantageous in many respects since the abuse crisis erupted in Boston and VOTF's headquarters and most of its conferences are located here. The movement against parish closures began in Boston and the Council of Vigiling Parishes (CoP) meets here. Because Massachusetts is home to many liberal Catholics, it has local chapters of nearly all of the national reform groups in this study. Boston College and Regis College (where I teach) sponsored numerous forums on Roman Catholic Church reform and the abuse crisis. My study received funding from several research grants that enabled me to attend a range of events in Wisconsin, New York, New Jersey, Maryland, Virginia, and Florida. When I attended national conferences of reform groups, I interviewed movement activists from all over the United States.[39]

Outline of the Book

This study presents an overview of the escalating struggles between church hierarchs and progressive reform groups in three major sections. Part 1, entitled "Burned Out, Bummed Out, and Thrown Out: Progressive Reformers Begin Their Wilderness Journey," describes the efforts of progressive reform groups from 1975 to 2010. During this period, reformers primarily applied the first and weakest form of nonviolent resistance in their struggle with church leaders (i.e., *protest and persuasion*), which included petitions, newspaper ads, demonstrations at the meetings of the USCCB, and, on rare occasions, face-to-face meetings with church officials. Strategies based on protest and persuasion represent a commingling of the insider and outsider approach, in that (in keeping with the insider approach) they often appeal to the goodwill of the opponent and downplay confrontation, but (in keeping with the outsider approach) pose at

---

[39] Although Massachusetts is among the most liberal states in the United States, at least until the founding of VOTF it is was not regarded as the location with the most liberal Catholics. In fact, when William D'Antonio presented his data on VOTF at a Boston College conference in 2005, he admitted to being surprised that VOTF began in Boston because the Midwest was considered the center of liberal Catholicism.

least the risk of public censure and an escalating crisis of legitimacy. The analysis outlined in part 1 traces both the growing tension within VOTF and CTA over the lack of leverage represented by their insider approach and the gradual shift of four reform groups, DignityUSA, CORPUS, Catholic Organizations for Renewal (COR), and WOC, toward sectarian status. This historical overview explains why so many Vatican II reformers no longer view insider strategies as an effective reform option.

Part 2, "Testing the Waters and Pushing the Boundaries," describes reform strategies that apply Sharp's second form of nonviolence, referred to as *noncooperation*, which include forms of resistance more intense and confrontational than mere protest and persuasion in that they involve some form of deliberate disobedience or defiance. Groups involved in noncooperation include conventional Roman Catholic parishes that model Vatican II principles; vigiling churches that resist closure decrees; sisters who conduct priestless liturgies; and Eucharistic communities with resigned priests and canonically active priests who experiment with liturgical innovations.[40]

All of the groups described above retain some formal ties to the institutional church—Vatican II parishes and vigiling parishes remain in their dioceses, Eucharist communities employ canonically active priests, sisters remain in their orders, and resigned priests retain canonical authority. Hence, practitioners of noncooperation have one foot in the system and one foot out as they engage in collective acts of defiance or violation of formal church rules.

Part 3, "Notes from the Underground" describes and evaluates the third form of nonviolent strategies in Sharp's model, namely *parallel institutions*, which include the alternative worship communities and networks of communities (sometimes referred to as dioceses) that operate outside the formal institutional Roman Catholic Church and often rely on presiders who have not been ordained in the Roman Catholic Church.[41] The parallel institutions described herein include four types of independent

---

[40] According to Canon Law #290, sacraments including the Eucharist are considered "valid" when administered by an ordained Roman Catholic priest even if he resigns in order to marry. However, the sacraments are referred to as "valid but illicit" if the resigned priest has not obtained approval to perform sacraments from the presiding bishop.

[41] Resigned Roman Catholic priests sometimes preside at underground rituals, but many underground communities rely on persons ordained by independent groups not recognized by the Vatican. Some groups rotate the role of presider and at least occasionally appoint presiders who have never been ordained. (See chapters 8 and 9 for a more extensive coverage of liturgies in underground communities.)

Eucharist communities and five independent parishes, one network of independent parishes, and two seminary-like organizations. These parallel communities attract Catholics who are often deeply alienated from the institutional church or who no longer feel welcomed or nourished by their local parishes. Many liberal reformers favor communities where they can retain their allegiance and connection to their Catholic tradition on their own terms. Thus, parallel institutions represent the most extreme form of nonviolent resistance and are the most sect-like in that they represent genuine (not just threatened or partial) defection by members who are no longer willing to "play by the rules" and who see little hope, at least in the short term, of reforming the institution from within.

Nonviolent theory rests on the premise that if and when parallel institutions become sufficiently strong, host institutions will fall of their own weight as they will consequently lack the resources and membership necessary for survival. The Roman Catholic Church is too vast and stable an institution to collapse in the short term; yet it is clearly losing its foothold among Catholics in the United States. Mass attendance has declined dramatically (M. O. Steinfels, 2003), the number of Catholics in the United States decreased by nearly four hundred thousand in 2007 (Catholic Culture, 2009), and one in ten Americans is estimated to be a lapsed Catholic (Paulson, 2008b).

The conclusion places the Catholic Reform Movement in a larger historical and cultural context and draws on a range of theory to interpret the findings of the study and to examine their implications for future strategic choices on the part of the Reform Movement.

PART ONE

BURNED OUT, BUMMED OUT, AND THROWN OUT
PROGRESSIVE REFORMERS BEGIN THEIR WILDERNESS JOURNEY

CHAPTER ONE

A SOWER OF MUSTARD SEEDS:
CALL TO ACTION

Dan and Sheila Daley share background characteristics with many couples who were drawn to the Catholic Reform Movement the Daleys helped build. Both came of age during the Vatican II era and spent years in religious life: Dan as a Chicago priest for six years and Sheila as a member of the Sinsinawa Dominicans for four years. Dan and Sheila's evolution as leaders of the Reform Movement was sparked by their participation in the 1976 Call to Action Conference sponsored by U.S. bishops. This historic conference, entitled "Call to Action: Liberty and Justice for All," generated a far-reaching liberal reform agenda, but most of the resolutions were dismissed by the bishops. Consequently, the Daleys formed the reform group Call to Action, which was originally Chicago-based but eventually blossomed into one of the largest and best known of the American Catholic reform groups.

Dan and Sheila's emergence as Catholic rebels was no doubt shaped by ancestors who challenged church officials. For example, Dan's great grandfather, Peter Binkowski, once led a group of "angry ushers" at Holy Trinity Church who sent "the tyrannical pastor fleeing for his life" (T. Roberts, 2008b, p. 12). In Sheila's case, her entire extended family became Lutherans after a pastor refused Christian burial for her grandfather due to his poor church attendance.

Both Dan and Sheila brought notable and complementary skills to their task of building a national reform organization. Dan exudes many of the trademarks of an effective community organizer: a lighthearted, low-key approach to conflict, an affable, gregarious personality, and a nonstop work ethic. Long-term CTA-er Robert McClory (2008a) describes Dan as resembling "an old style Chicago politician" (p. 3). For her part, Sheila has a more reserved and formal manner, consistent with her role as the detail-oriented, pragmatic manager who keeps "Dan's creative ideas under control" (p. 3).

One might describe Dan and Sheila as something of a "dream team" whose energy and dedication to their cause seemed inexhaustible for their thirty-two years as codirectors of CTA. CTA activists whom I interviewed describe the Daleys in exalted terms, emphasizing their "humble and openhearted nature," their willingness to live on a "shoestring budget" to keep CTA afloat, and their insistence on outreach to young Catholics. In 2008, the Daleys announced their resignation necessitated by Sheila's disabilities resulting from a catastrophic automobile accident (McClory, 2008b).

CTA publications include many testimonials to the Daleys, such as one by CTA members John and Carol Miles (2003) asserting that in contrast to the "inflated hopes" of those impressed by Pope Benedict XVI's recent visit, "Call to Actions' oft-scorned disciples are walking the harder, less traveled road toward a Church that truly inspires hope in and invites all sisters and brothers to work in solidarity in a socially just and peaceful world" (p. 3). In response to criticisms of the Daleys as "strident" and "iconoclastic," *National Catholic Reporter* editor-at-large Tom Roberts (2008b) describes the Daleys as "too self-effacing, not only about themselves, but also about Call to Action, to fit the description of ecclesiastically dangerous" (p. 12).

A New Movement Emerges

The founding of Call to Action (CTA) in 1977 marks the emergence of liberal Catholic reformers as a full-fledged religious movement. CTA aims to inspire a revivalist movement focused on insider reform strategies that would reclaim the liberal spirit of Vatican II and create a new model of Catholicism appropriate for the modern age. Increasingly, CTA embraces groups that have moved in a sectarian direction after exhausting avenues for achieving insider reform.

Since its founding in 1977, CTA, which claims twenty-five thousand members and fifty-three chapters, has served as a clearinghouse and facilitator for a range of progressive Catholic reform groups. CTA's *Mission Statement* (2008) states, "CTA is a Catholic movement working for equality and justice in the Church and in society.... CTA believes that the spirit of God is at work in the whole church, not just in its appointed leaders."

Reflecting the antibureaucratic ethos of the 1960s, which shaped CTA founders, CTA has remained a loosely structured movement organization dedicated to facilitating activism among a network of reform groups. The reform groups most closely associated with CTA include DignityUSA, the Corps of Reserve Priests United for Service (CORPUS), Women's Ordination Conference (WOC), FutureChurch, and Catholic Organizations for Renewal (COR), all of which sponsor information booths and workshops at annual CTA national conferences.

CTA experienced dramatic growth from 8,173 members in 1993 to 22,272 in 2000 (Thompson, 2001), but since 2000 its membership has hovered between 25,000 and 30,000. Attendance at CTA's national conference in Milwaukee usually draws thousands.[1]

---

[1] Attendances at CTA conferences reached a high of five thousand in 1996 and fell within the range of two to four thousand between 2001 and 2009 (N. S., personal communication, November 20, 2009).

Origins of CTA

As noted in the vignette above, CTA traces its roots to the now-legendary 1976 gathering sponsored by the United States Conference of Catholic Bishops (USCCB) entitled "Call to Action: Liberty and Justice for All," which was preceded by two years of hearings and discussions in parishes that solicited input from eight hundred thousand Catholics (CTA, *Our history*, 2009).[2] Catholic bishops took action on some conference resolutions focusing on peace and justice, but ignored resolutions focused on a range of hot-button issues among liberal Catholics, including the role of the laity in governance and a more inclusive priesthood. Disappointed by the outcome of the bishops' conference, nine existing Chicago-area organizations of priests, nuns, lay Catholics, and teachers formed a coalition and convened the first CTA conference in October 1978 that drew four hundred participants (Thompson, 2001).

CTA became a national organization when it published a petition entitled "A Call for Reform in the Catholic Church" in *The New York Times* on Ash Wednesday, 1990, that eventually attracted twenty thousand signatures. This ad outlined CTA's agenda of reforms that had been rejected by the bishops and includes (in abbreviated form):

- Reform and renew church structures.
- Incorporate women at all levels of ministry.
- Discard medieval discipline of mandatory celibacy.
- Consult with the Catholic people regarding teaching on human sexuality.
- Allow laity, religious and clergy to participate in selection of bishops.
- Support open dialogue, academic freedom and due process.
- Financial openness at all levels.
- Fundamental change to attract young people. (Thompson, 2001, pp. 4–5)

These positions were bold in that they obviously challenge many church policies, but CTA avoided taking explicit stands on questions of human sexuality (referring to reproductive issues). Thus, CTA sidesteps a few

---

[2] This USCCB conference was attended by 100 bishops, 11,341 delegates (64 percent of whom were church employees), and 1000 observers (including many representatives of reform groups) (Thompson, 2001, pp. 1–4).

issues that may be controversial among its own members. My own informal discussions with CTA members indicate that the question of abortion, especially "abortion on demand," remains controversial among many CTA activists.

A Mecca for Progressive Catholics

CTA spokespersons respond to critics who label them "too far left to be Catholic" by citing data on their membership revealed by conference registrations that portray participants as "thoroughly mainstream" (Thompson, 2001, p. 6). According to CTA data, 90 percent attend church regularly, 70 percent are active church volunteers, 75 percent are lay and 20 percent vowed religious, and 5 percent priests (as well as several bishops). Although attendees at CTA conferences are primarily middle-aged and older, CTA has made a concerted effort to attract young Catholics by sponsoring NextGeneration programs including an Internet chat room, annual retreats, and special outreach for young Catholics (defined as adults ranging in age from eighteen to forty-two).[3] In 2006 CTA recruited a young Chicana American, Nicole Sotelo, to oversee media relations and the NextGeneration programs. Speakers at CTA conferences often ask audiences to applaud the several hundred young CTA-ers visible at conference events. According to CTA codirector Sheila Daley, 15 percent of CTA members fall into the NextGeneration age category (S. Daley as cited in McClory, 2003).

Although CTA does not publish data on the social class or racial background of its members, one might assume that those who attend CTA conferences have comfortable incomes, judging by the fact that conference fees range between $160 and $300. For those who finance travel costs as well as meals and hotel costs, a weekend conference could easily cost $1,000-$2,000 or more. The fact that many conference attendees are well dressed, carry cell phones, and shop avidly at marketplace booths is further evidence that CTA members are relatively affluent. However, I did encounter some CTA members with modest incomes who financed attendance at conferences by economizing on food and lodging.[4]

---

[3] According to CTA staff member Nicole Sotelo, CTA's NextGeneration program has 300 members and its blog for young Catholics (http://youngadultcatholics-blog.com) has attracted 37,000 visitors since it was established in 2008 (personal communication, March 19, 2009).

[4] For example I did meet two Minnesota couples at the 2003 Conference who drove to Milwaukee in a single car, stayed in budget motels, and even brought hot plates to

Preaching to the Choir?

Most of the attendees whom I met at CTA conferences were regulars who considered CTA conferences a "can't miss" event and looked forward to connecting with friends and acquaintances from prior conferences. When I said good-bye to eight different persons at the 2003 conference, they responded with some version of, "See you at the next conference," assuming that I had now become a regular, like so many others who caught the CTA fervor.

Given that CTA describes itself as an organization of *progressive* Catholics and its agenda (stated above) favors liberal causes, it seems fair to conclude that CTA members are to the left in their political and theological orientation. This contention is supported by many of the liberal and radical speakers at CTA conferences.[5] In fact CTA members are often stereotyped by movement insiders as aging sixties-era leftists who have remained involved in peace and justice advocacy. However, there are clearly some participants who attend CTA events that are not easily categorized as liberal.

A case in point is Genevieve (a pseudonym), an elderly Caucasian woman I met at the 2003 conference from a rural town in northern Wisconsin, who proudly announced she was attending her fourth CTA conference, accompanied by her daughter and daughter-in-law (G. L., personal communication, November 8, 2003). These three women were so mesmerized by the first conference they attended that it has become an annual event, financed by splitting the costs of gas and a single hotel room. Genevieve explained that she had always been miffed by her husband's insistence on attending weekly Mass, as she found the lifeless liturgy and "dull, condescending sermons" intolerable. A turning point in her relationship to Catholicism occurred when she stumbled upon Matthew Fox's (1983) book *Original Blessing* in a bookstore. Although she found it difficult, she plowed through it and was delighted by the fresh perspective she

---

economize on food (J. S., personal communication, November 8, 2003). I met one elderly lady from Boston who took the train to Milwaukee on a budget fare and stayed with friends every year to attend the CTA conference. CTA also offers reduced rates for students and some scholarships, including ones marked for NextGeneration Catholics.

[5] Examples of liberal activists at CTA conferences include noted peace activists Kathy Kelly of Voices in the Wilderness (2003), John Dear, S.J., formerly of Fellowship of Reconciliation (2006), and Cindy Sheehan of Gold Star Families for Peace (2007). Examples of liberal theologians include feminist and environmental theologian Miriam Therese Winter (2003), originator of creation spirituality Matthew Fox (2005), and Vatican II scholar Bernard Cooke (2007).

gained regarding her faith. Far from hiding her new insights, with a mischievous grin she described taunting her pastor by citing Fox's book and bragging about her plans to attend CTA conferences. Genevieve appeared to be in her late seventies and relied on a cane to move about. Thus, while it seems unlikely that she would become a CTA activist, her middle-aged daughter and daughter-in-law, who "thoroughly enjoyed" CTA conferences, do represent potential recruits. Genevieve and her daughters represent laypersons for whom CTA was something of a conversion experience in terms of their relationship to Catholicism.

Another participant who captured my attention at the 2003 CTA conference was a tiny elderly woman with tightly permed hair and a stooped posture. This woman, whose name tag read Gladys, appeared anxious as she sat near me during a workshop by psychologist Richard Sipe entitled: "Clergy Sexual Abuse: The Crisis Behind the Headlines." During this workshop Sipe briefly reviewed some of the salacious details of papal history, revealing that some popes were married or had numerous mistresses and illegitimate children. He also stated his estimates of the extent of clergy abuse, warning that "the worst is yet to come," and that ultimately high-ranking clergy will be exposed as abusers. During the presentation Gladys's mouth dropped open in astonishment. At several points her face reddened and she frequently shook her head in dismay. At the end of the presentation Gladys trembled slightly as she raised herself from her seat and stumbled toward the exit. In response, several persons noted her distress and offered assistance. She replied by shaking her head from side to side while struggling to compose herself, and seemed relieved when she met up with a companion shortly thereafter. Gladys's demeanor suggests she was shocked to learn about scandals in church history and the extent of the abuse crisis that are probably not well known among many lay Catholics, who tend to think of popes and bishops as saintly persons. These two examples cited above suggest that CTA does not preach only to the choir of "progressive, enlightened" Catholics but at least in some instances, does also reach out to less-educated, ordinary Catholics.

Excommunication: A Badge of Courage?

Another significant feature of CTA's membership is that they welcome and even assign top conference billing to Catholics out of favor with the Vatican, in that individuals and groups who have been formally excommunicated or have voluntarily severed their relationship to the institutional church are featured speakers at CTA events. Examples include former Dominican priest Matthew Fox (who became an Episcopalian priest after years of conflict with the Vatican), priests Mary Ramerman and James Callan (who formed the breakaway Catholic Spiritus Christi parish in Rochester, New York), and priests and bishops ordained by Roman Catholic Womenpriests (RCWP) (all of whom have been excommunicated by Vatican decree).[6] CTA's embrace of these Catholics who have been censured by the Vatican seems logical, given that the speakers cited above chose to distance themselves from the institutional church to promote the very issues CTA embraces, including free intellectual inquiry (in the case of Matthew Fox) and women's ordination and lay decision making (in the cases of Spiritus Christi and RCWP).

Not only does CTA embrace excommunicated or defecting Catholics but it also faced a wholesale excommunication crisis of its own in March 1996 when Bishop Fabian Bruskewitz of Lincoln, Nebraska, imposed an excommunication edict on all members of CTA's Nebraska chapter.[7] Bruskewitz has become a principal foe of Catholic reformers, not only for his excommunication decree but also because his diocese is the only Roman Catholic diocese in the United States that refuses to participate in the annual audit of church policies on child abuse conducted by the USCCB Office of Child and Youth Protection (Reeves, 2006).

CTA's Nebraska chapter has carried on despite the excommunication decree, and even gained ten new members following the decree (Schaeffer, 1997a). Nonetheless, at the 2006 national CTA conference, a chapter member admitted, "Sometimes it's hard to convince Catholics they should join an organization when it translates into excommunication." In 2006 the CTA chapter announced it was appealing the excommunication decree after Bishop Bruskewitz released a letter from the Vatican upholding his decree (Call to Action, 2006c). Although the Apostolic Signatura, the Vatican's highest court, rejected CTA's appeal, the CTA-Nebraska chapter announced it would find "the proper avenue" for continuing the appeal

---

[6] See chapter 9 for more extensive coverage of Spiritus Christi and RCWP.
[7] This excommunication edict included not just the CTA Nebraska chapter but other groups as well, including several Masonic organizations, Catholics for a Free Choice (CFC), and Planned Parenthood.

(*Vatican tribunal won't*, 2007). These excommunications pose inescapable quandaries for CTA as an organization struggling to save a church whose highest-ranking officials seem intent on obliterating it.[8]

Accomplishments of CTA

CTA Conferences: A Can't-Miss Experience for Catholic Reformers

CTA's most outstanding achievement is its annual conference, which many observers have praised lavishly for its lively, upbeat spirit and its provocative, eclectic smorgasbord of presenters.[9] *National Catholic Reporter* editor Tom Fox (2003) wrote a glowing account of CTA's 2003 conference, proclaiming that

> every adult Catholic should at least once be enriched by the intellectual appeal that comes from mingling with several thousand hope-filled, renewal-minded Catholics. The environment is inclusive, which means that at a Call to Action gathering one feels the Church walking on both legs—and how different it is. (p. 7)

Swiss theologian Hans Küng (1981) also gave a rave review of CTA's liturgy in his speech to the 1981 CTA conference, stating,

> We had a beautiful liturgy before and a beautiful sermon also. I think the Eucharist proves that it was worthwhile to fight that we can now have such a liturgy ... we have to fight to see that we do not lose even women who are allowed to preach. (p. 5)

My own observations at five CTA conferences confirm Tom Fox's emphasis on the energizing, celebratory nature of these conferences. CTA keynote speakers are consistently high-profile authors and activists who deliver eloquent and sophisticated presentations that almost always evoke standing ovations from audiences. Examples of keynoters include

---

[8] Some members of the Reform Movement insist the excommunication by decrees (such as those applying to CTA's Nebraska chapter and RCWP) are not valid since Canon 1342 requires "a trial unless precluded by 'just causes' such as the accused person's refusal to appear" (Schaeffer, 1997b). Even when there are grounds for denying a trial, Canon 1720 requires the accused "be given an opportunity for self-defense."

[9] The priority CTA places on its annual conference is attested to by the high percentage of its budget devoted to this event: between 2005 and 2007 the percentage of CTA's revenues from conference fees ranged from 32 to 37 percent and conference expenses represented between 31 and 33 percent of total CTA budgetary expenses.

the Reverend James Lawson (2003), a leader in the American civil rights movement; Benedictine Sister Joan Chittister (2006), a prolific author and speaker on church affairs; and Dr. Clarissa Pinkola Estes (2005), Jungian analyst and author. Conference-goers feast on an enticing array of breakout sessions that include topics related to church reform, spiritual development, and peace and justice issues in the larger society. For those who tire of academic-style workshops, the conference program includes a "kaleidoscope of the arts: music, story-telling, theatre art, movement, dance and film" (Call to Action, 2006b, p. 4). For example the 2006 conference featured a dramatization of the play *The Story of Dorothy Day*, a workshop on mandala making, a musical performance by folk singers Kim and Reggie Harris, and a range of innovative liturgies.

Even during plenary sessions conference planners create a relaxed and festive mood by including a variety of skits, video clips, and audience participation exercises that are delivered with dramatic flair and wry humor designed to create a convivial atmosphere. For example, at the 2003 conference, the master of ceremonies invited everyone in the audience to stand if they were named Mary, next if they were related to someone named Mary, and finally if they knew someone named Mary, until finally everyone in the hall was standing and joking among themselves about the prevalence of the name "Mary" in Catholic circles.

CTA liturgies are highly flamboyant, participatory events that feature a dazzling array of liturgical dancers, live bands and choral groups, dramatizations of biblical readings, and homilists who are usually not ordained priests but well-known progressive theologians. If some attendees prefer less razzmatazz for their communal worship, CTA offers morning workshops featuring various forms of contemplative prayer, chant, meditation, and alternative liturgies.

CTA's Impact on Peace and Justice Activism

A *Time* magazine article describes CTA "as the premier membership organization" of Catholic liberals including "peace activist Daniel Berrigan, feminist Joan Chittister, and sociologist/author Fr. Andrew Greeley" (Van Biema, 2008). This article describes the influence of CTA as pivotal for Catholic reformers whose influence extended to "the highest reaches of the American Church as American bishops passed left-leaning statements on nuclear weapons and economic justice." Terrence Tilley, chair of Fordham University's theology department, is quoted as stating, "For a couple of generations, progressivism was an [important] way to be Catholic." Tilley also credits CTA with changing the attitudes of American Catholics, many of whom now agree with CTA's positions.[10]

CTA's Impact on Church Reform

Although it is often stereotyped as an outsider organization, CTA claims some insider credentials. For example CTA leaders have engaged in various dialogues with church hierarchs. In 2004 director Dan Daley participated in the Culture of Conversation Project in which five bishops and a variety of activists spent a weekend engaging in open dialogue "on all church issues, from sexual abuse to the availability of the Eucharist" (Call to Action, 2005, p. 2). For more than fifteen years, Dan Daley and other CTA staff attended USCCB's annual Social Ministry Gathering on Capitol Hill (Thompson, 2001). CTA also received an award from the late Cardinal Joseph Bernardin when he was Chicago's archbishop (T. Roberts, 2008b).

Documenting CTA's achievements is difficult because CTA newsletters primarily take the form of listing a whole range of activities by reform groups associated with CTA, rather than highlighting their own accomplishments. Looking back after thirty-two years with CTA, codirectors Dan and Sheila Daley do not claim to have achieved major reforms in church policies. Instead, Sheila describes their organization as "an alternative community within the church and that our contribution doesn't rise or fall on whether we've gotten the church to change" (S. Daley as cited in T. Roberts, 2008b, p. 13). Dan Daley acknowledges the effectiveness of outsider strategies, stating, "Once they're forced to disclose, whether it is because of sex abuse or financial accountability, ... the myth that they are somehow excused from that is gone" (D. Daley as cited in T. Roberts, p. 12). Consequently, Dan notes that Catholics are now more willing to speak out, and "the church in that respect has changed irrevocably."

Although CTA's major focus is not limited to church reform per se, there are a number of small-scale victories cited in its publications that can be attributed to primarily insider strategies including the following:

---

[10] Although Tilley makes a positive assessment of CTA's legacy in this article, this book cites a variety of sources (including Tilley) who believe CTA and the Reform Movement as a whole have reached an impasse and are in decline.

- CTA claims "partial credit" for the Vatican decision to lift the excommunication decree on Oblate Father Tissa Balasuriya[11] in 1997, citing CTA's efforts in rallying for his cause. (Call to Action, 1997, p. 1)[12]
- In 2003 a CTA chapter in North Virginia helped persuade Bishop Paul Loverde to take action on clergy abuse by calling for a boycott of the Lenten collection. Loverde responded by publishing names of his lay review board, naming a victim assistance coordinator, and setting up a separate lay advisory board to oversee work with victims. (Call to Action, 2003)
- CTA played an instrumental role in helping St. Augustine's parishioners in New Orleans persuade the archdiocese to reopen their church after it had been closed. St. Augustine's is the first African American Catholic parish in the United States. (Call to Action, 2006a)
- CTA members help initiate lay synods in various regions of the United States that give laypersons a chance to voice their concerns and engage in dialogue with bishops. (Call to Action, 2007)

CTA's victories attributable to insider strategies do not rise to the level of structural reform because they do not involve changes in formal policy at the diocesan or Vatican level.

Regarding outsider strategies, CTA emphasizes its role as a facilitator of the Reform Movement, most notably by hosting the Catholic Organizations for Renewal (COR), a network of twenty-four reform groups, which meets for several days before the CTA conference. CTA claims that COR, with the assistance of CTA staff, has had some impact on views of Catholic laity, as demonstrated by a 1992 Gallup poll of U.S. Catholics that revealed growing support for CTA's agenda items (Thompson, October, 2001).

CTA has also been a participant, alongside Voice of the Faithful (VOTF) and other reform groups, in the range of outsider strategies that include media and legislative campaigns pertaining to the abuse crisis and financial accountability. To the extent that these campaigns have succeeded in changing church policy, CTA can claim some measure of credit, although,

---

[11] Father Tissa Balasuriya is a Sri Lankan Catholic priest and progressive theologian noted for his work on interreligious dialogue.
[12] This reversal in Vatican policy regarding Tissa Balasuriya was not a total victory but reflected compromises on both sides. For an account of this case see: Stanton, H. (Ed). (1997). *Mary and Human Liberation: The Story and the Text*. Harrisburg, PA: Trinity International Press.

as chapter 2 documents, VOTF has played a more visible and significant role in these campaigns.

Criticisms of CTA

CTA: Is It Too Far to the Left to Be Effectual?

CTA is criticized by some mainstream and conservative Catholics for its leftist bent. Journalist Peter Steinfels (2003) refers to CTA as "a protean Catholic Church reform group that rather indiscriminately embraces thoroughly radical critics of the church alongside moderate Catholic liberals and even a few bishops" (p. 27). Some CTA members occasionally describe CTA as "all call, no action," meaning that CTA's energizing conferences are not followed up with activities at the local level to sustain and expand the energy unleashed at conferences (Moynihan, 2006, p. 12). Although CTA does boast fifty-three local chapters, many chapters are small and meetings are rare, so that chapters may not offer members ongoing opportunities for enrichment and activism they seek. Partly in response to this criticism, CTA has sponsored or organized a series of regional synods (noted above) in which laypersons gather to discuss church policies and, when possible, meet with local church hierarchs.

One can only speculate regarding how many potential church reformers reject the Reform Movement not because they are apathetic, but simply because it seems quixotic and futile. For some the cost of attending the conference in terms of time and money was too high, given their belief that, as one respondent explained, there would be "no practical outcome" or "concrete achievement" to justify their investment (A. K., personal communication, 2003).[13] Conference participants also complain that they want more open dialogue about the viability of the Reform Movement, particularly since, as one person put it, "the church is moving in the opposite direction" and "one might be excommunicated just for speaking out or joining CTA." Although these questions do occasionally come up at some conference sessions, most conference presenters adopt an "onward and upward" message that seems to take for granted conference-goers will remain loyal to Catholicism and the Reform Movement.

---

[13] Eight persons whom I interviewed described CTA conferences as "a great time" but decided not to return because they did not believe CTA could change church policy.

For example, during the plenary address by author Gary Wills at the 2003 CTA conference, an elderly man in a frustrated tone exclaimed, "We have been working for reform for twenty-five years now and we are no longer afraid of the hierarchy, but nothing seems to change." He suggested organizing a group to sit in at the Vatican that would announce, "We won't leave until our demands are met." In response, Wills nixed the suggestion of a sit-in, but assured the audience that he was convinced change would be forthcoming.[14]

Why Stay?

At the 2004 conference a debate about the question "Why stay?" did surface, in a workshop entitled "Why I Remain Catholic and Why You Should Too, Despite Everything." This workshop, conducted by long-term CTA leader Robert McClory, drew a standing-room-only crowd, thereby providing some evidence of the interest in this question among CTA conference-goers. During the workshop McClory (2005b) admitted many of his friends were leaving the Catholic Church, particularly women who were fed up with what they described as their "second class status" (p. 2). McClory took a defensive posture, citing the richness of the church's legacy—"its great scholars and saints, its great achievements, its sublime art and music, its zeal for human welfare and for a just world environment" (p. 2). McClory also cited the sense of community Catholics experience participating in a Eucharistic celebration and the spiritual enrichment he received from his exemplary parish, St. Nicholas in Evanston, Illinois. During his presentation, McClory urged his listeners to use humor to bolster their spirits and poke fun at the hierarchy, as he mocked the decision of the Trenton, New Jersey, diocese to declare invalid the first communion of a girl who received a host that lacked gluten, due to her dietary restrictions. According to McClory's satirical "ancient Gospel unearthed" passage, Peter asks, "Just what is so special about gluten?" and Jesus's reply parodies conservative hierarchs as follows: "It's a mystery and I don't want to talk about it anymore, so get busy washing the dishes" (p. 2).

---

[14] By 2008 Wills describes himself as "poped out," admitting he is no longer interested in commenting on the Roman Catholic hierarchy, and, while he remains Roman Catholic, he describes church reform as "not his business" (Wills as cited in J. Allen, 2008b, p. 1). Although Wills believes the church will eventually reform, he has no plans to become involved in the Reform Movement or devote any more writing to Catholic topics.

McClory's arguments were challenged by William Cleary, a former Jesuit priest and veteran of the Reform Movement. Cleary (2005) wrote McClory in advance of the conference and McClory encouraged him to attend the workshop. Cleary argued, "You should be saying (shouldn't you?) Catholic friends, the real God is speaking to us right now in history: leave the Roman Catholic Church behind" (p. 20). The very reasons Cleary cited for his decision to reject Catholicism correspond closely to items CTA hopes to reform: its "poisonous disdain for women," its "morally disgraced priesthood," its "reversal of Jesus' dearest teaching on service leadership," its rigid theology, its isolated papacy and "out of control" papal office, and its "intimidations of sexual minorities" (p. 20).

I heard this same debate over "Why stay?" repeated, albeit in a less sophisticated fashion, among many gatherings of reformers at CTA gatherings and in many other settings. Persons on both sides of the argument seem anguished and a bit tentative about their choice. Even in the debate above, McClory (2005b) concludes his defense of Catholicism by admitting, "I'm not rock solid on this" (p. 2), while Cleary (2005) ends his call to abandon Catholicism by extolling its "wealth of grace and its ethical beauty that stretches all the way to a preferential option for the poor to a borderless world aiming at international brotherhood and sisterhood" (p. 21). Thus, it seems fair to conclude that neither choice is entirely comfortable for progressive Catholics: staying in an increasingly punitive and rightward-shifting church evokes one sort of discomfort, while leaving one's deeply engrained religious heritage evokes a similar but distinct sense of estrangement.

What's Next?

For more than thirty years Call to Action has provided a community and network for Catholics caught in this "can't live with or without" dilemma. It remains to be seen how CTA will refashion itself under new leadership, and, indeed, whether CTA can survive in the new terrain facing reform organizations as the ranks of Vatican II Catholics dwindle and younger Catholics increasingly express a willingness to explore other religious denominations or reject any form of religious affiliation (Paulson, 2008b). One hopeful sign is CTA's selection of a youthful new executive director, Jim FitzGerald, a long-term CTA board member with an extensive background in theology and administration of nonprofits.

CHAPTER TWO

REBUILDING THE TEMPLE:
VOICE OF THE FAITHFUL

At first glance James E. Muller and James E. Post did not appear to be likely candidates for founding a new Catholic reform organization, Voice of the Faithful (VOTF). As lifelong Catholics, both were preoccupied with successful and demanding careers, Muller as a distinguished cardiologist and Post as a professor in the Strategy and Policy Department at Boston University. Both also found spiritual nourishment as members of an exemplary Vatican II-type parish, St. John the Evangelist in Wellesley, Massachusetts, whose pastor, Tom Powers, advised Muller, "You are the Church" when Muller requested meeting space to discuss the clergy sexual abuse crisis (Muller & Kenney, 2004, p. 25).

Like so many Boston-area Catholics, Muller and Post were shocked out of complacency when news of the abuse crisis broke in Boston in 2002 and the extent of Cardinal Bernard Law's complicity in protecting pedophile priests was exposed. Muller explains his response to the abuse scandal as follows: "It was my church and I could not leave it. But I also knew that I could not remain and simply accept what happened" (Muller & Kenney, 2004, p. 3). Thus Muller laid the foundations for VOTF by organizing a weekly discussion group in his own parish, and this group (which included Post) gradually expanded to form VOTF, which carved out a centrist path, distinguishing itself from other reform groups by making a "conscious decision to work for change from within the church" (p. 37).

As a principal founder of VOTF, Muller had undeniable star appeal as a Nobel Laureate recognized for his leadership role in the International Physicians for the Prevention of Nuclear War (IPPNW).[1] As an advocate for IPPNW, Muller successfully solicited a letter of support from none other than Pope John Paul II. Given his stature, Muller had much to offer a fledging organization like VOTF: he is a gifted meeting facilitator and polished public speaker, whose PowerPoint presentations at the early VOTF meetings contrasted his vision of a stable church structure buttressed by an active laity with a crumbling rightward-leaning pyramid structure representing today's dysfunctional church. Muller and Kenney's (2004) book about VOTF, *Keep the Faith, Change the Church* cites many examples of Muller's easy access to prominent theologians, church hierarchs, and media representatives.

---

[1] Dr. James Muller was a leader and founder of International Physicians for the Prevention of Nuclear War (IPPNW), an organization that was awarded the Nobel Peace Prize in 1985.

My interviews and observations of VOTF members revealed a high measure of respect for VOTF's founders, especially James Post, VOTF's president from 2002 to 2006, when his heavy lifting kept the organization afloat after the heady early days, when VOTF was energized by intense media attention. Post conveys a kindly paternal manner and confident, informed speaking style that weaves together apt quotations from scripture, church documents, and scholarly sources. VOTF members praise Post's generous donations of time and money, as evidenced by his willingness to attend VOTF events within and beyond the boundaries of the United States, often at his own expense. Clearly, the high level of respect accorded both Post and Muller suggests that the emergence and survival of VOTF reflects, in part, the quality and dedication of its first two presidents.

A Centrist Reform Movement

This chapter examines the newest and probably most visible Catholic Reform Movement in the United States, Voice of the Faithful (VOTF), which was founded in 2002 in Boston in response to the clergy abuse scandal that rocked Boston-area Catholics and eventually the entire country. VOTF is a type of revivalist movement, but it has a narrower focus than other reform groups because it does not challenge church dogma. VOTF describes itself as centrist and is focused on insider reform. Despite its more modest goals and philosophy, VOTF has not been noticeably more successful than other more liberal reform groups in its efforts at dialogue with church hierarchs.

VOTF is an important case study for an overview of Catholic reform for the following reasons:

1. VOTF is the first reform group that attempted to build a mass membership organization for lay Roman Catholics that included conservatives, moderates, and liberals.
2. While other reform groups have largely abandoned insider tactics,[2] VOTF hopes to achieve "a seat at the table" with church hierarchs.[3]

---

[2] As noted in the introduction, insider strategies aim to win the hearts and minds of the Vatican and American bishops through various forms of advocacy, education, and lobbying. Outsider strategies aim to achieve concessions by bringing to bear external pressure, especially negative media attention, legal maneuvers, and creation of independent worship communities that force the hands of institutional leaders.

[3] VOTF intentionally avoided the terms *renewal* and *reform* that were associated with "movements that had polarized and paralyzed the laity" (Muller & Kenney, p. 33), an unmistakable reference to chapter 1 and those described in chapter 3 and 4.

My analysis concludes that VOTF's insider strategies have demonstrated minimal effectiveness, but its embrace of outsider strategies has achieved some modest but significant gains in terms of promoting its three goals of (1) supporting victims of clergy abuse, (2) supporting priests of integrity, and (3) working for structural change in the church (*VOTF Mission Statement*, 2004).

I attribute VOTF's inability to build a mass membership base among a broad spectrum of Roman Catholics in part to difficulties in bridging the deep and ever-widening gaps in views of conservative and liberal Catholics over issues at the center of societal-wide "culture wars." Indeed, visions and reform objectives of the right and left wings of Roman Catholicism are the polar opposite of each other. Like other reform groups, VOTF encountered widespread apathy among laypersons, even in the midst of the abuse crisis, and had little success in efforts at dialogue with church hierarchs. VOTF's failure to unify the opposing sides within Catholicism reflects the conclusions of Wuthnow (1988) regarding increased polarization resulting from the widening gap in beliefs and opinions between liberals and conservatives within religious denominations.[4]

A New Lay Reform Group Emerges

The group of parishioners from St. John the Evangelist Parish in Wellesley, Massachusetts, who laid the groundwork for VOTF includes highly educated and influential Catholics who convinced each other that they were obliged to save the church they loved by taking steps to reform the flaws in church structures that allowed the clergy abuse crisis to occur.[5] This small founding group in Wellesley attracted a wider audience by holding open meetings on Monday evenings in the basement of St. John the Evangelist Parish.

On the two occasions I attended, these early VOTF meetings were packed, emotionally intense, highly charged events in which the audience listened attentively to every speaker and applauded them

---

[4] The implications of culture wars for the Catholic Reform Movement are discussed in the introduction.

[5] A study of VOTF members conducted in 2005 revealed that they have high levels of education: 87 percent have a college degree and 60 percent have graduate degrees (D'Antonio and Pogoeric, 2007). More information on this study is provided in the introduction.

enthusiastically. Meeting facilitators also led the audience in VOTF's Opening Prayer, which read, in part:

> We are the Church; we are the Body of Christ.
> Strengthen us, fill us with wisdom,
> Lead us to holy action in building up your reign.
> Help us to respect our voice and the voice of the faithful.
> (*VOTF national working group*, 2005, p. 2)

The prayer conveys the tone of VOTF meetings in that it has a reverential quality, but hints at a more assertive role for the laity by affirming "we are the Church," a phrase that became a mantra at VOTF gatherings. VOTF's mission statement reflects a similar tone as follows: "To Provide a Prayerful Voice, Attentive to the Spirit, Through Which the Faithful Can Actively Participate in the Governance and Guidance of the Catholic Church" (p. 2).

Both early VOTF meetings I attended featured a talk by a middle-aged Caucasian Susan Renahan, a "victim-survivor," who addressed the audience in a bitterly angry tone as she recounted her abuse in a Catholic grade school by a pastor who was later revealed to be a serial abuser. She described being dragged out of class by the pastor and raped in a variety of locations. Despite her caustic, even accusing tone toward the audience, Renahan received standing ovations following her speech at both meetings I attended, although the graphic descriptions of rape had elicited winces and embarrassed looks from many in the audience. This reaction reflects the background of VOTF members, who were raised in an era when sexuality was a taboo topic and priests were regarded as saintly persons.

These early VOTF meetings evoked mixed reviews from attendees whom I interviewed. Several persons had high praise for these meetings and eventually became VOTF activists. Others expressed an ambivalent reaction, praising the articulate speakers but questioning what the group hoped to accomplish. A few others expressed dismay over the survivor speech, which they found too strident and not entirely credible. They expressed concern that, by asking survivors to endlessly repeat their stories, VOTF was (as one person stated) "reinforcing their identification with the disempowering status of victim, making it difficult to move beyond their anger and bitterness and fashion a positive identity" (G. L., personal communication, May 6 & October 15, 2002).

One attendee who was a professional psychotherapist responded, "VOTF needs to learn that public meetings are not therapeutic settings.

As a therapist I know victims need to express memories and emotions related to the abuse in a private, supportive environment" (A. K., personal communication, September 14, 2002). She asked, "Was VOTF endangering victims by featuring them in a public setting where they continually recounted episodes of abuse and in which they flaunted their outrage, sometimes blaming all Catholics for failing to believe them or protecting abusers?"[6] Eventually VOTF decided testimonies by abuse victims would no longer be included in its weekly meetings.

A Path-Breaking Conference

VOTF's astonishingly successful 2002 convention entitled "Response of the Faithful" was held July 30, 2002, just five months after the small group in Wellesley had launched the organization. This hastily organized convention attracted more than four thousand Catholics to fill Boston's Hynes Convention Center. The convention evoked rave reviews as a lively, smoothly flowing event that included an entire day on issues related to church reform.[7] In his address to the conference, VOTF President James Post (2002) emphasized dialogue with bishops as a central VOTF objective, though he identified three conditions for the terms of the dialogue, namely, "our right to exist," "our right to be heard," and "our right to free speech as American Catholics."

Overall, the convention featured many eloquent, passionate speakers who did not hesitate to exercise their right to free speech, particularly canon lawyer Tom Doyle, O.P.J.C.D.[8] who received a standing ovation for his speech attributing the abuse crisis to the "fallacy of clericalism" that fostered "an unbridled addiction to power" (Doyle as cited in Muller & Kenney, 2004, p. 160) among church hierarchs.

Assessing the 2002 Convention, VOTF founder James Muller (2004) speculated that VOTF's "success had come off too well.... We had

---

[6] Two of the three critics suggested that VOTF should seek more mature "survivors" who had moved past the self-pitying, finger-pointing stage (A. K. and S. L., personal communication, July 26, 2002).

[7] Conference sessions included: clergy abuse ("Creating a Sexually Safe Parish"), the role of the laity ("The Authority for Lay Participation in Governance"), and organization building ("Starting a Parish Voice Affiliate: Chapter or Non Chapter").

[8] Father Tom Doyle was awarded VOTF's first Priest of Integrity of Award at this conference in recognition of his role in conducting an investigation of clergy sexual abuse for the Vatican. Doyle was fired by the Vatican following his intense efforts to convince church officials to adopt preventive measures.

demonstrated our movement had breadth and depth and potentially real staying power" (p. 224). Consequently, just two days after the convention, Cardinal Law launched a "public assault" on VOTF by announcing that the archdiocese would not accept funds from VOTF[9] and by voicing "scathing attacks on VOTF's convention" (Muller & Kenney, p. 228), charging that the convention included a speaker from a liberal group in Germany, We are Church, that favored married priests (p. 228).

Regarding VOTF's strengths, the convention brought together a massive and theologically diverse range of Catholics to reflect on their church in a thoughtful and civil manner. Although a few priests were present at the convention, the program was led by lay Catholics who declared their love for the church, but did not hesitate to hold Roman Catholic Church hierarchs to penetrating analysis and critique. For many attendees, this event was probably the first time they had attended a Roman Catholic event that was not led by clerics, and one in which the church's flaws were so openly and forcefully dissected and rebuked. Following the convention, VOTF continued to play a consciousness-raising role by organizing numerous forums on theology and church reform, and spirituality.

This 2002 VOTF founding convention showcased the professional and managerial backgrounds of its organizers, who created a well-designed, user-friendly website (www.votf.org) and orchestrated this impressive gathering with its range of high-profile speakers and near-flawless implementation.[10] VOTF's professionalism was also evident in its ability to attract extensive press coverage by cultivating relationships with local and national broadcasters and sending out timely press releases.

Many of the challenges that would plague VOTF in the years ahead were evident at the conference as well. While the professional credentials of VOTF's founding members had obvious advantages, VOTF tended to attract almost exclusively members like the founders: Caucasian, middle class, and midlife or older.[11] This development reflects a long-standing

---

[9] VOTF had created a Voice of Compassion fund, which earmarked contributions that could not be used for abuse settlements (Muller & Kenney, 2004). When the Boston archdiocese refused to accept $56,000 from the fund in 2002, VOTF gave the funds to Catholics Charities, who defied instructions from the archdiocese not to accept the funds.

[10] Many of VOTF's original founding group, including James Post, Steve Krueger, Scott Fraser, and Paul Baier, had managerial backgrounds and degrees (Muller & Kenney, 2004).

[11] VOTF's meetings and conferences tend to be highly cerebral and usually feature a range of experts whose academic vocabulary may have had little appeal to less-educated Catholics. VOTF's offices were based in Wellesley, one of the wealthiest Boston suburbs, a location that may have been off-putting to less privileged Catholics. In fact, at a parish

rule of community organizing that groups who start out Caucasian and middle class will remain that way, barring sustained efforts to attract underrepresented groups.[12]

Perhaps most important, the convention demonstrated that creating a centrist organization that could unite all types of Catholics was a daunting, perhaps impossible, endeavor. VOTF's 2002 conference revealed conflicts among liberal and conservative members over mission and strategy. Although VOTF leaders made a point of inviting several prominent conservative Catholics (including George Weigel, a conservative biographer of John Paul II), they all declined (Muller & Kenney, 2004). Frank Delacerate, a technical writer, expressed rather conservative views, arguing for "gradual, incremental and reasonable change" and pointing to "picketing for the ordination of women in front of the cathedral" (Delacerate as cited in Gibson, 2003, p.133) as the type of inappropriate strategy VOTF should avoid. Although his speech drew polite applause, it insulted members of the audience representing Massachusetts Women-Church, which sponsored the yearly demonstration during the ordination ceremony for new priests (M. S., personal communication, July 20, 2002).

Before the conference VOTF had hoped to avoid theological battles between liberal and conservatives and gain the respect of church hierarchs by taking the position that "we accept the teaching authority of the Catholic Church."[13] However, this position failed to placate many conservatives, some of whom mobilized to undermine VOTF. An organization calling itself Faithful Voice that pledged loyalty to the Magisterium claimed to have fifty members and created a website (www.faithfulvoice.com) that challenged VOTF's orthodoxy and motivations. VOTF also came under attack from a number of conservative intellectuals.

---

meeting I attended regarding VOTF on October 7, 2005, one parishioner remarked, "You can't trust people from Wellesley—they are not like the rest of us."

[12] Homan (1998) explains this principle as follows: "People from distinct cultural groups have different experiences, expectations, knowledge, and other qualities or attributes. These differences can become a source of conflict, separation and debilitation if they are unheeded or disregarded. They can become a source of harmony, richness and strength when they are recognized and valued" (p. 8).

[13] Several persons who participated in this vote told me that this position statement originally included the phrase "as interpreted by the laity," but this phrase was not included in VOTF literature. These sources also stated that VOTF leaders were persuaded to take this position by several Roman Catholic theologians who insisted VOTF would not have leverage with church officials if they failed to accept the teaching of the Magisterium, which refers to "the teaching office of the Church. It consists of the Pope and the Bishops" (Most, 1990).

Boston Globe reporter Charles Pierce (2003) described these conservatives as "waging a latter-day counterreformation" (p. 11) against liberal reforms which, in their view, threatened Catholicism's core beliefs. Pierce characterized them as "a conservative front wired into Washington and Rome" (p. 11). Pierce's article in the *Boston Globe Magazine* evoked expressions of concern and dismay among VOTF activists, some of whom were particularly troubled by remarks of the Reverend John C. McCloskey III, who reported "not feel[ing] troubled at all" that his confrontations with reform groups "could end in violence" (McCloskey as cited in Pierce, p. 12).[14]

Although VOTF has often ignored conservative critics, VOTF President James Post did respond to a criticism of Deal W. Hudson of *Crisis Magazine*[15] by sending an e-mail to members that apologized for featuring Debra Haffner as a conference speaker.[16] Haffner was an outspoken supporter of the right to abortion, a position "at odds with the Catholic Church's teachings on abortion and sexuality" (Post as cited in Muller, 2004, p. 236). Predictably, this rebuke of Haffner angered some Catholic feminists, and Haffner herself responded with "great dismay" (Bonavoglia, 2005, p. 143).

VOTF's decision to "accept the teaching authority of the Catholic Church" proved to be a point of considerable consternation among some liberal attendees,[17] who admitted that they came to the conference with little knowledge of VOTF, but were hopeful that the authority of conservative hierarchs was waning and perhaps, with VOTF's help, church leaders would be persuaded to "move forward toward becoming a Church of the modern world," as one person put it (C. C., personal communication, July 20, 2002). Several persons expressed shock at VOTF's decision to avoid challenging dogma, with comments such as: "That will never work." "They can't be serious." "Why would they want to cripple themselves in that way?" Although my sample was by no means representative,

---

[14] Rev. McCloskey is covered more extensively than other Catholic conservatives in the *Boston Globe* article, which revealed that McCloskey's extremism has "discomforted parts of it [the institutional church] including conservatives" (Pierce, 2003, p. 12).

[15] Deal W. Hudson resigned as editor of *Crisis Magazine* in 2004 following revelations of charges of sexual misconduct when he was on the faculty of Fordham University.

[16] Debra Haffner is described by journalist Angela Bonavoglia (2005) as a "Unitarian minister with twenty-eight years of experience as a sexuality educator who led a session on keeping children safe in faith communities" (p. 143).

[17] These conversations with thirty conference-goers were not formal interviews but rather casual conversations primarily with acquaintances. At various intervals during the day I jotted down notes about these conversations.

it does reveal that at least some conference-goers expected VOTF to challenge dogma.

Despite the inevitable tensions that arose, the 2002 convention overall had an upbeat, celebratory spirit and clearly strengthened VOTF's appeal and energized its followers. Speakers were quite candid in acknowledging the uphill battle they faced in negotiating reforms from deeply entrenched, staunchly conservative Roman Catholic hierarchs. President James Post (2002) even compared the prospects facing VOTF with the mythical struggle of Sisyphus, who heroically engages in a ceaseless effort to push a boulder up a steep hill, only to watch it roll back down as he nears the summit. Post reflected, "We must keep pushing the rock up the hill. It is a steep rock. It is a long hill. And it is a heavy rock."

A final issue that surfaced at the conference reflected feelings of discomfort and the awkwardness of finding an appropriate role for those victim-survivors who addressed the VOTF audience in graphic, accusatory language.[18] Even VOTF leaders acknowledge they were taken aback at the speech delivered at the 2002 convention by victim-survivor Arthur Ashe, who blasted the audience for not stopping to listen and learn the names of the victims who were picketing outside, and for their failure to attend a Solidarity Walk for victims several weeks earlier (Muller & Kenney, 2004, p 170).[19]

The Long Haul

VOTF'S landmark founding conference was followed by several other well-attended conferences.[20] Reflecting their managerial background, VOTF leaders quickly moved to transform VOTF from a movement of lay activism into a formal structure capable of sustaining their existence over the long haul.

---

[18] This discomfort regarding victims pertained only to those victims who were highly emotional and accusatory. Several spokespersons for victim-survivors are remarkably articulate and composed public speakers and are highly respected by VOTF. Examples include Barbara Blaine and David Clohessy, both of whom are officers in Survivors Network of those Abused by Priests (SNAP), the largest and oldest self-help group for victims of clergy abuse in the United States (www.snapnetwork.org/).

[19] Ashe's outburst did evoke some shock and anger, but had mixed results in that several hundred did respond to Ashe's command by joining a procession to the Boston cathedral for a demonstration on behalf of victims.

[20] Most notably, a 2003 conference in New York attracted fifteen hundred, and a 2004 regional New England conference attracted two thousand.

For starters, at the 2003 Fordham University Conference VOTF announced plans to achieve structural reform at the local level in a session entitled "VOTF: Where Do We Go from Here." The session was packed to capacity by several hundred who listened attentively as President James Post outlined a strategy of increasing the number of parish pastoral councils (PPCs)[21] and expanding them to include VOTF members and a greater role for laypersons. As Post's message was digested, several respondents responded with dismay. One middle-aged, well-dressed woman exclaimed, "But parish councils don't have any real power." Another male attendee shook his head and grumbled softly, "Oh, come on. That won't get us anywhere." While most of the audience remained silent, a few nodded in agreement, and several others raised questions about the technicalities of creating councils.

VOTF's goal of creating a nationwide network of local affiliates was hampered in part by its difficulty in attracting and sustaining affiliates. A case in point was evident at the June 7, 2003, Boston-area VOTF conference, where Judy, a tall, middle-aged woman with a shy demeanor and soft voice, explained that several VOTF members had been advised by their pastor that "if you don't like things the way they are, you should just leave." Judy returned to Mass in her parish a few times, but eventually concluded "there is nothing to be gained by staying," and moved to another parish nearby that had an active VOTF chapter. Judy's experiences were echoed by numerous other activists.

Despite VOTF's goal of creating a centrist organization, VOTF may have attracted more liberal than conservative activists. I recognized many CTA activists at VOTF meetings, particularly during the first two years. In 2004, a few female CTA activists shared with me their decision to abandon their involvement in VOTF, confessing that they felt more comfortable in CTA, where they were free to oppose church teachings, especially prohibitions on the ordination of women. These CTA activists were initially drawn to VOTF because they hoped it might have more leverage than CTA, given public outrage over the abuse crisis. They rather quickly came to feel disgruntled by VOTF's strict bureaucratic procedures that required multiple layers of clearances for simple events like organizing a rally or representing VOTF in a public forum. These activists also complained that VOTF was too much like the institutional church; one activist noted that "VOTF dictates what we should say and think."

---

[21] Parish pastoral councils (PPCs) are composed of lay members of the parish who advise the pastor on operations of the parish.

VOTF's strict controls on activists reflect the managerial orientation of many VOTF leaders, who were intent on protecting VOTF's centrist credentials. In this regard James Muller (2004) explained to Anne Barrett Doyle at a demonstration of survivors of clergy abuse, "I told Anne and the others that there were many Catholics who would never want to picket or protest. That's where I believed supporters of Voice of the Faithful would come from" (p. 51). One could argue that VOTF adopted a bureaucratic structure too early, thereby stifling the energy and imaginative ideas movements generate in their early stages. Like all social movement organizations, VOTF was highly dependent on volunteers whose incentives differ from the employees managed by VOTF leaders in their professional roles. VOTF's tight controls may have dampened the enthusiasm and participation of at least some of early VOTF activists, including liberals, and possibly conservatives as well, who could easily transfer their energies to other reform groups.

Despite difficulties in outreach, James Post (2004) proclaimed "slow but steady" growth as VOTF's membership rose to twenty-five thousand with more than two hundred local affiliates.[22] In 2005 VOTF conducted elections for a National Representative Council of twenty-six members from fourteen regions across the United States and held its second national conference in Indianapolis, Indiana, a central location, reflecting VOTF's goal of expanding beyond its base in the Northeast. More than five hundred VOTF members who attended the 2005 conference approved two priority items as follows: (1) working in state legislatures to extend the statute of limitations for filing claims of child abuse; (2) launching a campaign for financial accountability in parishes and dioceses (Post, 2006a). The emphasis on finances reflected VOTF's concern that the secrecy of church officials regarding financial matters enabled hierarchs to engage in secret payoffs for abuse claims and to hide other types of financial malfeasance. One year later, a 2006 study conducted by Villanova University supported VOTF's focus on financial accountability. Based on a nationwide survey of Catholic diocesan finance councils,[23] the study revealed that four of five dioceses included in the study admitted to experiencing at

---

[22] In 2003 VOTF claimed 190 affiliates. By July 2009, they listed only 60–70 parish affiliates (*Voice of the Faithful*, 2009).

[23] This survey included responses from seventy-eight diocesan chief financial officers, while ninety-six dioceses did not respond. The researchers did not estimate the amount embezzled, but data they did collect suggest the amount is "significant," with 11 percent of dioceses reporting at least $500,000 was stolen over the past five years (P. Feuerherd, 2006a).

least one case of embezzlement of parish funds within the past five years (P. Feuerherd, 2006b).[24]

CRITICS CHALLENGE VOTF

Many VOTF observers have raised concerns about its strategy and objectives since its inception. These critiques will be discussed in some detail, because they reveal the complex tradeoffs involved in VOTF's emphasis on insider strategies.[25]

A forum on October 23, 2005, sponsored by Boston College Church in the 21st Century offered varied presentations by academics who analyzed VOTF's strategies and achievements. This forum focused on a 2005 study by William D'Antonio and Anthony Pogorelc, which provided a demographic portrait of VOTF members based on extensive interview and survey data. A panel of theologians and social scientists responded to the findings of this study, noting VOTF's strong commitment to Catholicism and their dedication to church reform, but each panelist offered some criticisms of VOTF's mission and strategy.[26]

Voicing concerns from the right, two priests criticized VOTF's lack of deference to church authorities.[27] Voicing criticisms from the left,

---

[24] VOTF responded to this study by posting it on their website and featuring a running account of revelations of financial scandals in parishes and dioceses in the United States. They also hope to improve financial accountability by expanding the authority of finance councils in parishes and dioceses. The Villanova study was published four years after VOTF was founded and, hence, was not a catalyst for the formation of VOTF. CTA did include "financial openness at all levels" in its founding documents, but never made this issue a strategy priority.

[25] Chapters on other reform groups do not contain such extensive attention to critics, simply because no similar material is available. VOTF attracted a range of analysis and commentary perhaps because of its extensive coverage by the media and its focus on the abuse crisis, an important historical development.

[26] The presentations by academics at this Boston College forum on VOTF were later published in the book *Voices of the Faithful: Loyal Catholics Striving for Change* by William D'Antonio and Anthony Pogorelc. Hence my references include quotes both from newspaper articles covering the forum, the published articles of presenters, and my field notes from the forum itself. Some of the remarks quoted above were not included in the published papers.

[27] More specifically, Pogorelc noted that church leaders see VOTF as "adversarial," and he recounted the remarks of two bishops who complained, "I can't do anything right for the [VOTF] group" (Pogorelc as cited in Bole, 2005, p. 45). Fr. Robert P. Imbelli, a Boston College theologian, criticized VOTF's rhetoric, recommending that VOTF "purify our language" (Imbelli as cited in Bole, 2005, p. 45).

sociologist Michele Dillon (2007) and theologian Mary Hines (2007) challenged VOTF's unwillingness to question doctrinal issues, emphasizing that doctrine and structure were integrally related. Hence, they argued VOTF could not achieve its goal of structural reform if it remained unwilling to address doctrine.[28] Both Dillon and Hines urged VOTF to review church doctrine, especially the teachings of Vatican II, for principles that promote the right of laity to have a voice in both doctrinal and structural issues.

Sociologist John D. McCarthy (2007) noted the weak commitment of VOTF members to the organization, given that the majority of members are from New England and do not contribute to the organization or attend meetings. At several points during the presentations, when speakers noted that VOTF's current strategy "wasn't working," many in the audience nodded and groaned (presumably expressing agreement).[29]

VOTF strategies were also criticized by Father Tom Doyle (2008),[30] who urged VOTF to drop its objective of structural reform and focus solely on support for abuse victims, confessing,

> As far as reform etc. is concerned, I have lost all realistic hope that the institution will change for the better in my lifetime. The present crop of bishops, courtesy of John Paul II, is ... more clericalist and monarchical than any I can remember. (p. 1)

Thus, VOTF was unable to craft a strategy acceptable to both its conservative critics (for whom VOTF could not be deferential enough) and its liberal critics (for whom VOTF was failing to realistically appraise the mindset of church hierarchs and to assert its right to challenge church teachings).

---

[28] More specifically, Dillon (2007) argued that "it is sociologically and theologically naïve to assume that doctrine and structure, or culture and structure, are separate domains" (p. 118). Hines (2007) struck a similar note, insisting that "structure cannot be divorced from mission and doctrine without falling into the same overemphasis on institution that has led to the problems VOTF is addressing and ultimately to an impoverishment of our understanding of church" (p. 132).

[29] A second Boston College forum on VOTF was held on February 24, 2006, and featured four panelists, who praised VOTF's activism and timely response to the abuse crisis, but admitted the organization was in decline. When asked if VOTF had a future, there was a long pause before former VOTF president James Post haltingly responded, "There has to be," which was followed by silence from the other three participants. Post admitted there was controversy among VOTF leadership over the organization's future, but he favored retaining VOTF's original focus, allowing other organizations to challenge church dogma (Post as cited by Michalek, 2008, p. 1).

[30] Doyle's public letter to VOTF was posted on VOTF's website.

Contradictions in VOTF's Mission

Holding Clerics Accountable in a Culture of Clericalism

Church hierarchs view the abuse crisis as highly threatening to their reputation and job security. Although VOTF has rather vague policies on penalties for abusers and those involved in cover-ups, many VOTF leaders have called for resignations and criminal penalties. For example, in 2002 VOTF activist Mary Scanlon convinced VOTF leaders to post a letter to survivors on VOTF's website that pledged among other things to "advocate for criminal prosecution for the perpetuators of abuse and those who obstructed justice in the pursuit of these crimes" (Scanlon as quoted by Muller & Kenney, p. 153).[31] More recently, VOTF's full-page ad in the *New York Times* on April 8, 2008 (timed to coincide with Pope Benedict's visit to the United States), stated the following: "Pope Benedict should call for the resignation of those bishops who repeatedly reassigned predator priests" (*Calling all Catholics to*, 2008, p. A17).

VOTF has also called for resignations of specific hierarchs involved in cover-ups of clerical abuse, beginning with Cardinal Law in 2002 (Muller & Kenney, 2004). In its boldest move to date, VOTF issued a statement calling for the resignations of Cardinal Francis George, Cardinal Roger Mahoney, Bishops William F. Murphy and John B. McCormack, and Archbishop Daniel Pilarczyk, as well as the resignation of Cardinal Law from his ecclesial positions in Rome (*VOTF names bishops*, 2009).

Given that bishops and cardinals have traditionally enjoyed a high degree of job security and largely unchallenged authority within their dioceses, threats of criminal lawsuits probably are regarded as unthinkable, even sacrilegious, by at least some laypersons and church officials. *National Catholic Reporter* John L. Allen (2010) explained Pope Benedict's reluctance to accept the resignation of bishops reflects four principles upheld by the Vatican:

1. The Vatican doesn't want to convey the impression that "public opinion and media hostility can bring down a bishop."
2. One bishop's resignation can "create an avalanche which buries other bishops who don't share the same level of responsibility."

---

[31] VOTF had previously called for the resignation of Cardinal Francis George in a 2008 press release (*Unfit to Lead*, 2008c) and had earlier called for George to step down as president of the USCCB and Bishop Skylstad as vice president (*Voice of the Faithful Calls*, 2006).

3. Retirement is viewed as "a reward for a job well done" in which the cleric "has all the privileges of rank and few of the burdens."
4. The role of a bishop is regarded as sacramental such that the bishop serves as the "father of the diocesan family." (Allen, 2010)

According to the *Dallas Morning News*, two-thirds of American bishops have transferred abusive priests (*Special Report*, 2009).[32] To the extent that all or most of these bishops were forced to resign or serve prison time, or both, this development (whatever its merits in terms of fairness and prevention) would exacerbate the growing priest shortage and cause major administrative problems in affected dioceses. Even more to the point, if high percentages of priests and bishops were forced to resign, the church structure in the United States would be dramatically altered if not dismantled.

Even apart from penalties facings church officials, the abuse crisis has imposed a high cost on the American Roman Catholic Church including negative publicity and costs for abuse settlements that are expected to surpass three billion dollars (McClory, 2007a). Under these circumstances one should not be surprised at the defensiveness and hostility VOTF sometimes encounters from clerics. In fact, as noted in the two cases below, when VOTF called for penalties, their opportunities for dialogue were stymied.

In the first case, the New York VOTF chapter called for Bishop William F. Murphy's resignation in 2006,[33] following charges of "malfeasance when he handled priest sex abuse cases" (P. Feuerherd, 2006a, p. 7) as well as criticisms of a range of managerial decisions, including renovations of

---

[32] Two studies of the abuse crisis claim that knowledge of abusive priests was widely known not only by American bishops but also by the Vatican, including Popes John Paul II and Benedict XVI (Doyle, Sipe & Wall, 2006; Podles, 2008). These assertions were confirmed in 2010 when the media uncovered several cases of Benedict XVI's laxity in handling abuse cases during his tenure as Prefect of the Congregation for the Doctrine of the Faith (CDF) from 1981 to 2005. Despite these revelations, however, a Zogby poll of U.S. Catholics revealed that two-thirds believe Pope Benedict should not resign, although a majority gave Pope Benedict and American Catholic Bishops "largely negative ratings" (NCR staff, 2010) for their handling of the abuse crisis.

[33] Bishop William F. Murphy has a long-standing record as a foe of the Reform Movement. He served as the second highest official in the Boston archdiocese for eight years before being assigned to Rockville Centre, New York. During this time he forbade Massachusetts Women-Church from meeting on archdiocesan property (as described in chapter 4). In 2003 Massachusetts attorney general Thomas P. O'Reilly identified Bishop Murphy as a central player in the cover-ups of abusive priests in the Boston archdiocese (Rather, 2003).

his residence. Bishop Murphy responded by banning VOTF from meeting on church property in his diocese. Appealing to both sides, an organization of twenty-two current and resigned priests, called Long Island Voice of the Ordained, raised one thousand dollars for mediation services to arrive at a compromise between VOTF and Bishop Murphy. Their public statement read, "Among the values extolled by the life and teachings of Jesus, reconciliation, peace and unity are clearly preeminent" (Feuerherd, p. 7). One Long Island pastor who had contributed to the mediation fund criticized both VOTF and the bishop. He noted that the bishop's responsibility is to teach, and "what Murphy has done was to ban" (p. 8). Pointing to VOTF's self-defeating strategy, this pastor asked, "How could they expect that he would turn around and welcome them into parish facilities if they voted to call for his resignation?" (p. 8).

In this instance, VOTF's strategies were clearly counterproductive because their call for Bishop Murphy's resignation undermined their opportunities for organizing affiliates within parishes under Murphy's control. If they had organized a broad membership base first, their call for Murphy's resignation would have had more clout.

In the second case, a crisis erupted in the Chicago diocese in 2005 following revelations that Cardinal George failed to remove a priest who faced two legal charges of abuse of children in his parish. Five Chicago-area VOTF affiliates held joint meetings about this incident and decided to request a meeting with Cardinal George to voice their concerns. This meeting finally occurred on May 12, 2005. According to VOTF's account, when the cardinal arrived at the meeting he appeared "visibly agitated" and "his hands were shaking and he appeared red in the face" (*Dialogue with the Diocese*, 2007). Almost immediately the cardinal said, "You asked for me to step down from the USCCB!"[34] Cardinal George's anxious demeanor reflected his discomfort facing parishioners who had challenged his judgment. However, the meeting eventually "moved from contentious to cordial," and the cardinal became less defensive. As a conciliatory gesture, Cardinal George remarked, "I can see that you people really love this Church!" Both sides ended the meeting by agreeing to a follow-up meeting, which the cardinal subsequently cancelled, insisting it was no longer necessary since he had appointed an ad hoc committee to recommend solutions to the crisis.

---

[34] Despite VOTF's call for him to step down, Cardinal George was reelected as president of the United States Conference of Catholic Bishops on March 10, 2006, but this election was split rather than the unanimous vote traditional in these elections (Doucette, 2008).

One can infer from Cardinal George's behavior at this meeting that he was unaccustomed to being challenged by laypersons and could not contain his indignation over the fact that these parishioners challenged him to resign his leadership of the USCCB. At least Cardinal George made a conciliatory gesture by praising the parishioners' love for the church, even though he eventually cancelled the follow-up meeting. As in the instance with Bishop Murphy, VOTF adopted a contradictory strategy, because its call for George's resignation undermined their efforts to convince George to include them in deliberations over resolving a high-profile abuse case.[35]

Both of these incidents reveal the barriers to communication and relationship-building that occur when church hierarchs are faced with threats of resignation. They also expose VOTF's lack of leverage in negotiating concessions from bishops, who simply ignored their appeals. These examples suggest that insider strategies are better suited to a reform movement where targeted flaws are relatively minor in scope and relatively amenable to change. VOTF's efforts to resolve the abuse crisis revealed deeply entrenched problems in church governance and institutional priorities. Under these circumstances, insider reform strategies will, at best, achieve only marginal and easily reversible reforms. This theme is expressed by R. Scott Appleby, who noted,

> But if they choose to be a status quo organization, trying not to make waves and not to be confrontational, it's exceedingly likely that they won't attract attention and won't recruit new members and that they won't change anything. (Appleby as cited in Belluck, 2007, p. A16)

VOTF has occasionally been confrontational, as exemplified by the calls for resignation noted above. Yet its choice of insider strategies reflects the proverbial folly of putting the fox in charge of the chicken coop, whereby VOTF calls for cooperation and accountability from the very persons who are, in varying degrees, responsible for the sex abuse and financial scandals VOTF decries.

Compassion Fatigue?

Another contradiction inherent in VOTF's strategy centers on the high priority it has placed on the clergy abuse crisis. VOTF's decision to

---

[35] VOTF probably issued calls for resignations of bishops in order to emphasize its unwillingness to tolerate clergy abuse. Nonetheless, they undermined VOTF's legitimacy by revealing VOTF's lack of leverage.

prioritize the issue of extending the statute of limitations in state legislatures for abuse claims in 2005 reflects VOTF's longstanding commitment to victims, and the fact that these reforms can and have been won, since they do not require the consent of church hierarchs. The downside of VOTF's emphasis on abuse victims is that this goal may no longer appeal to large numbers of Catholics whom VOTF relies on for donations and new members.

During the beginning of the crisis, the revelations of the abuse crisis evoked an outflow of sympathy and support among many lay Catholics, some of whom contributed to reform groups and victim advocacy groups. More recently, however, at reform group gatherings that I attended, some activists are expressing reservations about the costs of abuse settlements. One VOTF activist questioned,

> Are we just exchanging one group of victims for another? Parishioners who lose their beloved parish communities also become victims, particularly since parishes selected for closure tend to be in poor neighborhoods, where the local parish may serve as a lifeline to disadvantaged persons. (O. R., personal communication, February 22, 2008)

Reformers also expressed concern over the range in settlements (in which the amounts of settlements varied greatly among victims), the possibility that some charges were fabricated, and that abuse settlements might "bankrupt the church" (G. L., personal communication, March 2, 2008). A VOTF activist involved in outreach to victims complained that "They [the victims] never seem to move beyond their anger and self-pity" (T. R., personal communication, November 4, 2007).

Such sentiments are on the increase among inactive Catholics, especially as the costs of settlements continue to grow. A Zogby poll of 803 self-identified Catholics indicated that 65 percent of respondents "expressed concern that the cost of settling child sex abuse cases would harm the church's ability to conduct its mission" (Bono, 2005, p. 2).[36]

"Is Liberal Catholicism Dead?"

The rave reviews Pope Benedict XVI received during his highly successful visit to the United States in May 2008 provoked speculation that perhaps

---

[36] Similar arguments were echoed by a group in Seattle who organized to oppose Bishop William Skylstad's settlement of $44.7 million to victims, arguing that "any settlement that places an extraordinary burden on parishioners is not acceptable" (Geranios, 2008).

Benedict had dealt a fatal blow to Catholic reform groups, especially VOTF and CTA, by pledging to end the crisis and by meeting with victims. The abuse crisis had given the Reform Movement a "second wind" that reenergized its base after its loss of membership and momentum during the 1990s. Father Thomas Reese, a fellow at Georgetown University's Woodstock Theological Center, predicts that Benedict's visit "changed the dynamic" whereby VOTF had been able to tap the anger among Catholics over the abuse crisis" (Reese as cited by Van Biema, 2008). Reese predicted that VOTF now lacks a visible enemy to mobilize against; since "most bishops have gotten their acts together on sex abuse, they look less like the enemy and more like part of the solution." Peter Steinfels, codirector of Fordham's Center on Religion and Culture, proclaimed, "It's a new ball game," (Steinfels as cited by Van Biema) such that a reemergence of progressive[37] Catholics would require new issues.[38]

Hence, the abuse crisis itself may no longer attract many members to VOTF, despite the new abuse cases that continue to appear on VOTF's website. This conclusion is supported by research conducted by the Center for Applied Research in the Apostolate (CARA), which revealed that the abuse crisis had no significant impact on parishioners' self-identification as Catholics, their mass attendance, and financial giving to the church (Gray and Perl, 2006).[39] This study also revealed that parishioners were relatively uninformed about the abuse crisis and expressed fairly strong support for church hierarchs. For example, 71 percent of respondents rated American bishops at least "fair" in terms of their handling of

---

This group was composed of priests, parish administrators, and laypersons. Although the group was not granted a role in negotiations, their efforts do represent an occasion in which members of a parish opposed a settlement because of the cost it would impose on parishioners.

[37] As detailed in this chapter, VOTF describes itself as a "centrist" rather than a "progressive" reform group. This distinction may not have been obvious to the sources cited in the article. Furthermore, VOTF is somewhat progressive in that it does include "structural reform" as one of its three agenda items, although it has never defined this goal very concretely.

[38] In response to these arguments, John Moynihan, VOTF's media representative, countered that reform groups are upbeat over their prospects, and claims, "We have made a difference, and if you stick with us we are going to make a further difference" (Moynihan as cited in Van Biema, 2008).

[39] This CARA study was based on a comprehensive analysis of ten polls conducted during the period 2001–2005. This study also revealed that diocesan giving had declined from 38 percent in 2002 to 29 percent in 2005, although only 34 percent cited the abuse crisis as the reason for the decline, while 64 percent cited changes in household income (Gray & Perl, 2006).

the abuse crisis.[40] Thus, while the crisis damaged the church's reputation, probably lastingly, overall most Catholics appear relatively complacent.[41]

Fifth Anniversary Marks Signs of Decline

Despite VOTF's sustained efforts to create a stable base, by VOTF's fifth anniversary in 2007 it was an organization in decline[42] (Burke, 2007). Even after staff reductions, VOTF's fiscal crisis accelerated and caught the attention of the media, including the *New York Times,* which reported VOTF's deficit had reached $100,000 in a budget of about $700,000 (Belluck, 2007). More seriously, VOTF leaders also admitted to being "in a stuck position" (p. A16) due to infighting over leadership and decision making.

The challenges facing VOTF were evident at VOTF's 2007 Regional Conference in Providence, Rhode Island, which drew more than five hundred participants. The one-day conference was picketed by a dozen victims, who charged VOTF with inadequate advocacy on their behalf (Colbert, 2007, p. 9).[43] Notre Dame theologian Richard McBrien admitted in his keynote speech that he struggled while preparing his remarks, recognizing that VOTF was at a "crossroads" that might lead it to "move in a new direction" (McBrien as cited in Dujardin, 2007). McBrien urged VOTF "not to give up or declare victory."

---

[40] Another CARA study revealed fairly high overall approval for American bishops, in that 61 percent reported being "somewhat or very" satisfied with "the leadership of the church in general," and 74 percent reported being "at least somewhat satisfied" with "the leadership of their local bishop or cardinal (*Five years later,* 2007). However, a shortcoming of CARA's studies is that their surveys include Catholics who remain in their parishes, and, hence, do not reflect the views of defecting parishioners, who probably have more negative ratings of church hierarchs.

[41] No doubt some VOTF members were dismayed to learn that several parishes in Los Angeles responded to the appeal of Cardinal Roger Mahoney to help close the gap in archdiocesan finances following a $720 million settlement with abuse victims. In fact, one parish contributed nearly $1.5 million, despite the fact that the donation evoked dismay among some parishioners (Trounson, 2008).

[42] In fact, VOTF annual reports reveal that VOTF had experienced deficit budgets with losses totaling $44,540 (FY2004), $75,647 (FY2005), and $3,807 (FY2006). VOTF has not published an annual budget since 2006.

[43] Michael Sweatt, a cofounder of a VOTF affiliate in Maine, was particularly incensed that VOTF had refused to honor his request to drop a Jesuit priest, Father Clark, from the conference's program because he led the board of trustees of a Catholic school in Maine that had failed to approve settlements for victims of a former coach at the school, Charles Malia. VOTF countered that the priest in question was not associated with the school when the abuse occurred and was not addressing abuse issues at the conference (Dujardin, 2007).

By July 2009, VOTF's funds had declined to critical levels, despite cutbacks. Chair of the board VOTF President Dan Bartley and Bill Casey (2009) pleaded to members for $60,000 in contributions to keep the organization afloat until the end of the summer. On July 21, 2009, VOTF jubilantly announced its appeal had raised more than $120,000 from twelve hundred donors as they devised plans to establish "a stable base of predictable income for the future" (*VOTF Gratified by*, 2009).

VOTF's financial meltdown can be attributed to several factors. First, due to its eagerness to attract a wide membership base, VOTF never required dues of its members, who joined the organization simply by signing on to its website.[44] Second, VOTF's visibility has waned following its high-profile early years, probably because many Catholics believe the abuse crisis has been resolved. Consequently, they are less likely to attend VOTF events or respond to fund-raising appeals. Third, according to John Moynihan, VOTF's former communication director, several major donors stopped contributing to VOTF in 2007. Moynihan explained that VOTF devoted little attention to fund-raising during its early years because they received many unsolicited donations from Catholics shocked by the abuse crisis (personal communication, March 11, 2007).

A New Direction

In spring 2008, VOTF's newly elected officers conducted their own "Strategy Survey" among five hundred members.[45] Based on these results VOTF leaders drafted a new strategic plan that emphasized five "strategic platforms," including spiritual and communal growth, local action, child protection and survivor support, universal church reform, and networking (*VOTF Strategic Plan*, p. 9).

In August 2010 VOTF fleshed out its new strategic plan with "Ten Steps toward Reforming the Catholic Church" that were somewhat bolder and slightly more liberal than past initiatives, including "developing inclusive governance structures" (that gave the laity a voice in selection of bishops), "inquiring into the causes of the crisis" (that recommended a greater role

---

[44] Following this fiscal crisis VOTF did require annual dues of $50 for those members who choose to vote in elections of officers. Members who simply want to remain on the listserve are not required to pay dues.

[45] Survey respondents identified the strengths of the organization as its dedicated leaders, sizeable membership, and centrist policies and its weaknesses as lack of funds, poorly defined structure, and lack of coherent strategy.

for women in the church and a study of mandated celibacy), and "empowering the laity" (that proposed educating laypersons about their rights). Thus, it seems fair to conclude that VOTF is moving in a direction that shows less concern for its more conservative members (who generally resist any effort to democratize church governance) and places slightly more emphasis on challenging rather than placating church hierarchs (by examining the causes of the crisis and engaging in global outreach).

Still Seeking a Seat at the Table

VOTF has not succeeded in gaining its goal of a seat at the table with church hierarchs, especially since VOTF leaders have not engaged in dialogue with formal decision-making structures in the Roman Catholic Church, such as the USCCB or Vatican officials. As one CTA activist put it, "All of VOTF's efforts to be mainstream and avoid offending the hierarchy [haven't] paid off. They are treated just like the other reform groups—they often can't meet on church property, have little interaction with bishops, and their appeals fall on deaf ears" (G. S., November 4, 2007).

VOTF's outsider status was evident early on at the USCCB meeting in 2002 in Dallas, which met shortly after the abuse crisis erupted. When a small delegation of VOTF members held a press conference outside the USCCB meeting place, a reporter queried, "Are you telling me that you have no communication with the bishops?" (Muller & Kenney, 2004, p. 127). As the reporter noted, VOTF was very much an outsider with no special insider privileges, which might have included observer status during the conference or even informal get-togethers with responsive bishops.

As of 2008, only 20 percent of dioceses explicitly prohibit VOTF from meeting on church property, but, according to John Moynihan, only "about a dozen" bishops are willing to engage in ongoing dialogue with VOTF affiliates in their dioceses (personal correspondence, July 4, 2008).

Insider Strategies—Achievements and Limitations

The primary area where VOTF can cite concrete achievements resulting from insider strategies is the creation of parish pastoral councils (PPCs) and parish finance councils (PFCs). In this regard VOTF cites a number of actions by VOTF chapters that produced tangible results by expanding the participation of lay members in parishes and dioceses.[46] These accomplishments no doubt represent considerable effort on the part of VOTF activists and point to some latitude in their ability to negotiate with clergy. VOTF's efforts to make inroads are hampered by the fact that pastors retain virtual control over every aspect of parish operations and, in some instances, parishioners active in reform activities have been denied roles in their parish by punitive pastors. One such case was a hot topic of discussion among a group of CTA activists at VOTF's 2002 conference. They expressed dismay over the firing of John Sheehan and his wife, of Springfield, Massachusetts, who were fired from their role as Eucharist ministers and lectors due to reform activity. CTA activists noted that Sheehan's pastor had shown a "shocking lack of compassion" given that this penalty was imposed during what the pastor knew to be a particularly difficult time for the family, who were mourning an adult daughter who had recently died.

According to Mark F. Fischer, associate professor at St. John's Seminary in Camarillo, California, PPCs were originally designed to be "deliberative bodies" (Fischer as cited in Gibson, 2003, p. 57), exactly the type favored by VOTF. However the role of PPCs was gradually scaled back so that the 1983 revision of the Code of Canon Law restricted PPCs to a "consultative vote only," and in 1997 the Vatican required that "priests must preside at all [PPC] meetings" (Gibson, p. 57). In fact, VOTF cofounder James Muller (2004) jokingly referred to these committees as "Yes Father, you are right" committees (p. 189).[47]

Thus VOTF's local victories, cited above, demonstrate a few noteworthy concessions VOTF can claim as a result of insider strategies, but they do not rise to the level of structural reform, since they do not significantly alter governance structures. Bishops have virtually unlimited control over their dioceses, and parish priests are granted considerable autonomy in administering their parish. A number of dramatic overhauls in parishes

---

[46] For example, VOTF members in Providence, Rhode Island, Tampa, Florida, and Brooklyn, New York, are working collaboratively with bishops to create PPCs and PFCs (Bartley, 2008). VOTF's Tampa affiliate has helped create a diocesan pastoral council, and VOTF members are assisting priests and dioceses to strengthen financial controls in a number of dioceses. In Maine VOTF members and other lay groups convinced a bishop to reverse his decision to "reinstate a priest who had protected a pedophile priest" (Doucette, 2008, p. 1).

[47] CARA's national parish inventory that covers 87 percent of all parishes in the United States revealed that, as of 2000, larger parishes are more likely to have PPCs than smaller ones, but overall percentages are high, ranging from 88 to 97 percent (*National parish inventory*, 2000).

and dioceses by newly appointed conservative clerics are recounted in chapter 6. Despite widespread protests by laity and priests in several dioceses, conservative clerics dismantled cherished programs, fired popular staff, and demanded compliance with their directives.

Even in cases where pastors are receptive to lay input, parishioners may be too intimidated by clericalist norms to assertively advocate their views, as evidenced by Pax Christi Community in Eden Prairie, Minnesota, whose parish is cited by Paul Wilkes (2001) in his book *Excellent Catholic Parishes*.[48] I interviewed two couples who had served on Pax Christi's parish pastoral council. They had the highest praise for their pastor, Tom Powers, emphasizing his "support for an involved laity" (C. P. and F. P, personal communication, November 9, 2003), but could not recall any incident where a council member had even disagreed with their pastor since they considered such behavior "rude" or "inappropriate."

Outsider Stategies—Modest Victories

VOTF: A Media Magnet

Many analysts point to media attention and the threat of lawsuits as critical factors that compelled church officials to institute new clergy abuse policies. For example, in his book on the abuse crisis, *Sacrilege*, Podles (2008) concludes, "Only under public pressure did the bishops compose a charter for the protection of children, only under public pressure did they set up a national review board" (p. 508). Doyle, Sipe, and Wall (2006) arrive at a similar conclusion, stating "the intense pressure brought to bear on the hierarchy from early in 2002 caused U.S. Catholic bishops to propose a policy that ruled out a return to ministry for perpetrators of sexual abuse" (p. 214). In his case study of clergy abuse litigation, Lytton (2008) pointed to "the critical role of litigation in achieving concessions: [clergy abuse] litigation was essential in bringing the scandal to light in the first place, focusing attention on the need for institutional reform, and spurring church leaders and public officials into action" (p. 4).

One of VOTF's (2008a) most impressive achievements stems from its Accountability Now Campaign, which promotes victim rights through campaigns that extend limitations for filing abuse claims and which was

---

[48] Tom Powers, who was pastor of Pax Christi in 2003, has subsequently retired.

successful in six states.[49] Post (2006b) attributes the Boston Archdiocese's decision to release extensive financial data in 2006 to VOTF's sponsorship of a 2005 bill that would require all churches in Massachusetts to release financial disclosure statements. Although this bill was defeated,[50] Post insists the threat of the legislation compelled then archbishop O'Malley to publicly commit himself to financial transparency.[51] O'Malley acknowledged his reason for this dramatic move was to "rebuild trust," affirming, "We are not trying to keep secrets from people. We are not trying to deceive them" (O'Malley as cited in Paulson, 2006a, p. A20).

VOTF's accountability campaign and the Villanova study on church finances cited above may also have contributed to a move by the USCCB meeting November 12–15, 2007, in which they tightened financial controls by requiring bishops to receive approval from their finance councils and college of consulters in five specific instances, including going in debt or approving legal settlements beyond $1 million ($500,000 for smaller dioceses), and going into bankruptcy (Allen, 2007b).

VOTF's Role in Anticlosure Movement

Lastly, VOTF's advocacy for parishioners who oppose parish closures is another area in which VOTF can claim some success. When the Boston archdiocese announced plans to close parishes, VOTF held a series of listening sessions for parishioners facing closure and sponsored a highly publicized Mass on the Boston Common on November 14, 2004, which was attended by one thousand and concelebrated by priests from parishes slated for closure (Tolfree, 2004). These actions by VOTF helped lay the groundwork for the emergence of the Council of Vigiling Parishes (CoP) 2005, which in turn inspired parishioners in many dioceses to resist closure decrees.

---

[49] The six state victories occurred in Delaware, Louisiana, New Jersey, Ohio, Virginia, and California.

[50] Post attributes the defeat of this bill to opposition from the Massachusetts Council of Church and Temples, which was concerned that the cost of legislation would be burdensome for small, independent churches.

[51] O'Malley's decision to open archdiocesan books may also have been influenced by the creation of the National Leadership Roundtable on Church Management (NLRCM), which describes itself as "an organization of laity, religious and clergy working together to promote excellence and best practices in the management of finances, human resources and development of the Catholic Church in the U.S. by greater incorporation of the expertise of the laity" (nlrcm.org). This group was created in 2005 following the abuse crisis.

It is beyond the scope of this study to identify the unique contributions of the many players involved in the reforms cited above, which includes a host of reform groups as well victim groups, attorneys, academics, clergy, and journalists. In the case of financial controls, the Villanova study exposure of mismanagement by diocesan officials may have captured bishops' attention because it was publicized when many dioceses were facing fiscal crises due to the abuse settlements, and were thereby especially sensitive to the threat of bad publicity and financial scandals. Nonetheless, VOTF clearly was the most skillful of the reform groups in attracting media attention, especially in response to the abuse crisis,[52] and thus bears a large measure of credit on this account.

VOTF's ability to attract extensive media attention is attributable to two factors. First the abuse crisis became a media magnet; it was covered extensively by print, television, and radio media in Boston and beyond. In fact, investigative journalism played a major role in uncovering the abuse crisis, especially the Spotlight Team of the *Boston Globe*, which won a Pulitzer Prize for its "courageous comprehensive coverage." The Pulitzer Prize board credited this coverage with "piercing secrecy, stirring local, national, and international reaction, and producing changes in church policy" (The Pulitzer Board as cited in Feeney, April, 2003). VOTF had a strategic advantage over other reform groups because it is headquartered in Boston where the abuse crisis first broke. Second, VOTF leaders made the most of its location by cultivating relationships with the media and sending out professionally designed press releases. Since VOTF leaders have professional backgrounds, most were highly articulate and came across as sincere and well informed in media interviews. To ensure a consistent tone and message, VOTF established strict policies about which members could serve as spokespersons for the organization.

VOTF's achievements do rise to the level of systemic change in that concessions resulted in policy-level changes, i.e., the Dallas Charter for the Protection of Children, tighter financial controls, and the appointment of

---

[52] One indication of VOTF's significance in attracting media attention regarding the clergy abuse crisis is revealed in *Betrayal, the Crisis in the Catholic Church*, a book by the investigative staff of the *Boston Globe* (2002). This book's index lists one page that refers to Call to Action (CTA) and eleven pages that refer to Voice of the Faithful (VOTF). No other reform groups were cited except for one reference to Catholics for Choice (CFC). Journalist David France's (2004) study of the abuse crisis refers to VOTF on thirty-eight pages, to CTA on two pages, and to the survivor advocacy group Survivors Network of those Abused by Priests (SNAP) on twenty-three pages.

a lay oversight panel that ultimately overturned several closure decrees of the Boston Archdiocese.[53] To the extent that VOTF influenced these outcomes, one can conclude that VOTF's efforts were enhanced by outsider strategies to a greater degree than insider strategies, particularly regarding systemic change.[54] Although the Vatican and American bishops as a whole have been largely unreceptive to VOTF's overtures, they have little choice in responding to negative publicity and lawsuits that damage their reputation and the financial stability of dioceses.

Peas in a Pod or Oil and Water?

Despite their obvious differences on issues of dogma, my analysis reveals the following similarities regarding CTA and VOTF. Both groups are similar in size and demographic composition, and both employ similar strategies, including sponsoring petition drives, newspaper ads, and educational conferences that often feature the same speakers. Both have relatively static and overlapping memberships that hover around thirty thousand members, have been prohibited from meeting in many parishes and dioceses, and have not obtained a formal role for laity in church governance or ongoing dialogue with church hierarchs. Finally, both make frequent reference to the documents of Vatican II to support their reform agendas. These striking similarities reflect that both organizations rely heavily on outsider strategies because they do not have insider status.

---

[53] Of course the categorization of "systemic change" is problematic in the case of the Dallas Charter in which compliance with audits was a "voluntary policy" that, as documented in chapter 6, allowed Bishop Fabian Bruskewitz to refuse to comply. In 2011, new disclosures revealed that the Philadelphia archdiocese had violated the Dallas Charter by failing to remove numerous priests despite credible charges of sexual abuse.

[54] VOTF may claim some measure of influence in the Vatican's decision to accept the resignation of Cardinal Law and the decision to approve a meeting of Pope Benedict XVI with victims of clergy abuse during his April 2008 visit to Boston. Assessing influence in these cases is all but impossible without access to decision makers. However, many reform groups and private individuals in Boston were demanding Cardinal Law's resignation, including a group of fifty-eight Boston-area priests whose petition demanding Law's resignation was published in the *Boston Globe* (Paulson, 2002, p. A34). VOTF's call for Law's resignation did not occur until Law had already left for Rome, presumably to confer with the pope on the resignation (Muller & Kenney, 2004). In the case of the meeting of Pope Benedict with abuse victims, Cardinal Sean O'Malley had lobbied for the meeting and selected the five Boston-area victims who met with the pope. Both of these decisions were one-time events that did not affect policy-level changes.

How Do They Expect Us to Respond to the Rape of Our Children?

At the Boston College forum on VOTF cited above, theologian Mary Hines (2007) challenged VOTF's tendency to emphasize its dissimilarity to CTA by urging them to review CTA history, tracing why it is considered "more dissident, more to the left and more involved in doctrinal matters" (p. 128) than VOTF. Consistent with Hines's suggestion, my analysis outlined above suggests the histories of both groups followed a similar pattern. To be sure, CTA has laid the more vigorous claim on what Hines refers to as the "ecclesiology from below" (p. 124) that validates the right of laity to both shape and challenge church teachings. However, the history of CTA demonstrates that, like VOTF, CTA members began as insider participants in the 1976 USCCB conference and moved to a marginal status only because (like VOTF) they were increasingly vilified by conservative critics and denied access to decision makers. Despite its efforts to establish insider credentials, VOTF has attracted its own critics whose rhetoric resembles that of CTA critics—"too strident," "too disrespectful of the hierarchy," "too arrogant" (terms I have heard assigned to VOTF). One VOTF member responded to criticisms by exclaiming, "How do they expect us to respond to the rape of our children?" (T. P., personal communication Nov. 13, 2004).[55]

A New Era

CTA and VOTF now face a similar challenge as they must somehow redefine themselves and their mission in the face of a dramatically altered landscape, whereby, according to a Pew Forum poll of thirty-five thousand Americans, religiosity among younger Catholics is on the decline, and Catholics nationwide are declining "faster than any other major grouping" (Paulson, 2008b, A11). Facing these challenges, there is some evidence that VOTF and CTA have begun working collaboratively, as

---

[55] For their part, at least some members of both CTA and VOTF have always been eager to collaborate. At the November 6, 2003, COR meeting, CTA codirector Dan Daley exclaimed (referring to VOTF), "We've got to love them to death" as he implicitly acknowledged the difficult road ahead for VOTF. He also described James Post, whom he met briefly, as "a terrific guy." CTA codirector Sheila Daley notes that VOTF can reach "a lot of Catholics in the pews that we can't get to because we've been marginalized by right-wing organizations" (S. Daley as cited in McClory, 2003, p. 4). For his part, VOTF's first president, James Post, was reportedly enthusiastic about working with CTA, but stymied by concerns of more conservative VOTF members (G. L, personal communication, November 4, 2004).

they were cosigners of a letter to Cardinal George requesting that he make good on his professed policy of "openness" regarding abuse complaints in his diocese (*Letter to Cardinal George,* 2009).[56] Although both CTA and VOTF joined a coalition of reform groups to organize a new coalition, the American Catholic Council (described in later chapters), CTA eventually dropped out due to financial and other considerations.

Are Insider Strategies a Blessing or a Curse?

Since its founding in 2002, VOTF's experiences contradicted its contention that insider status would strengthen its access to church officials and enhance its effectiveness. My analysis points to modest but noteworthy achievements of VOTF, but credits these reforms to outsider strategies. VOTF initially hoped its centrist credentials would enable it to build a broad-based membership of Catholics spanning right, center, and left. The goals were stymied as VOTF encountered deep-seated and perhaps insurmountable gaps in values and beliefs between the right and left wings of the Catholic laity. These gaps only intensified following the abuse crisis.

VOTF has indicated a slight tilt to the left by, as noted above, calling for a greater voice for laity in church governance and taking on a leadership role in the American Catholic Council, which aims to achieve far-reaching reforms in church governance. Although VOTF continues to espouse insider rhetoric, its increasingly bold stance suggests it recognizes that its insider approach to reform is ineffectual.

---

[56] The cosigners of this letter (including CTA, VOTF, SNAP, Coalition of Concerned Catholics, and Companions in Hope) expressed their concern regarding Cardinal George's decision to name a building in honor of Bishop Goedert, whose recent deposition revealed he acted "recklessly and deceitfully" in handling abuse cases (*Letter to Cardinal George,* 2009).

CHAPTER THREE

LEAVING EGYPT: DIGNITYUSA, CORPS OF RESERVE PRIESTS UNITED FOR SERVICE, AND CATHOLIC ORGANIZATIONS FOR RENEWAL

Sam Sinnett, former president of DignityUSA, regards both his Catholic faith and his homosexuality as a "gift from God." He believes that to deny his homosexuality would "put him in a position of not loving God, not loving myself and therefore not being able to love my neighbor, including my own children and family" (Sinnett as cited by Orso, 2006, p. 1). Sam's activism in DignityUSA strengthens his ability to reconcile his convictions regarding his sexual preference and his Catholicism. Despite his tireless efforts to strengthen Dignity, the organization has been losing members over the past several decades as the Vatican issued a series of punitive policies regarding homosexuality. In an effort to shore up Dignity's declining finances, Sam donated $5,000 from his own savings to create a matching fund to encourage membership donations.

Bill Manseau is a married priest who has played a central leadership role in a range of Catholic reform organizations over the past five decades, most notably Corps of Reserve Priests United for Service (CORPUS) and Federation of Christian Ministries (FCM). Bill is best known for his Pension Advocacy Campaign whereby he has advocated—successfully in some instances—that pensions be provided for Roman Catholic priests who resign the priesthood after many years of service. Bill and his wife, Mary, a former sister, raised three children as devout Roman Catholics who attended Mass and religious education classes as well as a range of home Masses and social events sponsored by reform groups. Following a trend of many children of progressive Roman Catholic reformers, the three Manseau adult children have all rejected the faith tradition of their parents. As the Manseau children became adults and began distancing themselves from the Roman Catholic faith, they faced considerable conflict with their parents over fidelity to Catholicism. Eventually, however, Bill and Mary came to accept their children's decision, realizing that many of their cohorts in the Reform Movement experienced this generation gap over religion. In 2005 the youngest child, Peter, wrote a widely praised book, entitled *Vows: The Story of a Priest, a Nun, and Their Son*, about his experiences growing up surrounded by reform-minded Catholics. Peter's speech about his book at the 2006 CORPUS convention evoked such an enthusiastic response that CORPUS chose to arrange a young adult panel for the 2007 conference, thereby encouraging ongoing dialogue among generations regarding the Catholic faith, which played such a central role in the lives of the rapidly aging CORPUS membership.

The reform groups described in this chapter and the next share a basic attitude of "can't live with and can't live without" Roman Catholicism that, in turn, has pushed them to the point where they must test the institutional boundaries of the church, if not to save it, at least to remain faithful to what they perceive to be the most valid legacies of their faith tradition. These groups are united (1) by their inability to make meaningful inroads with their agendas in their communication with Roman Catholic officials, (2) by their commitment to an authentic Roman Catholic tradition, and (3) by their experience of membership losses. After reviewing the protracted and often fruitless struggle of these groups to gain any foothold in the power structure, many may wonder why it took these groups so long to choose what they consider to be exile.

The organizations that have already begun their exodus from the institutional church include

> *DignityUSA*: The nation's oldest and largest organization of gay, lesbian, bisexual, and transgendered (GLBT) Catholics.
>
> *Corps of Reserve Priests United for Service (CORPUS)*: An organization founded by married priests who promote a "more inclusive" priesthood.
>
> *Catholic Organizations for Renewal (COR)*: A coalition of twenty-four reform groups that engage in information sharing and collaboration.
>
> *Catholic feminists*: Six closely connected Catholic feminist organizations described in chapter 4. They are Women's Ordination Conference (WOC), Women's Ordination Worldwide (WOW), Women-Church Convergence (W-CC), Women's Alliance for Theology, Ethics and Ritual (WATER), and Catholics for Choice (CFC).[1]

As one might expect of organizations embarking on an exile from their church, these groups are haunted by the question of their identity as Roman Catholics. This question cannot be ignored by these reformers, particularly given the high visibility of conservative, even fundamentalist, religious movements within and outside the Catholic Church. The example of Voice of the Faithful (VOTF) demonstrates that even centrist organizations that avoid hot-button issues come under hostile attack from Roman Catholic conservatives who question their loyalty to Catholicism. As long-term reformers, these groups have learned to brush off criticisms

---

[1] See appendix A for a chart with basic information and comparative data about these organizations.

of conservative Catholics. However, members of these groups do sometimes struggle to defend their efforts among friends and family who are often moderate or even slightly liberal but who remain loyal to Roman Catholicism. For example, one CORPUS member told me that his mother was troubled by his decision to leave the priesthood until the revelations of the clergy abuse crisis, which helped her understand his criticisms regarding the "deceptive and psychologically unhealthy" culture of the priesthood (J. S., personal communication, January. 23, 2005).

From the perspective of these "exodus organizations" described herein, they do not regard their departure as a rejection or abandonment of Catholicism. On the contrary, they have formed a revivalist movement aimed at reforming the Roman Catholic Church. They believe conservative hierarchs undermine the authentic character of the Catholic tradition, especially the legacy of Vatican II. As they move to the margins or outside the boundaries of the institutional church, these groups resemble some of the characteristics of a sect intent on reviving the tradition and restoring its authentic character. By endorsing policies expressly rejected by the Vatican (married priests, women's ordination, blessings of homosexual unions, and same-sex marriage) and by engaging in worship communities not approved by the Vatican, these organizations have moved in a direction clearly regarded as problematic, in some cases even schismatic by church officials, to the extent that the Vatican is aware of developments within these organizations.

There are a range of positions regarding how far these groups are willing to move in terms of severing their connections to the institutional church. Some individuals and groups remain nominally insiders, but risk censure by openly voicing criticism of the church's policies and governance. Others have risked or endured excommunication by joining worship communities condemned by the Vatican. Despite their differences, Vatican II reform groups are united is their emphasis on the centrality of Roman Catholicism to their group and to their individual identities. The phrases "Catholic in my DNA" and "Catholic in my bones" come up frequently at gatherings of these reform organizations.

Another factor pushing these organizations to distance themselves from the Vatican is that most of them have suffered membership losses, especially among members who no longer believe the Vatican will respond to their calls for reform. Many reformers also increasingly find local Roman Catholic parishes unwelcoming or off-putting (as documented in chapter 6), especially when conservative pastors adopt punitive policies toward reformers, for example by restricting access to Communion, by openly condemning feminists and GLBT persons, and by denying reformers roles as Eucharistic ministers or positions on parish committees.[2]

Consequently, members of these reform groups have gradually embraced an exile status, insisting that their spiritual well-being and allegiance to Roman Catholicism must be nourished by a welcoming, inclusive community that is willing to violate Vatican policies by allowing unrestricted access to the Eucharist, by blessing same-sex relationships, and by modeling an inclusive priesthood that does not exclude persons on the basis of gender, marital status, or sexual preference. Rather than engaging in fruitless battles with church hierarchs, these reformers devote their energies to creating underground communities that embody their vision of church.

An Exodus Model

Describing the Roman Catholic Reform Movement as a type of exodus is suggested by theologians and activists closely allied with reform groups. For example, Franciscan Michael H. Crosby (2005) recommends moving away from an institutionally defined "royal and clerical consciousness" toward a "spirituality of exile" in which one withdraws from the world, not to escape or drop out but rather to "recapture my understanding of what gives ... meaning" (p. 4). Further developing the exodus imagery, feminist theologian Rosemary Ruether (1985) proclaims that the organization Women-Church Convergence "represents the first time that women collectively have claimed the exodus community as a community of liberation" (p. 57). Drawing on this theme, DignityUSA published a full-page paid advertisement in the *National Catholic Reporter* (Nov. 11, 2005) entitled "Petition from a People in Exile" (p. 11). The ad decried the refusal of American Roman Catholic bishops to respond to Dignity's requests for meetings and urged readers to sign a petition supporting Dignity's right to engage in dialogue with church hierarchs and to defend the morality of their lifestyles.

---

[2] Examples of punitive behavior toward reformers are documented in chapters 1, 2, and 6.

Does the Vatican Care?

One might assume that church officials pay little attention to reform organizations, particularly since local bishops and Vatican officials often fail to even acknowledge receipt of correspondence from these groups, and over the past decade usually refuse to publicly or even privately engage in any sort ongoing dialogue. Nonetheless, CORPUS leader Bill Manseau (described in the vignette above) discovered the hierarchy was keenly aware of his association with reform groups when he filed a petition to be laicized twenty-five years after he left the priesthood to marry. Auxiliary Bishop Richard Lennon of the Boston archdiocese informed Manseau that Cardinal Francis Arinze, a high-ranking Vatican official, had ruled that his petition would be granted only if he resigned from CORPUS and several other reform groups (P. Manseau, 2005, p. 79). This response from the Vatican revealed that it keeps close tabs on reform groups, even to the point of maintaining records of members' reform activity.

However much Vatican officials may publicly ignore and reject reform groups, this surreptitious behavior suggests that they are not uninformed or apathetic about reform activities. This is evident in the reaction of Cardinal Sean O'Malley of Boston, in March 2006, to the announcement that a vigiling parish would engage the service of a married priest to say an Easter Sunday Mass for their community.[3] When O'Malley learned of their plans, he reversed his original refusal to supply a canonical priest, thereby forestalling the possibility of a "runaway church" (Paulson, 2005a, p. B1).[4] These two incidents suggest that, although bishops and cardinals claim to be impervious to pressure, they more likely are deeply concerned about the possibility of defection by the Vatican II reformers. Although some church hierarchs may be happy to part with the most activist reformers, many would not welcome widespread defections.

This chapter describes the exodus journeys of DignityUSA, CORPUS, and COR, all of which gradually revised the meaning of their Catholic

---

[3] According to canon law #290, sacraments including Eucharist are considered "valid" when administered by an ordained Roman Catholic priest, even if he resigns in order to marry. However, the sacraments are referred to as "valid but illicit" if the resigned priest has not obtained approval from the bishop.

[4] This incident is described further in chapter 7. Several groups from vigiling churches did explore the possibility of forming independent parishes if they lost their battle with the archdiocese over closure. Rumors regarding these options were circulating widely in Boston among those involved in the vigiling movement.

identity and their relationship with Roman Catholic hierarchs. By contrast, feminist Catholic organizations (described in the next chapter) realized almost from the beginning that their demands for equal rights for women within the church would not receive a fair hearing, and, hence, decided more quickly to adopt some characteristics of sects.

I will begin the discussion with DignityUSA, one of the oldest reform organizations, and the one most reluctant to choose exile.

Seeking Inclusion for the GLBT Community: DignityUSA

DignityUSA is a reform organization whose mission is "to unite lesbian, bisexual and transgender Catholics, as well as our families, friends, and loved ones in order to develop leadership, and be an instrument through which we may be heard by and promote reform in the church" (*Statement of Position*, 2008). Dignity identifies five areas of concern and commitment: spiritual development, education, social justice, equality issues, and social events.

Many reformers acknowledge that DignityUSA was the first reform group to create underground worship communities. Some reformers describe Dignity as one of the most conservative reform organizations, at least in terms of theology.[5] One must do a bit of digging to discover why DignityUSA has a reputation as conservative,[6] as reported by many reformers, who described the group with phrases such as, "They're sweet but very conservative." At first glance, what could be more liberal that a Catholic gay rights group, especially given the increasingly repressive stance of the Vatican toward homosexuality? Indeed, Dignity's statement of position and purpose does embrace many left-leaning political causes, including equal access to health care and the "eradication of all forms of sexism and patriarchy" (*Statement of Position*, 2008).

The most remarkable evidence of Dignity's theological conservatism is its March 18, 2005, protest over the refusal of Bishop Brom of the Diocese of San Diego to say a funeral Mass for John McCusker, a local gay businessman and community activist who owned two gay bars. Remarkably,

---

[5] One might interpret DignityUSA's rather theologically conservative stance to reflect a pattern among homosexuals noted by Humphreys (1970), whose landmark study revealed that homosexuals tend to be highly conformist in most features of their lives, other than their sexual preference, as a coping tactic for dealing with a stigmatized identity.

[6] Although formal positions taken by DignityUSA reflect a conservative orientation, Dignity members include a broad spectrum of Catholics.

Dignity's press release objected to Bishop Brom's refusal in part by stating: "Lack of access to the sacraments puts the very soul of a person in jeopardy" (*DignityUSA Calls*, 2005). It is hard to imagine the other reform groups in this study (even the centrist VOTF) claiming that one's inability to receive a Catholic funeral would jeopardize a person's soul. Further, when Bishop Brom subsequently apologized and presided at a memorial Mass for the family, Dignity issued an upbeat press release expressing gratitude for Bishop Brom's decision (McArron, 2005), but neither this statement nor the earlier one insisted that their rights as baptized Catholics in good standing had been violated nor that they were entitled to receive Catholic funerals.[7] Instead, Dignity left the question open by insisting that Bishop Brom made the decision to refuse a funeral Mass without knowing if McCusker was a "manifest sinner" (*DignityUSA calls*, 2005), the condition cited in canon law for refusing funeral rites. Other reform groups very likely would have portrayed the incident as a violation of the inclusive spirit of Jesus, who "welcomed everyone to the table," especially sinners and social outcasts. Regardless, Dignity played a role in influencing Bishop Brom's about-face, in part by drawing extensive publicity to the incident and helping mobilize six hundred people from all walks of life to attend a rally in support of the McCusker family at the GLBT center in San Diego.

Founded in 1969, DignityUSA maintains high visibility in the Reform Movement, participating actively in COR as a founding member and CTA, where it offers workshops and an information table at annual conferences. During its first decade, Dignity struggled to earn credentials as an insider organization by meeting with bishops and conducting liturgies in Catholic parishes (Dillon, 1999). Following a 1986 Vatican ban on the right of Dignity to use Catholic facilities, Dignity had little choice but to find "outsider" meeting space (McArron, 2003, p. 15).

Dignity has not escaped the internal debates over strategy and theology that characterize other reform groups. For example, in the 1970s the New York Dignity chapter engaged in a number of "more militant" actions

---

[7] GLBT Catholics have the same rights to the sacraments and Catholic funerals as other baptized Catholics, except for same-sex marriage, which is expressly forbidden. Gay men are still allowed to enter the priesthood, although criteria for acceptance have become more restrictive. Although church teachings disapprove of homosexual acts, they insist that persons should not be condemned or excluded due to their homosexual tendencies. Generally speaking, the decision to deny Catholic funerals to "manifest sinners" is left to the discretion of priests and bishops.

than those favored by the national president, including "quiet watch-ins" in front of St. Patrick's Cathedral "to inform people about alternative understandings of sexuality than those articulated by the Vatican" (Dillon, 1999, p. 91). The analysis below suggests that Dignity's leadership remains relatively reserved and nonconfrontational in their overall orientation toward Roman Catholic hierarchs.

Restrained Rhetoric

The most striking feature of Dignity's highly professional website (www.dignityusa.org) is its rather bland, reserved language that contrasts with the more hard-hitting, provocative rhetoric characteristic of other reform groups. DignityUSA takes a strong stand in favor of GLBT rights but it does so with abstract, academic-sounding language. Although Dignity's depersonalized rhetoric is not inherently conservative, Dignity consistently avoids a polarizing offensive tone when referring to Roman Catholic officials, even when Dignity's leaders are deeply offended by the positions of these officials. The deferential tone of Dignity's rhetoric reflects traditional, "old-fashioned" Catholicism that accords clerics a high degree of courtesy and respect.

Dignity's restrained rhetoric is evident in their *Declaration of Non-Reception of the Letter on the Pastoral Care of Homosexual Persons* (1987), which rejected a letter issued by the Congregation for the Doctrine of the Faith (CDF) on the pastoral care of homosexuals, describing it as "pastorally inadequate to meet the needs of American gay and lesbian Catholics, their families and friends" (p. 1). In their statement, they base their right to reject the document on the tradition of *sensus fidelium*, whereby the laity may reject a teaching that "finds no effective expression in the lives of the faithful" (p. 1). This mild statement avoids any criticism of the authors of the pastoral letter.

In contrast to many GLBT advocacy groups, Dignity does not use the term *homophobic* in referring to church leaders or documents, despite the disparaging rhetoric used by church officials to refer to homosexuality. One example of this rhetoric is the Congregation for the Doctrine of the Faith's (CFC) statement on homosexual unions, issued in July 2005, which describes homosexual acts as "intrinsically disordered" and homosexual persons as "objectively disordered" (*Congregation for the Doctrine*, 2005, p. 2). In a famous 1986 document, then-Cardinal Ratzinger used even bolder and more provocative language that defined homosexuality as "a more or less strong tendency ordered toward an intrinsic moral evil" (Ratzinger as cited by Allen, 2005, p. 155).

Dignity's most critical language appears in a press release in response to Joseph Ratzinger's election to pope. In it they describe Ratzinger as having "the most virulently anti-gay, anti-GLBT rhetoric in the last papacy" (*DignityUSA Sees Challenge*, 2005, p. 1). His election is viewed by many GLBT Catholics as "a profound betrayal by the leaders of the Catholic Church." Despite its claim that many GLBT persons feel "betrayed" by the choice of Ratzinger, Dignity does not claim that the organization felt betrayed. This relatively hard-hitting language of betrayal is counterbalanced by the fact that criticism is directed at Ratzinger's *rhetoric*, but not personally against the new pope.

In contrast to DignityUSA, other reform groups intentionally avoid a subservient tone or clerical-sounding language when they find the actions of Roman Catholic hierarchs objectionable or repugnant. For example, in referring to church officials, reformers ventured to use terms such as "bullies" (several W-CC publications) and "power-hungry residents of the Vatican" (in a May/June *CORPUS Reports* article); and a WOW convention speech by Harvard Divinity School professor Elisabeth Schüssler Fiorenza (2005) that depicted church leaders as "morally bankrupt" and "more like the Roman empire than the ekklesia of Christ" (p. 3).

Catholics by Right, Privilege, and Duty

Although all reforms organizations reviewed in part 1 defend their right to call themselves "Catholic," DignityUSA is particularly emphatic in their claim, asserting, "It is our right, our privilege, and our duty to live the sacramental life of the church, so that we might become more powerful instruments of God's love working among all people" (*Statement of Position*, 2008). Despite its conciliatory orientation, however, Dignity was censured in 1986 when Catholic bishops issued a ban forbidding GLBT groups from meeting in church properties and relying on canonically active priests to conduct their liturgies.[8] Consequently, DignityUSA chapters meet in non-Catholic churches and rely on priests who have

---

[8] The term *canonically active* refers to Roman Catholic priests who have not resigned or been defrocked. As noted earlier, church officials typically use the term "valid but illicit" to refer to services conducted by priests who left ministry after being ordained in the Catholic Church and conduct sacraments without approval from a Roman Catholic bishop. Priests ordained in non-Catholic denominations may be recognized by the Vatican as having the

resigned from Roman Catholic ministry or who are not Roman Catholic. Ironically, the reform organization most eager to retain ties to the institutional church became the first group to create worship communities outside formal church boundaries. Dignity acknowledges that the 1986 ban on use of church facilities was the last straw for many members "who just could not stand to be associated with a Church that condemns and punishes" (McArron, 2003, p. 15).

The deep division between the goals of Dignity and the policies of church officials was particularly evident in Boston in 2004 during the legislative battle at the State House over attempts to challenge the legality of same-sex unions, which followed the decision of the Massachusetts Supreme Court allowing same-sex marriages in Massachusetts. While Boston's Dignity chapter rallied alongside an interfaith coalition of many Jewish and Protestant denominations that favored same-sex marriage, the Boston archdiocese was among the most vigorous and visible proponents of overturning the Massachusetts Supreme Court decision, even to the point of circulating in parishes petitions opposing same-sex marriage (Associated Press, 2005).[9]

Dignity remains connected to the Catholic tradition in the sense that chapter get-togethers are centered on a liturgy that closely resembles the traditional Mass, though it does use gender-inclusive language.[10] In its sharpest deviation from traditional liturgies, DignityUSA has developed a "Blessing of Relationships Liturgy"[11] that includes elaborate procedures for celebrating and sanctifying gay unions (Welch, 2007). Nevertheless, Dignity's weekly liturgies are considerably more conventional than many feminist gatherings, which often conduct improvisational Eucharist celebrations that are not referred to as a Mass (Dierks, 1997).

Public Protest on Solidarity Sunday

DignityUSA's primary protest and publicity event is "Solidarity Sunday," designed as a "faith-based anti-violence initiative" held every year on the

---

authority to conduct valid sacraments if they have a valid line of apostolic succession that can trace its lineage to the original twelve apostles.

[9] In 2006 the United States Conference of Catholic Bishops released a document entitled *Considerations Regarding Proposals to Give Legal Recognition to Unions between Homosexual Persons*, which strongly opposes marriage among homosexuals as well as civil recognition of homosexual unions.

[10] For a detailed description of Dignity liturgies, see chapter 8.

[11] This "Blessing of Relationships Liturgy" includes a Gathering Prayer, a Liturgy of the Word, a Reflection on Love, a Rite of Reconciliation, and a Rite of Blessing.

Sunday before October 11, which is National Coming Out Day. Members are encouraged to wear rainbow ribbons throughout the day as a way of "making [their] opposition to anti-gay violence visible" (*Solidarity Sunday*, 2007). Solidarity Sunday has been endorsed by a number of notable persons, including President Clinton and Vice President Gore in 1997 and the Gay and Lesbian Alliance Against Defamation, as well as Bishop McCarthy of Austin, Texas (*History of Solidarity Sunday*, 2007). The purpose of this symbolic protest is directed not at church officials but against antigay violence, which is condemned by the Vatican's own statements opposing homosexuality. Thus, Dignity's major symbolic protest centers on an issue that actually meets with Vatican approval. Rainbow ribbons provide a subtle method of enabling Dignity members to publicly acclaim their status as GLBT persons or as supporters of those persons.

Dignity's rather tepid protest stands in stark contrast to the Rainbow Sash Movement, which sponsors an annual protest every Pentecost Sunday at which GLBT Catholics and their sponsors attend Mass wearing rainbow sashes as a method of "highlighting the ugly wound of homophobia" (*Why we wear*, 2009). The movement's board of directors asserts that "this wound [homophobia] has become a spiritual cancer on the Mystical body of Christ." Some church hierarchs view these protests as a defiance of church teaching. Consequently, they do not allow sash-wearers to receive Communion in a variety of dioceses in the United States, England, and Australia (McNeill, 2007).[12]

Staving Off Membership Decline

Responding to a decade-long membership attrition that followed the 1986 ban on access to church facilities, in 1996 DignityUSA hired Basile Ryan, a consulting firm, to develop a strategic plan for increasing membership. Subsequently, it announced it would eliminate dues at the national level, although dues at that time were only $20 annually.

Dignity publications claimed a membership of 5,000 in the 1980s that shrank to 2,400 by 2007.[13] Dignity spokespersons have also acknowledged

---

[12] Although the DignityUSA website does have a link to the Rainbow Sash website, the fact that it does not explicitly endorse the Rainbow Sash Movement is yet another indication of its relatively conservative orientation.

[13] Membership trends for DignityUSA are difficult to track since their website and publications include very little data about membership or annual budgets and they did not respond to my request for data. As with other reform groups, only a small percentage of

that Dignity now faces competition from underground churches or other denominations that also offer "welcoming liturgies" for GLBTs. As several speakers at Dignity's 2000 convention put it, "Dignity is no longer the only game in town" (Stone, 2003, p. 18).

The most startling revelations occurred in May 2007 when Dignity published its budget, revealing that the organization was almost broke (DignityUSA, 2007). In his speech at the 2007 Dignity convention, President Sam Sinnett (2007) acknowledged Dignity's pressing financial crisis, candidly stating that current funding patterns, where only seven hundred members donate $50 or more, are "neither healthy nor sustainable" (p. 2).

Dignity members rallied to save the organization by pledging $150,000 to hire staff for vacant positions (P. B., personal correspondence, May 5, 2008). A surge of new energy was generated as members elected new officers, hired new staff, and raised dues to $50. Since its resurgence in 2007, Dignity has solidified its membership and financial base.

Despite Dignity's more conservative theological orientation, one could argue that Dignity's target constituency of GLBT Catholics has received harsher treatment from the Vatican in the past decade than other reform groups, given that opposition to homosexuality and same-sex relationships has become a political priority on the part of the Vatican and American bishops following the abuse crisis. Further, it is possible that, as Sinnett suggested in his convention speech, the increasingly hostile stance by the Vatican on homosexuality[14] may have hampered Dignity's fundraising endeavors.[15] Perhaps donors no longer view the Roman Catholic Church as a viable target for advancing GLBT rights, especially since some Christian denominations now bless gay and lesbian unions and ordain openly gay and lesbian clergy. Most notably, the Episcopal Church took the unprecedented step of ordaining the Reverend Gene Robinson, openly

---

members attend national conventions. Dignity's newsletter *Dateline* reports attendance at Dignity's biannual conventions as ranging from two hundred to three hundred over the past decade. The Dignity website in 2007 lists fifty-six local chapters, substantially less than the seventy-five chapters reported in 1996.

[14] As previously noted, in 2006 the Vatican released a document that strongly opposes marriage among homosexuals as well as civil recognition of homosexual unions. In 2005 the Vatican issued a statement restricting access to the priesthood for homosexual men.

[15] This assertion is suggested by the fact that Dignity received two grants of $7,500 (one in 2001 and another in 2003) from the Gil Foundation, described by Dignity as "the preeminent GLBT organization," as well as a $52,000 donation from two members in 2001. Dignity did not report grants from Gil after 2003.

gay, as bishop in 2003.[16] Perhaps Catholic GLBT persons see little reason to support Dignity's advocacy on their behalf, given the uncompromising stance of the Vatican, and, therefore, Dignity's efforts to increase membership have fallen flat.

Many potential or former members share the sentiment expressed by a youthful Asian gay man, who explained at a March 7, 2004, Dignity Boston meeting that he "had moved past" the need to seek validation or support from the Boston archdiocese. As he put it, "I just don't give a [expletive deleted] what they say anymore, though I respect those who are trying.... I think it is more important to reach out to other Catholics."

Thus, as the stigma and discrimination against homosexuality declines in American society, the need and desire of many GLBT Catholics for approval and validation from the institutional church has declined as well. This is a shift with potentially negative consequences for Dignity's outreach to donors and members. One might imagine Catholic GLBTs asking Dignity why they should endure all indignities imposed by the Vatican when gays are welcome in many churches. Beyond the confines of the Roman Catholic Church, gays face considerably fewer barriers to full inclusion in many religious communities, including established denominations and underground parishes.

Spillover Strategy

Although Dignity leaders continue to participate in various types of protest activities, their political activism is increasingly targeted at legislation involving civil rights for GLBT persons rather than at church reform. By devoting a portion of its energy to promoting acceptance of homosexuality in the broader community, Dignity hopes that a more tolerant public attitude in society might have spillover effects, ultimately convincing hierarchs to reexamine the church's position on homosexuality. In fact, Dignity's vision statement expresses this spillover strategy as follows:

> Dignity envisions and works for a time when GLBT Catholics are affirmed and experience dignity through the integration of their spirituality with

---

[16] The Episcopal Church's decision to ordain a gay bishop did result in a schism between conservative clerics who oppose homosexuality and those who oppose discrimination on the basis of sexual preference. Some reformers do mention this schism when discussing the controversies surrounding the teachings of the Roman Catholic Church on GLBT issues.

their sexuality, as beloved persons of God who participate fully in all aspects of life within the Church and society. (*DignityUSA Vision*, 2008)

In other words, if Dignity cannot make inroads under the current papacy, they hope to create external pressure (an outsider strategy) by winning support from the larger society. As the larger society becomes more tolerant toward GLBTs, the church's policies regarding homosexuals are likely to evoke a rising tide of negative reaction from insiders (laypersons and clerics) within the Roman Catholic Church. Unlike other reform groups, DignityUSA was forced to form independent communities by Vatican decree. Clearly, Dignity would prefer to remain within the confines of the institutional church, but was forced to accept a pariah status by the Vatican's increasingly hostile stance toward GLBT persons.

Redefining Fidelity—CORPS of Reserve Priests United for Service

The Corps of Reserve Priests United for Service (CORPUS) is a reform organization that has for decades advocated to end to mandatory celibacy for the Roman Catholic priesthood. Its membership is composed primarily of resigned Roman Catholic priests, some of whom are principal leaders of the Reform Movement as a whole.[17]

In 2009 CORPUS redefined it mission as follows:

> CORPUS is a faith community affirming an inclusive priesthood rooted in a reformed and renewed Church, ... CORPUS is defined by the Roman Catholic tradition and also by the charisms and decisions of conscience which the Spirit inspires. (W. Manseau, 2009, p. 13)

CORPUS's decision to abandon insider reform strategies reflects recognition by CORPUS leaders that the Vatican would not approve optional celibacy in their lifetimes. It also reveals the evolving views of CORPUS leaders who became more liberal and less bound to the institutional church due to their participation in the Reform Movement.

---

[17] Founded in 1974, CORPUS was designed as an alternative organization for married priests who wanted to focus almost exclusively on optional celibacy rather than the more diffuse and radical agenda of Federation of Christian Ministries (FCM). FCM is a six-hundred member organization with roots in the Catholic Reform Movement. It provides certification for ministry for both married and single men and women, support for small faith communities, and online religious studies programs and regional and national gatherings (Powers, 1992, p. xvi).

Until 2004, the strategy of CORPUS resembled CTA in that it primarily worked for reform from within institutional Roman Catholic structures. CORPUS secretary Ray Grosswirth (2004) recalls, "CORPUS, in the spirit of the Council [Vatican II], was formed both as a support mechanism for married priests and their families, as well as a vehicle for dialogue between the organization members and the church hierarchy" (p. 24).

In contrast to other reform groups, however, CORPUS's decision to become a sectarian organization was the most protracted, but individual members had started to defect from the institutional church when they chose to terminate their status as "canonically active" Roman Catholic priests. To be released from their priestly vows, Roman Catholic priests must request a laicization process whereby church authorities assign them status as a lay member of the church.[18] This laicization process was a momentous step for many CORPUS members, as evidenced by the painful accounts of their individual transitions that were frequently included in the bimonthly magazine *CORPUS Reports*. Inevitably, their decisions to leave the priesthood disappointed at least some superiors, fellow priests, parents, and others, and often evoked charges of infidelity to their vows. At CORPUS's first national convention in 1988, CORPUS leader Anthony Padovano delivered a path-breaking speech, "Broken Promises," in which he forcefully rebutted charges of betrayal, insisting,

> We are still faithful but to a different Church, a new Church, one which all God's people need us to help them build. We are the bridge between the old and the new since we have lived in both Churches, between clerical and lay life, since we have known both profoundly; between celibacy and marriage, since we have been given both gifts. (Padovano as cited in Powers, 1992, p. 277)

Two years later Padovano (1994) once again defended CORPUS's loyalty by defining CORPUS's bedrock commitment as "allegiance and fidelity to

---

[18] Some CORPUS priests simply resign without undergoing the laicization process, as in the case of Bill Manseau, described in the vignette at the beginning of this chapter. CORPUS member Patrick Callahan (2008) reports that the option of leaving without dispensation became more common under John Paul II, who reformed the process in a manner Callahan describes as "vindictive and demeaning" (p. 16). A process that used to be resolved in several months, then took several years and required the priest seeking dispensation to "demonstrate that, in effect, the priest, due to clear character flaws, should never have been ordained in the first place" (p. 18). A priest who leaves without dispensation forfeits the right to marry in the Catholic Church. However, in June 2009 Pope Benedict XVI responded to criticisms from bishops by granting expanded authority to the Congregation of the Priesthood to dismiss "priests who have married, are living with women, or have abandoned the priesthood" (Wooden, 2009). The new law quickens the laicization process but does not apply to priests accused of sexual abuse.

the Catholic tradition, its unalterable definition of itself as Catholic and its desire to join with the Pope and Bishops in every issue which brings the Church and its people life" (p. 2).

Although every resigned priest has to come to terms with the issue of fidelity, each priest follows a unique path as he reconstructs his career, and often his religious identity, following resignation. CORPUS leaders are unrelenting in their insistence that mandatory celibacy is detrimental to the institution. Members affirm their decision to marry, as evidenced by many articles in *CORPUS Reports* by married priests describing the rewards of long-term marriages and family life. For his part, Anthony Padovano emphasized at a COR meeting on November 6, 2003, that "the decision to marry and the decision to become a priest" are "the two best decisions I ever made, in that order."

CORPUS director of member services Stu O'Brien admitted that when he left the Roman Catholic priesthood "in the heady days of Vatican II," he and many of his colleagues thought "change was right around the corner and the end of celibacy was at hand" (personal communication, February 3, 2003). Decades later O'Brien and many of his CORPUS colleagues confess that removal of the celibacy requirement would not entice them back into a church they regard as exceedingly dysfunctional. Rather, for the immediate future, CORPUS has decided its efforts to "be Church" will take place at the outermost margins of the Roman Church, a location that might have been unthinkable during CORPUS's early years.

Early Conversations with Church Hierarchs (1971–2004)

Even before the formation of CORPUS, several of its future leaders engaged in a variety of communication with church officials over the issue of celibacy, but the dialogue usually fell short of expectations. In his homily at the 2004 CORPUS convention, Frank Bonnike (2005), one of the founders of CORPUS, recounted a meeting of a priests' council with Cardinal Dearden in 1971, just before the bishops' synod in Rome. When pressed to bring up the issue of optional celibacy at the synod, Dearden replied, "Well, you know, I am just one bishop from one country." Everyone laughed when Father Walter Barr responded, "Cardinal Dearden, you are not just one of the boys. You are a big boy in this church, a big, big boy" (Barr as cited in Bonnike, p. 22). Bonnike also recalls the failed attempt of Father Frank McNulty, who was chosen by the bishops to represent American priests during Pope John Paul II's visit to the United States in

1987. On that occasion, McNulty made an appeal for optional celibacy, which fell on deaf ears.

By its thirtieth anniversary in 2004, CORPUS leaders were willing to admit publicly that their organization needed a change of direction. CORPUS member Carl J. Hemmer (2005) admits that, under existing conditions, insider strategies have little value, given that many of the bishops who befriended CORPUS in the 1970s have been replaced with bishops "who are far less open to dialogue with married priests" (p. 26).[19] Hemmer also acknowledged CORPUS faced a rapidly declining and aging membership.[20] In fact, membership in CORPUS slipped from 11,000 in 1990 (Powers, 1992, p. 255) to 605 in 2010 (Pinto, 2011).[21]

Joining Forces with Others in Exile (2005–present)

In 2005, after assessing these stark realities, CORPUS considered a range possible options, including disbanding altogether. As in the case of DignityUSA cited above, CORPUS members rallied when faced with the prospect of closure. The March/April 2005 edition of *CORPUS Reports* adopted an upbeat, forward-looking tone as CORPUS leaders announced several new initiatives. First, CORPUS joined with other reform groups—Federation of Christian Ministries (FCM) and Women's Ordination Conference (WOC)—to create a National Catholic Ministerial Alliance. The purpose of this alliance is to promote "the grass roots reformation of the Roman Catholic Church's ministries" (W. Manseau, 2005, p. 28) by supporting renewing forms of ministry within and outside the church. Groups not affiliated with the Roman Catholic Church would be included if they demonstrated a "high level of spiritual maturity" (p. 28).

---

[19] Hemmer also cited other factors influencing CORPUS: (1) new priests are more conservative; (2) CORPUS's allies, CTA, and FutureChurch, have little influence; (3) lay ministers have assumed priestly duties in many parishes (Hemmer, 2005).

[20] One factor influencing the decline in CORPUS membership may be the fact that many Vatican II priests have severed their connection to Roman Catholicism. In this regard, CORPUS members Patrick Callahan (2008) reports that at a reunion of students from St. Edward's Seminary in Seattle, Washington, only 25 percent of the twenty men who attended indicated "active membership" in the church (p. 16).

[21] Membership dues for CORPUS (which include a subscription to the bimonthly magazine) rose gradually from $15 in 1990 to $85 in 2007 in an effort to strengthen the financial stability of the organization. However, CORPUS has a policy of accepting any contribution a person can afford. *CORPUS Reports* was a simple mimeographed newsletter in 1990 but is now a glossy, attractive magazine with color photos and a professional layout.

Several months after forming the alliance, CORPUS and the Ecumenical Catholic Communion (ECC) announced the establishment of a new religious and ecumenical community, named the Community of John XXIII. The purpose of the community is "the spiritual development and apostolic work of its members" and its strategies include "blending traditional and contemporary experiences with religious life" (Padovano, 2005a, p. 33). This community was to be modeled after formal Catholic religious communities, which Anthony Padovano of CORPUS (2005a) describes as "one of the great glories of Catholicism, indeed one of its most creative contributions" (p. 32). Membership in this community, which is open to any Christian, includes three vows (later renamed commitments): fidelity (chastity), frugality (poverty), and solidarity (obedience).[22] As of summer 2009, the Community of St. John XXIII reported seventeen members and holds periodic conference calls, functioning as a virtual community (Pinto, 2009, p. 15).

Thus, after more than three decades of struggling for reform from within, by 2005 CORPUS had essentially become a sectarian organization. Two years earlier Russ Ditzel (2003a), CORPUS president, admitted, "At some level, it would be easier to just walk away. We believe, however, in the charism of sacramental ministry" (p. 22). Ditzel's pessimistic tone reflected his dismay evident in a follow-up letter to Bishop Wilton Gregory, USCCB president, who had declined CORPUS's invitation for a dialogue. In the letter, Ditzel (2003b) adopts a confrontational tone, noting that "you are being dishonest, Bishop, when you state: 'We are in the long haul for a lot of honest, open, heart-to-heart conversation.'" Ditzel notes that far from engaging in dialogue, Catholic bishops have stifled communication by suppressing VOTF in many dioceses, silencing theologians, including Roger Haight, S.J., and refusing to meet with CORPUS the previous October.

CORPUS's decision to endorse more inclusive forms of ministry did alienate some of the more conservative members. Over the course of this study I encountered several married priests, active in CORPUS during its

---

[22] The Community of John XXIII redefines celibacy as "a call to witness authentic human relationships at every level of creation" and to challenge oppressive practices "which exploit our sacred creation." The vow of poverty is redefined as the vow of justice-making based on Elisabeth Schüssler Fiorenza's concept of a discipleship of equals and O'Murchu's concept of justice as "egalitarian rather than patriarchal, essentially distributive rather than hierarchical." The vow of obedience is renamed the "vow of mutual collaboration," whereby people work together to "build a culture of right relating humanly, earthly and cosmically" (Scaine, 2007, p. 30).

formative years, who did not support women's ordination and who favored a more moderate approach to church reform than the one embraced by progressive CORPUS leaders (L. P., personal communication, October 24, 2005).

Bill Cleary's column, a regular feature in *CORPUS Reports*, takes an extreme position by encouraging members to abandon the Roman Catholic Church altogether.[23] Cleary's views are more extreme than most CORPUS members, but the fact that his columns are published suggests such a move is not considered "off the table" by his editors. In his review of *The Church that Forgot Christ* by journalist Jimmy Breslin, Cleary urges Catholics to defect. Breslin is an accomplished investigative journalist, who has been on the staff of several New York newspapers and won a Pulitzer Prize in 1986 for commentary. In his book review, Cleary (2004) concludes, "From my perspective that church we all think of when we say the word 'church' has already disappeared. Alas, the leaders forgot the Gospel, having neglected the wind of the Spirit, and must now reap the whirlwind" (p. 46). For those who share Cleary's perspective, the choice of exile becomes essential to one's integrity and spiritual well-being.

Not coincidentally, Breslin (2004) proclaims his own decision to leave the church following the revelations of clergy abuse, despite a lifelong pattern of regular church attendance. "Why should I be in a church like this?" he asks. "The answer is I'm not" (p. 7), as he walked out in disgust at the revelations of hypocrisy and deceit by church officials.

Mentoring New Models of Ministry (2005–Present)

Since 2005, CORPUS has developed its role as mentor for new models of ministry, particularly its support for a series of ordinations by the organization Roman Catholic Womenpriests (RCWP). CORPUS members have attended RCWP ordinations in many locations, and some have developed mentoring relations with newly ordained women.[24]

While engaging in this research, I encountered several current and former CORPUS members who questioned the alliances CORPUS was

---

[23] Cleary's arguments regarding abandoning Catholicism are also cited briefly in chapter 1.
[24] Corpus has also collaborated with RCWP on several conferences, including a preconference session at the CTA national conference in 2006: "Bridging the Gender Gap, Gender Equality, Sex and Ordination." The second conference held in Boston in 2008 was entitled "Inclusive Ministry and Revival in a Complex Age."

forming in its efforts to mentor noncanonical priests. For example, one member expressed skepticism about ECC Bishop Peter Hickman, a member of CORPUS's National Catholic Ministerial Alliance and a formal partner of the Community of John XXIII. This member referred to Hickman as a "two-bit" bishop, implying that as a bishop ordained in the Old Catholic Church,[25] he did not undergo the same rigorous process of training and selection required of Roman Catholic bishops (J. L., personal communication, October 22, 2005). The most intense controversy within CORPUS focused on the decision of some of its members to participate in a highly publicized convocation for married priests on December 8, 2006, which was sponsored by Married Priest Now! and included ordinations of three men, including long-term CORPUS leader Ray Grosswirth. Two hundred priests, bishops, and their wives attended this convocation,[26] which was linked via satellite to reportedly twelve hundred priests and their wives in Europe, Asia, and Latin America (Fujimori, 2006, p. 1).

Emmanuel Milingo, the founder and principal leader of Married Priests Now!, is a former Roman Catholic archbishop from Zambia, who engaged in a highly publicized dispute with the Vatican following his marriage to a South Korean woman in a mass wedding ceremony presided over by the Reverend Sun Myung Moon, founder of the Unification Church. After the ceremony, Pope John Paul II convinced Milingo to renounce the marriage, but he subsequently reunited with his wife when he returned to the United States in 2006.

CORPUS has long-standing connections to several organizations of married priests, most notably the North American Alliance for a Renewed Catholic Priesthood, but Married Priests Now! is the proverbial new kid on the block that has attracted considerably media attention. Some members of CORPUS were troubled by Milingo's connection to Rev. Moon, a cult leader who was involved in a series of financial scandals in the United States and South Korea (Fisher and Leen, 1997). *CORPUS Reports* featured two articles defending Milingo—one by Bill Manseau (2007) emphasizing

---

[25] The Old Catholic Church was once affiliated with the Vatican but chose to become independent in 1870 because it refused to accept the doctrine of papal infallibility that was adopted at the first Vatican Council. More detailed information on the Old Catholic Church and the Ecumenical Catholic Communion is included in chapter 9.

[26] Priests in attendance included CORPUS members, Protestant clergy, members of the American Clergy Leadership Conference (ACLC), an interdenominational and interfaith association organized by Reverend Moon, and priests and bishops from independent dioceses (including Bishop Jim Burch of One Spirit and Dom Luis Castillo Mendez, the patriarch of the Catholic Apostolic Church in Brazil), as well as priests and bishops ordained by Archbishop Emmanuel Milingo (Burch, 2007).

Milingo's highly developed spirituality, and another by Jim Burch (2007), bishop of the Catholic Diocese of One Spirit, presenting a positive account of Milingo's December 8, 2006, convocation.[27]

Eventually CORPUS issued *CORPUS Position Statement regarding Married Priests Now!* (2007), a formal document that acknowledged the "goodwill" of CORPUS members and others involved, but also expressed concern about the following four points: (1) Married Priests Now!'s "insufficient public emphasis on the charisms of women and their yearning for ordination," (2) a "marginalization of homosexual candidates," (3) a "heavy clericalization" of the organization, and (4) a reliance on "funding sources that are questionable" (p. 36).

Where Is Jesus?

CORPUS's defection from the institutional church is perhaps best summarized by CORPUS secretary Ray Grosswirth (2005) who argues that "our leaders in Rome have left Jesus out in the cold, whereby it is difficult for the Holy Spirit to guide the actions of our power-hungry residents of the Vatican" (p. 39). One could infer from Grosswirth's remarks that CORPUS members, who once answered a call from Jesus by being ordained in the Catholic Church, are now claiming a call to move outside the institutional church, where the spirit of Jesus is largely absent.

Redefining Catholic Identity: Catholic Organizations for Renewal

Catholics Organizations for Renewal (COR) is a coalition of twenty-four Catholic reform organizations that meets biannually to share information and plan joint strategy around reform issues.[28] COR describes itself as

---

[27] According to Bishop Burch (2007), Rev. Moon insisted on no "public thanks for his financial assistance to Married Priests Now!" because "all it would bring would be more persecution" (p. 16). Further, Burch explained that Rev. Moon's support for Married Priests Now! reflects his theology, which revolves around "the sanctity of the family and the family unit as the great strengthener of society" (p. 16). Although Milingo's convocation also received funding from the Mormons and the Seventh Day Adventists, Burch claimed that exposing its connection with Rev. Moon became a media "frenzy" (p. 16).

[28] The number of reform organizations listed on COR's website has varied somewhat during the period 2004–2007. As of June 2010, twenty-four reform organizations are listed on COR's website.

"not an organization but a forum, a table where we talk" (*Brief History*, 2007). COR invites member organizations to present proposals to other COR groups, and each group decides for itself whether to publicly endorse the proposal. This decision-making process "preserves the autonomy and diversity of individual organizations, which differ considerably in the range of issues they choose to address" (*Brief History*). This flexible approach to coalition building reflects the different philosophies and strategies of its member organizations, which include insider reform groups (including FutureChurch and the Coalition of American Nuns) as well as outsider reform groups (CTA, CORPUS, and DignityUSA) and independent worship communities (Spiritus Christi and ECC). COR's collaboration among member organizations primarily involves press releases, petitions, and letters to church officials. For example, fifteen COR member organizations signed a press release drafted by DignityUSA (2006) protesting the U.S. Catholic bishops' statement entitled *Ministry to Persons with a Homosexual Inclination: Guidelines for Pastoral Care*. This statement charged that the bishops' guidelines were based on the mistaken premise that "homosexuality is a choice rather than a deeply ingrained emotional and psychological attraction" (*Press release by the*, 2006).

Initially COR required that "all members and applicants were baptized and formal members of the Roman Catholic Church," but eventually included some groups who were "institutionally marginalized" (due to issues such as censure by the Vatican, noncanonical marriages, resignations by priests without dispensation, etc.). More recently, COR has chosen "to define church identity as 'Catholic' rather than 'Roman Catholic,' sensing a tension between the letter and the spirit of Vatican II and a Roman institution which seems monarchical and restorationist" (Padovano, 2005a, p. 34). Consequently, in 2003 COR expanded its membership base to the independent network of parishes ECC and the independent parish Spiritus Christi.

COR does not want its policy statement to be interpreted as abandoning the Roman Catholic Church altogether. In fact, it establishes "seven indicators of Catholic identity," summarized as follows: (1) *sacramentality*, referring to baptism in any Christian church; (2) *intentionality*, meaning the desire to access more fully the values of the Roman Catholic tradition;[29] (3) *law*, that is, the fullness of the Church of Christ is not present in

---

[29] Although COR has decided to abandon its exclusive focus on Roman Catholicism, Padovano (2005a) explains that COR members may desire to "access more fully the

only one church; (4) *history*, divisions within Church are no longer necessary; (5) *conscience,* the Vatican II emphasis on individual conscience; (6) *pastoral life*, the Christian emphasis on inclusiveness; and (7) *ecclesiology*, belief in an institutional expression of four signs of Catholicism—one, holy, catholic, and apostolic (Padovano, 2005a, pp. 34–35). Thus COR claims credentials as a Catholic organization, but claims its right to include groups that it regards as inappropriately excluded from the institutional church.

Moving Toward an Authentic Spirituality

In some instances, spokespersons for reform groups come close to suggesting that they are more loyal to the authentic Catholic tradition, particularly as it emerged from Vatican II, than the church hierarchs intent on restoring a pre-Vatican II church. Consider, for example, the following quote from the COR statement: "Yet COR seeks to remain within the tradition of a Church both Catholic and, indeed Roman, where that further adjective defines legitimate and not expropriated institutional structure" (Padovano, 2005a, p. 32). This rather ambiguous statement implies that current church leadership may not be "legitimate" because it has "expropriated" the institutional structure—in other words, engaged in improper power grabbing.

Similar ideas are expressed by CORPUS secretary Ray Grosswirth (2005) who asks, "Who is leading our church? ... Is Jesus Christ our primary guide, or have we allowed our cardinals and bishops to replace his pastoral leadership with an authoritative and dictatorial hierarchy?" (p. 39). Although he admits being "perhaps presumptuous" in his assertions, Grosswirth is, nonetheless, convinced that Christ would favor "the inclusiveness of CORPUS over the oppressive policies of Rome" (p. 40).

Thus members of these reform groups consistently argue that the Reform Movement makes it possible for them to stay connected (or to reconnect) with the Catholicism that they would otherwise have to abandon. For example, some gay Catholics describe Dignity as a "lifeline" enabling them to reconcile being both gay and Catholic. Alice Knowles of Boston rekindled her childhood Catholicism in 1998 at age forty-five when a friend introduced her to Dignity (Knowles as quoted by Price, 2005).

---

values of Roman Catholicism, because they have no desire to be at odds with it, and because they feel they are distant from it for less than essential reasons" (p. 34).

CORPUS member Paschal Baute (1994) insists that the marginal status of exile is the ideal environment for fostering an authentic spirituality; in his words, "For the apostles and the church, the experience of marginality was an essential step for genuine conversion" (p. 1). Baute raises the question as to whether an ordained priesthood is even necessary or desirable, given the dangers of clericalism and egoism that it engenders. He suggests that

> When embraced with joy, the priesthood of the resigned is in a profound sense an offering of a new "Mass" of a more cosmic order of the mystical priesthood of Emmanuel, more truly able to be brother with the excluded, the lonely and the lost, the least, the little, the lame and the last of the world. (p. 2)

Echoing Baute's reflections, one could conclude that persons involved in the exodus experience are seeking a more mature spirituality, rejecting the childlike status imposed on them by authoritarian Roman Catholic hierarchs where "Father always knows best." This theme is echoed by CORPUS member Joe McCool (2004), who challenges Catholics to interact with the pope and church officials from the standpoint of an adult. He explains that "as an adult, the Church's word would not and could not substitute for my God-given ability to think and be responsible for my own thoughts and behavior" (p. 33).

Thus, the reform groups cited above believe that by moving outside the boundaries of the institutional church they are liberating themselves from a form of religiosity that prevents free intellectual inquiry and the primacy of individual conscience. Thus, they are demanding that the Roman Catholic Church nurture rather than hamper their spiritual development and heed rather than silence the legitimate demands of feminists, gays, and married clergy.

Stage theories of spiritual growth shed light on the perspective of reformers who view their exile from the institutional church as a spiritual leap of sorts, intended to bring them closer to God, thereby affirming their roots in the Catholic tradition. Looking to James Fowler's (1981) stage theory, one notes that as an individual advances toward spiritual maturity, he or she recognizes the cultural biases of his or her own tradition and denomination and interprets religious mythology as conveying metaphorical rather than literal meaning. One cannot conclude that reformers are necessarily more spiritually advanced than their opponents, given that stage theories assess individual (not group) development and require in-depth study and evaluation of individual biographies. Nonetheless,

Fowler's theory is helpful in interpreting the journeys of reformers described above, who regard their decision to move outside institutional boundaries as essential to their efforts to achieve spiritual maturity. Hence, Fowler's theory is consistent with reformers' conviction that moving beyond formal church boundaries need not be interpreted as a rejection of the tradition or an abandonment of the spiritual search.

CORPUS leader Anthony Padovano (2006b) describes CORPUS's legacy this way: "A sense of gratitude for all the official Church made possible in our lives, even gratitude for its resistance, which led us into deeper waters and different harbors" (p. 28). Thus, Padovano acknowledges and celebrates the new spiritual insights that reformers have attained by challenging and, in some ways, moving beyond the limitations of the Roman Catholic tradition, while at the same time struggling to remain true to its most authentic and enlightened core of beliefs.

CHAPTER FOUR

CATHOLIC FEMINISTS CONFRONT GOLIATH:
WOMEN'S ORDINATION CONFERENCE, WOMEN'S ORDINATION
WORLDWIDE, WOMEN-CHURCH CONVERGENCE,
WOMEN'S ALLIANCE FOR THEOLOGY, ETHICS AND RITUAL,
AND CATHOLICS FOR CHOICE

As she entered her eightieth year, Marie Sheehan had a devastating stroke that limited her capacity to maintain her organizing efforts on behalf of Massachusetts Women-Church, which had been her major focus for the past three decades. Before being captivated by the women's movement, Marie resembled no one so much as Mother Teresa in her staunch fidelity to Catholicism and her reputation as a saintly woman who heeded the call of Jesus to care for "the least of our brethren." Marie raised seven children single-handedly on a meager budget when her husband died, just several years after she gave birth to her youngest child. Marie's relatives were so impressed by her strength and stamina that they offered little assistance, assuming she could easily manage the tasks of raising a family on her own. Though Marie appeared brave and calm on the surface, she endured intense emotional suffering and feelings of inadequacy following her husband's death. Despite juggling a full-time job and the challenges of raising a large family, Marie maintained a practice of daily prayer and scriptural reading that she credits with sustaining her during these difficult years (personal communication, May 24, 2004).

As the division director of a local branch of Catholic Charities, Marie won numerous awards for her remarkable record of kindhearted and capable service to disadvantaged members of her community. Marie's burgeoning interest in feminism was fueled by her work with many desperately poor women, whom she recalls as "so beaten down, so helpless" (personal communication, May 12, 2005). After attending an early national conference of Women-Church Convergence (W-CC) in 1987, Marie tapped into what seemed to onlookers as a bottomless reservoir of energy to build and sustain a Massachusetts chapter of Women-Church. The chapter held annual conferences and conducted an annual silent vigil outside the Boston cathedral during the ordination ceremonies for new male priests. They even raised funds for an advertising campaign that featured boldly printed ads proclaiming "Ordain Roman Catholic Women," which were posted atop taxicabs all over Boston. Marie and her circle of Women-Church activists know that ordination for women probably will not happen in their lifetimes, but they remain deeply committed to their cause and convinced that it will inevitably prevail.

As a woman in her eighties, Marie takes a long-range view that enables her to make light of the decision of Bishop William F. Murphy in 2000 to ban Massachusetts Women-Church from meeting on Catholic property. Marie referred to the bishop as "little Billie Murphy," whom Women-Church board member Gerry Finn knew as a child. Marie is both amused and angered that this "young upstart" had the gall to deny space to Women-Church members, most of whom have a lifetime record of volunteer work in Catholic parishes and whose families contributed for generations to the Catholic properties from which they are banned.

No Room at the Inn for Catholic Feminists

Growth in feminist consciousness among Catholic women led to their growing dissatisfaction with the status of women within the Roman Catholic Church and to a longing for more gender inclusivity. The vision of a more inclusive church is articulated by a core of feminist theologians and activists who have created and sustained a variety of Catholic feminist reform groups in United States over the past four decades. Catholic feminist organizations described in this chapter include the three best-known and most influential Catholic feminist reform groups: Women's Ordination Conference (WOC), Women's Ordination Worldwide (WOW), Women-Church Convergence (W-CC), and two feminist think tanks: Women's Alliance for Theology, Ethics and Ritual (WATER) and Catholics for Choice (CFC).

These five Catholic feminist organizations have close ties and engage in many collaborative efforts. From a very early point, these organizations recognized there was little hope of winning significant concessions from Roman Catholic Church hierarchs and, hence, devoted minimal energy to insider strategies. Instead, beginning in the 1980s these groups experimented with a variety of outsider strategies, including demonstrations and press releases that focus negative media attention on the church's sexist behavior, and participation in rituals and ordination ceremonies that violate formal Roman Catholic doctrine. WATER codirector Mary Hunt (2003) explains that early on in their movement Catholic feminists realized that there was "no room at the Inn ... nowhere for us as Catholic feminists called to priesthood and prophecy to work" within the institutional structures of Roman Catholicism (p. 2). Reflecting on the futility of insider strategies, she explained, "It is all but fruitless to knock on the doors of the patriarchal/kyriarchal institution and beg to be allowed in on their terms. Rather it is fruitful to live the alternative—whether ordination, socialization of resources, or the like—and let the good life speak for itself" (p. 2).

Hunt's prognosis was confirmed in 1994 when Pope John Paul II (1994) issued his apostolic letter *Ordinatio Sacerdotalis*, which stated that his stance against women's ordination was a "definitive" teaching and not open to discussion. The more Catholic feminists pushed for women's ordination, the more marginal they became from the standpoint of the Vatican, and their marginal status in turn forced them to move in a sect-like direction in order to give voice to their rage and visions for a renewed Catholicism. Catholic feminists cite the story of David as symbolic of their struggle as a small, marginal group of women who dared to challenge the giant Goliath (the Vatican, a seemingly impenetrable and immovable foe). For example, feminist theologian Mary Hunt (2006) comments on the battle over same-sex marriage legislation by noting the "David and Goliath nature of the relationship between these small groups [feminists and GLBT groups] and the colossal power of the Vatican." She claims that only scholars who have distanced themselves from the Vatican feel free to support same-sex marriage:

> The less institutional connection an individual or group has, i.e., the scholars cited by Dignity or the Conference for Catholic Lesbians (CCL), the more likely they are to publicly promote a pro-sex position. The more institutional connection, the more likely individuals and groups are to remain timid and tentative in calling at most for gay civil rights, avoiding the claim that same-sex love is healthy, good, natural and holy, subject to the same criteria as heterosex with regard to its morality. This is how the lines are currently drawn.

As Hunt asserts, Vatican has Goliath-like power because it exerts overarching power in policy making and access to decision makers, while groups that dissent from Vatican policies are ostracized.

Defecting in Place: Catholic Feminists, Inside, Outside, and on the Edge

Leaders of Roman Catholic feminist organizations have no difficulty acknowledging that the decision to reexamine their faith is a painful one for many women whose Catholic roots go very deep. For example, the novelist Alice McDermott (2005), an outspoken proponent of women's ordination, confesses, "I could no more stop being Catholic than I could stop being a native New Yorker or of Irish descent, my parents' child or my children's mother." In a CFC article in 1998, Valerie Stroud (1998), the United Kingdom representative for the International Movement We are Church, commented,

> Catholicism is not something one can discard like a piece of clothing. It penetrates the roots of one's being.... Practiced in accordance with Gospel principles, Catholicism is healthy, life-giving and brings joy to the heart. (p. 1)

In a similar vein, Mary Hunt (2004) defends her Catholicism among those who would dismiss the entire tradition based on distaste for the current leadership, arguing, "I do not look kindly on those who would miss the fact that Catholicism, like all the other world's major faiths, can produce what Daniel C. Maguire calls the 'renewable moral energy of religion'" (p. 2).

For her part, feminist theologian Elisabeth Schüssler Fiorenza offers a definition of Catholicism that totally contradicts the pronouncements of Vatican officials. Speaking at a WOW conference, Schüssler Fiorenza (2005) echoed the theme of CORPUS that the Reform Movement offers a more authentic spirituality than that of current church hierarchs. She defines "radical democratic feminist catholicity" as "an all-embracing inclusive church in which all are truly equal but not the same; an ekklesial culture where differences are respected and people are truly free ..." (p. 19). Schüssler Fiorenza asserts that her radical version of Catholicism is rooted in the vision of Old Testament prophets and early Christian communities. WATER cofounder Mary Hunt (2004) shares Schüssler Fiorenza's dismissal of Vatican definitions of Catholicity, insisting that "I am not worried about being told that I am not Catholic enough, or that I am not a good enough Catholic. Such value judgments by others have no part in any faith I would embrace" (p. 3). Adopting a rather defensive posture, Hunt claims her only reason for maintaining any connection to Catholicism is her commitment to transforming the institution so that its energy can become a force for social justice. Like Hunt, Fran Kissling of CFC is not troubled by charges of heresy—if anything, the hostile reaction she evokes from the church fuels her energy to continue challenging "the unjust political system that I can and am committed to overturning" (Kissling as cited in Bonavoglia, 2005, p. 132).

While some of the best-known Roman Catholic feminists cited above have largely resolved concerns regarding their Catholic identity, the same cannot be said for many Catholic women who are still struggling to reconcile their newly emerging feminist consciousness with their longstanding ties to Roman Catholicism. As they began to examine their church with a feminist lens, many Catholic women do experience a gradual learning curve that resembles the transformation of CORPUS members, which was described in an earlier chapter. Dierks (1997)[1] explains the gradual awakening that occurs:

> To pray with people we love and know as faith-family, we must ignore excluding language, insensitive homilies, and poor liturgy. The pervasive nature of sexism in the church, indeed sexism deified and presented as religious necessity, is a burden of stone strapped to the backs of women. (p. 14)

Many of these feminists were once "pay, pray, and obey" Catholics who became transformed as they began to apply feminist insights to their church. For example, one sister admitted,

> I never questioned the church. Now I belong on a day-by-day basis. I keep asking: Why am I still religious? Why am I am member of the Catholic Church? Those questions are very real and I know that I am not the only one who struggles with them. (Winter, Lummis & Stokes, 1995, p. 88)

Not surprisingly, a large-scale study of interdenominational feminist spirituality groups in 1995 revealed that Catholics were the angriest with their denomination, and further that 82 percent of Catholic sisters and 81 percent of Catholic laywomen reported often feeling alienated from the church.[2] In contrast, the proportion of Protestant women (including laywomen and clergy) who report feeling alienated was only 62 percent (Winter et al., 1995, p. 102). The finding that Catholic women are more alienated than any other denomination in the study probably reflects the fact that the Catholic Church has been among the most resistant of all denominations to demands for women's ordination. Further, the highly authoritarian structure of the Roman Catholic Church prevents women from any meaningful voice in policy making, given that doctrinal and governance decisions are confined to male clerics, in contrast to denominations such as Congregationalists, Episcopalians, and Unitarians that allow some degree of democratic governance.

---

[1] Dierks's book *Women Eucharist* documents more than one hundred small Eucharist communities across the United States. These communities are composed of Catholic women at various stages of developing feminist consciousness. The findings of Dierks's book are described in detail in chapter 8.

[2] This study was conducted by three scholars who were themselves participants in feminist spirituality groups and the Women-Church movement. The study was based primarily on surveys of 3,746 women who belonged to a church and a women's spirituality group and represented diverse geographic backgrounds, ethnic groups, and ages. Approximately 80 percent of those surveyed were classified as "more or less feminist" (Winter et al., 1995, p. 31).

The 1995 study intentionally included one-third Roman Catholic and one-half Protestant respondents (Winter et al., p. 30).[3] Findings reveal that many Catholic women who feel alienated from the church remain members of a parish, irrespective of whether they attend Mass. These Catholic women who stay decide for themselves the meaning of their Catholic identity. The authors of this study use the term "defecting in place" to describe the decision to "leave the old way of relating and to stay on one's own terms, to be present in a whole new way" (Winter et. al., p. 114). However, some of the feminist women in the study did in fact leave, and the authors predict many more will follow. Those who are the verge of leaving express their tentative position with some of the following statements: "I have one foot in and one foot out." "My spiritual experience is that of being in exile." "About every three days I want to leave the institution" (Winter et al., p. 116).

The Catholic women in all three categories (inside, outside, and on the edge) have followed distinctly individual paths to reach their decisions, and their journeys will continue to evolve. Catholic women who favor women's ordination (which, according to polls, comprise a majority of all Catholic women)[4] are pushed to the margins, and some of these increasingly disenchanted and outspoken women have become activists in Catholic feminist reform organizations.

WOMEN'S ORDINATION CONFERENCE AND WOMEN'S ORDINATION WORLDWIDE

Origins of Women's Ordination Conference

The formation of the Women's Ordination Conference (WOC) followed a historic conference in Detroit in 1975 where nineteen hundred women met to discuss the ordination of women within the Catholic Church.

---

[3] Four out of five of Protestant respondents were from "old-line" denominations including Episcopal, Lutheran, Presbyterian, Methodist, United Church of Christ, and Disciples of Christ (Winter, et al., p. 30). This study included a sample of 3,746 women and 112 men ranging in age from under 30 to over 70, but most were 35–55.

[4] A poll conducted in spring 2005 by the Gallup Organization and sponsored by the *National Catholic Reporter* revealed that 61 percent of female Catholic respondents favor ordination of celibate women and 54 percent favor ordination of married women (Gautier, 2005, p. 21). Based on extensive 2006 survey data, Putnam and Campbell (2010) report that 75 percent of Anglo Catholics favor female clergy while only 57 percent of Latino Catholics do.

WOC describes itself as "the world's oldest and largest national organization working solely for women to be ordained as deacons, priests and bishops into a renewing priestly ministry in the Roman Catholic Church"[5] (WOC, *About Us*, 2009).

During its early years, WOC played the insider role by demonstrating outside the annual meetings of the USCCB, and in 1979 was invited to meet with the Bishops' Committee on Women in the Church. Although these talks continued for three years, WOC leaders ultimately described these meetings with the bishops as "a non-meeting of the minds," as theologian Rosemary Radford Ruether put it, due to the bishops' lack of responsiveness (WOC, *History*, p. 2). Later, WOC opposed efforts by the bishops to write a pastoral letter on women because the letter "made women rather than sexism the problem" (p. 3). The pastoral letter underwent four increasingly conservative revisions and never won final approval, in part because these drafts met with dissatisfaction among bishops themselves and "prominent American Catholic women" (Burns, 1994, p. 128).

The Current Focus of WOC

Consequently, WOC has designed a three-pronged strategy as follows: first, *the Ministry of Irritation*,[6] which encourages dramatic actions to shine light on the issue of women's ordination;[7] second, *the Ministry of Walking with Women Called in the Catholic Church*, which offers an online community for women called to priesthood within the Roman Catholic Church; and third, *the Ministry of Prophetic Obedience*, which helps groups that want to move forward with "community-based ordinations" (J. B., personal communication, June 23, 2004).

---

[5] More specifically, WOC identifies its long-term goals as follows: "to reform the governance structures of the Catholic Church, including canon law, to be more inclusive, accountable, and transparent"; "to bring about equality and justice for women in all dimensions of life and ministry in the Catholic Church"; and to "incorporate feminist, womanist, mujerista, and other liberating theologies in every-day Catholicism" (WOC,. *About Us*, 2009).

[6] The title "ministry of irritation" evoked a negative response from some members. Although WOC elicited suggestions for a new title, the title remains on its website (www.womensordination.org).

[7] In support of its "ministry of irritation," WOC has sponsored a series of petitions to the Vatican over the past several decades and has joined other reform groups in a range of advocacy activity.

Over the past several decades, WOC increasingly has emphasized focusing negative media attention on the refusal of the Roman Catholic Church to ordain women. For example, on April 18, 2005, WOC members in five cities held demonstrations that sent pink smoke signals, mimicking the practice of the Vatican conclave meeting in Rome that sends smoke signals to announce its progress in choosing the next pope (*Catholic Women's Ordination*, 2005). WOC also organizes a yearly World Day of Prayer for Women's Ordination into a renewed priesthood when small groups of WOC members gather to conduct prayer services in homes and, occasionally, even in Catholic parishes (with the consent of pastors). WOC's newsletters increasingly highlight ordinations by Roman Catholic Womenpriests (RCWP) and other independent groups that have ordained women as priests or deacons.

Defiant Voices of Women's Ordination Worldwide

WOC has played a central role in the networking and collaboration of all the Catholic feminist organizations described below. In the case of Women's Ordination Worldwide (WOW), WOC was a cofounder and played a central role in the evolution of Women's Ordination Worldwide particularly from 1996 to 1998 when it served as WOW's principal coordinator. WOW's primary activities to date have centered on its two international conferences in 2001 and 2005, which received international coverage due, in part, to the extraordinary acts of defiance that occurred at both conferences.

The first conference of WOW in 2001 in Dublin, Ireland, attracted 350 women from twenty-six countries and became a noteworthy event when Sister Joan Chittister, a long-time leader of the Reform Movement, attended the conference in defiance of orders from the Vatican forbidding her attendance. The Vatican never made good on its threat to impose "grave penalties" because Chittister's decision was supported by 127 of the 128 members of her Erie Benedictine community as well as by the prioress of her order, Christine Vladimiroff, who responded to the Vatican order by explaining,

> Obedience in Benedictine life is not a matter of someone in authority telling someone to do a task or not to do a task.... Benedictine authority and obedience are achieved through dialogue between a [community] member and her prioress in a spirit of coresponsibility. (Vladimiroff as cited in Bonavoglia, 2005, p. 14)

Chittister's defiant spirit in 2001 was mirrored at the 2005 WOW conference in Ontario, Canada, which was scheduled to precede an RCWP ordination ceremony. Adding fuel to the fire, theologian Rosemary Ruether issued a call to reject the choice of Cardinal Ratzinger as the new pope. Ruether explains, "This papacy may forfeit the respect that modern Popes have won from the non-Catholic world. There needs to be a real debate and action that defies the strategies of silencing and forced submission" (WOW, *Speaker Calls for,* 2005).

Ruether's reference above to silencing and forced submission refers to Ratzinger's role, as Prefect of the Congregation for the Doctrine of the Faith (CDF), in silencing or removing from office 107 theologians (M. Fox, 2006), as well as the more recent Vatican decision to fire *America* editor Father Tom Reese.[8] These precedent-setting actions by Chittister and Ruether, as well as their endorsement of "illicit" ordinations, are outsider strategies, clearly not designed to curry favor with church officials. While Chittister remains a Benedictine nun, she was willing to risk expulsion rather than muffle her support for women's ordination. Chittister explained that her decision to defy the Vatican ban was essential to her integrity, given that she could not credibly advise other women to resist abuse if she succumbed to the Vatican's threat. In her words, "Maybe one significant act of conscience, however small, is worth more than all the books and all the words ever written, ever said" (Chittister as cited in Bonavoglia, 2005, p. 11).

Controversies in WOC: Mainstream versus Radical Feminists

WOC's attempt to straddle the insider-outsider divide has generated tension throughout its history,[9] and these tensions resurfaced at the 2005 WOW Conference in Ottawa, Canada, where controversy erupted in reaction to a speech by Schüssler Fiorenza (2005), who urged women to move beyond ordination toward creating a "discipleship of equals" that does not require clerical and hierarchical distinctions. Many women involved in

---

[8] *America* is a Jesuit magazine designed to "boldly engage American culture, neither running from contemporary trends nor failing to promote the values of Catholic thought, culture, and faith in American society" (Gibson, 2006, p. 282).
[9] The issue of whether Catholics feminists should pursue ordination or create a more egalitarian model of ministry has been debated throughout WOC's history (Dillon, 1999, pp. 96–103).

the ordination movement interpreted Schüssler Fiorenza's comment as a criticism of their efforts. This point was raised by Denise Donato (2005), an ordained priest in the independent parish Spiritus Christi, who rejected Schüssler Fiorenza's arguments that ordination was inherently inegalitarian. Donato insisted her ordination does not imply she is "holier" or "higher" or "more important" than others (p. 6). Donato also objected to WOC's policy of not mentioning the RCWP ordinations on the St. Lawrence River that followed the 2005 conference. Donato claimed this policy was a deliberate attempt to "protect" women who might lose their jobs in Catholic parishes or organizations by attending an event associated with these "illicit" ordinations. While acknowledging this dilemma, Donato objected to the policy of "operat[ing] out of fear," noting that "Rome does not need to issue decrees to silence us—we do it to ourselves and each other" (p. 6). Addressing these disputes, WOC executive director Joy Barnes (2005b) noted that "diversity of opinion is a sign of maturity and health" (p. 4), and urged members to tolerate differences and focus on "common ground."

WOC's inclusion of more conservative perspectives was evident in an article in WOC's newsletter by Kate Kuenstler, P.H.J.C., criticizing the "illicit" ordinations by RCWP. Kuenstler (2007) argued that these unsanctioned ordinations are regarded as "premature and out of season" (p. 10) by some Catholics and may "drive a wedge" on the issue by polarizing supporters of ordination and those who are neutral or opposed to ordination.[10]

In many respects, WOC resembles the reform organizations described earlier (CORPUS, DignityUSA, and COR) in that it has a small budget ($247,212 in 2008) and small membership (two thousand), and has increasingly embraced outsider strategies in its advocacy efforts. Another similarity is that all four organizations have encountered dramatic declines in attendance at their national conferences.[11] Although WOC has not held its

---

[10] Kuenstler (2007) is concerned about the impact of the ordinations, not on WOC members but on potential supporters of women's ordinations among the laity and hierarchy. Kuenstler favors an incremental approach that would focus initially on ordaining women as deacons. She notes that "the laws of the Church are changed by organic, gradual change," and she is concerned that the fallout from the illicit ordinations would undermine advancement opportunities for women who seek positions within the institutional church (p. 10).

[11] It seems unlikely that WOC could attract the sizeable crowds numbering in the thousands who attended earlier conventions, when women were just beginning to request ordination. For example 3,000 persons attended WOC's second conference in Baltimore

own conference since 2000, two recent conferences that were heavily promoted by WOC attracted only several hundred,[12] in contrast to the thousands who attended the earlier conferences of Catholic feminists. On a more positive note, WOC has also recently demonstrated signs of strength, especially WOC's 2007 World Day of Prayer for Women's Ordination, which was the largest ever. On March 25, 2007 (the Feast of the Annunciation of the Blessed Virgin Mary), twenty events were held in the United States and twenty-eight in other countries and regions across the globe, primarily Latin America[13] (Taylor, 2007, p. 1). The global network of WOC contacts may prove to be a powerful source of strength for the organization. Very possibly the issue of women's ordination has a fresh appeal to Catholic women in countries where the feminist demands and critiques of Vatican policies have only recently been voiced. WOC's outreach in this regard may have been strengthened by the fact that its three-pronged strategy appeals to women at different stages of defining their loyalty to the institutional church.[14]

Dismantling Institutional Power: Women-Church Convergence

Women-Church Convergence (W-CC) is a coalition of thirty-six "autonomous Catholic-rooted organizations/groups" and describes itself as "raising a feminist voice and committed to an ekklesia of women which is participative, egalitarian and self-governing" (*Women-Church Convergence, Working,* 2008). W-CC, founded in 1984, is even more loosely structured and poorly funded than WOC. W-CC emerged following a 1983 conference

---

in 1978. Roughly equivalent crowds attended conferences of Women-Church Convergence—3,200 in 1987 in Cincinnati and 2,400 in 1993 in Albuquerque (Neu, 1995, p. 245).

[12] The 2007 W-CC conference attracted 250 people and the WOW conferences attracted only 350 in 2001 and 400 in 2005. Admittedly, the WOW conferences held outside the United States (in Dublin, Ireland, and Ontario, Canada) meant that travel was more expensive for many WOC members than earlier WOC conferences in the United States. However, WOW's conferences drew from an international audience as well.

[13] WOC's World Day of Prayer events were held in Argentina, Brazil, Bolivia, Canada, Chile, Colombia, Ecuador, Germany, Ireland, Mexico, Peru, Spain, South Africa, Spain, the United Kingdom, and Venezuela.

[14] WOC experienced a setback in 2008 when its offices were destroyed by fire. In 2009 WOC reported only twelve cities in the United States that participated in the World Day of Prayer Event.

in Chicago entitled "Women Church Speak" that drew thirteen hundred women. Feminist theologian Rosemary Radford Ruether (1995) explains that the Women-Church movement (that ultimately formed W-CC) intentionally chose a loose structure to avoid the pitfalls of institutionalization. In her words,

> By refusing to link these distinct groups into a superstructure or to provide any ongoing central office for the movement, other than as a clearing house for the coordination of the distinct groups, Women-Church also refuses to become an institution in itself. (Ruether, p. 250)

By avoiding institutionalization, the Women-Church movement avoids the polarizing options of leaving or staying in the institutional church, joining one denomination or another, choosing Christianity or post-Christianity. Instead W-CC members and organizations "favor a process approach that allows members and groups to choose from a spectrum of options" (Ruether, p. 250). Membership organizations in W-CC range from small Eucharist communities to six local Women-Church chapters to other membership organizations, including DignityUSA, the National Coalition of American Nuns (NCAN), and WOC.

W-CC embraces broadly defined, visionary, and radical social goals, including elimination of all forms of patriarchy and racism and all forms of violence.[15] These radical goals are translated into concrete actions primarily at the chapter level, where members engage in networking, public education projects, rituals, and theological discussions.[16]

Although W-CC includes groups that could be labeled both insiders (for example, Sinsinawa Dominican Women's Network) and outsiders (for example, A Critical Mass: Women Celebrating Eucharist), W-CC adopts essentially outsider strategies by directing its efforts primarily at networking and conferences and devoting little energy to seeking concessions from church officials. W-CC's outsider status was reinforced by the experience of one of its local chapters, Massachusetts Women-Church (described in the vignette above), which was banned from meeting on church

---

[15] W-CC's goals include (1) the equal distribution of economic resources in local, national, and global communities; (2) rooting out racism in personal lives and in structures of church and society; (3) elimination of heterosexism/homo-hatred, patriarchy, and racism; and (4) elimination of all forms of violence, especially against women and children (*WC-C Common Commitments*, 2008).

[16] As noted above, over the past twenty years, W-CC has sponsored a number of national conferences, though attendance has dwindled from thousands in the 1980s and 1990s to 250 in 2007.

property following its refusal to meet with Bishop William F. Murphy in 2000 when he rejected their request to meet on neutral ground rather than in the bishop's office.[17] This ban did little to dampen the activities of Massachusetts Women-Church in the short term, particularly since it received many offers of meeting space from non-Catholic parishes and campus ministers. By 2007, however, it chose to disband due primarily to the declining health of its aging leadership team. They also acknowledged that their annual conferences, which once attracted hundreds, had been experiencing low turnout as other local groups (especially Boston College's "The Church in the Twenty-first Century" series) were sponsoring feminist theologians and forums on women's issues in the church (M. S., personal communication, April 14, 2004).

A Feminist Think Tank: Women's Alliance for Theology, Ethics and Ritual

Founded in 1983, Women's Alliance for Theology, Ethics and Ritual (WATER) describes itself as a "feminist educational center" and a "network of justice-seeking people" and is run primarily by the partnership team of Mary E. Hunt, Ph.D., a leading Catholic feminist theologian, and Diann L. Neu, D.Min., who is nationally known for her feminist liturgies, which are widely used by feminist spirituality groups. Hunt and Neu have played central leadership roles through the histories of WOC and W-CC and continue to make presentations at their conferences. WATER publishes a quarterly newsletter, which includes in each issue a ritual marking significant events in the lives of women or the women's movement. These rituals are feminist and ecumenical in nature and weave together poems, prayers, music, and dance from a variety of religious traditions and feminist literature. Over the years, WATER has received a variety of foundation grants that have funded a range of education programs aimed particularly at young women and Third World women.

In 2003, WATER, along with W-CC, was reminded of their outsider status when the president of Washington Theological Union (WTU) refused

---

[17] The leaders of Massachusetts Women-Church had heard rumors before the meeting that they would be threatened with excommunication if they did not drop their public advocacy for women's ordination. They were not given a reason for the ban on their right to use church property, but they believe it was imposed because of their refusal to agree to a meeting in the bishop's office.

to rent space to WATER for their twentieth anniversary celebration. WATER's request for space was denied because WATER codirector Mary Hunt served on the Clergy Advisory Board of the Religious Coalition for Reproductive Choice, which supports women's right to choose, even in a number of controversial late-term cases.

Perhaps not surprisingly, a dour mood permeated WATER's anniversary celebration, reflecting that the WTU rejection was simply part of what Hunt described as a growing trend of repression and backlash against feminist organizations in religious settings, particularly Catholic ones. During this event, WATER announced that it is the only remaining women's spirituality center of its type, as similar groups in the Midwest and California had recently folded. Reflecting on these setbacks, theologian Elisabeth Schüssler Fiorenza admitted she was basically a "pessimist," but responded to the question "Will feminist work in religion survive?" by stating that "it depends on the dreams and visions we seek to realize today." Other speakers described a growing backlash against feminist theologians in academe and burnout among feminist activists, whose best efforts had evoked little in the way of concrete reform.

Not One of the Pack—Catholics for Choice

Catholics for Choice (CFC)[18] presents an interesting contrast to the Vatican II reform groups described in this study. Like WATER, CFC is not a membership organization but rather a research and advocacy think tank funded primarily by grants and donations from individuals and foundations. CFC describes its mission as follows: "CFC shapes and advances sexual and reproductive ethics that are based on justice, reflect a commitment to women's well-being and respect, and affirm the moral capacity of women and men to make sound and responsible decisions about their lives" (CFC, *About Us,* 2009). Inevitably, CFC focuses on countering the Vatican's efforts to restrict reproductive rights through government legislation across the globe.[19]

---

[18] In 2008 the organization changed its name to from Catholics for a Free Choice (CFFC) to Catholics for Choice (CFC). I use the more recent initialism throughout this manuscript.

[19] CFC identifies five foci for its research and advocacy including abortion and contraception, HIV/AIDS, sex and sexuality, new reproductive health technologies, and religion in public policies.

A Unique Mission

CFC can claim to be a Catholic reform organization, in some sense, since it does maintain ties to the Reform Movement as a member of Catholic Organizations for Renewal (COR) and W-CC. In sharp contrast to other reform groups in this study, CFC has become increasingly institutionalized and well financed since its founding in 1973, when it was primarily a grassroots volunteer organization. In 2006, CFC boasted annual budget of 3.5 million dollars (J. O'Brien, 2006),[20] which marks CFC as the wealthiest Catholic feminist organization, whose budget and staff size probably surpass the resources (budget and staff) of all the other reform groups combined.[21]

The fact that CFC is so much more successful at fund-raising than other Catholic reform organizations is testimony to the marketing, research, and advocacy skills of its leaders, as well as the salience of the issue of reproductive rights over the past several decades. CFC's ability to tap such extensive resources may reflect that donors who favor CFC's advocacy of reproductive rights need no convincing that the Vatican and American bishops are formidable adversaries, who exert their considerable symbolic power in the pulpit and in legislative bodies where they aim at restricting or prohibiting reproductive rights. In contrast, convincing donors to support reform groups intent on democratizing an institution whose leaders are known to be authoritarian and staunchly conservative may seem a poor investment, especially given that so many worthy causes are more likely to bear fruit in the short run.

Embracing Outsider Strategies

From the beginning, CFC targeted its efforts at public opinion rather than Vatican policies. Pat McMahon, CFC's first executive director, "understood that CFC's principal niche was not lobbying but education, and that achieving our goals would require well-produced material" (*A Mouse that*, 1998). Until her resignation in 2007, Fran Kissling, who served as CFC president for twenty-five years, shaped the organization's reputation for professional, reliable research and an iconoclastic approach to Catholicism.

---

[20] From 2007 to 2010, CFC claimed a budget of three million dollars and twenty staff.
[21] A chart in appendix A reports budgetary information for those reform groups that publish this information.

CFC's ability to muster media attention stemmed in part from Kissling's role as CFC spokesperson—her acerbic wit and clever one-liners made her an appealing media "star," whereby she was frequently quoted or interviewed by national press, especially during the clergy abuse crisis and later during the papal transition in 2005.

Kissling's position papers, particularly "Is There Life after Roe?," have attracted considerable attention, even evoking rave reviews, including one by Notre Dame theologian Richard McBrien (2005a). McBrien described this paper as "ground-breaking" and "remarkable," (p. 10) praising Kissling's balanced presentation of both sides of the abortion debate. In this article, Kissling (2004/5) continues to expand on her long-standing position favoring a middle ground between demands on the part of some pro-choice advocates for unrestricted access to abortion and the uncompromising antiabortion stance of the Vatican.[22] On the one hand, she acknowledges that the fetus has value and may suffer pain, and expresses concern about the "coarsening of humanity" that may result from taking human life. On the other hand, she favors a woman's right to control the decision and exercise her own conscience in weighing the consequences of an unwanted birth.

Like other reform groups, CFC had made some attempts to develop lines of communication with church hierarchs. For example, in the 1990s when the battle over abortion intensified, CFC called for dialogue and succeeded in convincing some bishops to meet with individuals and small groups (Dillon, 1999). However, in sharp contrast to the deferential approach of reform groups CORPUS and DignityUSA, from the beginning CFC asserted itself as an organization that would be provocative and unapologetic in its interaction with the Vatican. For example, in 1974 on the first anniversary of the *Roe v. Wade* Supreme Court decision, CFC cofounder Patricia Fogarty McQuillan, in a dramatic gesture, crowned herself pope on the steps of St. Patrick's Cathedral in New York City. A further bold step was CFC's full-page ad in the *New York Times* containing its petition, signed by ninety-seven prominent Catholics, asserting "A Diversity of Opinions Regarding Abortions Exists Among Committed Catholics" (October 7, 1984, p. E7). The petition noted that church

---

[22] Kissling's article was published in the Winter 2004/5 edition of *Conscience*, CFC's quarterly magazine. Although Kissling's article is not presented as a CFC policy statement, it is cited as a resource in CFC's web page on the issue of abortion.

teachings on abortion are not consistent, and support for abortion adheres to "principles of moral theology, such as probabilism, religious liberty, and the centrality of an informed conscience."[23]

As one would expect, CFC's ad evoked a quick and hostile response from the Vatican. The two priests, two religious brothers, and twenty-six nuns who signed the ad were ordered to recant and, in the end, only two nuns chose to leave religious life rather than recant. However, twenty-four women religious who signed the ad held out for two years of negotiating before arriving at a compromise position that avoided resignation (Henold, 2008).[24] Subsequently, CFC has come under sharp attack from the Vatican, which accused CFC of "leading [Catholics] into sin" (Bonavoglia, 2005, p. 112), as well as from conservative Catholics, such as the Catholic League for Religious and Civil Rights, that termed CFC "one of the most devilish anti-church organizations operating in America today" (p. 112).

In response to these attacks, CFC has countered the Vatican at every turn, grounding its arguments in political and moral principles as it advocates reproductive rights, including emergency "morning after" pills, condom use, and "contraceptive equity laws," which require employee prescription drug coverage to include contraceptives. Kissling (2000) cites the following principles from Roman Catholic theology to justify CFC's claim that Catholics have the right to choose abortion and support the legal right to abortion: (1) The Catholic Church has "no firm position ... on when the fetus becomes a person"; (2) Catholicism respects the right of its members to exercise their individual conscience; (3) the church's formal prohibition on abortion is not an infallible teaching.

CFC board member and sociologist Susan Farrell (2005) grounds support for reproductive choice in Roman Catholic social justice teachings. Farrell contends that although the church teaches that "women and men are equal and made in the image of God," this principle is violated by church policies that "deny sex education and contraception to poor

---

[23] This *New York Times* ad was organized partly as a defense of vice presidential candidate Geraldine Ferraro, who was sharply attacked by New York Cardinal John O'Connor for her pro-choice position (Bonavoglia, p. 115).

[24] Hunt (2008) asserts that "the 97 signers of the ad were in fact penalized every thinkable way." The twenty-six nuns were threatened with dismissal from their order and the sixty-seven nonreligious signers "lost jobs, tenure, and/or promotion in Catholics institutions," and "virtually all" lost speaking or teaching engagements.

women and teenagers throughout the world, contributing to childbirth and abortion-related deaths and the spread of HIV" (p. 4).[25]

CFC's confrontational stance against the Vatican was nowhere more evident than in 2002 when CFC adopted a "See Change Campaign" advocating that the Holy See, recognized as an independent state,[26] be denied its special status in the United Nations as a Non-member State Permanent Observer. This status allows the Vatican to speak and vote at UN conferences, a right not granted to representatives of any other religion. CFC argues that the Roman Catholic Church should not enjoy a status that does not apply to any other of the world religions and that was never approved by the General Assembly. This special status claimed by the Holy See entails "significant power" because UN conferences operate on consensus. Predictably, the Holy See has used its privileged status to resist UN consensus on reproductive rights, including family planning and condoms for AIDS prevention (*See Change Campaign*, 2007). John L. Allen (2004), Vatican correspondent for the *National Catholic Reporter*, concurs with CFC's claim that its See Change Campaign attracted much media attention, but noted that "it did not go anywhere politically" (p. 46). For its part, CFC claims it won the support of "hundreds of nongovernmental organizations involved in development and thousands of individuals" (J. O'Brien, 2007a, p. 19), including parliamentarians in Sweden, the United Kingdom, Ireland, and Germany.

Notable Victories vis-à-vis the Vatican

To a larger extent than other Catholic reform groups, CFC claims a number of notable victories in its battle with the Vatican. Bonavoglia (2005) credits CFC with contributing to legislative successes at the state level[27] as well as helping to convince the 1995 United Nations Conference on

---

[25] Farrell also references a book by reform leader Anthony Padovano (2004) entitled *Life Choices: Toward a Catholic Theology of Reproductive Options* (CFC Press, Washington, DC). It outlines a theological justification for "reproductive justice."

[26] According to Vatican expert John L. Allen Jr. (2004), the Holy See is the "proper term for designating the authority of the papacy to govern the Church. It is a nonterritorial institution" (p. 23). The Holy See is distinct from the term *Vatican*, which refers to the 108 acres of property in Rome where the Vatican Palace and St. Peter's Basilica are located.

[27] According to Bonavoglia (2005), CFC helped pass laws mandating availability of contraceptives in emergency rooms in four states and contraceptive equity laws (requiring that if health packages include prescription drug coverage, they must include contraceptives) in twenty-one states.

Women in Beijing to pass a resolution opposed by the Vatican that affirmed women's right to "have control over matters related to sexuality" (p. 126), including reproductive rights. As testimony to its influence at the United Nations, CFC has also been granted special consultative status by the Economic and Social Council at the United Nations. Additionally, CFC's "Condoms4Life Campaign" has documented the disastrous consequences of the Vatican's policy of lobbying against access to condoms in poor countries. As a result of this campaign, CFC claims a role in convincing increasing numbers of Catholic bishops to come out publicly against the Vatican's ban on condoms, most notably Bishop Kevin Dowling of South Africa (J. O'Brien, 2007a, p. 20). CFC also points its role in legislative victories regarding reproduction rights in predominately Catholic countries, including Brazil, where the government announced a plan to make cheap birth control available in drugstores, Mexico City and Portugal, where abortion has been legalized, and the state of Connecticut, which approved legislation mandating all hospitals supply emergency contraception to rape victims (J. O'Brien, 2007b).[28]

Reviewing its strategies and achievements, one notes that CFC makes almost no claims regarding transformation of Roman Catholic Church structures or policies,[29] but instead emphasizes its role as a counterforce to the Vatican's opposition to women's sexual and reproductive rights. By publishing opinion polls that reveal a majority of Catholics favor reproductive rights for women (including abortion) and by grounding its arguments in Catholic teachings that protect individual conscience, CFC is well positioned to identify itself as a valid voice for many Catholic laypersons in policy making, thereby fracturing the Vatican's monopoly in this regard.

A Prophetic Voice?

CFC's emphasis on counteracting rather than transforming Vatican officials is evident from Kissling's in-your-face style that flaunts her disdain

---

[28] In achieving these legislative victories, CFC worked in coalition with many groups. It is beyond the scope of this study to uncover the relative significance of CFC's role in this regard.

[29] In 2011, CFC did claim "a victory for our Condoms4Life Campaign when the Pope supported the use of condoms in HIV/AIDS prevention" (CFC, *Support Catholics*). However, the meaning and implications of Pope Benedict XVI's statements regarding the use of condoms to prevent AIDS are still being debated. It is also not clear what role CFC's campaign played in influencing the pope's statements.

for church officials, choosing gestures that in no way will curry favor or mend fences. For example, a CFC ad that appeared on billboards and in print in 2001 on World AIDS Day pictured Catholic bishops in ceremonial robes with the caption, "Catholic people care. Do the bishops? Banning Condoms Kills."

Indeed, Kissling prides herself on her revolutionary credentials. When journalist Angela Bonavoglia interviewed Kissling for her book *Good Catholic Girls*, she expected Kissling to regret her notorious quote, often cited by conservatives, in which she bragged, "I spent twenty years looking for a government that I could overthrow without being thrown in jail. I finally found it in the Catholic Church" (Kissling as cited in Bonavoglia, 2005, p. 131). Far from being repentant, Kissling jubilantly declared, "I think it's a great quote" (p. 132). Kissling concludes that CFC is aligned with the prophetic tradition, which involves "provoking," in contrast to the Catholic Reform Movement as a whole where "there is very little that is prophetic" (p. 132). Kissling struck a similar chord in her interview in the *National Catholic Reporter* in which she describes reform groups (VOTF, CTA, ARCC,[30] WOC, and Dignity) as "so small in number that the movement doesn't exist" (Kissling as cited in J. Feuerherd, 2007, p. 7). Kissling points to the damages the Reform Movement inflicts on itself by currying favor from church hierarchs rather than distancing itself from Vatican control. By emphasizing insider strategies, reform groups often silence themselves so as not to offend church hierarchs. As Kissling points out, reformers can reclaim their gifts of prophecy and imagination by moving outside institutional structures. This generalization is consistent with Turner (1969), who describes *communitas* as the realm of artists and prophets, which contrasts with church structures that demand conformity to the institution's "party line."

Kissling's willingness to be prophetic reflects the fact that her organization has a different audience and objective than other Catholic reform organizations. CFC can afford to be more confrontational precisely because CFC's strategy is aimed at developing support for its goals among policy makers and politicians involved in issues of reproductive rights rather than among Vatican officials. If CFC were engaged in transforming

---

[30] The initialism ARCC refers to the Association for the Rights of Catholics in the Church, a think-tank type organization dedicated to substantive structural change in the Roman Catholic Church. It has designed a "Proposed Constitution of the Catholic Church," which is available on their website: (www.arcc-catholic-rights.org).

rather than counteracting Vatican policy, it would almost certainly be forced to adopt deferential language and insider strategies.

Conversely, now that reform groups have moved in a sect-like direction, we do see some evidence of bolder rhetoric and more provocative strategies, such as the defiant statements of Chittister and Ruether at WOW conferences (cited above) and WOC's support of independent ordinations. Precisely because CFC has a distinctive mission, it logically follows that its impressive achievements cannot be measured against those of Vatican II reform groups, many of which, until fairly recently, emphasized primarily insider strategies in the belief that the church would incrementally adopt their reform agenda.

Losing the Battle but Winning the War?

Just Treading Water?

The following example demonstrates both the dismay of many Catholic feminists over their disenfranchised status and the limitations of insider strategies. A 2004 protest by Catholic feminists in Boston over then-archbishop O'Malley's refusal to include women in the ritual foot washing on Holy Thursday, despite the fact that his predecessor, Cardinal Law, had included women in this ritual. O'Malley further aroused the ire of feminists when in a Holy Week homily he listed feminism as one of the negative factors, along with the drug culture and divorce, influencing the "religious practices of the baby boom generation" (O'Malley as cited by Bodengraven, 2004, p. 7).[31] The widely publicized outcry over O'Malley's remarks did achieve some tangible results in that O'Malley publicly clarified his comments and, after consulting with Rome, included women in the foot-washing ceremony the following year. Although in this instance an insider strategy (appeals to the archbishop) did win concessions, the nature of the victory did not break new ground, but "treaded water" by enabling feminists to hold on to a previous liturgical role.

---

[31] The public outcry over this incident was strengthened by the fact that, shortly afterward, six hundred women attended a feminist conference entitled "The Church Women Want" as part of Boston College's "Church in the Twenty-first Century" series. The conference featured noted Catholic feminist theologians, including Ada Maria Isasi-Diaz and Elizabeth Johnson.

One Door Closes and Another Opens

Despite WOC's inability to effect change, Regina Bannan, Ph.D. (2005), president of WOC's board of directors from 1997 to 2000, defends WOC by stating, "There has been a major statement about women's ordination from the Vatican about once a year for the last decade" (p. 2). So, at a minimum, WOC's efforts to rally public dissent have forced the Vatican into a defensive posture.

The tone and overall message of WOC's newsletters and press releases are generally upbeat and optimistic, but WOC leaders and Catholic feminists as a whole undoubtedly recognize that women's ordination within the Roman Catholic Church is not imminent. Not only did their long-time foe in the Vatican, Cardinal Joseph Ratzinger, become pope in 2005 but also Cardinal Ratzinger enacted the most formidable barrier to women's ordination by declaring that John Paul II's letter banning women's ordination belonged to the "deposit of faith," which thereby had been taught "infallibly" (Ratzinger as cited by Gibson, 2006, p. 214). Although Ratzinger's claim of infallibility has been hotly contested,[32] Pope Benedict's stance against women's ordination is unequivocal, and hence an insurmountable obstacle for Catholic feminists as long as he is pope.

While Catholic feminists can hope for a more flexible pope to replace Benedict in the future, that hope is undermined by the fact that Pope John Paul II appointed all but three of the 117 cardinals who elected Benedict (Gibson, 2006, p. 75).[33] Benedict already has followed in John Paul II's footsteps by appointing cardinals who share his conservative theology.[34]

While prospects for women's ordination within the institution are fading, the pent-up desire of Catholic women for ordination is evident in the growing numbers of women seeking ordination by independent groups.

---

[32] Theologian Richard P. McBrien (2005b) insists that "not everything that is said or written by the pope or other bishops, individually or collectively, is necessarily doctrinal" (p. 10). McBrien further notes that there are "different levels of teaching authority, for even teachings that are doctrinal."

[33] Catholic feminists can always hope for a surprise candidate like Pope John XXIII whose liberalism did not become evident until after he became pope (Küng, 2003), but the odds suggest that women's ordination in the Roman Catholic Church is not likely for the foreseeable future.

[34] Benedict has already appointed "50 of the 121 electors who can pick his successor from among their own ranks, raising the possibility that the next pontiff will be a conservative in Benedict's own image" (Pullella, 2010). Benedict's selections of cardinals also included Archbishop Donald Wuerl of Washington, DC, who is regarded as a moderate.

Thus, as Benedict XVI closes the door to *insider* ordinations, he inadvertently pushes women in the direction of *outsider* options.

Another irony often pointed out by feminist theologians is the fact that while men are entering religious orders in dramatically declining numbers, women are willing to undergo extensive training, often at their own expense,[35] for the privilege of serving in the ministerial roles. Indeed, even within Catholic parishes, as of 2005, women comprise 80 percent of lay ecclesial ministers, and in the United States there are 31,000 lay ministers, whose numbers surpass the 29,000 diocesan priests (Allen, 2007, p. 13). Presently, 18,000 Catholics are preparing to become lay ecclesial ministers, who comprise "roughly six times the number of seminarians in training to become Catholic priests" (p. 12). If these trends continue, the majority of Catholics in ministerial roles may, in the near future, be women. Thus, while Benedict may be winning the battle in terms of preserving an all-male clergy, he may be losing the war to women who are increasingly serving in ministerial roles. The visibility and preponderance of women in these roles will probably strengthen support for women's ordination among Catholic laity. However, a countermovement may stifle this trend. A 2009 report from the Center for Applied Research in the Apostolate (CARA) revealed a 10 percent decline in active lay ministry programs (whose participants are two-thirds female), as well as a decline in the number of "parish life coordinators, often women" (Sotelo, 2009, p. 18).[36]

The Vatican Loses Ground

Thus, CFC plays the role of outside agitator in tackling the Vatican head-on and, occasionally, beating it at its own game as protector of moral decision making regarding reproductive rights. WOC takes a more indirect, underground, "guerilla warfare" approach to sap the Vatican's strength by

---

[35] Since women are not allowed to enter the Roman Catholic priesthood, they obviously are not granted the no-cost education and training available to male seminarians. However, some Catholic women do receive scholarships to Catholic colleges and grants from ministry education programs in Catholic parishes. Religious sisters often receive funding for education from their orders.

[36] Sotelo (2009) suggests "that while budgetary reasons are often cited for such reductions, many believe that bishops take such actions due to ideological differences with the lay leadership, preferring programs or parishes coordinated by male priests or sometimes women religious, who "support older models of ministry with less emphasis on lay participation" (p. 18).

exposing discriminatory behavior and supporting new forms of ministry expressly forbidden by the papacy. In both instances, the Vatican is forced into a defensive posture as its power to control reproductive policies wanes, even in staunchly Catholic countries, and its ability to command the loyalty and obedience of growing numbers of women within its ranks dissipates. The Vatican resembles all patriarchal structures, which initially seem deeply entrenched and impermeable but eventually buckle in response to clever and timely feminist challenges designed to expose patriarchy's flaws and systemic injustices.

CHAPTER FIVE

TOWARD A NEW CITY OF GOD

Jan Leary, a cradle Catholic, fits the profile of Vatican II reformers. As a lifelong Catholic, she had an intense identification with her faith, delighting in its elaborate rituals, its sophisticated theology, and the tight-knit communities she encountered in the parishes she joined, first as a child and later as a wife and a mother of three daughters.

She attended Catholic primary schools and the Catholic College of St. Rose when Vatican II was being celebrated as a new and invigorating crossroads for Catholicism. She returned to school in her forties and earned masters degrees in psychology and divinity, and later a Ph.D. in psychology. Jan discovered the Reform Movement in her late forties following a divorce. Although Jan worked part time as a therapist and as a professor at local colleges, she became a virtual full-time volunteer reformer, playing leadership roles in local faith-sharing groups and in local chapters of Call to Action (CTA) and Women-Church Convergence (W-CC). On the national level, she served on the board of Catholic Organizations for Renewal (COR) and was a cofounder of Voice of the Faithful (VOTF). In 1995 Jan cofounded a new reform organization called "Save Our Sacrament: Reform of Annulment and Respondent Support" (www.saveoursacrament.org) with Sheila Rauch Kennedy, the ex-wife of former Massachusetts congressman Joe Kennedy. Jan and Sheila opposed the decision of a Boston Roman Catholic tribunal granting their husbands annulments of their first marriages in order to remarry in the Catholic Church. Their issue was not the right of their husbands to remarry but rather the declaration that their long-term marriages would be declared not sacramental. Jan and Sheila appealed these initial annulment decisions to the Vatican Roman Rota tribunals. Later Jan set up a website that provided free counseling to other Catholics involved in annulment cases. In 2007 Jan and Sheila learned that the Vatican Rota had approved their long-standing appeals and reversed the annulment decisions of the Boston tribunal. Actually, these favorable decisions had been made years earlier, but Vatican courts never informed either one directly. Jan and Sheila ultimately learned of these decisions through indirect sources.

Jan believes her experience with the annulment process was the tipping point that led her to reassess her role in the Reform Movement. She gradually recognized that the meaning she derived from the movement and Catholicism itself had waned as well. Following the 9/11 tragedy, Jan transferred her energy into political reform in support of the Palestinian struggle for justice. Now in her early seventies, Jan worships at a newly formed Spirit of Life community led by a married couple considered "illicit" by church hierarchs. Although Jan enjoys her new community's warmth and its inclusive ministry, she finds the service a bit "too traditional" as she longs for a new, more cosmologically centered and ecumenical form of liturgy (personal communication, April 20, 2007).

Nearly all of the reform groups reviewed in part 1 have become more sectarian, to a greater or lesser extent, by abandoning efforts to change an unresponsive, closed system and by embracing new spiritual communities. Although VOTF remains focused on insider reform, even it has been forced to refashion its mission after acknowledging declining contributions and a loss of momentum. Reformers recognize that the exodus and the David and Goliath myths have relevance for their movement, since both myths suggest that seemingly invulnerable opponents have vulnerable points. Hence, to succeed, challengers must learn to identify and penetrate those sensibilities. The achievements of Catholics for Choice (CFC) demonstrate that the Vatican is not omnipotent, and that reformers could potentially win public relations battles targeted at Vatican teachings that do not enjoy widespread public support.

After Benedict, What?

Reform groups chose to embark on an exodus journey prior to the election of Cardinal Ratzinger as pope in 2005, though their choice was no doubt reinforced by this development. Upon the death of John Paul II, each of these groups issued a press release praising positive aspects of John Paul II's papacy, but noting his staunch conservatism and controlling leadership style that stymied reform on their priority issues. For example, Women's Ordination Conference (WOC) executive director Joy Barnes (2005a) commented:

> In feminist circles, Pope John Paul II will long be remembered as the pope who was full of contradictions. He talked about the value of the feminine, yet he did not allow women to live out the fullness of our gifts in our own church. (p. 1)

Reform groups also responded to the news of Ratzinger's election with "dismay" (DignityUSA), "alarm" (W-CC), and "deep concern" (CFC). Corps of Reserve Priests United for Service (CORPUS) President Russ Ditzel (2005) commented, "The more things change, the more they stay the same" (p. 19), noting that the election of Ratzinger crushed hopes that a new pope would signal a "refreshing change in the Vatican's public persona" (p. 19). CORPUS Ambassador Anthony Padovano (2005c) struck a defiant pose, proclaiming, "I seek to affirm even a reactionary Papacy cannot withstand totally the powerful forces for reform which, I believe, come from a Council and the Spirit" (p. 40). Perhaps most telling was the response of Sister Maureen Fiedler of the Interfaith Voices radio show, who was in St. Peter's Square when the choice of the new pope was announced. Fiedler (2005), a long-term ally of Catholic feminists, lamented, "My heart sank when I heard the announcement. The Church needed a healer, and Ratzinger's record is that of a lightning rod—a creator of divisions not a healer of them" (p. 3). Fiedler concludes her remarks in a despairing tone: "My only consolation is that it [the church] survived the Medicis and other such popes ... We can survive this one ... I hope" (p. 3).

In some respects, Pope Benedict's papacy has not been as hostile to the agendas of Vatican II reform groups as they anticipated. Notre Dame theologian Richard McBrien has noted many surprisingly positive gestures of the new pope, including his decision to meet with the censored Catholic theologian Hans Küng (a favorite of Vatican II reformers), his decision to allow open discussion at the 2005 Synod on the Eucharist (where the celibacy requirement for the priesthood was debated), and his ruling that Father Marcial Maciel Degollado, founder of Legionaries of Christ, could no longer exercise a public ministry following credible charges of sexual abuse (McBrien as cited in Devine, 2007, p. 8). According to McBrien, all of these decisions contrasted sharply with policies of Pope John Paul II and indicated an unexpected degree of flexibility and openness on the part of Benedict.[1]

Even some Catholic feminists found cause for hope in Pope Benedict's highly publicized comments on March 2, 2006, when he stated that "it is right to ask oneself if more space, more positions of responsibility, can be given to women, even in the ministerial service" (Pope Benedict as cited in Zagano, 2006, p. 6). As expected, Benedict affirmed that ordination was not available to women, but mentioned the contributions of many Catholic women, including Hildegard of Bingen, Catherine of Siena, Teresa of Avila, and Mother Teresa. Feminist scholar Phyllis Zagano (2006) characterizes the pope's remarks as a "bombshell" (p. 6) because the pope suggested some roles in policy making and ministry within the church

---

[1] Pope John Paul II repeatedly rebuffed Hans Küng's request for a meeting, imposed strict limits on topics for discussion at synods, and protected Marcial Maciel Degollado from censure.

might be open to women, despite the fact that these domains have traditionally been restricted to clergy. Zagano (2007) is hopeful that if women are allowed to fill these roles, this move would lay the groundwork for the restoration of female deacons, which in turn might strengthen the case for women's ordination to the priesthood at some future point.

Benedict's positive gestures evoked only brief mention in the periodicals published by most reform groups, where the most extensive coverage has been devoted to the growing number of independent ministries they are sponsoring. Perhaps their hopes have been dashed too many times in the past, particularly since reformers have actually lost ground on their reform agendas over the past several decades.[2] Many reformers believe that any paltry reform that might be forthcoming would fall far short of their goals. One reformer characterized such concessions in biblical terms, describing them as "mere crumbs from the master's table" (G. S., personal communication, November 18, 2007).

The unenthusiastic response of reformers to these moves by Benedict reflects that some of them have been radicalized by enculturation in the Reform Movement, where they have been educated in new and challenging theologies and social critiques. As Vatican II reformers moved to the left, the church was moving in the opposite direction and shutting down opportunities, not only for substantive reform but even for dialogue.[3] Under these circumstances, the choice to form independent churches became the favored option of many Vatican II reformers.

Dancing in the Street

The strategic dilemmas facing reformers and the exile status of reform groups was very much on display during the April 15–20, 2008, visit of

---

[2] For example, when reform groups began forming in the 1970s, reforms such as women's ordination, an end to mandatory celibacy, and homosexual rights were still open for discussion with church hierarchs, and the USCCB still included liberal and moderate bishops who were willing to engage in dialogue with reformers. As detailed in chapters 3 and 4, for the past several decades the Vatican has issued a series of documents restricting rights for GLBT persons and prohibiting women's ordination. Although the Vatican has not prohibited discussion of mandatory celibacy, it has repeatedly defended mandatory celibacy in spite of the growing priest shortage, and its waiver of the celibacy requirement for Anglican and other previously ordained priests who defect to Catholicism.

[3] Letters and petitions sent to the Vatican and to American bishops by liberal reformers are often not acknowledged in any way under the papacies of both John Paul II and Benedict XVI.

Benedict XVI to the United States. Journalist Eileen Markey (2008) noted that, unlike angry protests during previous papal visits, this time reform groups (including WOC, DignityUSA, CFC, and VOTF)[4] designed celebratory protests to "show the pope how the church in the United States differs from the Vatican view." Reformers were targeting public opinion—both Catholics and non-Catholics—as much as the pope, given that protestors wanted to highlight the justice of their demands for reform and the fact that "change is already happening," referring to independent ordinations. Thus, as exile groups, reformers were no longer waiting for the approval of the pope but rather rejoicing in their emergence as free subjects claiming their voice as the people of God in a renewed church. The fact that reformers are reaching out primarily to the wider public rather than the Vatican reflects their recognition that insider reforms may have failed (the pope rejected their pleas). Nevertheless, reformers can tap the power of public pressure to win legal and public relations battles that weaken the pope's power. They can also create worship communities not under his control.

Pope Benedict received high marks for his 2008 visit to the United States. Vatican *National Catholic Reporter* correspondent John Allen (2008a) described the pope's demeanor during the visit as "gracious and surprisingly humble" (p. 8) and credited him with winning "points for graciousness and breadth of vision." Survivors Network of those Abused by Priests (SNAP)[5] and VOTF applauded Benedict's decision to meet with victims and to publicly acknowledge the abuse crisis, but also emphasized that these actions would have to be followed by concrete reforms to ensure genuine changes in policy. For its part, VOTF sent a petition signed by eight thousand people to Pope Benedict asking him to "hold bishops accountable for their actions in the abuse crisis" (*VOTF petitions Pope,* 2008b) by, among other things, requiring "accountability and transparency in all governance matters."

Although some reformers may view Benedict XVI's visit as a first step toward ongoing reform, others view it as an exhibition of the stronghold of clericalism among American Catholics (and even the American media), many of whom appeared dazzled by Benedict's kindly manner, regal attire, and majestic gestures. Televised images of the visit depicted pious, adoring crowds, who seemingly reverted to the docile behavior of

---

[4] Other organizations cited in this article include Pax Christi USA, a Catholic peace group, and the Rainbow Sash Movement, an advocacy organization for GLBT persons.

[5] Founded in 1989, SNAP is a victims' self-help group that engages in a range of advocacy and educational activities.

pre-Vatican II Catholics, as if the deceit and dysfunction exposed by the abuse crisis had never occurred. One might reasonably surmise that reformers who have chosen exile once shared this deeply engrained deference to the pontiff, but now claim to see through his facade of omnipotence that had terrified them. Now that they no longer fear him, reformers conduct their protests with elated spirits, proclaiming their release from a form of deference that had once enchanted them.

No Turning Back

Reflecting on the future direction of the Reform Movement, feminist theologian Rosemary Radford Ruether articulated a rather sobering but candid vision in her speech at the 2006 Boston College conference entitled *The Church Women Want*. Ruether (2006), one of the earliest and most influential Catholic feminist theologians, states,

> My commitment to Roman Catholicism is not based on the idea that it is the true church—or even that it is the best church—but simply it is a very important expression of historical Christianity in the West, and its reform and renewal are vital to Christian and indeed human betterment.

Ruether acknowledges that the Roman Catholic Church may not be "totally reformable according to my vision," but that the "reform vision of Catholicism needs to be defended as a vital option, even though other views will probably prevail and even seek to drive out the reform option."

Similar themes are expressed by Anthony Padovano (2007a) of CORPUS, who describes the Reform Movement as facing the same struggle as Virgil's Aeneas, who escaped from the flames of Troy carrying his father (a symbol of the past), his young son (a symbol of the future), and the household gods (a symbol of the values of life). Drawing on this myth, notably a type of exile myth, Padovano explains that reformers will find hope by maintaining strong links to the Catholic identity of their past, creating a new model of church appropriate to the modern age, and following the dictates of the Spirit who sustains them amidst conflict and rejection. Padovano insists that to abandon the church altogether would be to "lose our identity, the DNA of our memories and our heritage" (p. 20). However, reformers cannot cling to a past "that has been razed by the flames of the future" (p. 20).

These statements by Ruether and Padovano contradict those who characterize Catholic reformers as naïve or unrealistic. In fact, many reformers do not mince words in their stinging rebuke of current church leaders, sometimes using terms to describe church hierarchs that would be considered off-limits by many non-Catholics. For example, at the 2006 CTA convention, two of the Reform Movement's most revered spokespersons, Anthony Padovano and Joan Chittister,[6] suggested that the Roman Catholic Church risked becoming a "cult" by cutting off debate and the possibility of reform. Both described the present impasse faced by the movement as "perilous."[7]

As reformers have become increasingly critical of the Roman Catholic hierarchy, it has become easier for reformers to consider outsider strategies, particularly forming coalitions with parallel institutions such as Roman Catholic Womenpriests (RCWP) and the Ecumenical Catholic Communion (ECC). These outsider strategies flow logically from the slogan "We are the Church," which is commonly cited at meetings of reform groups. In other words, if leaders are out of touch, unresponsive, and tyrannical, reformers have little choice but to move forward without the approval of hierarchs. Padovano (2007a) explains that "there are no credible authorities left" (p. 20), so that reformers must "reach for a spirituality and ecclesiology, a vision of authority and Christology we did not know before" (p. 20). Hence, reformers must undertake a new spiritual journey that will leave behind their roles as "pay, pray, and obey" Catholics and enable them to give shape to their vision of a renewed Catholicism.

Another slogan expressed by reformers is "We didn't leave the Church, the Church left us," meaning that the Roman Catholic hierarchy has abandoned the promise of Vatican II, in contrast to reformers who are struggling to sustain and build upon what they regard as the best of their Catholic heritage. Padovano (2007a) explains, "The deepest Tradition in

---

[6] In his speech entitled "Boundaries," Anthony Padovano (2007a) concluded, "The end result of rejecting the culture of one's own era is not a Church but a cult" (p. 19). Joan Chittister's (2006) remarks were more subtle, making thinly veiled references to the Vatican by stating, "As long as we go on making the poor poorer and turning this democracy into an oligarchy of the rich, by the rich and for the rich, we cannot possibly be a renewed church. We can only be a cult committed to our private agenda, our own personal liturgies, and our new/old set of pious but abstruse devotions remote from the spirit of Vatican II" (p. 3).

[7] Padovano and Joan Chittister described Vatican leaders as a cult due to their isolationist and authoritarian tendencies and their disconnect from contemporary culture. However, their characterizations do not match the sociological definitions of a cult, which specify "a group without much internal discipline with a loose-knit structure" or a group that represents "the beginning phase of a new religion" (K. Roberts, 2004, p. 188). In sociological terms, Padovano and Chittister are describing a sect, which has exclusive membership policies and fundamentalist theology.

Church law is that the law is less than the Spirit and the care of the people is the supreme law of the Church" (p. 18). Thus, to the extent that reformers are responding to an authentic call of the Spirit and are acting on behalf of the people, they are justified in violating existing rules. By leaving behind an outmoded form of Catholicism, reformers must chart their own path, breathing new life into a tradition that they charge is becoming irrelevant to the modern world. In keeping with the prophetic nature of sects, reformers increasingly challenge a papacy whose credibility and viability are dissipating due to what reformers describe as its dysfunctional, outmoded governance system.

One could also argue that outsider strategies have enabled reform groups to move beyond stalemate and create communities that give once-excluded groups, especially women and the GLBT community, hands-on experience in ministry and inspirational, supportive environments, where they can retain their allegiance to Catholicism while refusing to support or endure liturgies and teachings that are sexist, homophobic, and exclusionary. These newly emerging communities represent concrete achievements of the Reform Movement, which has little to report in terms of concessions from church leaders.

DignityUSA provides a welcoming network of underground communities where GLBT Catholics can obtain blessings for gay unions, promote GLBT rights in the larger community, and challenge restrictive Vatican policies regarding GLBTs. By forming the National Catholic Ministerial Alliance, CORPUS members can draw on their pastoral experience and theological training to help newly ordained "outsider" priests compensate for their exclusion from formal training in Roman Catholic seminaries.

Although insider ordination remains an elusive goal for WOC for the foreseeable future, events such as the World Day of Prayer for Women's Ordination help rally new supporters to WOC's cause. Although WOC's support of "illicit" ordinations is troubling to their more conservative members, these ordinations provide models of women priests who claim the Catholic tradition and who create worship communities that, to some degree, reflect feminist principles. WOC's outsider status was evident on October 14, 2008, when eleven WOC representatives were forced to surrender their passports by Vatican and Italian police when they attempted to deliver a petition calling for restoring women's ordination to the diaconate (Women's Ordination Conference, 2008). WOC's Vatican action was timed to coincide with the 2008 International Synod on the Word, which included twenty-five women delegates, nineteen of whom were auditors and six were biblical experts (FutureChurch, 2008). The fact that this synod included more female representatives than any previous synod did not deter WOC from reasserting its demand for women's ordination.

OUTSIDER PRESSURE STRENGTHENS INSIDER REFORM GROUPS

FutureChurch is an insider reform group that defines itself as a "national coalition of 5,000 parish-based Catholics[8] who seek the full participation of all baptized Catholics in the life of the Church" (*About Us*, 2004).[9] During the period when many reform groups largely abandoned insider reform, FutureChurch effectively used insider tactics to achieve two notable accomplishments:

   a. Its Women in the Word campaign solicited eighteen thousand postcards and e-mails to U.S. and Canadian bishops asking for inclusion of women biblical scholars at the 2008 International Synod on the Word. FutureChurch claims this campaign resulted in historic representation of women at the synod and the approval of two propositions promoting attention to women's concerns (FutureChurch, 2008).[10]
   b. In 2010 FutureChurch announced that its campaign to draw attention to women in the early church had resulted in 303 celebrations on the Feast day of St. Mary of Magdala,[11] including thirty outside the United States[12] (FutureChurch, 2010a).

FutureChurch has attracted considerably more members and organized more celebrations than the feminist reform groups discussed in chapter 4.

---

[8] Executive Director Sister Christine Schenk reports that, in addition to its five thousand members, FutureChurch includes seven thousand "activists" who purchase their advocacy and educational material and participate in various programs (personal communication, August 3, 2010).

[9] Although FutureChurch publicly supports opening ordination to "all baptized Catholics" and other liberal reforms, it avoids confrontational tactics by "work[ing] with an attitude of respect for church teachings" and avoiding support for "gay marriage" or "pro-choice" positions (*FutureChurch-separating*, 2010).

[10] FutureChurch also asked for more opportunities for women to preach and more attention to the role of women in biblical and church history.

[11] Sister Christine Schenk explains that Mary of Magdala celebrations were important because, in her words, "retrieving historical memory was touching something very deep in the psyche of women because, much as we love Jesus and revere our Catholic tradition, most of us never saw ourselves in the Jesus story because it had always been presented as Jesus and twelve men" (Schenk as cited in T. Roberts, 2009c).

[12] Celebrations were announced in Australia, Columbia, Finland, Kenya, the Netherlands, Nicaragua, South Africa and Zambia.

FutureChurch's achievements in this regard reflect the skills of its leaders in community organization, as well as the fact that it is probably less threatening to mainstream Catholics than more radical groups. The very public and outspoken advocacy and education efforts of groups like WOC, W-CC, WATER, and CFC have strengthened support among lay Catholics for a more equal role for women within the institutional church and have generated more receptivity to women's concerns on the part of Catholic bishops. Hence, outsider groups may give insider groups like FutureChurch more leverage in promoting its reform agenda, which in turn is more palatable to church hierarchs because it does not involve doctrinal issues. It may also strengthen claims of hierarchs that their objections to women's ordination are not based on discrimination. For outsider reform groups, FutureChurch's achievements represent primarily symbolic reforms, given that bishops made no commitment to representation of women at future synods, and their resolutions promised merely a reexamination of the role of women in the lectionary.

A Last Hurrah for the Reform Movement?

Despite the formidable odds they face, reformers have organized a last hurrah of sorts by forming a coalition (including CORPUS, FutureChurch, and VOTF) entitled the American Catholic Council. This council is designed to promote more democratic and accountable governance structures, which are identified as a prerequisite for moving forward on respective reform agendas of reform groups. *The Declaration of the American Catholic Council* (2008) decries a "serious deterioration in the life of the Catholic Church" in the United States, citing closed parishes, lack of access to sacraments, sex abuse victims, declining membership and finances, and "paternalistic, monarchical leadership that is often unresponsive, repressive and ineffective." Their mission embraces the goal of reforming church governance structures to reflect positive features of "the American experience: a democratic spirit, concern for human rights, freedom of speech and assembly, and a tradition of participation and representation." This council represents a last-ditch effort for many reformers, since it will explore strategies for enabling the American Catholic Church to remain connected to the Vatican but attain some measure of autonomy.[13]

---

[13] The American Catholic Council is discussed more extensively in the conclusion.

Toward a New City of God

Those reformers with a thorough knowledge of biblical history recognize that the exile is often lonely, perilous, and seemingly foolhardy to outsider observers. Reformers know they will not see church renewal in their lifetimes, but they also believe the tradition itself is imperiled if conservative factions retain control. Some reformers have been subject to penalties in the form of excommunication, denial of access to sacraments, and loss of jobs and speaking engagements. Reformers also express concern about the future viability of their struggle given the graying of the Reform Movement and the declining revenues and memberships of reform groups. Nonetheless, I did not encounter any reformers who wanted to return to a pre-Vatican II church. Rather, expressions heard frequently at both formal and informal gatherings of reformers include: "We know too much," "We've come too far," and "It [the traditional church] no longer feeds my spiritual hunger." As noted previously, members of Dignity USA, CORPUS, and VOTF rallied to shore up their organizations when they appeared to be on the brink of collapse.

Some reformers do encounter despair and burnout, like CORPUS member George Clements (2007), who concludes that thirty years of effort have produced "largely ineffectual reforms" (p. 35). He describes CORPUS members as "nice people" who are no match for "hard-nosed bishops" (p. 35). Although many have abandoned the Reform Movement, reformers who remain insist they are responding to a call from the Spirit that their Catholic training taught them to heed wholeheartedly.

Moreover, despite its drawbacks, the Reform Movement offers a type of inclusive community where activists connect with others who share their memories of both the pre- and post-Vatican II church and their dreams for a renewed Catholicism that they believe could guide American society in promoting the common good, restoring community, and creating more just and equitable societal structures.

Many Vatican II reformers argue that the dangers of exile pale in comparison to what they describe as "spiritual suicide,"[14] which one experiences upon silencing the voice of one's conscience. The reformers' view of the institutional church is graphically expressed by Eugene Kennedy (2005), a psychologist and former priest, who uses the image of a beached

---

[14] The term *spiritual suicide* was used repeatedly by a variety of reformers at conventions and meetings attended as part of this research study.

whale to characterize the Roman Catholic Church suffocating from outmoded structures and doctrine. Yet he notes the church "refuses to create a healthy type of authority based on respectful human relationships" (pp. 11–13). Perhaps reformers lack the strength to push the whale back into the ocean, but they are not willing to participate in a death watch. Thus, if reform efforts are unsuccessful, the only remaining option is to keep the tradition alive at or beyond the outermost boundaries of Roman Catholicism.

While outside observers often wonder what sustains reformers, those who are deeply invested in the Reform Movement regard their journey as essential to their own spiritual well-being and perhaps the only hope for salvaging the best of their Roman Catholic heritage. Padovano (2007a) predicts this journey leads to an "Easter encounter with a Christ we do not recognize as easily as we once did but whom we shall follow wherever he leads us" (p. 20). Hence many reformers are convinced that this treacherous and challenging journey is their only hope for realizing the biblical vision of "a new city of God, on a distant mountain, in an alien land" (p. 20).

PART TWO

TESTING THE WATERS AND PUSHING THE BOUNDARIES

CHAPTER SIX

PROPHETS WITHOUT HONOR
VATICAN II PASTORS ARE DISAPPEARING

Father Walter Cuenin is a classic example of a Vatican II priest whose firing by Archbishop Sean O'Malley in September 2005 attracted a firestorm of media attention and protests. Cuenin's reputation as a Vatican II pastor was on display during his tenure as pastor of Our Lady Help of Christians Parish in Newton, Massachusetts, that served as a mecca for many progressive Catholics. In his book *Excellent Catholic Parishes,* Paul Wilkes (2001) identifies Cuenin's parish as one of the seven most outstanding Catholic parishes in the United States. During his seven-year term at Our Lady's, Cuenin revitalized a dying parish by restoring decrepit buildings, recruiting competent staff, and creating vibrant liturgies and innovative programs that reach out to those "some might consider outside the normal Catholic axis," including "gays and lesbians, the divorced, those who had left the Church for a variety of reasons" (Colbert, 2006a, p. 9).

When the clergy abuse crisis erupted in Boston in 2002, Father Cuenin became one of Cardinal Law's most outspoken critics and played a leadership role in organizing fifty-eight Boston-area priests to sign a letter (published in the *Boston Globe* on December 8, 2002) urging Cardinal Law to resign following revelations of Law's role in cover-ups of abusive priests. Cuenin also provided space in parish buildings for Voice of the Faithful (VOTF). The Boston archdiocese justified its decision to fire Cuenin by pointing to his acceptance of a stipend and loan of a car in violation of diocesan policies. In response, Cuenin asserted that these expenditures were common practice in the archdiocese and were approved by his finance council and reported for years in the parish's financial statements (Colbert, 2006b). Cuenin's supporters insisted the finance charges were a "smear campaign" (Colbert, p. 9) designed to discredit one of the archdiocese's most outstanding critics.

Cuenin made no secret of his anguish over his dismissal, confessing at his farewell service, attended by more than one thousand people, that "It is with a very heavy heart that I speak to you for the last time from this pulpit" (Cuenin as cited by Viser, 2005, p. B1). If Cuenin's firing was designed to silence him, it seems to have had the opposite effect, as the publicity surrounding his firing made him, as he put it, "more of a public figure who receives thanks and praise" (Cuenin as cited in Black, 2006) for speaking out. On July 10, 2006, Cuenin's defiant spirit was on display when he preached at the main worship service associated with Boston's Gay Pride Week, citing Catholic social teachings that defended the "fundamental human rights of homosexual persons" (Cuenin as cited in Paulson, 2006b, p. B1). Cuenin now serves as campus chaplain at Brandeis University.

This chapter documents a range of censures of Vatican II parishes and dioceses by conservative bishops who, in some instances, fired or defrocked defiant Vatican II priests and replaced them with conservative priests. These repressive measures are relevant to the Reform Movement for two reasons. First, the decline in the availability of Vatican II parishes helps explain why many liberal reformers are exploring or forming the marginal and underground communities described in upcoming chapters. Second, reform group leaders helped organize a range of protests aimed at challenging repressive measures imposed by conservative bishops. Although these protests did not prevent censure or dismissal of Vatican II priests, they did attract media coverage that in turn drew supporters to their cause.

A Generation Gap in the Priesthood

The declining availability of Vatican II parishes throughout the United States results primarily from the attrition of Vatican II priests, who are in many cases replaced by younger priests who never experienced the tumultuous Vatican II era, and who tend to be more conservative and authoritarian than older cohorts (Hoge & Wenger, 2003). As documented below, a secondary factor influencing the composition of today's priesthood is the less prevalent but significant repression of Vatican II priests, especially those who are outspoken risk takers engaged in resisting and sidestepping what they consider the more objectionable dictates of presiding bishops and the Vatican. Even those Vatican II pastors who remain discreet and circumspect in their relations with church authorities are not immune to the bishops' repressive policies, which impose an atmosphere of intimidation and defeatism among those Vatican II pastors left standing.

Because of this generational shift among priests, parishes once known as havens for liberals may now be presided over by conservative clerics who emphasize rules-minded theology and old-fashioned liturgy. During a speaking tour in Boston, Miami, and Baltimore, I heard from seven persons who described problems in their parishes resulting from the replacement of Vatican II priests with more conservative pastors.[1]

---

[1] This speaking tour, which occurred during 2005–2006, was sponsored by Celibacy Is the Issue (CITI) on the theme of "Catholics, Yesterday, Today, and Tomorrow."

These parishioners requested anonymity, since they remained uncertain whether they would remain in their parish and wanted to avoid offending their new pastor.

The growing generation gap in the American priesthood had been extensively documented (Hoge & Wenger, 2003). Journalist Peter Steinfels (2003) concludes that contrasts between the older generation (referred to as Vatican II priests) and newer priests (referred to as John Paul II priests) are perhaps exaggerated, but nonetheless observes that "there is no doubt a shift—think of it as a shift in the center of gravity—has taken place" (p. 320). According to Steinfels, not only are newer priests more conservative, they also enter the seminary later in life and, "by many reports, are less academically qualified" (p. 321).[2]

The declining number of Vatican II priests parallels a decline in the number of Vatican II bishops, a trend acknowledged by many sources. Steinfels (2003) describes the American church hierarchy, "especially Cardinals and Archbishops" (p. 39), as strongholds of conservatives in the contemporary church. Catholic theologian Richard McBrien of Notre Dame University explains,

> As the Catholic hierarchy became more conservative under Pope John Paul II, bishops who were open to a diversity of viewpoints in the church either died or retired, and were replaced by bishops who were more, let's say, attuned to the desires of the Holy See. (McBrien as cited in Paulson, 2008e, p.A10)[3]

Thus, the repression of Vatican II priests and parishes cited below almost certainly reflects the desire of conservative hierarchs to weed out liberal priests and stifle dissent.

---

[2] The gap between Vatican II priests (born between 1943 and 1960) and John Paul II priests (born after 1961) was documented in a *Los Angeles Times* poll that surveyed 1,854 priests from 80 U.S. dioceses, which represents "the most extensive independent nationwide poll of Catholic priests since a similar *Times* poll conducted in 1993" (Watanabe, 2002, A1). This study found that nearly 40 percent of younger priests identified themselves as conservative, compared to 28 percent of priests overall, and that younger priests "expressed more allegiance to the clerical hierarchy [and] less dissent against traditional church teachings." In contrast, Vatican II priests were more likely than younger priests to support ordination of married men and women deacons, and to favor more lay participation.

[3] Further evidence of the conservative drift of the Vatican is suggested by the fact that in 2006, Catholic bishops voted 173 to 29 on a dramatically revised translation of the Order of the Mass. Reporter John Allen (2005) declared this vote an overwhelming victory for conservative clerics. The new translations bring liturgical language closer to the original Latin and impose a uniform code for every parish (p. 5).

Repressive Measures by Conservative Bishops

Although evidence regarding the conservative drift of the priesthood is widely available, documenting punitive measures toward liberal clerics is challenging because many pastors may not reveal their censure to parishioners or fellow priests, and others may leave the priesthood or retire to avoid censure. Evidence presented herein regarding these measures to remove or silence liberal priests is primarily anecdotal—most of the cases I cite came to my attention when they received considerable media attention or evoked protests from reform groups.

Reasons for Repression

All of the examples of punitive measures cited below revolve around three central "culture wars" issues that Pope John Paul II and Pope Benedict XVI oppose. These issues include (1) expanding roles for women, resigned priests, and GLBT persons; (2) serving Communion to non-Catholics and Catholics considered ineligible for Communion;[4] and (3) engaging in rebellious behavior considered inappropriate by church hierarchs.

The Hunthausen Case Foreshadows Growing Power of Conservative Bishops

The case of Seattle Archbishop Raymond Hunthausen who was censured in 1985 foreshadows the more recent censure of liberal priests cited below. These incidents reflect efforts by conservative hierarchs to penalize clerics who implement liberal reforms.[5] The Vatican charged Hunthausen with, among other things, allowing divorced Catholics and non-Catholics to take Communion, allowing a local DignityUSA chapter to use the cathedral, and "underemphasizing the authority of hierarchical teachings" (Briggs, 1992, p. 17). According to Schilling (2003), Hunthausen was able to retain his office following this Vatican investigation due in large measure

---

[4] Excommunicated Catholics and those who divorce and remarry without obtaining an annulment are ineligible for Communion. Some American bishops have announced bans on Communion for other reasons, including, for example, politicians who openly support abortion.

[5] Hunthausen had a reputation for peace and justice advocacy, due to his strong advocacy for the poor and his decision in 1982 to protest the stockpiling of nuclear weapons by withholding half of his income tax. The IRS recouped the unpaid taxes by garnishing his wages.

to his success in rallying support from fellow bishops at a time when liberal bishops still held a slight edge of power in the United States Conference of Catholic Bishops (USCCB). Schilling described Hunthausen as "a favorite among Church progressives" (p. 18) for whom his status as a victim of "a Vatican clampdown" (p. 18) only enhanced his stature. Further, according to a bishop interviewed by journalist Kenneth Briggs, the infractions cited in Hunthausen's case were "common" in many dioceses, so that many bishops were supportive of him because they allowed similar practices in their own dioceses.[6] However, other bishops responded to accusations by "smooth-talking the Vatican" (Bishop Sawicki as quoted by Briggs, p. 132), in contrast to Hunthausen who refused to show the attitude of expected deference and obedience.

Hunthausen did not escape censure altogether since Bishop Thomas J. Murphy was appointed coadjutor bishop to oversee Hunthausen's curtailment of objectionable practices. Hunthausen reportedly became more risk avoidant after this ordeal, and colleagues described him as "less bold, more subdued—though unbowed" (Briggs, 1992, p. 571).

Censure of Vatican II Priests in Massachusetts

Supporters of the Reverend Cuenin (cited in the vignette above) believe that his dismissal took place in the context of a broader movement against liberal Vatican II priests within the Boston archdiocese, and perhaps more broadly in the United States. Consequently, the firing of Cuenin unleashed a barrage of criticism, even ridicule, from Boston journalists, several of whom repeated rumors pervasive among reform groups that Cardinal Law was still exercising indirect control over the Boston archdiocese from his basilica in Rome (Vennochi, 2005; McGrory, 2005). For their part, parishioners at Our Lady's sponsored a whole series of demonstrations demanding Cuenin's reinstatement, although Cuenin urged them to accept his dismissal because the archdiocese had the authority to reassign him. VOTF President James Post (2005) put aside his usual restraint in denouncing Cuenin's firing, suggesting, "The months ahead will determine whether our Church will make it possible or impossible for our children and grandchildren to practice the Catholic faith."

---

[6] Briggs uses the pseudonym "Bishop Sawicki" to refer to the cleric who requested anonymity.

After Cuenin's dismissal in September 2005, the Council of Vigiling Parishes (CoP) claimed that many priests who had signed the petition requesting Cardinal Law's resignation had suffered negative career consequences. They noted that half of the forty diocesan priests who signed the Law petition have resigned or been reassigned to new parishes, and that several chose to retire or resign in an effort to spare their parishes from being shuttered.[7] (Szaniszlo, 2005, p. 22).[8] Rev. Tom Mahoney, of the Priests' Forum, lamented,

> Certainly, there is some truth to the idea that some people have been targeted. I would expect to find in the church a community of love, but instead it feels more like living in a war zone, where there's intrigue and spies. It's an atmosphere where many priests are reluctant to speak publicly for fear of punishment. (Mahoney as cited by Szaniszlo, p. 22)

In contrast, an article on the same topic in the *Boston Globe* found a lack of evidence to support the claim that priests who signed the letter requesting Law's resignation were being expelled from public ministry (Paulson, 2005e).[9]

It is beyond the scope of this study to investigate these allegations regarding Boston priests. Nevertheless, the statement of Rev. Mahoney cited above indicates that the firing of Cuenin and controversies over assignments of other dissident priests created an atmosphere of intimidation and mistrust that probably translated into more cautious and conformist behavior on the part of liberal Boston priests. Three other examples of censure in Massachusetts cited below also document a tense and repressive atmosphere. I use pseudonyms to describe these cases since my sources expressed a desire to protect themselves and the priests involved. Both incidents occurred in 2005 and 2006, the same time period as the firing of Father Walter Cuenin.

One case involved a Catholic campus center (referred to here as St. Bridget's) located on a suburban campus that was not technically a

---

[7] As documented in chapter 7, parishioners from several parishes closed during the reconfiguration process in 2004–2005 contend their parishes received closure decrees as retribution against their outspoken pastors, especially those who signed the Law petition.

[8] Of the fifty-eight priests who signed the 2002 letter to Cardinal Law, eighteen belong to religious orders or hold jobs outside the archdiocese, and consequently were not under diocesan control.

[9] The article noted "the overwhelming majority of the fifty-eight signers appear to have suffered no negative career impact" (Paulson, 2005e p. A1), and several signers forcefully denied charges of retaliation. However, four of the most outspoken priests from shuttered parishes did not receive new parish assignments.

parish but operated much like one under the supervision of a very capable nun (whom I call Sister Judy). She, in turn, drew on the gifts of an active committee of parishioners.[10] This community had its own spacious chapel where Sunday liturgies often attracted several hundred worshipers who were seeking an alternative to the dull liturgies at their local parish. This campus center had operated without a permanent priest for several years but was actively searching for one.

I attended Sunday Mass at St. Bridget's on February 27, 2005, when students, families with small children, and elderly persons packed the chapel. At this Mass a youthful Franciscan priest (Father Paul) presided, delivering a spirited homily, which he began by singing a few lines from the popular song, "I Will Always Love You." As she introduced Father Paul, Sister Judy announced that he was a candidate for the position of permanent chaplain. The entire liturgy was lively and jubilant, enhanced by a four-piece string band that led the congregation in singing conventional Catholic hymns. The congregation warmed up to Father Paul, laughing at several of his jokes and greeting him enthusiastically after the service.

Months later, the archdiocese refused the recommendation of parishioners to hire Father Paul, and instead assigned them a conservative priest without soliciting their input. Shortly thereafter, Sister Judy resigned her position, believing that "the theological perspective and pastoral style of the newly-assigned campus minister" would not be complementary to her own (J. D., personal correspondence, June 16, 2008). Likewise, Dorothy (my contact in the community) and her small circle of friends who were stalwart volunteers at St. Bridget's chose to explore other parishes in the vicinity, eventually finding one at a considerable distance, where a Vatican II priest was attracting disaffected Catholics from a wide span of surrounding towns. Dorothy and her friends from St. Bridget's also attend a monthly Mass presided over by a local married priest who is listed on the Rent-A-Priest website.[11]

According to Dorothy, the newly appointed priest at St. Bridget's was reassigned after less than a year, and plans are underway to merge the St. Bridget's community and the local diocesan parish into a single unit with one newly appointed priest (D. J., personal communication, October 16, 2007).

---

[10] This community came to my attention because I had interviewed a lay leader of the community (Dorothy, a pseudonym) as part of my research on Eucharistic communities.

[11] Rent-A-Priest is a website managed by Celibacy Is the Issue (CITI). For more information on CITI, see chapter 7.

Another example centers on a parish I refer to as Blessed Sacrament in the Worcester Diocese, where the priest (whom I refer to as Father Dan) narrowly escaped being fired in 2006 after parishioners intervened on his behalf following a transfer assignment from his local bishop. I learned of this incident when two parishioners (referred to by the pseudonyms Mary and Deb) contacted me for advice. They explained that their bishop was acting on complaints from a conservative parishioner, who opposed the dramatic restructuring of parish programs by a lay board that included Mary and Deb, though this was not the reason cited by the bishop for the firing. Mary and Deb pleaded with the bishop to reverse his decision, and ultimately he allowed Father Dan to remain at Blessed Sacrament (M. P., personal communication, February 18, 2006).[12]

A final example of censure in the Boston area centers on St. Luke's Parish in Westborough, Massachusetts. On the same weekend Father Cuenin was ousted from his parish in Newton, Bishop of Worcester Robert J. McManus showed up unannounced at the Saturday evening Mass and "pulled the pastor [Rev. George Lange] from the pulpit" (Levenson, 2005) during Mass in order to express his rebuke of the pastor. The rebuke centered on the pastor's decision to disobey the bishop's request that every parish in his diocese circulate a petition supporting a constitutional amendment banning same-sex marriage.[13] In this case, the two resident priests at St. Luke's remained in the parish, though several sources claim the associate pastor received some form of censure.

An End to Lay Preaching in Minnesota

In January 2008 Archbishop Harry Flynn of the St. Paul-Minneapolis diocese ordered an end to lay preaching in diocesan parishes, calling such a practice a "liturgical abuse" (Flynn as cited in Berggen, 2008), although twenty-nine parishes engaged in the practice, and some even offered

---

[12] I was unable to obtain any information as to whether Father Dan agreed to conditions or restrictions to secure his position. Most members of the parish never learned of this episode, and this is the only example I encountered that resulted in a favorable outcome for a liberal priest. I do not know to what extent, if any, Mary and Deb's advocacy influenced the bishop's decision.

[13] In his homily, described by several parishioners as "stunning," Bishop McManus criticized the parish pastor for a notice that appeared in the September 29, 2005, bulletin, stating, "The priests of this parish do not feel they can support this amendment. They do not see any value to it and they see it as an attack on certain people of our parish, namely those who are gay" (Levenson, 2005).

formal training for lay preachers. Flynn reportedly took this action as a form of "cleaning house" to prepare for his conservative successor, Archbishop John Nienstedt. When Nienstedt took control of the diocese, blogger N. Coleman (2008) decried Nienstedt's decision to appoint a conservative pastor for Coleman's liberal "improvisatory" parish, St. Stephen's in Minneapolis, that had relied on lay preachers for decades. Consequently, after celebrating their last tearful service in the school gym on March 30, 2008, two hundred members of St. Stephen's defied diocesan control by defiantly moving five blocks to a new location, where they planned to continue their Sunday lay-led prayer meetings. N. Coleman (2008) claims that several progressive parishes in the diocese are also "being brought into line" by Nienstedt so that all parishes conform to the uniform standards of the General Instruction of the Roman Missal (GIRM).

Suspension in Ontario and Firing in Australia

The Reverend Edward Cachia (2006) from Cobourg, Ontario, is another example of a priest whose outspokenness evoked censure.[14] Bishop Nicola De Angelis suspended him from the priesthood for his public support and participation in ordinations by Roman Catholic Womenpriests (RCWP). After Cachia refused to recant his support for RCWP, Bishop De Angelis excommunicated him (Cachia, 2006). For roughly one year, Cachia served as pastor of Christ the King Eucharistic community of more than one hundred members, which meets in a memorial hall in Cold Springs near Peterborough (Owens, 2006). In 2006, Father Cachia announced that he missed his priestly community and returned to the priesthood (L. D., personal communication, December 12, 2006). Canadian RCWP Marie Bouclin (2008) replaced him as the associate part-time pastor for the Christ the King community, though she must travel three hundred miles to conduct their liturgies.

In February 2009, Archbishop John Bathersby fired Father Peter Kennedy as pastor of St. Mary's Parish in Brisbane, Australia, in response to complaints about irregular practices, including use of parish facilities by homosexuals, a Buddhist meditation group, and political groups

---

[14] Although these cases took place outside the United States, they are included because they closely resemble several of the most famous examples of censured liberal priests in the United States cited in this chapter. It is possible the bishops in these cases received orders from the Vatican to censure these dissident priests.

(Edman, 2009). Following a lengthy mediation process, Father Kennedy agreed to resign and hand over the keys to St. Mary's in April 2010, but he vowed to continue ministering to his parish in another setting. He claimed that 90 percent of his congregation would follow him (E. Allen, March 29, 2010).[15]

Repression Spurs Resignation by Vatican II Priests

The Reverend Tim Stier, Freemont, California

My research uncovered several examples of Vatican II priests who resigned or took leaves of office in the face of increasingly restrictive policies by church hierarchs. For example, the Reverend Tim Stier, a former pastor of Corpus Christi Church in Freemont, California, publicly announced he is no longer active in the diocese and is challenging church teachings on celibacy, women's ordination, and the inadequate response by clergy to the sexual abuse crisis. Stier confessed "I'm not a perfect person and I do have weaknesses and sin. But there is a level of dishonesty and arrogance in this that just tells me we need systematic, radical change" (Stier as cited in Jones, 2005).[16]

Resignations in Boston

In a February 2006 interview, the Reverend Walter Cuenin (featured in the vignette above) stated that he knew of three priests in the Boston archdiocese who have "taken a leave from the priesthood and they're all very dynamic excellent priests" (Cuenin as cited in Black, 2006). I interviewed a Boston priest who confessed he planned to resign in the near future after taking steps to safeguard his own parish. He confessed that he had "given up hope" that progressive change would happen in the church

---

[15] This story of Father Peter Kennedy is remarkably similar to the story of Father James Callan of Spiritus Christi in Rochester, New York, which is described later in this chapter. Both Kennedy and Callan had personal histories of defying church policies and both created dynamic parishes with reputations for social justice outreach. Both chose to form sectarian parishes rather than accept dictates of their bishops. Both cases attracted considerable media attention and generated considerable controversy.

[16] Stier was dismayed that his efforts to generate dialogue on solutions to the priest shortage (including the issue of celibacy and women's ordination) had failed, and he characterized the priesthood as "a burned out, disillusioned, low morale group of people."

in his lifetime, and found working under the thumb of current leadership "intolerable" (T. L., personal communication, June 18, 2005).

Resignations by Gay Priests

Some gay priests considered resigning from the priesthood because of their objection to the 2005 Instruction from the Vatican's Congregation for Catholic Education on the ordination of homosexuals.[17] In a *New York Times* article, Laurie Goodstein (2005) reported that her interviews with gay priests and seminarians evoked "a wave of anger and sadness among some gay priests and seminarians who say they may soon have to decide whether to stay or leave, to remain silent or speak out" (p. A10).[18]

Benedictine Father Robert Pierson did publicly resign as director of campus ministry in protest over the new Vatican policy on gays. In an e-mail to students and administrators at St. John's University in Collegeville, Minnesota, Pierson confessed that, as a "celibate gay priest" (Pierson as cited in Young, 2006, p. 6), he objected to the language in the church statement on homosexuality, noting that "the language it uses is really mean-spirited and nasty, and it hurts people" (p. 6).

CENSURE OF VATICAN II PARISHES RESULTS IN SCHISMS

Corpus Christi, Rochester, New York

One of the best-known censures of a Vatican II parish occurred in 1998 at Corpus Christi parish in Rochester, New York, whose pastor, James Callan, enjoyed a reputation among Catholic reformers as a maverick, due to his willingness to implement liturgical reform and his relentless advocacy

---

[17] This Congregation for Catholic Education document is entitled *Instruction Concerning the Criteria for Discernment of Vocations with Regard to Persons with Homosexual Tendencies in View of Their Admission to the Seminary and Holy Orders*. This document has evoked considerable controversy on the right and the left. Some liberals have expressed relief that the document states homosexuals are entitled to dignified treatment and may remain priests if they remain celibate and do not have "deep-seated homosexual tendencies." Some conservatives are disappointed that the document does not forbid all homosexuals from the priesthood.

[18] Thirty-nine Italian priests expressed similar sentiments in a public letter that stated "homosexuality has not stopped them from being good priests" (*Gay clergy issue letter*, 2005). They claimed that the Vatican's new policy made them feel like "unloved and unwanted children."

for peace and justice. During his tenure, Callan transformed Corpus Christi from a dying inner-city parish of six hundred people into a vibrant community of three thousand (Patterson, 2001). This parish became a magnet for progressive Catholics and something of a testing ground for liturgical innovations, including blessings of gay unions, inclusion of women in central roles during the celebration of Mass, and offering Communion to non-Catholics.[19]

Many observers credit Corpus Christi's avoidance of censure for many years to the protection they received from Bishop Matthew Clark of Rochester, who was "considered one of the more progressive voices within the episcopate" (Patterson, p. 11). Callan (1997) insists that Bishop Clark was aware of the irregular practices at his parish and tacitly approved them. In fact, Bishop Clark had modeled some path-breaking liturgies himself, for example, by holding a "Gay and Lesbian Mass" at Sacred Heart Cathedral. By 1998, however, news of the liturgical aberrations at Corpus Christi reached the Vatican, and Cardinal Ratzinger ordered Bishop Clark to fire Callan. After a protracted series of events, Callan and staff members at Corpus Christi severed their ties with the Rochester diocese by forming a schismatic Catholic parish they named Spiritus Christi.[20]

Cardinal Ratzinger probably believed his quick and decisive move to fire Callan would send a bold message regarding the Vatican's refusal to tolerate liberal revisions to the liturgy. His message may have backfired. As documented in chapter 7, the schismatic parish Spiritus Christi eventually became a mecca for reformers because it exemplified the type of Vatican II liturgy and inclusive ministry that liberals were unable to create within institutional structures. Paradoxically, the uncompromising stance of Ratzinger may have strengthened the resolve of reformers to move in a sectarian direction.

St. Stanislaus Kostka Parish, St. Louis, Missouri

St. Louis, Missouri, attracted nationwide media attention due to a landmark battle over parish assets that occurred at St. Stanislaus Kostka (hereafter referred to as St. Stan's). In 2005 St. Stan's, a parish built by Polish

---

[19] The Vatican probably became aware of liturgical innovations at Corpus Christi Parish because of a front-page photo of pastoral administrator Mary Ramerman at the altar in liturgical garb in the February 12, 1998, edition of the *National Catholic Reporter* (Callan, 1997).

[20] For more information on Spiritus Christi Parish, see chapter 9.

immigrants, severed its ties with the St. Louis archdiocese in order to avoid turning over its 9.5 million dollars in assets to the archdiocese. This decision followed a protracted battle with Archbishop Raymond L. Burke, who had a reputation as "the most outspoken of conservative bishops" (Wittenauer, 2008). Burke claimed he was entitled under canon law to control the assets of the parish.[21] Parishioners claimed their charter dated back to an 1891 deed assigning parish property to a "civil corporation made up of parishioners" (Zaiger, 2005, p. A3).

This battle over fiscal control was not a liberal-conservative contest, since it was primarily over autonomy and survival of the parish. Parishioners feared that Burke might sell their property to fund abuse settlements. With slogans that included "Our Polish parish's 9/11" and "Pray with us, not on us," parishioners were determined to resist what they viewed as a "hostile takeover" by Burke (AP: *Polish Church Defies*, 2004).

St. Stan's has had a reputation as a conservative parish, although Pastor Marek Bozek challenged this stereotype, noting that the parish includes a range of Catholics and a sizeable group of gay Catholics (personal correspondence, Nov. 4, 2006).[22] Both liberal and conservative parishioners at Stan's clearly evidenced a defiant spirit by risking excommunication for refusing to allow diocesan control of its finances. Fifteen hundred people turned out for a triumphant Christmas Eve Mass presided over by Bozek in 2005, despite a warning from the archbishop that attending the service was a mortal sin (*Banished Priest Gets,* 2005). In his homily, which evoked a standing ovation, Bozek adopted a slogan of the Reform Movement, exclaiming, "Rules and regulations were not the church but we are the church" (Bozek as cited in Kaintz, 2005, p. 1), as he extended a special welcome to nonparishioners and non-Catholics.

In May 29, 2008, the Congregation for the Doctrine of the Faith (CDF) upheld Burke's excommunication of St. Stan's board and Father Bozek, declaring the church a "schismatic church" (*Schismatic St. Louis Parish,* 2008). During Father Bozek's first three years at St. Stan's, the parish grew from 260 to 550 members and word spread of his "droll sense of humor and a knack for delivering intelligent homilies" (Cooperman, 2008a, p. 6).

---

[21] Burke's predecessor, Archbishop Justin Rigali, initiated the move to take control of St. Stanislaus's assets. Rigali proposed putting the parish's assets in an archdiocesan trust fund (*Church History*, 2005).

[22] Bozek, a Polish immigrant, became pastor of St. Stan's after he left his position in another diocese in order to express support for St. Stan's struggle against Archbishop Burke. Although parishioners at St. Stan's welcomed Bozek's offer to serve as their pastor, the archdiocese never approved his assignment.

However, the parish has also become a hotbed of controversy as Bozek took high profile stands on behalf of liberal issues by participating in the ordination of two local women by RCWP.[23]

Bozek has chosen not to challenge his laicization. Meanwhile the parish remains embroiled in a legal conflict with the archdiocese, which filed a lawsuit in January 2009 asking the courts to restore archdiocesan control of the parish. They claimed changes to the parish's new bylaws violate canon law and the parish's 1891 bylaws (O'Malley, 2010). Bozek's bold moves have alienated some parishioners, who unsuccessfully challenged his authority.[24] Two hundred families left the parish following these conflicts. Despite these losses, Bozek claims the congregation has grown under his leadership, since he has attracted many new members. Nonetheless, Bozek has become a polarizing figure. He may have violated a basic tenet of community organizing, which discourages moving too far outside the beliefs and values of the community.[25]

The example of St. Stan's demonstrates that the uncompromising stance of conservative clerics like Archbishop Burke often weakens church authority rather than bolstering it. In this instance, St. Stan's Parish would almost certainly have not chosen schism if it had been allowed to retain control of its assets. At least some of its parishioners were conservative Catholics who were reluctant to sever ties with the Vatican. In fact, Archbishop Robert J. Carlson, who replaced Burke as archbishop, offered to restore parishioners' control over parish assets.[26] This offer won the

---

[23] Bozek also proclaimed his beliefs that laity should control finances and select their own priests, and that the priesthood should be open to women and married clergy.

[24] St. Stan's board deadlocked twice in June 2008 on a vote to fire Bozek. At a third meeting Bozek broke the deadlock and dissolved the board. When parishioners elected a new board in October, the archdiocese threatened to excommunicate the two newly elected board members. The archdiocese had already excommunicated the four reelected board members (Townsend, 2008). In December 2009, Bozek issued a public offer to resign following revelations that he had sought and received affiliation from two independent groups, the Reformed Catholic Church, which dissolved shortly thereafter, and Married Priests Now!, which Bozek abandoned following exposure of its connections to the Reverend Sun Myung Moon (Townsend, 2009).

[25] The second rule of legendary community organizer Saul Alinsky's (1972) rules for radicals is "Never go outside the experience of your people" (p. 172). One could argue that current church leaders are also violating this principle by repressing Vatican II principles that most Catholics support.

[26] In 2010 Archbishop Carlson made an offer to allow the parish to retain control of its assets in return for allowing the archdiocese to control the appointment of new board members. Parish members rejected the offer by a vote of 257 to 185 because the offer would require Bozek to resign. It also did not guarantee that the parish would remain open (Kenny, 2010).

support of a sizeable minority of parishioners, but it was too late because by then Bozek had won the support of a majority of parishioners (Kenny, 2010). Archbishop Burke's overreach backfired and resulted in schism.

Conservative Bishops Transform Dioceses

Excommunication Decree in Lincoln, Nebraska

Bishop Fabian Bruskewitz of Lincoln, Nebraska, is a notorious foe of liberal reformers; he imposed an excommunication decree on members of Call to Action (CTA) and several other reform groups in his diocese, which Vatican courts later upheld. Reformers also challenge Bruskewitz for his refusal to comply with the National Review Board's audit of compliance with the USCCB's Charter for the Protection of Children and Young People, except for the first audit in 2003 (Reeves, 2006). In defense of his position, Bruskewitz claims his diocese complies with church and civil laws, and he does not recognize the Review Board, particularly since some of its members support abortion.[27] As noted earlier, the Nebraska CTA chapter has survived Bruskewitz's excommunication decree, despite the fact that the Vatican courts have upheld the decree.

Loyalty Pledge in Oregon

In 2004, CTA undertook proactive measures to combat a crackdown in Portland, Oregon, where Bishop Robert Vasa initiated a requirement that every lay minister in his diocese sign a 6,200-word "Affirmation of Personal Faith Loyalty Pledge." The pledge assented to church teachings in a number of areas, including "homosexuality, contraception, premarital sex, abortion, euthanasia, the Real Presence, Mary, hell, purgatory, and the authority of the church" (McClory, 2005a, p. 3). In response to this ultimatum, CTA members formed an Oregon chapter and invited CTA leader and author Robert McClory to conduct a speaking tour based on his book *Faithful Dissidents: Stories of Men and Women Who Loved and Changed the Church*. McClory's presentation on January 23, 2005, attracted more than

---

[27] According to a *National Catholic Reporter* editorial, Bishop Bruskewitz receives "no public support" from other bishops because "he is so far out by himself on ice so thin that it would hardly support another" (*The shock fades in*, 2006, p. 24).

two hundred people, including Bishop Vasa himself. McClory insisted that Catholics who object to a church teaching have the right to engage in dialogue and to refuse unquestioning obedience. In response, Bishop Vasa insisted that CTA's "understanding of dissent" contradicts "profession of faith in the Catholic Church" (Vasa as cited in McClory, p. 3).

Upheavals in Midwestern Dioceses

Two Midwestern dioceses faced considerable turmoil in 2006, following the appointments of two highly authoritarian, conservative bishops, Edward K. Braxton for Belleville, Illinois, and Robert Finn for Kansas City-St. Joseph, Missouri. Even before Braxton's installation as bishop, seven priests in the diocese protested the choice of Braxton (based on his prior record) and their exclusion from the selection of a new bishop, citing canon law. They also cited the precedent of collaboration in the selection of Braxton's predecessor, Bishop William Gregory (McClory, 2006). Following Braxton's installation, fifty Belleville priests signed a letter to Cardinal Francis George protesting the selection process. In reply to the priests' objections, the papal nuncio, Monsignor Gabriel Montalvo, simply advised them that the pope appoints bishops and no one had ever presumed to question the procedure before.

The script played out in Belleville resembles the drama in the Kansas City-St. Joseph, Missouri diocese under Bishop Robert W. Finn, who is one of four Opus Dei bishops in the United States. After Finn became bishop on May 24, 2006, he implemented a broad-sweeping and highly contested makeover of the diocese, which included massive staff changes and dramatic alterations in diocesan programs. Most notably, he cancelled a diocese lay formation program that had received the 1998 Tribute Award for its contributions to lay ministry (Coday, 2006).[28]

The *National Catholic Reporter* interviewed a variety of staff and parishioners, who insisted that Finn implemented his far-reaching overhaul of the diocese with little or no consultation, even among "the senior

---

[28] The overall rationale and thrust of Finn's leadership aimed to transform the diocese into one consistent with his own Opus Dei version of Catholicism, which includes "an affinity for indulgences and Latin" (Coday, 2006, p. 7). Hence, Finn dramatically cut funding for the Diocesan Bolivian Mission and the Office of Peace and Justice, while setting up a Respect for Life Office (to handle pro-life issues) and upgrading a Latin Mass community. Finn also censored the diocesan newspaper, banning a column by theologian Richard McBrien and rejecting articles about the Catholic peace group Pax Christi.

leadership of the diocese or the people in the programs affected" (Coday, 2006, p. 6). A *National Catholic Reporter* editorial on Finn's tenure in Kansas City concluded, "We have learned through difficult experience in this country that bishops are, indeed, monarchs," noting that "the legitimate exercise of leaders and of authority are quite other matters" (*No Rationale for,* 2006, p. 24).

Mixed Signals

In 2008 the fallout from the repressive measures by bishops cited above sent mixed signals. In several of these cases, reformers and previously inactive Catholics rallied to resist conservative takeovers of their parishes and dioceses by conservative bishops. Reformers took heart from the news that forty-five priests (representing a majority of the priests in the Belleville diocese) sent a public letter demanding Bishop Braxton's resignation, citing his "lack of cooperation, consultation, accountability, and transparency" and claiming "he lost his moral authority" (*Belleville Priests Call,* 2008, p. 3). Following this action, Frank S. Ladner, eighty-one, a Catholic philanthropist, financed a quarter-page newspaper ad in *USA Today* calling on the pope to remove Braxton (McClory, 2008a).[29] The tension between Braxton and Bellevue priests reached a crisis in 2008 when diocesan committees discovered that Braxton had made unauthorized expenditures totaling eighteen thousand dollars.

Although Braxton refused to resign, reformers could interpret developments in Belleville positively because priests and parishioners in the diocese launched a concerted and well-orchestrated resistance against Braxton's violation of diocesan procedures. This effort may reflect the contagion effect of the 2002 letter signed by fifty-eight priests in Boston, which some credit with forcing Cardinal Law's resignation. The examples from Boston and Belleville suggest that, at least in some instances, extremes of autocratic or ineffective governance may evoke counter movements by priests and laity, especially in cases as severe as those in Boston and Belleville.

In the case of St. Stan's and Spiritus Christi, censure resulted in schism. Both parishes now serve as examples that it is possible to survive and

---

[29] The publication date for this ad was April 17, 2008, the third day of Pope Benedict XVI's visit to the United States.

even thrive as independent parishes. Consequently, schismatic parishes may encourage other disaffected parishes and Eucharistic communities to pursue a sectarian path. Dramatic transformations of dioceses and repressive measures by conservative bishops also motivate liberal Catholics to abandon the church or explore underground communities.

Many reformers expressed dismay at the Vatican announcement on June 27, 2008, that Archbishop Raymond Burke, a canon lawyer, has become the first American appointed to head the Vatican's top canonical tribunal, the Apostolic Signatura.[30] The fact that the Vatican chose a highly controversial figure like Burke for this position, and later promoted him to the rank of cardinal, is an ominous sign for reformers regarding Pope Benedict XVI's stance, given Burke's prominent and controversial role in penalizing dissidents.[31]

No Room at the Inn for Vatican II Pastors or Parishioners

For five decades after Vatican II, many liberal Catholics, especially those from large metropolitan areas, could find a hospitable Vatican II parish that preached and practiced the type of liberal Catholicism they favored. Although some Vatican II parishes remain, pastors in these liberal strongholds have almost certainly become less bold and outspoken due to the ever-present threat of sanctions by conservative bishops or the Vatican. Hence, liberal Catholics in many areas are unable to find a parish that they find nourishing and uplifting, especially since many Vatican II parishes now lack a rebellious spirit and innovative liturgy.[32]

---

[30] The Reverend Thomas Reese, senior fellow at the Woodstock Theological Center at Georgetown University, said the Vatican highest court "has a focus on narrow procedural issues, rarely tackling substantive issues" (Wittenauer, 2008).

[31] In addition to his uncompromising stance at St. Stan's (cited above), Archbishop Burke censored or penalized public figures and Catholics in his diocese for issues he considered contrary to Catholic teachings. For example, he excommunicated three women ordained in St. Louis by RCWP and imposed severe canonical penalties on Sister of Charity Louise Lears for her support of RCWP ordinations. He also vowed to refuse Communion to Senator John Kerry during his 2004 presidential campaign due to his pro-choice stance (T. Roberts, 2008a, G1).

[32] In an Internet blog, Eugene Cullen Kennedy (2010) cites further examples of strong-arm tactics by conservative clerics, including Bishop Thomas Paprika, newly appointed to the Springfield, Illinois, diocese, who claimed the devil caused the abuse crisis; Bishop Thomas Olmstead of Phoenix, Arizona, who excommunicated a nun who allowed an abortion necessary to save the life of a young mother; and Bishop Frank DeWayne of Venice, Florida, who has eliminated parish councils, ruled out any role for women in the liturgy, and used "spy-like" agents to monitor pastors in his diocese.

Several reformers cite the attrition and repression of Vatican II priests as factors influencing their decision to commute to the closest Vatican II parish in their vicinity or to explore the alternative worship communities like those described in the next three chapters. A case in point is a small group of parishioners from Our Lady Help of Christians Parish (featured in the vignette at the beginning of this chapter) who refused to return to their parish following the firing of Father Walter Cuenin. This group, who named themselves "A Pilgrim People," served as a catalyst for the formation of an underground community referred to as The Holy Spirit Catholic Community, which rents space from the Unitarian church in Wellesley, Massachusetts, and has affiliated with the Ecumenical Catholic Communion (ECC). Holy Spirit is a small community of fewer than fifty members, including several CORPUS priests, two female priests ordained by ECC, and activists from the vigiling movement.

Some disaffected Catholics abandon Catholicism altogether by joining Protestant parishes. *National Catholic Reporter* editor-at-large Tom Roberts (2010) coined the term "the 'had it' Catholics" to describe Catholics who leave the church, in part because they no longer support its teachings. Roberts noted that the 22.8 million people who have left the Catholic Church (representing 10 percent of all Catholics) make up a group larger than any other religious denomination in the United States.[33]

Thus, one can conclude that Pope Benedict is making good on his preference for a "smaller, purer church" in which liberal Catholics are not welcomed or accommodated. Hence, the movement to restore the progressive principles of Vatican II increasingly survives in sect-like groups where the Vatican cannot silence prophetic voices. While this break is painful and protracted for some reformers, others are eager to move past culture wars between conservative and liberal Catholics that show no sign of resolution or reconciliation.

---

[33] Tom Roberts's blog (2010) on "The 'had it' Catholics" describes Jim Fitzpatrick, a lifelong Catholic who defected to a Disciples of Christ Church due to his dismay over the conflict in the Kansas City-St. Joseph diocese following the appointment of Bishop Robert Finn (described above). Jim followed the lead of his wife, Mary, who had joined the new parish years earlier in protest over John Paul II's pronouncement that women would never be ordained.

CHAPTER SEVEN

WHAT THEREFORE BELONGS TO CAESAR? MARGINAL COMMUNITIES

Louise Haggett, a cradle Catholic, discovered the Catholic Reform Movement in midlife in 1992 when she was unable to find a priest to visit her mother in an assisted living facility. As she investigated the priest shortage, she discovered there were twenty-five thousand married Catholic priests in the United States (one hundred thousand worldwide). Consequently, she set up a website to advertise the services of married priests for weddings and other forms of ministry. Next Louise founded a professional organization called Celibacy Is the Issue (CITI) that provides certification for married priests and educates Catholics about their ministries. In establishing the CITI ministry in 1992, Louise drew on her considerable skills as an advertising executive for thirty-five years. As of 2008, CITI priests have served more than half a million people. Currently more than two hundred priests are listed on CITI's website.

In her advocacy on behalf of married priests, Louise developed a deep respect for "the holiness, warmth, kindness and pastoral gifts of married priests." She also recognized that "their humble, self-effacing nature inhibited them from advocating on their own behalf" (L. H., personal communication, September 18, 2008). Louise's persistent and passionate advocacy of married priests won her widespread recognition, including a 1999 award from the Corps of Reserve Priests United for Service (CORPUS). Although some CITI priests are troubled by CITI's catchy but rather commercial sounding slogan, "Rent a Priest," it has proven an effective, easy-to-remember brand. CITI hopes to sneak in through the back door, as it were, in the same fashion as altar girls gained Vatican approval after they became increasingly commonplace in many parishes in the late 1980s. CITI describes its strategy as "Just do it," citing Canon Law 27 that reads, "Custom is the best interpreter of laws" (*Celibacy Is the Issue*, n.d.).

Currently Louise retains her connection to Catholicism by attending masses celebrated by married priests, where she believes the strong sense of community "brings the group much closer to the Divine Presence." In 2005 Louise authored a sociological study entitled *The Bingo Report* that documented a relationship between mandatory celibacy and clergy sex abuse. Although the Vatican refuses to budge on mandatory celibacy, Louise is hopeful that CITI's record of exemplary ministry by married priests will keep the issue alive, as the priest shortage continues to worsen and American Catholics seek new ways to practice their faith.

Marginal Communities: Neither Church Nor Sect

This chapter focuses on marginal communities whose boundaries intersect the insider-outsider divide within Roman Catholicism. These communities struggle with Jesus's command to "render therefore to Caesar the things that are Caesar's, and to God the things that are God's" (Matthew 22:21). In the case of progressive Catholics, Caesar refers metaphorically to church hierarchs who suppress Vatican II principles that progressive Catholics regard as essential to their faith. Thus, in questioning "what therefore belongs to Caesar?" reformers must examine what they owe to the institutional church (in terms of loyalty, obedience, donations, etc.). In questioning what they owe to God, they must consider the longings of their own soul, which may be nourished by alternative worship communities. Thus, progressive Catholics drawn to these marginal communities struggle to carve out a middle path between the dialectical tensions of church and sect. They have one foot in the church, in terms of a long history as Catholics and a love for many features of the tradition, and one foot out, in that they are searching for a more authentic and less restrictive spirituality than is fostered by the institutional church.

Four types of marginal communities are described below as follows: (1) small Christian communities (SCCs), including Eucharistic Centered Communities (ECCs) that participate in the Network of Intentional Eucharistic Communities;[1] (2) Celibacy Is the Issue (CITI) communities; (3) religious communities of sisters who conduct their own liturgies; and (4) vigiling groups that resist closure of their parishes. On the one hand, these four types of communities remain nominally connected to the institutional church as members of SCCs and CITI communities whose liturgies are conducted by priests with canonical authority, as sisters who belong to Roman Catholic orders, and as vigiling parishioners who are struggling to save their parishes. On the other hand, these four types of communities are moving toward an outsider status as they progress beyond mere protest and engage in the second stage of nonviolent resistance referred to as noncooperation, whereby groups "deliberately withdraw the usual forms and degree of their cooperation with the person, activity, institution" (Sharp, 1973, p. 183).[2]

---

[1] The Network of Intentional Eucharistic Communities maintains a website and holds periodic conferences for small Christian communities, which include networking and educational forums on liturgy, canon law, and church renewal. For more information, see: (www.intentionaleucharistcommunities.org)

[2] In contrast, ECCs and parishes that operate totally outside the boundaries of Roman Catholicism are classified as underground and are described in chapters 8 and 9.

Small Christian Communities (SCCs)

The last several decades have witnessed explosive growth in the number of small Christian communities (SCCs), in which small groups averaging in size from thirteen to seventeen members meet voluntarily on a weekly or biweekly basis to explore issues of faith among a close-knit community of like-minded seekers. Lee (2000), who has conducted extensive research on small Christian communities, estimates that in 2000 there were "minimally 37,000" SCCs (p. 16) in the United States, whose members total at least one million. Lee and Cowan (2003) further speculate that by 2003 the number of SCCs may have risen to 45,000–50,000.

Lee (2000) attributes the dramatic growth of SCCs to a desire for a more intense religious experience than is possible in a conventional parish, and to a "hunger for community with emotional depth" (p. 7).[3] As one might expect, the demographic characteristics of SCC members resemble, to some degree, members of reform groups in that members of both groups are predominately female, middle-aged and older, and, with the exception of Latino SCCs, are more affluent and well educated than the general Catholic population.

ECCs as Resistance Communities

Only Lee's (2000) fourth category of ECCs qualifies as *resistance communities* because they openly criticize the church and violate some church rules regarding liturgy. His fourth category includes Call to Action (CTA) communities and Eucharistic Centered Communities (ECCs), each of which includes slightly fewer than 100 communities.[4] In comparison with other types of SCCs, members of CTA and ECC communities express higher levels of social awareness and engage in more social justice activism.

Lee (2000) estimates that these CTA and ECC communities represent less than 1 percent of the SCC population. Some ECCs trace their roots to the underground church movement of the 1960s that included hundreds of small "house churches" (p. 12), where Catholics and Protestants engaged

---

[3] Although members of SCCs constitute only about "one-in-twenty regular church attending Catholics" (Lee, 2000, p. 10), they have higher rates of attendance at Mass, participation in devotional practices, and involvement in parish activities than parishioners who do not belong to SCCs.

[4] CTA communities in this study are not necessarily formally affiliated with CTA, but refer to communities who have asked to be listed on the CTA website.

in informal participatory liturgies and extensive social activism. My own research findings parallel those of Lee, who found that SCCs allow Catholics, especially those who are highly educated and have attained professional status, to leave "an institutional Catholicism they find untenable, but remain connected with a community that has been shaped by Catholic culture" (p. 128).[5] Leaders in the communities I observed describe their communities as something of "an alternative church or parish" that enabled members to remain connected to the features of Catholicism they cherished most, which they identified in the following order of importance: the Eucharist, the liturgy of the Mass, and Catholic social teaching. Most of these leaders also confessed they were "relieved" to avoid the rigid rules and judgmental pronouncements that are increasingly prevalent in many parishes.[6]

The ECCs I observed are not "underground" or "illicit," because their priests have canonical authority to confer the sacraments. These communities have never been restricted or prohibited by diocesan officials. Nonetheless, these communities operate in the margins, so to speak, of diocesan control, particularly since local bishops did not assign their priests.[7] For this reason, during the tenure of Pope John Paul II, Cardinal Ratzinger expressed some reservations about these "base ecclesiastical communities"[8] that emerged as a central component of liberation theology in Central America (Lee, p. 119). However, John Paul II did note the positive impact of these communities on evangelization and community building, and, consequently, allowed them to proliferate.

As voluntary groups with weak links to the church bureaucracy, ECCs can bend and sidestep rules to a greater extent than is possible in most

---

[5] At a June 8, 2009, gathering of Eucharistic communities attended by 230 people representing at least forty-two communities, some participants favored no connection to the institutional church while others had some involvement in local parishes. Sociologist William D'Antonio described intentional Eucharistic communities as "a leading edge of the future" (D'Antonio as cited in T. Roberts, 2009b).

[6] Some ECC members do occasionally attend liturgies in their local parishes. In fact, the oldest ECC in my sample meets only twice a month during most of the year so that members have the option of attending Mass at a local parish on alternate weeks.

[7] The ECCs in this chapter invite priests with whom they are acquainted to conduct their liturgies. These priests receive modest stipends from ECCs, but their income is derived primarily from other forms of employment.

[8] Base ecclesiastical communities have been attributed to liberation theology and Vatican II documents. The base ecclesiastical communities' movement began in Brazil and the Philippines in the 1960s and has spread worldwide. These communities are usually connected to a parish, but meet in small groups to explore theology and its implications for their lives and the spiritual, political, and economic realities they face.

parishes, particularly during the current repressive climate described throughout this study. Unlike liberal parishes, the ECCs I visited reported no problem with "spies"[9] who might report their alleged transgressions to diocesan officials.[10] Several members of the five ECCs I observed expressed concern that my research might evoke punitive action from local church hierarchs by calling attention to some of their more daring liturgical practices. Consequently, I have decided to use pseudonyms in describing the communities and their presiding priests.

Liturgies at Boston ECCs

The five ECCs I attended in the Boston area share many similar characteristics. Attendance ranged from fifteen to roughly one hundred people on the occasions I attended, but even in the largest groups most attendees seemed well acquainted. They greet each other on a first-name basis and are familiar with recent events in each other's lives. All five groups went far beyond a simple handshake of peace during the liturgy as they engaged in something of a love fest, whereby embraces and kisses on the cheek were exchanged among almost every group member (including the priest-presider, me, and other newcomers). Each group had at least one physically or mentally challenged member, who was showered with special attention and affection.

The demeanor of attendees at these ECCS was highly cooperative and reverent, as they followed the script of the Mass closely, chiming in enthusiastically with the lines designated for the congregation and receiving the

---

[9] Several Boston members of Catholic reform groups advised me that during his tenure Cardinal Law reputedly sent "spies" to liberal communities in his archdiocese, particularly the Paulist Center and Jesuit Urban Center, which had reputations for innovative liturgies, resulting in disciplinary action in several instances. At the Paulist Center in 1986 the archdiocese objected to allowing a woman to preach the Good Friday homily, and in 1993 the Reverend Bill Larkin was rebuked for using inclusive language in conducting a baptism. At the Jesuit Urban Center, staff member Sister Jeanette Normandin was fired in 2000 for her role in a baptism in which she performed tasks reserved for priests (J. N., personal communication, September 12, 2005). Chapter 6 also cites the example of Blessed Sacrament Parish (a pseudonym) in suburban Boston where a Vatican II pastor was almost dismissed, possibly due to complaints of conservative members of the parish.

[10] Spies who were sufficiently resourceful could infiltrate at least some of these groups rather easily, because many have websites or are listed in the CTA church renewal directory. Brochures describing these communities consistently emphasize that they are open to all and welcome new members. However, it is obviously easier to remain anonymous when attending liturgies in a large parish, whereas attending a small community gathering might be awkward, especially if one were asked to offer explanations for one's presence.

Eucharist with bowed heads and attentive, solemn facial expressions. During liturgies, I never witnessed participants carrying on private conversations among each other or gazing around with bored, distracted looks. Only the largest of the five ECCs I observed had children (ages four to nine) present during the liturgy, and, perhaps coincidentally, the three children remained fairly quiet and subdued during the service. Although the communal atmosphere and attentive demeanor of members might impress church hierarchs, they would likely disapprove of some of the more rule-bending features of their liturgies, particularly given the new regulations on the form and language of the liturgy that have been imposed over the past decade.

The homily is the principal feature of these liturgies that deviates from the requirement that the priest must deliver the sermon (Hitchcock, 2000).[11] Only two of the five communities in this study restricted sermons to the priest-presider. A community I shall call Disciples of Jesus occasionally adopted a practice referred to as a *dialogue-homily* in which the priest sets the stage for the discussion by sharing a few of his own reflections, and then invites members of the community to respond. For example, at a 2004 Twelfth Night liturgy, members discussed their own troubled relationship to the institutional church. Several confessed that that they were uncertain to what extent they could "consider themselves Catholic." Others claimed that this community would be their only connection to Catholicism.[12]

Several communities rotate the responsibility for the homily among members on a volunteer basis. The quality of these "home-grown" lay homilies was excellent. I observed one rather stale and lackluster sermon, delivered in a rather didactic style with prosaic language to drive home the point that extravagant lifestyles were a form of greed that "robbed the poor of their share of the world's resources." In contrast, the other homilists delivered carefully crafted, highly articulate sermons in an engaging manner. A husband and wife delivered a sermon designed as a dramatic dialogue between the two of them, which in turn generated a discussion among the audience about the tensions and joys of family life in the contemporary world.

---

[11] Church rules state that the sermon may be "entrusted to a concelebrating priest, or in some cases a deacon," but "never by a lay person" (Hitchcock, 2000, n.p.)

[12] One year later this Twelfth Night liturgy discussion focused on the story of the magi, reflecting on the manner in which the story transcended barriers of race and class (as three kings from foreign tribes pay tribute to a child born in a stable), the mystery and majesty of the star, and the drama of the search itself.

Rule-Bending Practices of Boston ECCs

Priests in these communities occasionally delivered sermons on reform issues. For example, I observed one sermon by an ECC priest (Father Stan, a pseudonym) that was a not-so-subtle rebuke of the highly punitive directives of some church hierarchs. Stan named in particular Archbishop Raymond Burke of St. Louis, who threatened to forbid Communion to politicians that took pro-choice positions on abortion. Stan's sermon centered on the Gospel story of the Good Samaritan (Luke 10:25–37). In a tone of wry humor, Stan contrasted Archbishop Burke's authoritarian pronouncements with Jesus, who encouraged his listeners to think for themselves rather than offering pat answers. Stan asked his audience the same question posed by Jesus: "Which of the three followed the law in this story—the priest, the Levite, or the Samaritan who helped the man beaten by the robbers?" Stan's message resonated with his audience, who responded to the homily with sustained applause. Stan acknowledged the applause by holding out his open palms and in a humorous tone, exclaiming, "Applause is cheap, I want money, money!"

Ironically, one community (I shall refer to it as the Fatima Community) attracted persons from non-Catholic backgrounds, in part because they enjoyed a reputation as a nonjudgmental community that placed no litmus test on new members or restrictions on eligibility for the Eucharist. Shirley, a former Baptist, was drawn to Fatima where she could worship with her lesbian daughter and her partner and their two adopted children. (S. L., personal communication, July 11, 2004). On the day I attended services, Shirley could have easily passed for a lifelong Catholic as she carried oil and water decanters at the offertory, stopping very deliberately to reverently bow her head as she approached the altar. Molly, another regular at the Fatima community, was a middle-aged divorcée who developed deep bonds with the community after members showered her with support and attention following the death of her only son, who had died of AIDS several years earlier.[13]

All five of the communities had ties to reform groups, as announcements about CTA or Voice of the Faithful (VOTF) events were posted in their meeting places and literature. Several communities send at least

---

[13] Although Molly is strongly attached to this community, she refused an invitation to serve on the pastoral board because she had never been baptized Catholic, and she felt this disqualified her from serving in a leadership role (M. L., personal communication, July 11, 2004).

several members to attend VOTF or CTA conferences held in the Boston area and they occasionally invited reform group leaders[14] to give talks or lead retreats.[15]

Celebration of the Eucharist is another aspect of liturgy that involved nonstandard adaptations. In all of the liturgies I attended, the Communion service included both bread and wine, and, in all but one community, the entire congregation participated in the distribution of Communion. After the priest consecrated the hosts and wine, they were passed among members, each one saying, "the body of Christ" or "the blood of Christ" as they passed the basket of hosts and goblet to the person on their right or left, who replied "Amen," and served the next person in similar fashion.

On one occasion at an outdoor Mass sponsored by two communities, the presiding priest asked all those present (thirty-two people) to raise their outstretched palms and join him in saying the words of consecration. Participants dutifully raised their hands and most at least attempted to repeat the words of consecration, drawing on memory, as there were no printed texts of the Mass available. No one in the audience seemed the least bit shocked or put off by this practice, judging by the calm facial expressions, relaxed body language, and cooperative efforts to follow the priest's request.[16] Another community created a group process of consecrating the Eucharist, whereby several group members read statements from a program that complemented the words of consecration by the priest.

Challenges Facing Boston ECCs

In sum, all five communities described herein remain vital; they maintain a consistent core of members and an ongoing schedule of weekly or

---

[14] For example, one community scheduled a retreat with Edwina Gateley, founder of the Volunteer Missionary Movement and a noted Catholic author, who is a regular speaker at CTA conferences. The fact that Gateley had been censured in several dioceses did not deter this community from organizing this retreat. The Disciples of Jesus community received correspondence and occasional visits from a prominent Roman Catholic theologian, whose work had been recently censured by the Vatican. This theologian had served as a priest for this community for several years when he lived in Boston.

[15] All of these communities on an annual or biannual basis hold retreats that usually draw high turnouts of more than 50 percent of their members. These retreats are usually conducted at a retreat house under the direction of a formal retreat director.

[16] All five of these communities have a governance structure in the form of a pastoral council or steering committee that oversees the operations of the group. Fatima, the largest community, has the most formal structure with a board of twelve persons who serve

biweekly liturgies and, in varying degrees, serve as *resistance communities* where dissent from Vatican rules and teachings is permitted and condoned.[17] The rule-bending practices described above (including homilies delivered by laypersons and group participation in the consecration and delivery of the Eucharist[18]) are ones that may still occur in some Roman Catholic parishes.

I did uncover a number of problems common to these groups, most notably their lack of young members. Only two communities had attracted a few members under forty. Even adult children who had been raised in these communities chose to leave. Further, the relationship of the groups to the institutional church remained tenuous. In fact, the youngest spokesperson whom I interviewed bragged that she and other members of her community had severed all connection to the institutional church, except for her participation in this community, which met at a local Catholic monastery. The stability and rationale of these groups is threatened if they fail to identify any connection to the Roman Catholic tradition that forms their core identity. While each community does attract new members from time to time, they also lose members due to death, relocation, and other forms of attrition.

The Fatima community, the largest and fastest growing of the five groups, continues to attract new members from those parishes in Boston that were shuttered under the archdiocesan reconfiguration. In July 2007 the Fatima community lost several families with young children due to the lack of a religious education program. In response, Father Stan sent an e-mail to the community explaining that the community was unable to offer religious education, given that its meeting space had no separate area for classes and young children became restless after sitting through a one-hour liturgy.[19] This example indicates a downside of small ECCs that

---

rotating terms of three years. These five communities take up regular collections to cover their own expenses and to support charitable causes.

[17] On May 23, 2005, the Winchester, Massachusetts, VOTF chapter organized a forum that features spokespersons from eight ECCs in the Boston area, including several of the communities described above. All of these speakers described their communities in glowing terms, emphasizing the close bonds of community members, spirited liturgies, and flexible interpretations of Catholicism.

[18] The task of distributing Communion is generally restricted to priests and trained Eucharistic ministers. The consecration of the Eucharist is usually performed solely by the presiding priest(s). The USCCB's policies for distribution of Communion specifically forbid passing the chalice among parishioners (www.nccbuscc.org/liturgy/current/norms.shtml).

[19] Father Stan suggested the community might become more appealing to children by providing them liturgical roles such as greeters, musicians, participants in processions, and taking up collections (S. M. personal correspondence, July 2, 2000).

resemble sects, which often lack the resources and stability available in conventional parishes.

CELIBACY IS THE ISSUE (CITI) COMMUNITIES

The vignette at the beginning of the chapter highlights the organization CITI, whose website lists twenty-three Eucharistic Centered Communities (ECCs) across the United States, where resigned Roman Catholic priests (most of whom are married) preside at regularly scheduled liturgies.[20] Church hierarchs go to great lengths to undermine the legitimacy of married priests, describing their sacraments as "valid but illicit," since hierarchs take strong exception to CITI in particular and the resumption of a priestly role by resigned priests in general.[21] In an *LA Times* interview, Tod Tamberg, a spokesperson for the Archdiocese of Los Angeles, described CITI sacraments as "less-than-legitimate" (Tamberg as cited in Mehren, 2005, p. A1), and warned that Catholics who allow CITI priests to conduct marriages, baptisms, etc., may encounter "problems, even pain" in the future if they want these sacraments recognized by the church.

CITI communities meet in a variety of settings, including Protestant churches, private homes, and chapels in retirement centers and retreat centers. At a forum on ECCs, CITI priests described presiding at liturgies around their dining table with family and friends as well as in more formal settings. Some also serve as guest homilists and substitute ministers at a range of Protestant parishes. CITI priests are in highest demand to perform wedding services, and most charge a fee of roughly three hundred dollars, which includes a consultation and the wedding service itself.[22] CITI priests often charge no fee or accept voluntary donations for many services, such as funerals and Masses for SCCs.

---

[20] Several of these CITI communities are Dignity chapters (described in chapter 8) and several of them are communities where married priests share liturgical roles with Roman Catholic Womenpriests (RCWP), such as the Jesus Our Shepherd community in Nenno, Wisconsin, and the St. Mary of Magdala community in Harwich Port, Massachusetts (described in chapter 9).

[21] An example of church hierarchs' negative reaction to CITI is included later in this chapter under the section "The Movement against Parish Closures."

[22] CITI priests are popular among Catholics who do not meet the criteria for marriage in their local parish due to divorce, lax attendance at Mass, refusal to attend marriage preparation classes, and other factors. Some couples who no longer practice Catholicism chose to have a priest perform their wedding due to the preferences of their parents.

Future Prospects of CITI Ministries

Like VOTF, CITI has relied primarily on insider strategies because it hoped that, as married priests assume more liturgical roles, the Vatican would eventually relent and condone their ministry. CITI has not been any more successful than VOTF in its use of insider strategies. The Vatican shows no signs of softening the celibacy requirement, except in the case of conservative married priests who defect to Catholicism from other denominations. On the contrary, CORPUS has lost ground in its efforts to communicate with church officials over the celibacy question. Consequently, the most viable option for CITI priests would be to form and serve underground communities, which are not dependent on Vatican approval.[23]

WORSHIP COMMUNITIES OF CATHOLIC SISTERS

On several occasions I was approached by Catholic sisters who were eager to describe "underground" activity in their own convents or other locations. These sisters confided to me that sisters in their community were increasingly conducting their own priestless liturgies (including Eucharist). One sister (whom I will refer to as Phyllis) explained that this practice was increasing in her community because priests were often not available. Several sisters had recently died, and her community had been unable to find a priest willing to preside at funeral Masses. Consequently, her community in Pennsylvania conducted their own funeral liturgies. When I asked if the Eucharist had been consecrated by a priest prior to the service, Phyllis replied, "I don't know, no one asked. Even the elderly sisters, who tend to be conservative, did not raise any objections. The whole thing ran very smoothly." (P. G., personal communication, January 14, 2004).

Priestless Liturgies: A Preferred Option?

One sister explained that her community had become increasingly perturbed by the poor quality of funeral Masses conducted by many priests, who often "arrived late, seemed unprepared, and didn't know enough

---

[23] Like other reform groups, the membership of CITI is rapidly aging and few younger priests join CITI after resigning. Consequently, CITI may be short-lived.

about the deceased to say anything personal or meaningful about her life." She also admitted that the more feminist members of her community had objected "for some time" to rules restricting sacramental roles to male priests. All the sisters in her community shared discontent over "lifeless, hurried, impersonal" liturgies, although the situation was not universally dismal. Occasionally "capable, caring priests" would devote sufficient time and attention to their tasks, but the opposite pattern was becoming more frequent. Consequently, there was "almost a sense of relief" at the several recent priestless funerals, where sisters fashioned a liturgy they found to be a moving and appropriate tribute to their colleagues (P. G., personal communication, January 14, 2004).

I interviewed three sisters about these developments and engaged in informal conversations with scores more. In every case, the sisters emphasized "these sorts of things are becoming commonplace in many orders." One admitted, "We've been doing our own liturgies for decades, even before the priest shortage"[24] (J. L, personal communication, March 12, 2006). In some communities, sisters were crafting their own liturgies to mark special events such as anniversaries of the order. These sisters emphasized they still loved the Mass, but believed that their spiritual lives were enriched by different types of rituals. Some sisters consult with feminist theologians to develop liturgies with inclusive language that portray positive female images and feminist themes.

Ordinations of Catholic Sisters

Two independent bishops report that they have ordained Roman Catholic sisters or have corresponded with sisters who have been ordained by independent bishops. One bishop stated that "I personally know of two sisters from two different congregations who have been ordained by independent bishops, in one case with the full knowledge and tacit consent of her superiors" (J. P., personal communication, October 13, 2006). These sisters seek ordination for its own sake, and also as a means of claiming apostolic succession, which enables them to conduct "valid" sacraments.[25]

---

[24] Kaiser (2006) cites a similar development among sisters in the Philippines, where he interviewed Sister Mary John Mananzan, who said, "We don't call for priests to say mass for the community anymore. We celebrate our own community mass" (p. 161).

[25] Roman Catholic doctrine specifies that only ordained priests with authentic apostolic succession can perform valid sacraments. The issue of apostolic succession is covered more thoroughly in chapter 8.

Of course, the sisters who are ordained by independent bishops keep their status secret to avoid censure. In one instance, a sister who was ordained as a priest by an independent order left the convent for a period, but ultimately returned, because she missed her religious community (J. P., personal correspondence, October 13, 2006).

Repression of Catholic Sisters by the Vatican

The three sisters whom I interviewed admitted to being deeply concerned about the prospect of censure by church officials, as they consistently requested anonymity in their interviews and rejected my requests to tape-record them. On the one hand, they sought me out to share their stories with mischievous grins and impassioned, petulant tones of voice that conveyed their sense of intrigue and rebelliousness. On the other hand, their repeated requests for confidentiality revealed all too clearly their concern for retribution. Precisely because sisters are so vulnerable in the current situation, I have chosen not to attempt to document the extent or prevalence of priestless liturgies in convents.

In his revealing historical overview of American sisters, Briggs (2006) documents the extensive backlash launched by Pope John Paul II to thwart and reverse many of the progressive reforms in women's religious congregations as part of his campaign to reverse Vatican II reforms. Although the movement to reform women's congregations began even before Vatican II, the pace and scale of reforms accelerated after this watershed event. American sisters abandoned habits for secular forms of dress, embraced a range of career options and living arrangements, and adopted democratic forms of governance within their congregations. In response to pressures from the Vatican, American sisters remained steadfast in preserving these reforms, even refusing to accept the Vatican's attempt to change the name of their official organization, the Leadership Conference of Women Religious (LCWR) or to replace this organization with an alternative group controlled by the Vatican (Briggs, p. 187). Although some sisters have resisted Vatican control for some time, until recently these dissident sisters avoided media attention, which likely would have evoked a harsh response from the Vatican.

Briggs insists that the conservative crackdown on women's congregations contributed to the vast decline in vocations among American women, which dropped from a high of 185,000 in 1965 to a low of 69,963 in 2005. Briggs's final chapter is hauntingly entitled "Will Sisters Survive?"

Vatican Investigation Backfires

In February 2009, the Vatican announced plans to conduct a "doctrinal investigation" of the largest U.S. women religious organization, the LCWR (T. Fox, 2009a). In explaining the purpose of the investigation, William Joseph Cardinal Levada pointed to concerns about the extent to which American sisters promote church teachings on three important doctrines, namely, homosexuality, a male priesthood, and salvation for non-Catholics. Reportedly, the vast majority of U.S. women religious "did not comply with a request to answer all questions in a document of inquiry" (T. Fox, 2009d, p. 1) that made up this first phase of this study. For their part, the Catholic reform groups cited in part 1 have issued press releases and petitions decrying the investigation, including a resolution passed at the 2009 National CTA Conference (*Call to Action*, 2010).

In spite of, or perhaps in some measure because of this investigation, the fifty-five heads of women's religious orders and umbrella groups, including Marlene Weisenbeck, president of LCWR, took a bold step in publicly endorsing President Obama's health-care bill, which had been rejected by the United States Conference of Catholic Bishops (USCCB) (Boorstein, 2010). This stance demonstrates a newly emerging assertiveness by religious sisters, who, at least in this instance, were willing to take a public stance that contradicts the position of the bishops.[26]

By the end of 2010, the Vatican showed signs that it recognized their investigation of American sisters had backfired; it had evoked mistrust and dismay among broad sectors of American Catholics, including sisters and laypersons. In a candid interview, Archbishop Joseph Tobin, the Vatican's "No. 2 official for religious life," advised, "Rome must acknowledge the depth of anger and hurt" among American nuns in response to the visitation (Tobin as cited by J. Allen, 2010b, p. 5).[27] In an obvious

---

[26] Commenting on this divergence between Catholic bishops and Catholic sisters, journalist Kevin Eckstrom (2010) states, "This dispute [like the dispute over Obama's honorary degree from Notre Dame] has resurrected the fight over who can lay claim to the title 'Catholic,' and whether there can be principled disagreement on political questions." Thus, this controversy is at the center of the culture wars, since conservative Catholics oppose Obama due, in part, to his pro-choice stance, while liberal Catholics, including many religious sisters, praise Obama's policies for improving the well-being of disadvantaged persons.

[27] The term *nun* is used in the two *National Catholic Reporter* articles cited here, but I have used the term *sister* throughout this book because it accurately describes the vowed religious women whom I interviewed. The term *nun* refers to a "woman who leads a

attempt to quell these concerns, Tobin stated that "he does not expect any 'punitive fallout' from the visitation" (p. 5) and he committed himself to be a "strong advocate" to ensure that sisters will be allowed to engage in dialogue about the findings.

A Potential Feminist Uprising among Religious Sisters

If the Vatican imposes punitive policies on religious sisters, the Vatican risks alienating and possibly even provoking schism among some orders of American sisters, who could disband or form lay communities, or at a minimum engage a public and high-profile battle with the Vatican over control of their orders. According to Zagano (2010), American sisters could potentially attract widespread support among Catholic laypersons, particularly since sisters are on the front lines in their capacity as teachers, nurses, and counselors. Zagano also points to potential financial losses facing the Vatican if women's religious orders defect and claim their extensive property and financial holdings.[28]

Sisters have played a significant role in strengthening the American church for generations by providing low-cost labor and dedicated services in a vast range of roles. It is reasonable to conclude that church hierarchs can no longer take for granted the unquestioning obedience and subservience of American sisters. Feminist theologians from within religious orders have played central leadership roles in cultivating a feminist consciousness among Catholic women, especially those involved in the Catholic feminist organizations described in chapter 4. This feminist enculturation is reflected in the tilt in power relations between church hierarchs and Catholic sisters. By refusing to comply with the Vatican investigation and by taking a public stance contrary to that of the bishops, Catholic sisters demonstrate a bold and concerted form of noncooperation. According to Sharp's model (1973, 2005), loss of obedience from key players represents a potentially significant weakening of an institution's power.

---

contemplative life in a monastery which is usually cloistered (or enclosed) or semi-cloistered." The term *sister* is a "woman who does live, minister, and pray within the world." (anunslife.org/resources/sisterornun/ - Cached). Nuns and sisters take different types of vows.

[28] Phyllis Zagano (2010) notes, "U.S. women religious control huge properties and, in many cases, significant amounts of cash and security. They're not that thrilled with how they've been treated either" (p. 24).

The Movement Against Parish Closures

Beginning in August 2004, Boston's reputation as the "epicenter of the clergy sexual abuse crisis" (Guntzel, 2005, p. 13) was enhanced when a series of nine parishes defied the decision of Archbishop Sean O'Malley to close 83 of the 357 parishes in the archdiocese.[29] The archdiocese justified its decision to close parishes by pointing to budgetary shortfalls and shifting demographics of Boston-area Catholics that left many parishes without enough members to sustain themselves.

The outrage and criticism directed at the Boston archdiocese during the clergy abuse crisis seems to have had a spillover effect, mobilizing parishioners to question and ultimately challenge the archdiocesan reconfiguration plan. Initially, parishioners in nine Boston-area parishes slated for closure announced they would hold round-the-clock vigils in their churches to prevent the archdiocese from shuttering their parishes. These vigils were maintained by small groups of parishioners who occupied the parish in shifts on a twenty-four-hour basis so that the archdiocese could shut down and lock the parish buildings only by calling on police to arrest and remove vigilers. Vigiling groups were hopeful that the archdiocese would be responsive, if for no other reason than to avoid a showdown. Following the abuse scandal, the archdiocese did not need another crisis that would attract negative media attention and offend parishioners.

This anticlosure movement in Boston ultimately spread to other dioceses facing closure decrees, where parishioners began vigiling campaigns and filed civil and canon law challenges in civil and Vatican courts.[30] Many reform groups have lent support to this movement, especially FutureChurch,[31] which received two grants from Catholic foundations to

---

[29] Archbishop Sean O'Malley was installed as a cardinal in 2006. Throughout this book, the author describes O'Malley as an archbishop in the period before he was appointed cardinal and as cardinal thereafter.

[30] The FutureChurch website has a link (*Save our parish* communities) to a list of "Parishioner websites dealing with parish closures" that includes postings in the following states: three in Massachusetts, two in New Jersey, four in New York, four in Ohio, and two in Pennsylvania.

[31] FutureChurch describes itself as a "coalition of parish-based Catholics which works to preserve the Eucharist by advocating for ordination for all the baptized" (www.futurechurch.org). Chapter 5 describes FutureChurch's activities promoting women's issues within Roman Catholicism.

support its Save Our Parish Community project.[32] (Updated accounts of these anticlosure campaigns are chronicled on the FutureChurch website, www.futurechurch.org.) By 2008, fifteen parishes in Massachusetts and New York had filed canonical appeals in Vatican courts to prevent parish closures.

"Your Parish Is Not a McDonald's Franchise"

Groups involved in this anticlosure movement acknowledge that some parish closures may be warranted in cases of dwindling membership and growing deficits, but they oppose closures for "vibrant parishes" that have balanced budgets and stable or growing memberships.[33] As a FutureChurch slogan put it, "Your parish is not a McDonald's franchise" (*FutureChurch*, 2005), but rather "parish communities are the lifeblood of the Catholic Church and anything that damages their well-being is a threat to the body of Christ."[34]

The first vigil in Boston emerged almost spontaneously on August 29, 2004, when parishioners at St. Albert the Great Parish in suburban Weymouth decided to occupy the parish after the last Mass on the day it was slated for closure. When I visited St. Albert's, it struck me as a highly conventional parish. Most of the rather modest cars in the parking lot were decorated with bright yellow bumper stickers emblazoned with the slogan "Keep St. Albert's Open." When I arrived before the liturgy on Sunday morning, the church was about half-full of middle-aged and elderly parishioners who were engaged in a group recitation of the rosary. Despite its conventional atmosphere, there were several characteristics of St. Albert's that observers believe marked it for closure, namely, it was the home of an active VOTF chapter and its pastor, the Reverend Ron Coyne, was an outspoken liberal who in 2002 had signed the now-famous petition demanding Cardinal Law's resignation (English, 2004).

---

[32] This project includes publications such as a *Crisis Kit for Parishes*, with advice for parishioners facing closure, and a petition endorsed by many reform groups, aimed at preserving vibrant parishes (FutureChurch, 2006).

[33] Boston vigilers drove home this message in 2005 by purchasing space on billboards near archdiocesan headquarters. The billboards depicted a blue sky dotted with clouds emblazoned with a "commandment-like" message, seemingly heaven–sent, that read, "Do Not Close Vibrant Parishes."

[34] FutureChurch (2005) insists that "the most fundamental right of a parish in canon law is the right to come into existence, be acknowledged and continue in existence"

Accomplishments of the Vigiling Movement in Boston

Ultimately, a total of twelve Boston-area parishes facing closure decrees engaged in vigils for varying periods. The vigiling movement can claim some successes as follows. First, due to discontent over the reconfiguration process, Archbishop O'Malley appointed an external review committee, and their recommendations convinced O'Malley to reverse "roughly one-quarter of his 83 suppression decrees" (Guntzel, 2005, p. 13).[35] Second, vigilers added their voices to those of other reform groups demanding financial transparency, which VOTF leaders claim convinced O'Malley's to open archdiocesan books in 2005. Third, due to the contagion effect of the Boston vigils, campaigns against parish closures spread to other dioceses.[36]

Embodying the Reform Movement slogan "We are the Church," many vigilers took responsibility to run their own parishes by holding Sunday services, conducting religious education programs, and sponsoring a range of events usually supervised by clergy. Vigilers also described the experience of engaging in round-the-clock vigils as uplifting, due to the strong communities that emerged among vigiling groups.[37] According to Thomas Groome, a Boston College theologian, the Boston vigils were the longest lasting in the history of the American Roman Catholic Church, commenting, "It is amazing they have kept it up" for more than one thousand days (Groome as cited in McCabe, 2007, p, B2).

Vigiling Movement Reflects Conservative-Liberal Divide

The Council of Vigiling Parishes (CoP) and the vigiling groups in each parish reflect a range of Catholics who often differed on questions of insider versus outsider strategies and their loyalty to the institutional church.

(c. 374.1), and that "to be suppressed the impossibility of continued life must be clearly demonstrated." FutureChurch further claims canon law does not allow churches to be closed due to a priest shortage, but rather recommends group "liturgies of the word and group prayer in the absence of priests."

[35] Reversing closure decrees resulted in a variety of outcomes: one parish was converted to a chapel, others were merged, and the fate of others remains ambiguous (as decisions were postponed).

[36] Appeals against parish closures were filed in the following locations outside Boston: two in Buffalo, New York, one in Syracuse, New York, and two in New York City (*Parishioners nationwide appeal,* 2008).

[37] After St. Albert's was reopened, parishioners announced they would conduct brief vigils every year to commemorate their vigil and renew their communal bonds.

For example, the two cochairs of CoP, Cynthia Deysher of St. Anselm's in Sudbury and Peter Borre of St. Catherine of Siena's in Charlestown, reflected the two extremes of the movement. Both Peter and Cynthia were business executives and dedicated leaders, but their personalities and orientation offered a sharp contrast. At the four CoP meetings I attended in 2005, Cynthia played a conciliatory role and, during press interviews, often complimented the cardinal for positive gestures. In contrast, Borre exhibited an aggressive stance, frequently adopting militant-sounding slogans, for example by declaring that the movement must decide to "follow Martin Luther" (by leaving the church) "or follow Martin Luther King" (by engaging in nonviolent resistance).[38] Referring to the Boston archdiocese, he quipped, "Is this Boston or Baghdad?" (comparing church hierarchs to the archenemy of the United States, Saddam Hussein).[39]

Better Strident than Silent

At a January 15, 2005, CoP meeting a member from St. Bernard's wondered aloud if she was "a bit too strident" during a recent meeting with the archbishop. Another CoP member responded, "Better strident than silent," which evoked sustained applause from the entire group. At the same meeting, a middle-aged man from St. Bernard's reported that the archbishop had advised them that "it would be easier to deal with you without the vigil," which again evoked enthusiastic applause from several persons who ridiculed this suggestion. One member remarked, "Yeah, and then you'd be closed, and that would be the end of it." At this same meeting several members would occasionally question (as one vigiler put it) "whether we can believe anything the archdiocese tells us given how often we have been misled."

One big controversy among CoP members was whether to approve hiring married priests from CITI Rent-A-Priest (described above) to conduct

---

[38] Borre's slogan asking vigilers to follow either Martin Luther or Martin Luther King poses the choice of forming a sect versus remaining in the church. The implication of church-sect theory for the vigiling movement is discussed below.

[39] Borre met with sharp criticism from some of CoP's more conservative members because he provided "contraband Eucharist" to vigiling groups (meaning that he found priests willing to consecrate hosts in advance, which Borre delivered to vigiling groups). Conservatives also criticized Borre for putting some vigiling churches in contact with Rent-A-Priest, which offered the services of married priests. Conservatives feared Borre would evoke negative reactions from church officials because these actions violated archdiocesan policies.

masses for vigiling groups when the archdiocese denied their request for priests. This question came to a head in 2005 when CoP members from closed parishes in Natick and Quincy announced plans to have married CITI priests preside at Easter Mass. The Boston archdiocese condemned this action as "schismatic," and hastily agreed to provide a diocesan priest for the Quincy group, after meeting with their representatives at a last-minute meeting at 10:30 p.m. on Holy Thursday (Paulson, 2005a).[40]

This whole flap over married priests received extensive media coverage, particularly the Natick group whose request for a diocesan priest was denied. They went ahead with plans for a dramatic outdoor Easter Mass on March 27, 2005, which was presided over by two CITI priests in a park near its closed parish. It received massive coverage by local newspapers and television stations. Following this controversy, the small cores of vigilers in several shuttered parishes continued to debate strategies, with the more liberal members suggesting the formation of an independent parish, while slight majorities opposed any action that would threaten the preservation of their parish (L. H., personal communication, February 15, 2005).[41]

Who's Minding the Store?

The protest movement that emerged in the wake of parish closure decrees revealed many errors in communication and decision making on the part of church hierarchs, particularly in Boston. These management shortcomings suggest that insider strategies were hindered not only by the rigid conservatism of church leaders but also by their lack of understanding of public relations and community building, perhaps because they had been previously sheltered from public scrutiny.

Archbishop O'Malley's awkwardness in handling conflict was evident in his confession that the dissent and turmoil over his reconfiguration

---

[40] Although the Quincy group was reluctant to cancel their invitation to the CITI priest, they ultimately agreed to O'Malley's offer, upon the advice of CITI's Louise Haggett, who warned that canon law only allowed for married priests when diocesan priests were unavailable (L. H., personal communication, March 16, 2005).

[41] A vivid example of the magnetizing power that church hierarchs wield over at least some laity is revealed in the following remarks of Sean Patrick Glennon from the Quincy parish following his meeting with the archbishop: "It was a profound experience because I believe Archbishop O'Malley is probably the closest person to the pope I'll ever meet, and I was extremely grateful that he took the time to meet with me personally" (Glennon as cited in Paulson, 2005a, B6).

plan evoked great personal anguish, admitting to a *Boston Globe* reporter that "at times I ask God to call me home and let someone else finish this job, but I keep waking up to face another day of reconfiguration" (O'Malley as cited by Paulson, 2004, A1). Before the abuse crisis such a plea by an archbishop might have evoked shame and empathy, but when I interviewed vigilers at St. Anselm's parish about the remark, one vigiler quipped, "We're not falling for that Catholic guilt trip" (S. B., personal communication, November 17, 2004). Several other vigilers responded that they knew from their experience in executive positions that conflict and complaints "come with the territory" (a phrase used by two vigilers) and should not evoke surprise or defensiveness on the part of the archbishop. (G. S., personal communication, February, 23, 2005).[42]

Another indication of poor communication is the fact that an organization as highly centralized as the Roman Catholic Church failed to present consistent rationales for its decisions, thus adding to the mistrust generated by the abuse and closure crises. Most important, O'Malley originally explicitly denied that revenues from closures would be used to finance abuse settlements (Belluck, 2004).[43] However, the Vatican Supreme Court later cited abuse settlements as a reason to justify parish closures (Paulson, 2008d).

Another contradiction centers on the decision of "a subset of bishops and cardinals who sit on the Vatican's highest court, the Apostolic Signatura," which in June 2008 rejected an appeal filed by eight groups of Boston-area parishioners (Paulson, 2008d, B4). This ruling criticized parishioners appealing closure for "focusing on their own concerns, rather than those of the archdiocese as a whole" (p. B4). This argument incensed many vigilers. Susan Hurley, a leader of the vigil at St. James the Great in Wellesley, Massachusetts, emphasized the failure of hierarchs to create an honest and collaborative process, noting, "With the Archdiocese it's a matter of: 'We mismanaged the money you gave us, we moved and promoted priests who should not have been allowed with children, and now

---

[42] Ironically, seven years after the crisis, Cardinal O'Malley is cited by journalist Jason Berry (2009) for his exemplary handling of the vigiling crisis, noting that "his restraint toward the vigiling movement ... might be a model for other bishops confronting parishioners who sit rather than vacate" (p. A13). Berry contrasts O'Malley's restraint with the recent missteps of Archbishop Alfred Hughes in New Orleans, who evoked outrage by ordering raids on two vigiling churches in which police bashed in a door and arrested vigilers. However, as documented above, O'Malley's restraint emerged only in response to negative media reaction evoked by his own mishandling of closure decrees.

[43] O'Malley claims that abuse settlements would be funded by insurance settlements, sale of the chancery, and other funds not related to parish closures.

we're asking you to pay even further by giving us your churches'" (Hurley as cited by Guntzel, 2005, p. 14). Thus, from the standpoint of vigilers, the church hierarchs were focused "on their own concerns," and were willing to sacrifice their parish communities in the process.[44]

Finally, the theme of community is regarded as a hallmark of the Catholic tradition, (Groome, 2002).[45] However, church officials in Boston designed a reconfiguration process that undermined community by organizing clusters of parishes in geographic regions, which would then recommend the most appropriate parish or parishes within their cluster for closure. This process undermined community for the following reasons:

1. Closure disrupts long-standing communal bonds. Asking a group of parishioners to decide which parish should be closed is like asking a group of employees to decide who among them should be laid off. These decisions were painful for all concerned and, not surprisingly, evoked resentment and misunderstanding.
2. Closure decrees were secretive. The archdiocese refused to explain or justify why or how parishes were selected for closure. Although the clusters were probably designed to solicit lay input, they heightened mistrust and resentment. Many vigilers believed the outcome was based on favoritism, the market value of parish property, and retribution against outspoken pastors.
3. Adding fuel to the fire, parishioners from shuttered parishes were directed to join nearby "welcoming parishes." Parishioners described these parishes as "anything but welcoming" because they often were unable or unwilling to accommodate new arrivals in religious education and other programs. This outcome intensified the disruption and sense of loss for those whose community had dispersed.

---

[44] Other contradictions included the fact that O'Malley claimed the archdiocese owned all parish funds and property, but lawyers representing other dioceses claimed parish property was not owned by the chancery in order to protect it from creditors (Guntzel, 2005). In August 2005, the Vatican ruled that "Boston erred in claiming the financial assets of closing parishes," and these parishes are now required to voluntarily transfer assets from shuttered parish (Paulson, 2005d).

[45] Groome (2002) identifies three overlapping features of Christian communities that "are called to be catholic": They "(1) welcome and extend care to all people; (2) affirm the integrity of each local church and the communion of all particular churches into a universal whole; and (3) maintain unity as reconciled diversity—not through uniformity" (p. 249). By these criteria, one could argue that the struggle to preserve parishes is a struggle to express one's catholicity.

In 2008 Cardinal O'Malley revealed that the archdiocese was spending $880,000 annually to maintain closed parishes until the appeal process was exhausted (Paulson, 2008a). Some might speculate that O'Malley's patience and generosity in waiting out the appeals process is a public relations tactic, while others might interpret it as a heartfelt recognition of parishioners' rights to due process.[46]

Relative Merits of Insider-Outsider Strategies

One would be hard-pressed to make the case that insider strategies resulted in CoP's modest victories. At the beginning of the anticlosure movement, Archbishop Sean O'Malley refused to even meet with vigiling groups, and letters and phone calls requesting meetings and information were usually not even acknowledged. One of the first concessions they obtained from the lay review board was an agreement that their letters to the archdiocese would receive the courtesy of a reply (G. L, personal communication, June 12, 2005). The archdiocese's failure to honor this agreement was a source of complaint at CoP meetings. When O'Malley began meeting with vigiling groups in 2005, vigilers described these meetings as tense and uncomfortable.[47]

The vigiling movement attracted a range of Catholics, including some conservative and moderate parishioners who were not interested in issues of the "culture wars" but had strong ties to their local parish. The issue that created the strongest unity among CoP activists was their outrage over what they perceived as strong-arm tactics of archdiocesan officials, who initially planned to close their beloved parishes without a word of explanation or justification. By shutting down opportunities for insider reform, archdiocesan officials strengthened the resolve of vigilers to launch and sustain a vigorous outsider campaign to save their parishes.

Outsider strategies created a public relations nightmare for the archdiocese. Vigilers received press coverage on radio, television, and print

---

[46] Vigilers at St. Jeremiah's in Framingham were disappointed that O'Malley assigned an Eastern Rite Catholic Community to worship at their parish without their consent or input. Although the archdiocese cites this development as "testament to improved relationships," vigilers "denounced what they said was a lack of consultation, though they welcomed the new community" (Paulson, 2008c, B1).

[47] For example, the Weymouth group berated O'Malley for his treatment of his priests (especially their pastor Ron Coyne) and, on one occasion, a representative from the St. James Parish in Wellesley described engaging in a "shouting match" with O'Malley over the relative merits of her parish and those of poor Catholics in the inner city.

media in the Boston area and beyond. The photo-ops of elderly parishioners and families with children camping out in their churches evoked considerable public sympathy. Neighboring non-Catholic churches and businesses would drop by with food and words of moral support.

Two incidents in particular evoked considerable public outrage and negative publicity for the archdiocese. First, when two parishioners at Natick's Sacred Heart Parish decided to begin their vigil on Christmas Eve 2004, their pastor called the police, who escorted the vigilers out of the parish.[48] The insensitivity of arresting parishioners on Christmas Eve evoked rebukes from reform groups and a *National Catholic Reporter* editorial (*Time for a Few*, 2005).

A second controversy erupted on June 10, 2005, when Archbishop O'Malley shut down Our Lady of Presentation School in Brighton several days before it was scheduled to close. This was done to prevent a rumored vigil by parents opposed to the decision to close the school. Teachers and students were denied access to their belongings, including certificates and mementos for the end of year celebrations. Outraged parents and teachers responded by holding a preschool graduation ceremony in the traffic circle outside the school. Boston Mayor Tom Menino provided a historic downtown building for the older children's graduation ceremony. These events evoked scathing criticism from journalists and politicians, including Mayor Menino, who called O'Malley's action "reprehensible, unconscionable" and "a heartbreaking insult" (Menino as cited by Paulson, 2005b, B4).[49] Father Bryan Hehir, president of Catholic Charities, who served as an advisor to O'Malley during this period, acknowledged that the negative fallout from the Presentation School fiasco was "horrendous because it tended to reinforce a lot of fears and attitudes and there was anger at a new level" (Hehir as cited in Paulson, 2005b, B1).

---

[48] At a CoP meeting, Peter Borre, cochair of CoP explained that he joined the two Sacred Heart parishioners at the beginning of their vigil, but left later in the evening, confident that the archdiocese would never arrest vigilers on Christmas Eve. The two vigilers were transported to police headquarters but released when the archdiocese dropped charges. Police were called in this instance because the pastor received approval to call the police from the archdiocese. At many of the vigiling churches, pastors were supportive of the vigilers and did not take action to prevent vigils.

[49] The *Boston Globe* weighed in with its own editorial, describing the incident as a "new chapter in clerical clumsiness for the Archdiocese" and commenting that Archbishop O'Malley "should have been able to find a way to broker a deal" that would have allowed the graduation ceremonies to take place (*Tussle at Brighton*, 2005, A18).

Consequently, advisors convinced O'Malley to assert control over closure decisions rather than delegating them to subordinates.[50]

In October 2006, in a move that was clearly designed to promote goodwill, Cardinal O'Malley sold the Brighton school to a citizen group, voluntarily dropping the asking price from two to one million dollars (Colbert, 2006b).[51] Clearly, the Boston archdiocese has honed its public relations skills and is taking constructive steps toward polishing its image, which was besmirched by the abuse crisis and its mishandling of closure decrees.

The outsider strategies of vigils and canon law appeals strengthened the leverage and visibility of insider reform groups, especially VOTF and FutureChurch. Concomitantly, the vigiling movement generated new energy and new networks of activists, who were spurred to action by loss of their parish community. Some vigilers eventually joined reform groups or attended their meetings and read their literature. CoP meetings included many testimonials by vigilers who expressed a growing willingness to challenge church hierarchs. Sharon Harrington, an attorney and CoP activist, often remarked, "Even if we lose, our relationship with the Boston archdiocese is unalterably changed."

Most probably, the high visibility and widespread public support enjoyed by vigiling groups in Boston had a restraining effect on bishops in other dioceses, who may have scaled back some closure decrees in order to ward off or end vigils. Dioceses outside Boston probably have become more willing to communicate and possibly even negotiate with parishioners in affected parishes, recognizing that the Boston archdiocese's secrecy and lack of dialogue heightened anger over parish closures.

Future Options for Shuttered Parish Communities

As this juncture, reformers have little to show for their remarkable vigiling campaign. On May 7, 2010, the Vatican rejected appeals from ten closed

---

[50] As noted in chapter 6, members of reform groups claimed that, for several years after Archbishop O'Malley replaced Cardinal Law, he delegated much of his authority to subordinates who had been appointed by Cardinal Law. Reformers frequently insisted, "The Boston Archdiocese is still being run by Cardinal Law."

[51] This agreement stipulated the building could not be used as an elementary school because it might draw students from a nearby Catholic school. O'Malley was lauded for his role in the agreement, and Tom O'Brien, a parent from the school and member of the foundation board, called the agreement "a seminal moment" (O'Brien as cited in Colbert, p. 8) for improving community relation with the Boston archdiocese.

parishes to the full board of the Apostolic Signatura, so that they had exhausted all legal recourse through Vatican courts. Nonetheless, CoP announced that parishioners would continue their fight to preserve their parishes and were considering filing a federal lawsuit as well as other strategies, including maintaining vigils that had persisted for more than five years (Lavoie, 2010).[52] Jon Rogers, a leader of the vigiling St. Frances X. Cabrini, in Scituate, Massachusetts, proclaimed, "We're ready to schism, if it comes to that" (Rogers as cited in Spitz, 2010, p. A8).[53] Although the St. Frances community is remarkably determined and resourceful, it remains unclear how many, if any, of the vigiling communities will survive, given that the archdiocese has announced its plans to move forward on closures. Interestingly, a spokesperson for the archdiocese, Terrence C. Donilon, predicted a peaceful resolution to the closure movement, declaring, "Our hope is through continued respect and mutual dialogue, they [vigiling groups] will respect the decisions that have been affirmed by the Vatican (Donilon as cited by Wangsness, 2011, p. B8). However, CoP members no doubt recall that dialogue with hierarchs became available only in response to their vigiling campaign.

FutureChurch (2010a) reports on successful anticlosure campaigns outside Boston, which include the Immaculate Conception Roman Catholic Parish in Springfield, Massachusetts, and the San Martin de Porres Mission in Dayton, Oregon. Another notable victory occurred in 2011 when the Vatican Congregation for the Clergy ruled that bishops had not adequately justified their decision to sell twelve parish buildings in several dioceses (Filteau, 2011). Parishioners from these reprieved parishes are hopeful their parishes will now reopen, but the Vatican ruling only requires preserving church buildings. Bishops have the right to appeal the decision and retain considerable discretion over implementation (Lavoie & Lindsay, 2011).[54]

Although St. Peter's Parish in Cleveland, Ohio, has been shuttered, parishioners chose to preserve their parish community by forming a nonprofit organization and leasing a new rental space. Their former pastor

---

[52] CoP also lost its appeal to Pope Benedict XVI, who responded to their letter requesting reconsideration by rejecting the request but offering prayers on their behalf (Wangsness, 2010, B8).

[53] Remarkably, the staying power of Rogers's parish is attested to by its claim that it attracted "some 1,000 people to lay-led services during the 2010 Christmas weekend, despite or possibly because of the negative decision from the Vatican.

[54] The decision required the churches to be reopened but did not require their status as a parish would be restored.

Father Bob Marrone agreed to serve as their pastor and the new organization celebrated their first Mass on August 15, 2010. Although Marrone regards this move as "an act of disobedience, not a schism," he acknowledges that the bishop would probably describe his community as schismatic (Marrone as cited by O'Malley, 2010). Parishioners defend their decision by citing Cleveland Bishop Richard Lennon's advice to preserve their community following closure. Bishop Lennon has not attempted to suppress their new community, although he advised them that "their salvation was in jeopardy if they conducted worship services outside a sanctioned church" (Lennon as cited by O'Malley, 2010).

The Potential Impact of the Vigiling Movement

Although the vigiling movement has salvaged some parishes, these victories are highly fragile because parishioners have not gained any significant reforms in church structures or canon law that would prevent future parish closures, including parishes that escaped closure due to vigiling campaigns. In Boston several parishes that were allowed to remain open describe their newly assigned pastors as less liberal than previous pastors, and, consequently, the character and ambience of the parish has changed.

The option of forming independent parishes is increasingly being considered by vigiling groups. Some vigilers are familiar with the story of St. Bridget in Indianapolis, Indiana, which became an independent parish in 2000 following an unsuccessful anticlosure campaign. Boston vigilers have attended liturgies in independent parishes and others participated in forming the Holy Spirit Community now affiliated with ECC. St. Peter's Community in Cleveland has formed an independent community and the St. Frances X. Cabrini Parish in Massachusetts is considering schism. Hence, while this movement began as an insider movement, some of its groups have already adopted a sect-like status, and more parishes may consider schism when closure is imminent.

Many sources have predicted that large-scale closures will continue in dioceses throughout the United States, given ongoing demographic shifts in the Catholic population and financial difficulties in many dioceses resulting from abuse settlements, the economic recession, and defections of disaffected Catholics. Bishops in these dioceses will probably avoid some of the mismanagement that occurred in Boston, which was widely covered in Catholic publications. Nonetheless, the vigiling movement provides dramatic evidence that many Catholics retain deep ties to their parish, and therefore closure decrees may remain an ongoing source of conflict in the years ahead, especially if parishioners in targeted parishes join the anticlosure movement.

A Middle Path Between Church and Sect

My study outlines a range of options whereby liberal Catholics carved out a middle path in the dialectic tension of church and sect by creating marginal communities that avoid the type of repression prevalent in many Vatican II parishes. These communities remain within the boundaries of the institutional church, but increasingly indicate a willingness to engage in public struggles over control of their communities and religious orders. However, these communities remain fragile because of their aging population, the danger of burnout among the small cadre of volunteers who organize these groups, and their vulnerability to crackdowns by conservative bishops. By choosing a middle path between church and sect these communities face hard choices, given that their status within the church is endangered by their defiant behavior, but they cannot claim the autonomy of a sect.[55] Some shuttered parishes may follow the lead of St. Peter's Community in Cleveland by forming independent communities. However, the tradeoffs involved in this choice have received little attention by the groups involved.

This chapter has revealed more examples of backlash, especially among sisters who refused to comply with the Vatican's investigation and the anticlosure movement that mobilized to preserve parishes. Other examples of backlash were included in chapter 6, in which the parishes of Corpus Christi and St. Stanislaus chose schism rather than accept Vatican directives. Hence, my analysis demonstrates Gene Sharp's (1973) basic premise that leaders are dependent on the support of their followers, and the credibility and viability of organizations diminish when members withdraw their support.

My analysis also confirms the superior effectiveness of outsider strategies. The example of the Vatican investigation of American sisters suggests the possibility of defection by some religious orders, which could

---

[55] In the case of CITI communities, these tensions are less pronounced because they have no formal connection to or dependence on the Vatican. Nonetheless, they could be subjected to excommunication decrees. In the case of St. Peter's community in Cleveland, they have formed an autonomous community but have not yet been subjected to excommunication or other penalties. Hence, they remain "marginal" rather than "underground."

result in financial losses to the Vatican and the American Catholic Church. Similarly, widespread defections by American laity might translate into substantial loss of revenue. MSNBC reporter Steve Johnson (2005) estimates that eighty million American Catholics make up only 6 percent of Catholics worldwide but contribute "as much as a third of the Vatican's annual fund-raising for the pontiff's charities" and donated "$20 million per annum in recent years to the Vatican's general revenues." Despite Pope Benedict's preference for a "smaller, purer" church, he may be forced to make some concessions to protect the church's financial security if Americans substantially decrease donations.

The well-educated liberal Catholics who make up the Reform Movement are the Catholics most likely to abandon the church or withdraw contributions, since their views are increasingly out of step with the conservative drift of the Vatican. If marginal and underground communities attract a substantial number of liberal Catholics, their growing numbers (and the concomitant loss of contributions to the Roman Church) might convince the Vatican to compromise in some areas. Once again, outsider strategies are more effective than insider ones. Liberal reformers can exert more meaningful pressure on the Vatican by defecting than by working for reform from within.

PART THREE

NOTES FROM THE UNDERGROUND

CHAPTER EIGHT

THE CATACOMBS REVISITED
UNDERGROUND CATHOLIC FAITH COMMUNITIES

Sheila Durkin Dierks has experimented with the entire range of resistance communities outlined in this book in her journey from conventional Catholic to ordained deacon and later priest in her Light of Christ parish, which is affiliated with the independent Ecumenical Catholic Communion (ECC). Dierks (2008b) described her ordination on March 14, 2008, in an article entitled "When Grandmothers Get Ordained." Reveling in her unconventional status as a sixty-four-year-old female seminarian, Dierks wonders if Roman Catholic seminarians prepare for their ordinations as she did by designing their own ceremonies and planning meals and housing for friends and family. Dierks explains that ECC Bishop Peter Hickman, as presider at her ordination, was simply affirming "what had already been accomplished ... when the community publicly, in one voice calls me forth, and says they believe I am ready to be diakonos to them" (p. 19).

Dierks shares many background characteristics with members of Catholic reform groups: she has twelve years of Catholic education and a long history of service and leadership roles in a range of Catholic agencies, including serving on the liturgical commission and teaching theology in a Catholic school in the Kansas City-St. Joseph diocese.

Through her participation in Catholic feminist groups, including Women's Ordination Conference (WOC) and Women-Church Convergence (W-CC), Dierks (1997) gained an in-depth understanding of the unequal status of Roman Catholic women and the extent to which the institutional church was (in her words) "an impediment to spiritual maturity, as it often seems to encourage infantilism in adults, especially female ones" (p. 18). Consequently, Dierks formed several feminist Eucharistic communities and in 1997 authored *WomenEucharist,* a study of one hundred such communities.

Dierks (2008b) remains involved in two WomenEucharist communities but has found her spiritual home in the Light of Christ community, which she describes "as humble and hopeful a community as I have had the pleasure to know" (p. 19). In this community Dierks can reimagine Catholicism amidst a community of fellow seekers. She explains that "ordination within such a Communion is blessedly full of the old-into-new" (p. 20).

Dierks recently earned a graduate degree from the Iliff School of Theology and has coauthored her fourth book, *Eucharist Prayers for Inclusive Communities (Volume II): Possibilities for the Liturgical Year* (2008a), which offers "liturgies to celebrate the liturgy of life with everyone and everything" (*About Us, Woven Word,* 2008).

Chapter Eight

Choosing a Schismatic Path

The worship communities described in this and the next chapter are "underground" because they operate without the approval or support of the Roman Catholic Church. and have relatively low visibility to Roman Catholics outside the confines of the Reform Movement. In most instances, their low visibility simply reflects their small size and marginal status. Precisely because these underground communities are not part of the institutional church, most of them are not secretive and not concerned about retribution from church officials.[1]

By severing or not claiming affiliation with the institutional church, underground communities are more sect-like than the advocacy groups or marginal communities described in earlier chapters. Nevertheless, these underground communities only partially match the criteria of sects proposed by Weber-Troeltsch.[2] Consistent with Weber-Troeltsch, these communities are part of a revivalist movement within Roman Catholicism, have voluntary membership, and have chosen a schismatic path. To some extent, underground communities evidence the conversion experience characteristic of sects, in that persons attracted to underground communities have gradually replaced conventional religious beliefs with a liberal theological orientation.

In sharp contrast to Troeltsch's concept of sect, however, these communities do not impose exclusive attitudes and structures or standards of "ethical austerity." On the contrary, these communities are less demanding and conformist than a conventional Catholic parish, particularly since they allow members to determine their own beliefs and contributions in terms of time and money.[3] Founders of these communities favor informal structures and promote experimental and individualistic approaches to religion by introducing a smorgasbord of liberal theologies and forms of

---

[1] The fourth group of communities in this chapter, the Diaspora of Resigned Sisters and Priests, includes some members that prefer to operate in secret because they remain active in Roman Catholic parishes and are concerned about retribution.

[2] Weber-Troeltsch define sects as characterized by (in abbreviated form) (1) separation from general society, (2) exclusivity in attitude and social structure, (3) emphasis on prior conversion, (4) voluntary membership, (5) "spirit of regeneration," and (6) "attitude of ethical austerity" (O'Dea as cited in Stark & Bainbridge, 1981, p. 21). The applicability of the church-sect dichotomy to my research is discussed in the introduction.

[3] These communities depend on contributions, but many do not collect donations during services and do not impose formulas for the amount of contributions expected of members. Most communities do not recite the Apostles' Creed or amend it to reflect their theological orientation.

spiritual practice that sometimes include sources from non-Catholic denominations and non-Christian religious traditions.[4]

Debates over Apostolic Succession and Eucharist

One issue that evokes some controversy within the Reform Movement is the question of the validity of Eucharistic services if the presiding priest is not Roman Catholic. Catholic social teachings specify that valid consecration of the Eucharist requires a priest with apostolic succession, which refers to the belief that "each validly ordained bishop can trace his episcopal consecration in an unbroken line to one of the original apostles or to the apostles collectively" (McBrien, R. 2008).[5] Only priests with apostolic succession can transform the Eucharist bread and wine into the real body and blood of Christ. This process is referred to as *transubstantiation* (Von Lehmen, 2010).[6]

Catholic dogma regarding the validity of Eucharistic services did not prevent underground groups from deliberately forming schismatic communities, in part because they had developed a high degree of skepticism toward threats from church officials.[7] Moreover, most of the priests who minister to the underground communities and parishes in this study claim apostolic succession because the bishop who ordained them has a valid claim to apostolic succession.[8]

---

[4] Both the introduction and the conclusion explore in more depth the extent to which underground communities and the Reform Movement as a whole correspond to the definition of "sect."

[5] Notre Dame theologian Richard McBrien (2008) cites numerous Catholic scholars who reject the belief that bishops can trace their ordination back to the apostles. However, McBrien states that "to say that the church is 'apostolic' means that it continues to be faithful to the word, worship, witness and service of the apostles."

[6] Father Jeffrey D. Von Lehman explains that the "real presence of Jesus in the Eucharist" is important to Catholics because "Jesus in the Eucharist wants to be present to us and is deeply present to us in love and in compassion. Only when we begin to understand the Eucharist as a time when Jesus is not distant, but close; not aloof, but very intimate; not above us, but profoundly near us; not judging us, but compassionate toward us, will we truly be able to relate this teaching to the Church in our faith and devotion" (p. 4).

[7] Due to the fact that church officials do not condone any of the underground communities in this study, they cannot employ the services of Roman Catholic priests who have not resigned or been expelled.

[8] Several of the underground churches in chapter 9 are affiliated with the Old Catholic Church and other independent orders, which are recognized by the Vatican as having apostolic succession. Roman Catholic Womenpriests (RCWP) demonstrates the complexities involved in this issue because their bishops were secretly ordained by Roman Catholic

The Reform Movement would prefer to avoid debates over apostolic succession and "the real presence of Jesus in the Eucharist." My conclusion is based on the fact that I have never heard these issues discussed at reform gatherings or in literature of reform groups. The question of the "real presence" is one that does not lend itself to empirical research, given that a scientific investigation of the contents of the Eucharist would be controversial, to put it mildly. Furthermore, church teachings emphasize the mysterious nature of the Eucharist, which involves a spiritual dimension not accessible to empirical research.

Reformers avoid this issue because they do not want to offend Catholics who cherish traditional teachings regarding the Eucharist. Reform groups have little to gain by stirring up controversy over these questions, in contrast to debates over contraception, celibacy, homosexuality, and women's ordination, which have more concrete consequences for people's lives. Reformers can cite scientific research and historical precedents to challenge church teachings on these issues of the "culture wars," while debates over the Eucharist do not lend themselves to rational analysis.

Catholics highly value the Eucharist. Liberal Catholics often defend their allegiance to Catholicism by citing the deep sense of meaning they derive from the sacraments, especially the Eucharist. The next chapter cites reports from underground priests that lapsed Catholics joined their communities because Protestant communities did not provide weekly Eucharistic services.

Eucharist with a Small e

Feminist theologian Sister Miriam Therese Winter (2005) cleverly sidesteps the question about apostolic succession in her book *Eucharist with a Small "e,"* which is widely ready by liberal reformers. Her book outlines an informal priestless type of eucharistic celebration that she defines as a "parallel practice with Christian tradition" (p. 17). This alternative form of Eucharist occurs when a small group of Christians gathers to break bread together as they remember Jesus and call forth his spirit. She describes the Roman Catholic tradition of the "Sacrament of the Eucharist" as evolving from "the table fellowship of the followers of Jesus after he had died" (p. 26). In contrast, *eucharist* with a small *e* "reflects the experience

---

bishops. It is unlikely that the Roman Catholic Church would recognize their claims to apostolic succession, given that the Vatican has prohibited the ordination of women.

of Jesus eating and drinking with others while he was still alive" (p. 26). According to Winter, even the Last Supper, which many Catholics describe as the "first Eucharist," has been misinterpreted. The Last Supper was not a Christian rite but a Passover celebration presided over by Jesus, who was never ordained and who never intended to found a new religion. Thus, the Last Supper corresponds to Winter's description of *eucharist* with a small *e*, which refers to a community gathering where members nourish each other by sharing food and expressing vows of solidarity and remembrance of their common values and heritage.

Winter (2005) is a clever wordsmith who validates the legitimacy and symbolic power of her approach to eucharist without launching a frontal attack on formal church teachings. She describes her form of eucharist as an "alternative" to the Sacrament of the Eucharist rather than "a substitute" (p. 18). She defends its legitimacy by noting that "it requires no permission, breaks no law," and requires "no prerequisite training nor any expertise" (p. 18). Winter also redefines the meaning of the term *real presence* by explaining that

> God who is real and really present may not be real or really present to me in certain images or names. Therefore, it is essential that we trust our own experience of God, who is beyond all names and transcends every one of our images even while inhabiting them. (p. 128)

Winter redefines *eucharist* as "whatever nurtures and nourishes faith or the ever resilient wellspring of hope, or gives rise to the manifold facets of love" (p. 11). The small *e* eucharist has room at the table for reformers who have been banished or have defected from conventional parishes. Winter explains, "Seeds of systemic change are sown where there is a place at the table for persons and perspectives that custom or tradition would exclude" (p. 42).

In conclusion, Winter's form of small *e* eucharist is the one emphasized by underground communities, which are explicitly designed to make room for persons who are not welcome or do not feel at home in Roman Catholic parishes. Members of these communities craft their liturgies to reflect their evolving understanding of Eucharist and Christian community. Some members may be reassured by their priests' claims to apostolic succession, but their primary orientation is renewing and reformulating their Catholic heritage. Thus, even the Eucharist, perhaps Catholicism's most cherished rite, does not escape reconsideration. Just as reformers do not accept the church's monopolistic claim to apostolic succession, so too, they do not accept the church's restrictions on access to the Eucharist.

Consequently, underground communities generally offer unrestricted access to the Eucharist.[9]

Roots in Early Christian Communities

Many underground communities claim that they recreate the communal spirit and informal egalitarian structure that characterized early Christian communities. Plummer (2004) documents that this claim is common in many independent worship communities that have ties to both Catholic and non-Catholic denominations.

In fact, debates between some early Christian communities and the first church hierarchs resemble points of contention between liberal reformers and the Vatican. According to biblical scholar Elaine Pagels (1981), when a hierarchy of priests and bishops was being instituted in the second century, Gnostic communities challenged this development. They believed a hierarchical structure contradicted their belief that "one's own experience offers the ultimate criterion of truth, taking precedent over all secondhand testimony and all tradition, even Gnostic tradition!" (p. 30). Gnostics organized their communities on the basis of "strict equality" (p. 49), and the presider role was selected by lot to prevent ranking among members. Tertullian, a defender of orthodoxy, accused the Gnostics of heresy in their refusal to accept the legitimate authority of church officials. He took special exception to the position of women in Gnostic communities who "shared with men positions of authority" (p. 50). In response, Gnostics accused church officials of lust for power. One Gnostic document describes church officials as "want[ing] to command one another, outrivaling one another in their empty ambition" (p. 48).

The contrasting theological orientations of church hierarchs and underground communities resemble the debates between the Gnostics and the early church hierarchs. Liberal reformers accuse contemporary church hierarchs of power grabbing and self-promotion, while hierarchs accuse reformers of heresy.[10] Liberal reformers emphasize the rights of

---

[9] Several communities do include notices in church bulletins that all "baptized Christians are welcome to participate in the Eucharist," while others do not impose any restriction and invite all present to partake of the sacrament.

[10] Although the term *heresy* is not commonly used by contemporary clerics, conservative hierarchs insist that Catholics in good standing must accept the teachings of the Magisterium. Chapter 9 describes a diocesan trial against Ned Reidy, a priest in the Ecumenical Catholic Communion, who was found guilty of heresy and schism.

individuals to choose their own beliefs and spiritual practices, while hierarchs emphasize conformity to church teachings. Underground communities also resemble early Christian sects in their emphasis on egalitarian structures and inclusive rituals (especially eucharist with a small *e*). Although some underground communities have ordained presiders, their structure and norms are considerably more egalitarian and flexible than a conventional Roman Catholic parish.

The polarization between the beliefs and orientation of liberal reformers and church hierarchs confirms the analysis of Hunter (1999) and Wuthnow (1988) regarding the profound and far-reaching differences in philosophy and values of conservatives and liberals. These opposing camps were present in Christian history from the beginning and have erupted in various forms throughout Christian history. The marginal and underground communities in this study reflect both the strengths and the weaknesses of those early communities that favored an egalitarian, sect-like model. On the one hand, they create warm, inclusive communities and respect the right of members to a self-directed spiritual search. On the other hand, they may be short-lived if they do not develop more stable structures. The expansive size and long history of the Roman Catholic Church is testimony to the endurance of the church model.

Underground Worship Communities

This chapter includes underground communities that meet the following criteria:

1. They do not meet in Roman Catholic parishes.
2. They do not rely on canonically active Roman Catholic priests.
3. Members are usually not active in Roman Catholic parishes.[11]

Listed below are descriptions of four contemporary examples of underground Catholic faith communities: Community of God's Love, DignityUSA communities, WomenEucharist communities, and the Federation of

---

[11] As noted in chapter 7, examples of both marginal and underground communities are not pure types. In order to classify them as "underground" communities, they must meet two out of three of the stated criteria.

Communities in Service, composed of former Glenmary Sisters. These underground communities represent a type of parallel institution that moves outside the structures of its host institution where members can practice their faith on their own terms and design a new model of Catholicism.

Community of God's Love

The Community of God's Love (CGL) is an excellent example of a Eucharistic community that gradually evolved from its initial status as a parish-based community to a marginal community (as described in chapter 7) in the 1980s and 1990s then to its current underground status. CGL had the reputation in the 1990s as being the largest and most stable intentional community for liberal Roman Catholics in the Boston area, renowned for its lively, imaginative liturgies and its emphasis on social justice activities and church reform.

Evolution of CGL

CGL traces its roots to the Christian Formation Center, where Franciscan friars began celebrating a Sunday morning Eucharistic liturgy in 1968. Several current members of CGL were among the over five hundred members who attended these liturgies until the late 1970s. The fifty individuals who remained together after the center closed in 1985 formed the nucleus of a new intentional community that named itself Community of God's Love.[12] During the 1990s, CGL's membership reached its peak of several hundred as its members became active in church reform activities. CGL members cite two reasons for CGL's loss of members. First, the community had offered religious education for children at various intervals, but, when these programs were cancelled, members with small children moved on to parishes in their community. Second, some members became involved in creation spirituality groups associated with the theologian Matthew Fox[13] (C. G. L., personal communication, October 18, 2003).

---

[12] Over the past three decades, CGL has moved to four separate locations in the northern suburbs, including Lazarus House, a homeless shelter where members heightened their social awareness by celebrating liturgy with "the homeless and poverty stricken" (*CGL Welcome Packet*, n.d., p. 5).

[13] Matthew Fox is a former Catholic theologian who became an Episcopalian priest after being censured by the Vatican. He is a featured speaker at many reform gatherings. His theology of creation spirituality emphasizes environmentally oriented theology. He founded the University of Creation Spirituality in Oakland, California, whose faculty

CGL Liturgy

When I attended a worship service of this group in fall 2003, the group had dwindled to roughly fifteen members, who met in a modest building located on a summer camp for deaf children in Chelmsford, Massachusetts. Members of the group all appear to be middle-aged or older Caucasians, and several appeared to be well past retirement age. In fact, one elderly woman now lives in Florida in the winter and connects with the group only when she returns during summer months. Another member had just died, and the community had conducted their own priestless funeral liturgy for her at a funeral home.

Although CGL's liturgy is conducted every Sunday, attendance varies and on some occasions only two or three members show up. Despite their declining numbers and rapidly aging membership, members are deeply committed to each other, and the group plans to continue meeting, as member Marty Swett put it, "as long as we are physically and mentally able." As the youngest member of the group, Swett insists that she would remain in the group "until she is the last one left if necessary" (personal communication, August 14, 2003).

CGL is fairly isolated from connections to other Roman Catholic groups. They conduct their own annual retreat, but found Roman Catholic retreat houses too expensive. The only consistent connection they maintained was the Call to Action (CTA) national conference, which several of their members attend on a rotating basis. The group takes up collections among themselves and offers funds to those who volunteer to attend the conference. CGL members have an elaborate range of material for liturgy, including their own custom-made liturgy packets, which reflect a strong emphasis on themes of equality, inclusiveness, anticlericalism, and environmentalism. For example, they have thirteen different Eucharistic prayers, each of which contains some of the standard language used during the blessing of the Eucharist, such as "Take this, all of you, and eat, this is my body given up for you" (*CGL summer liturgy*, n.d., p. 17). Statements expressing CGL's philosophy are interspersed with conventional prayers. For example, an ecumenical emphasis is evident in the following prayer: "We are grateful for the courage and fidelity of those who came before to

---

included many prominent scientists, environmentalists, and liberal theologians. A website (www.originalblessing.ing.com) lists fifty-nine primarily small creation spirituality communities. Most of these communities are small, but Jubilee! Community in Asheville, North Carolina, claims eight hundred members and has built a circular meeting space to dramatize its egalitarian ethos.

prepare a path for us to follow—the holy women and men of every age, and culture and spiritual tradition" (p. 16). Expressing the theme of inclusiveness, another petition reads, "We pray that by the Wisdom of that same Spirit we may know that all people are our sisters and brothers, so that wherever we are, peace and justice will be the signs of your presence among us" (p. 26).

The CGL community has its own creed, which makes no reference to the litany of beliefs in the Apostles' Creed, but instead lists four separate "because" statements, each of which is followed by five or six statements of community commitments that flow from these beliefs. For example, the first category of CGL's creed states, "Because of our belief in God as Creator, we choose to be a people who use the gifts of the earth to enhance all of life and who respect the well-being of the planet and its life system" (*CGL summer liturgy*, p. 13). Their egalitarian commitment is reflected in the fourth and final section of the creed as follows: "Because of our belief in Church as Community ... We choose to have no superiors among us" (p. 14). CGL's list of songs and chants includes conventional Catholic hymns alongside many contemporary songs by Marty Haugen, Dan Shutte, S.J., Kathy Sherman, C.S.J., and others. The community uses *Cycle C lectionary readings* published by Priests for Equality, a group of priests dedicated to create inclusive language texts for Catholic liturgies.[14]

CGL's *Welcoming packet* identifies the community's core values as follows: "We value the Eucharist, Christian fellowship, support and care for one another, prayer, and service to neighbor" (p. 2). These values were evident in the liturgy I attended in October 2003. Members greeted each other warmly as they arrived and seemed familiar with events in their lives. A married couple who appeared to be in their early sixties, arrived early to place chairs in a circle, distribute prayer books, and set up a small table in the center of the circle that was covered with a small quilt, candles, and goblets. Members handcrafted the quilt in memory of their recently deceased member Sally.

According to guidelines entitled "Flow of liturgy," members rotate all liturgical roles (setting up for liturgy and presiding at the service). The couple who led the liturgy began by announcing the name and page

---

[14] Priests for Equality are associated with the Quixote Center, centered in Hyattsville, Maryland, which describes itself as "a band of 'impossible dreamers' who joined together in 1976. We are a multi-issue grassroots social justice organization with roots in the Catholic social justice tradition" (*About the Quixote*, July 5, 2005).

numbers of songs and prayers read during the liturgy. The husband provided live music from a small electronic keyboard to accompany singing by the community. This gathering included eight women and two men, all Caucasian over age forty. Two members who were not the presiders held up the wine goblet and plate of hosts during the Eucharist service, but the whole community participated in saying the consecration and distribution of the Eucharist. Consistent with Eucharistic communities, the handshake of peace was highly expressive as members embraced and chatted with each other.

Following this liturgy, I had planned to go out to lunch with a community member Marty Swett, who was a former student. As Marty mentioned our plans, six other group members agreed to join us and we engaged in a two-hour discussion of CGL at a nearby restaurant. The group seems to enjoy spending time together and sharing stories of their spiritual journeys as an enduring intentional community.[15]

CGL exemplifies the drawbacks of sectarian groups that isolate themselves from connections to an umbrella-type organization. Despite the devotion of its core members, CGL is on the brink of extinction because it has not attracted a younger generation of members. This inability to survive beyond one generation is characteristic of sects.

DignityUSA Communities

DignityUSA,[16] the advocacy organization for gay, lesbian, bisexual, and transgender (GLBT) Catholics, is recognized by many in the Catholic Reform Movement as a pioneer in the formation of alternative worship communities. DignityUSA's website claims that Dignity has a reputation for outstanding quality liturgies that "nourish and sustain its members to live the Gospel admonition to feed the hungry, comfort the afflicted, cloth the naked, visit the prisoner, support the grieving and lonely." During the 1970s and early 1980s some Dignity chapters met in Roman Catholic parishes but were forced to locate new meeting spaces following a 1986

---

[15] During this meeting I asked community members if they preferred anonymity in order to prevent any negative fallout from church officials. Several weeks later, the community informed me that they had no desire for anonymity and nothing to fear from church officials, given that they had totally cut themselves off from the institutional church.

[16] DignityUSA's role as an advocacy group for GLBT Catholics is described in chapter 3.

United States Conference of Catholic Bishops (USCCB) ban on the use of Catholic facilities by homosexual groups.[17]

Dignity Liturgies

As of 2011, the fifty-three Dignity chapters listed on the website meet primarily in liberal Protestant churches. All but three Dignity chapters meet on Sunday afternoon or evening, with meeting times ranging from 4:00 p.m. to 7:00 p.m.. This suggests that Dignity attracts primarily adult singles or couples without children, given that Sunday evening would likely be an unpopular time for families. The Boston Dignity chapter I attended attracted primarily persons middle-aged and above.

DignityUSA's website includes a special link for resources on liturgy. These materials, including hymnals and lectionaries, are conventional Catholic publications and do not list sources specifically designed for GLBT Catholics. My description of Dignity liturgies is based on Dignity/Boston, which has its own professionally bound *Order of the liturgy* (2003) that includes revisions to the standard Roman Catholic liturgy designed to reflect gender inclusiveness and petitions on behalf of Dignity members.

DignityUSA made an explicit decision to include gender inclusive language in response to pressure from feminists within their own ranks (Dillon, 1999). The most explicitly feminist example of inclusive language appears in Eucharistic Prayer 5, where the presider proclaims "Loving God open our hearts to the Spirit ... May She lead us to a life of love and service, full of confidence in you." The congregation responds, "We pray that wherever we are, justice will shine forth, and that all women and men can approach each other as equals as brothers and sisters living in the light of your presence" (*Order of the,* 2003, p. 19).

Three prayers in Dignity/Boston's *Order of the liturgy* (2003) refer implicitly and explicitly to Dignity and the marginalized status of GLBT Catholics. The most subtle reference occurs in Eucharistic Prayer 1, which states, "We pray for those who have been damaged or excluded by the Church, as well as those whose gifts and vocations are not yet recognized by your Church on earth" (p. 9). Dignity's appeal for acceptance by church hierarchs is stated most assertively by the presider in Eucharist Prayer 8 as

---

[17] This ban by American bishops followed a *Letter to the Bishops of the Catholic Church from the Vatican* issued on October 30, 1986, which instructed the bishops to withdraw all support (even the "semblance" of support) from any group that does not oppose homosexual acts.

follows: "May the Spirit take away all that divides us. May this Spirit bless our Dignity community, and bring us to that day when we will share this table with N., the bishop of Rome" (p. 25).

Presiders at Dignity/Boston rituals are usually ordained persons from Protestant denominations or former Roman Catholic priests who "are no longer in official Church ministry due solely to their sexual orientation or partnered status" (*Liturgy at Dignity/Boston*, 2009). Although canonically active Roman Catholic priests presided at Dignity liturgies during its early history,[18] it has become increasingly risky given the 1986 letter from the Vatican banning support for homosexual groups.[19] Dignity/Boston's website states emphatically that "ordained presiders are not assigned by the Archdiocese of Boston or any other Roman Catholic religious organization, but are active members of our community whose ministry to us is affirmed by the community." Dignity/Boston members play central roles in the liturgy alongside the ordained presider as guest homilists or lay ministers (including Eucharistic ministers, ministers of hospitality, lectors, sacristans, healers, dance ministers, and bread bakers). At least quarterly, Dignity/Boston offers occasional lay-led liturgies, and lay ministers officiate when ordained ministers are not available. Dignity/Boston proclaims, "We welcome all to the Eucharistic table, regardless of faith tradition" (*Liturgy at Dignity/Boston*).

The Dignity/Boston liturgy I attended on March 7, 2004, was held in St. John the Evangelist Episcopal Church, several blocks from the Massachusetts State House. The congregation of sixty-one adults was dressed casually and maintained relaxed but attentive postures during the service. The overall mood of the service was both reverent (in that participants maintained a respectful, attentive demeanor) and participatory (in that most attendees added their voices to the songs and congregation responses in the *Order of liturgy*). The celebrant (who was not introduced or named in the bulletin) was a rotund and balding man who

---

[18] As noted in previous chapters, "canonically active" refers to Roman Catholic priests who have not resigned or been excommunicated.

[19] Dignity brochures make reference to several priests who have been censored for their work with homosexuals, including Father John McNeill, who was expelled from the Jesuit Order, and Sister Jeannine Gramick and Father Roger Nugent, who were barred from active ministry to homosexuals in 1999 by the Congregation for the Doctrine of the Faith (CDF). More recently, Archbishop Harry Flynn of the St. Paul-Minneapolis Archdiocese denied New Ways Ministry the right to have a Mass during its symposium, entitled "Catholicism and Homosexuality," scheduled for March 16–18, 2007 in Minneapolis.

appeared to be in his fifties. His calm, jovial, and gentle manner suggested that he enjoyed his role as celebrant.

The following characteristics of the liturgy distinguish Dignity/Boston's liturgy from a Mass in a conventional parish:

- Three lesbian couples and four gay couples in the congregation occasionally held hands or put their arms around each other's back during the liturgy.
- One participant was dressed ostentatiously in highly sexualized clothing associated with drag queens.[20]
- Just before the consecration of the Eucharist, the entire congregation surrounded the altar and participated in saying the Eucharist prayer. When members were asked to exchange the handshake of peace, they enthusiastically exchanged vigorous hugs, pecks on the cheeks, and warm greetings.
- At the end of the service I was approached by a formal greeter (a plump grandmotherly woman) who offered me a welcoming packet.
- Dignity/Boston's choir, composed of six males and six females, led the singing by the congregation, as their melodious, spirited voices resounded through the chapel, validating the reputation for superb music that Dignity enjoys among Catholic reform groups.
- During several songs, one beaming pixie-like member of the congregation dramatized the theme of the song with body prayer (a series of symbolic bodily gestures and facial expressions).

Dignity/Boston's Activism

Following the liturgy, most of the congregation attended a special meeting regarding the chapter's plans for advocacy on behalf of the landmark Massachusetts Supreme Court ruling on May 17, 2004, upholding the legality of same-sex marriage. Members spoke very candidly and passionately about the political tailspin surrounding the same-sex marriage decision. Several persons proclaimed (in reference to the Boston archdiocese's opposition to the decision), "I'm pissed and I'm not going to take it anymore," "We are the Church," and "We will not be sheep." One middle-aged

---

[20] This participant wore flamboyant feminine clothing—knee-high boots with stiletto heels, a tight-fitting miniskirt, a low-neckline chiffon blouse, and a flashing gold necklace and earrings.

woman advised the group, "We need to support one another so we are not infected, so we don't hate back."

Attendees at the meeting also expressed support for Russ (a pseudonym), a frail, elderly member who began by discussing the case of Patrick McSorley, a Boston-based clergy abuse victim who had recently committed suicide. Russ's comments drifted into revelations about himself, admitting that he had a history of abuse and alcoholism, and "hated my existence" until he became involved in the Dignity community, which he proclaimed "has helped me tremendously." Russ assured the group that "God loves you as much as anyone else." Confessing his own vulnerability to harsh judgments, he explained, "I need to know I won't go to hell."

Dignity/Boston is a very active chapter; its brochure lists sixteen separate committees and a Friday night supper program for indigent people, which they conduct in collaboration with Arlington Street Church.[21] As documented in chapter 3, DignityUSA chapters have declined in number over the past several decades and they vary in size and degree of activism. Chapter reports in DignityUSA's newsletters indicate that many chapters remain vibrant, offering their members a supportive environment that affirms their sexual preference and their right to remain Catholic. Although Dignity liturgies have some innovative features, they conform much more closely to the standard Roman Catholic liturgy than the other three communities described in this chapter. This relatively more traditional orientation of Dignity liturgies reflects the preferences of its members.

Future Prospects

Although Dignity communities retain a significant core of members, they compete with non-Catholic churches and underground groups that welcome GLBT persons. DignityUSA communities are less isolated than CGL because they belong to DignityUSA, which provides resources and networking on its website and at national conventions. National officers and staff also periodically visit chapters to bolster morale and share news of national developments. Despite these assets, the long-term prospects of Dignity communities seem dim, because they have not attracted

---

[21] Located in the center of Boston, Arlington Street Church is Unitarian and has a reputation for welcoming GLBT persons and its social justice ministry.

many members from younger generations who share their strong ties to Catholicism.

WomenEucharist Communities

In her book *WomenEucharist,* Dierks (1997), featured in the vignette at the beginning of chapter, documents the emerging nature of more than one hundred feminist spirituality groups composed almost exclusively of Catholic feminists.[22] Given that her book is now more than ten years old, I contacted the author to assess the status of these groups. In response, Dierks was uncertain how many of these WomenEucharist (WE) groups still exist, though she belongs to two that still meet regularly. Dierks describes these communities as bridge-type communities that helped women move away from their dependence on conventional parishes and introduced them to new models of practicing their faith (personal communication, July 6, 2008).[23]

Dierks's (1997) own experience in a feminist spirituality group inspired her to examine the range and nature of these groups by surveying individuals (that netted 126 respondents) and by visiting five communities. Dierks obtained her contacts by word of mouth because there was no centralized list of these communities. Like other underground communities, these communities arose spontaneously to fill a gap in the lives of Catholic feminists who were seeking ways to practice their faith in a manner consistent with their emerging feminist consciousness.

WE Liturgies Reflect Feminist Principles

Dierks (1997) does not present these WE communities as a "final answer" (p. 18) or a replacement for the institutional church. On the contrary, she shares the perception of feminist theologian Rosemary Radford Ruether that ultimately women will move past their need for separate

---

[22] In Derek's sample, ninety-two respondents identified themselves as Catholic in some fashion, while of the remaining twelve, eight identified themselves as belonging to another denomination, and four failed to answer (though two of these four identified themselves as Catholic in other survey questions).

[23] Several members of Massachusetts Women-Church informed me that the dozen W-CC communities they helped form have all folded, but they did encounter several members from active W-CC groups across the country when they attended a Women's Ordination Worldwide Conference in Ontario in 2005 (M. S., personal communication, October 12, 2007).

communities in favor of communities in which women will participate as coequals with men.[24]

In the short term, however, feminist spirituality groups are designed to foster the spirituality of Catholic feminists who face the "virtual certainty that their voices will not be heard, their talents never fully employed in the church of their baptism" (Dierks, 1997, p. 14). The groups in Dierks's study adopted structures and forms of celebration that reflected principles of feminist theology as follows (in abbreviated form):

> Community without hierarchy (sitting in a circle)
> Community without sexism (imaging God as female)
> Community without rigidity (reflecting members' journeys and insights)
> Community without slavery to fixed space (dances and gestures in ritual)
> Community without judgment (offering gifts without fear of rejection)
> (p. 16)

Dierks (1997) attributes the emergence of WE groups primarily to dissatisfaction with "poorly developed liturgies, male dominance of ritual, scandal in the institution, and a lack of awareness of justice issues within parishes, as well as a felt push from the Spirit" (p. 41).[25] Some members describe their emergence as a type of "Pentecost experience," which one member expressed as follows:

> Then the spirit came, and we were filled up and began to express ourselves in foreign tongues (for it is certain that to say that women can celebrate is two thousand years foreign) and we began to make bold proclamations (for to say that all we need do is ask and Jesus is with us is audacious indeed). (p. 53)

As women begin to participate in these groups, Dierks asserts that they gained a more mature understanding of Eucharist and community. She identifies six key components of women's experiences emphasized in WE communities, which enhance their spiritual development (in abbreviated form):

---

[24] In Ruether's words, "I assume the name for this liberated humanity would then no longer be 'Women-Church,' but simply 'Church,'" that is the authentic community of exodus from oppression that has been heralded by the traditions of religious and social liberation" (Ruether as cited in Dierks, 1997, p. 18).

[25] Some of these groups had connections to other organized groups: one received instruction from the Medical Mission Sisters in the sixties, another from a Catholic Worker House. Some emerged from parish women's groups and others from Women-Church Convergence (described in chapter 4).

Affirming Ourselves (recognize one's worthiness in relation to oneself, God, and the earth community)
Power of Role Models (affirm women's capability to perform diverse roles)
Power of Reading (transformation by exposure to feminist literature)
Power of Education (influence of progressive and feminist theologians)
Power in the Workforce (paid employment empowers women)
Power of Prayer (grounded in feminist theology) (pp. 61–70)

By reflecting women's special style of celebration and prayer, WE communities reflect the spiritual preferences and priorities of their members. WE members come to regard their personal lives as worthy and essential to their spirituality, and thereby become a central focus of their prayer life. Consistent with the theories of feminist psychologist Carol Gilligan (1982), Dierks found the theme of human relationships to be a primary value among the women in her sample, as revealed by the fact that "friendship" was mostly frequently cited reason for participation in a WE community. Dierks describes WE communities as essentially informal, egalitarian, and responsive to the interests and orientations of members, characteristics that apply to feminist spirituality groups from diverse denominations and religious backgrounds (Winter, Lummis, & Stokes, 1995).

The Eucharist at WE Liturgies

The distinctive character of WE communities is their "deliberate active contact with our heritage of Eucharist" (Dierks, p. 114), though WE gatherings are never referred to as a *Mass*. Scripture is included in many WE liturgies, but participants analyze the readings through the lens of feminist biblical scholarship. Increasingly, WE rituals include readings from non-Catholic sources, including women's poetry, biography, and feminist theology. WE gatherings do not close with a song but rather by gathering around a communal meal. Dierks explains that "It is the continuation of the banquet.... We do not fast when the bridegroom is present" (p. 131).[26]

Inevitably, WE communities face the same question posed by other underground communities as to whether their Eucharist contains the real

---

[26] One of the most common complaints regarding WE communities is their new and evolving nature, such that, as Dierks terms it, "the spiritual garments don't always fit just right" (p. 220). For some the gatherings are too unstructured, too therapeutic, too messy or experimental, while others find these qualities appealing. Some want more frequent meetings while others desire inclusion of husbands and children. Dierks concludes that members rate their experiences in WE communities very positively.

presence of the body and blood of Jesus, given the absence of a canonical priest. Dierks (1997) raises this question in her survey, and 56 percent of her 102 respondents indicated "a positive belief that at WomenEucharist the bread and wine become the body and blood of Christ" (p. 156) while only 4.5 percent indicated that they were "fairly certain" (p. 156) Jesus was not present. Dierks asserts that precisely because WE liturgies are so deeply moving and transformative for many participants, they represent a more profound sacramental experience than participants attain in a typical parish liturgy. Dierks explains, "Jesus is no longer seen as the possession of the clergy. Rather, he is understood to be freely willing and ardently present to those who gather and ask him to be with us" (p. 157). Dierks insists that WE celebrations resemble early Christian communities that did not have elaborate rules and designated celebrants.[27]

Since there is no comprehensive listing of WE groups, it is impossible to estimate their current numbers, composition, or focus. During my research, I came across references to similar groups while attending "The Church Women Want" conference series at Boston College,[28] where participants described small faith-sharing groups that are formed in workplaces, parishes, or reform group meetings. In fact, the conference series itself was initiated by a faith-sharing group of Boston College faculty and staff that emerged through informal connections among women on campus.

WE's Uniqueness

WE Communities have some sect-like features, most notably their decentralized and communal nature. Unlike most sects, however, their mission is unique because they are not designed to replace parishes but rather to raise the feminist consciousness of members and experiment with liturgical innovations. The bridge-type nature of these communities enables them to avoid debates over structure and leadership and to craft a diverse and eclectic range of liturgical forms.

---

[27] The type of Eucharist celebrated by WE communities corresponds to Winter's (2005) description of "eucharist with a small 'e,'" which does not involve ordained presiders. Dierks's book was published before Winter's *Eucharist with a Small "e,"* so she was unable to apply Winter's terminology.

[28] The first conference, "Envisioning the Church Women Want," was held at Boston College April 16–17, 2004. The second conference, "Creating the Church Women Want," was held at Boston College on July 15, 2006. Both conferences were sponsored by Boston College's Church in the 21st Century Center.

Disaspora of Resigned Sisters and Priests

During my research I was contacted by several resigned sisters and priests who described participating in periodic rituals with their former colleagues in religious orders, many of whom had also resigned. These sources described liturgies that had been adapted to reflect participants' changing theologies and lifestyles. I do not identify the communities described by my sources because they requested confidentiality. Some of their members continued to worship in Catholic parishes and feared retribution for participating in an unsanctioned worship community. Although these groups are difficult to locate and study, they represent another layer of underground communities. Like other underground groups, there is no comprehensive directory, but they may be numerous. Powers (1992) estimates that, between the close of Vatican II in 1965 and 1992, 20,000 American priests resigned from the priesthood. Briggs (2006) reports the number of women in religious orders in the United States dropped from 185,000 in 1965 to 69,963 in 2005.

I will describe one example of a community of former religious sisters who continue to meet at regular intervals for ritual and socializing. My account is based on a book entitled *Mountain Sisters*, by retired sociologist Helen M. Lewis and former Glenmary sister Monica Appleby (2003).

Defection by Glenmary Sisters

Glenmary Sisters, a progressive religious community, experienced a mass defection of sisters in 1967 after they had reached stalemate in their efforts to negotiate with church authorities.[29] The seemingly prophetic motto of this community was "Honor and Trespass Boundaries as Love and Justice Demand" (Lewis & Appleby, 2003, p. xix). Conflict centered on the rigid rules regarding curfew and cloister, and on prohibitions pertaining to "eating with the seculars" that interfered with the Glenmary Sisters' organizing efforts among poor rural families in Appalachia. In a letter to Glenmary Sisters, Mother Mary Catherine asserted that the sisters needed to move beyond outworn structures and risk creating something new. In her words, "It is a question of whether we are willing to 'walk on the water'" (p. 67). After leaving their order, forty-five of the seventy sisters who left made a collective attempt at "walking on water" by creating a

---

[29] Lenore Mullarney, a Glemnary Sister quoted by Lewis & Appleby, estimated the size of the order to be approximately one hundred (p. 72).

secular organization, Federation of Communities in Service (FOCIS), to continue their community organizing work in Appalachia.[30]

FOCIS Liturgies

FOCIS evolved over its forty-year history from an organization with central headquarters to a dispersed community that engaged in new models for working with oppressed populations. Although some former Glenmary Sisters moved on to other denominations, others remained Catholic while struggling to "forgive the Church" (Lewis & Appleby, p. 215).[31] Eventually FOCIS became something of an alternative church for many former Glenmary Sisters as they conducted liturgies at FOCIS's annual meetings and on other occasions. As FOCIS members became more feminist, their liturgies became more innovative and experimental. Originally, FOCIS tapped married priest John Rausch for FOCIS liturgies conducted during weekend meetings, especially for important events.[32] Eventually FOCIS member Anne Leibig became a co-celebrant, answering her decades-old call to serve in this role.

FOCIS liturgies include many of the innovative, participatory features exemplified by other underground communities. For example, the Liturgy of the Word would typically include readings from the Gospel alongside other readings from poems or books that a member found particularly meaningful. During the service, the celebrant would include references to comments from people at an earlier meeting or newsworthy events in people's lives such as births, illness, etc. Spiritual practices from other traditions were occasionally included. For example, Anne Leibig often conducted breathing exercises or guided meditation to help people focus at the beginning of the service. At a gathering in 1992, Mary Herr drew on her Cherokee heritage to create a sweat lodge experience and talking circle.

Drawing on their Catholic appreciation for mystery and symbol, the FOCIS twenty-fifth anniversary celebration included a range of artistic

---

[30] The four hundred member Immaculate Heart Sisters encountered a conflict similar to the Glenmary Sisters, in which members of the order elected to become a lay ecumenical community in 1970. Like the Glenmary Sisters, the Immaculate Heart Sisters renounced diocesan control over their order following ongoing conflicts with the conservative Los Angeles Cardinal James Francis McIntyre. The conflicts centered on initiatives of Immaculate Heart Sisters to implement Vatican II reforms (Caspary, 2003).

[31] Some of the sisters who remained Catholic also participated in "an alternative women's church" (p. 215).

[32] John Rausch was listed on the website Rent-A-Priest, sponsored by Celibacy Is the Issue (CITI), an organization described in chapter 7.

material, such as a symbolic nature trail, a spiral cake walk (that formed a maze), and a friendship quilt, with a block for the name of each member, that subsequently has been used regularly at FOCIS events. FOCIS members also created their own theology study group, which in turn prompted a theological focus at their gatherings. In the words of FOCIS member Linda Mashburn,

> As a Protestant, I feel comfortable saying that FOCIS is my church, but I understand it is difficult for people brought up in the Catholic Church to label it as church. Yet for me it has always epitomized the best of what church is: the Body of Christ. It is wonderful that other FOCIS members could name it in that way. (Mashburn as cited by Lewis & Appleby, p. 221)

Thus, the Glenmary Sisters who remained connected through FOCIS created a sect-like underground community in which members could maintain a connection to their shared history while adopting liturgies to reflect their evolving spirituality and theology. Glenmary Sisters did not view their decision to leave as a violation of their vows but rather as an effort to redefine these vows in a manner more suited to their work as community organizers and more in keeping with the liberating vision of Vatican II. Hence the community reinterpreted poverty to mean "sharing with all our human and material resources" (p. 69), charity became "caring for others in their need" (p. 69), and obedience became "bearing responsibility for the self, religious community, [and] the non-Catholic community" (p. 69). These newly defined vows resemble the redefinitions of celibacy, poverty, and obedience defined by CORPUS's newly emerging Community of John XXIII, as described in chapter 3.[33]

Walking on Water

The story of the Glenmary Sisters is particularly dramatic because a majority of sisters in the order chose to leave rather than succumb to the

---

[33] The Community of John XXIII redefines celibacy as "a call to witness authentic human relationships at every level of creation" and to challenge oppressive practices "which exploit our sacred creation." The vow of poverty is redefined as the vow of justice making based on Elisabeth Schüssler Fiorenza's concept of a discipleship of equals and O'Murchu's concept of justice as "egalitarian rather than patriarchal, essentially distributive rather than hierarchical." The vow of obedience is renamed the "vow of mutual collaboration," whereby people work together to "build a culture of right relating humanly, earthly and cosmically" (Scaine, 2007, p. 30).

authority of their local bishop.[34] Their motto of "walking on water" is a fitting metaphor for the underground movement, which no longer relies on institutional structures to keep them afloat but must find their own sense of balance and resolve in this turbulent era, as old certitudes dissolve and newly evolving forms of consciousness pose challenges and opportunities. The sect-like communities in this chapter vividly demonstrate the fragility and instability of sects, because they are very grassroots in nature, lacking the type of structure and resources necessary to sustain themselves over the long term. By the same token, these communities are designed as bridge-type groups that can sustain disaffected Catholics (GLBTs, feminists, and other types of liberal Catholics) who hope the church will eventually reform. Some members of these groups may eventually gravitate to the more stable type of underground parishes described in the next chapter. One example of this potential trend is Sheila Durkin Dierks, featured in the vignette at the beginning of this chapter, who is now an ordained priest in the Light of Christ community, which is affiliated with the Ecumenical Catholic Communion.

---

[34] The Glenmary Order still exists and lists nine sisters on their website (www.glenmarysisters.org).

CHAPTER NINE

SOMETHING NEW UNDER THE SUN?
UNDERGROUND PARISHES

Roman Catholic Womenpriests (RCWP) Jean Marie Marchant and Marie David were both ordained in Canada on the St. Lawrence River in 2005, both are married to resigned Roman Catholic priests, and both are building Eucharistic communities in Massachusetts.

Marie David discovered her call to the priesthood while doing retreat work with her husband, Jim, at a facility they purchased on Cape Cod and named Evensong by the Sea Retreat and Spirituality Center. This facility generates income as a bed and breakfast during the tourist season and doubles as a retreat center during off-season months. Marie explored the option of ordination in other traditions, but became convinced that she was called to remain Roman Catholic and to minister to the growing numbers of disaffected Catholics who visit Evensong (M. D., personal communication, September 14, 2007). Several years ago, Marie and Jim built a small chapel on their property. Named St. Mary of Magdala Chapel, it serves as worship space to a small but growing faith community of roughly sixty members from the surrounding area, including members of Massachusetts Women-Church, who are thrilled to encounter ministry from husband and wife copastors who take turns presiding at Sunday liturgies. Visitors to the Sunday services rave about the lovely chapel, with streams of natural light and a stone fountain, as well as the inspiring and thoughtful homilies delivered by Marie and Jim. Commenting on their first encounter with a woman priest, several visitors to the chapel have exclaimed about Marie's "beatific smile" and her "jubilant spirit," which fosters a celebratory spirit among attendees.[1]

Jean Marie Marchant felt a lifelong calling to the priesthood that inspired her to earn a master's degree in theology from Weston Jesuit School of Theology. Jean's devout practice of Roman Catholicism sustained her through many personal difficulties, including the loss of two children during childbirth and a traumatic divorce. Eventually, Jean married her current husband, Ron Hindelang, S.T.L., Ph.D., a resigned Roman Catholic priest, and pursued a successful career, culminating in her position as director of Health Care Ministry for the Boston archdiocese, where she supervised more than two hundred chaplains. To protect her position, Jean did not

---

[1] I attended a liturgy at St. Mary of Magdala Chapel in August 2007 and informally interviewed seven people who had attended services on different occasions. I also attended a service at the Spirit of Life community on December, 31, 2006, when the community was still in the formative stage.

reveal her status as a RCWP until one year after her ordination, when she broadcast her ordination and decision to resign her position with the archdiocese in a *Boston Globe* article (Paulson, 2006c, p. B1). In February 2007, Jean and Ron founded Spirit of Life community, which meets at 5:00 p.m. every Sunday in the Congregational Church of Weston. Spirit of Life now boasts more than thirty members, several of whom served as volunteers at the RCWP ordinations that took place in Boston on July 20, 2008.

Schismatic Parishes

This chapter describes the most path-breaking and parish-like communities in this study, which are prefigurative models of a renewed Catholicism. As long as conservatives control the papacy, these communities do not seek and would not be granted affiliation with the Roman Catholic Church. They openly defy church teachings regarding homosexuality, women's ordination, divorce, celibacy, and restrictions on access to the Eucharist. Church officials have declared many of these communities "schismatic" and imposed excommunication decrees.[2]

All of communities in this chapter resemble sects because they have severed their connections to the Roman Catholic Church and emphasize their divergence from the institutional church in their literature and religious education programs. Like sects, they claim to embody the most essential truths of their tradition. These communities include five independent parishes, one independent network of communities, and two independent seminaries. The five independent parishes described in this chapter are distinguishable from the underground communities described in chapter 8 based on the following criteria:

a. They refer to themselves as a parish.
b. They have regular meeting places and conduct at least weekly liturgies.
c. They have professionally trained clergy.

---

[2] The Vatican never censured some of the underground communities in this chapter because they never had any formal connections to the institutional church. These communities include Grace Church of Dover, the Inclusive Community, the Ecumenical Catholic Communion, and the Diocese of One Spirit. Consequently, these communities do not fully correspond to the definition of sect as "branch[ing] off from a larger established religion." However, this distinction is imprecise because these communities never bothered to seek affiliation, since they rejected many Vatican doctrines. Most of these

One could argue that these underground groups are not a new or unusual development but simply another version of schismatic groups that have plagued Catholicism throughout its history, most notably the Orthodox schism in the eleventh century and the Protestant Reformation in the sixteenth century. Indeed, these groups do bear some resemblance to these historic schisms in that, in each case, defections from Roman Catholicism occurred because these communities wanted autonomy from a Vatican hierarchy regarded as either corrupt or tyrannical. In contrast to these major schisms, many of the contemporary underground groups described below view their exiled status from Roman Catholicism as temporary and hope to rejoin the institutional church under more progressive leaders.[3]

The type of sect-like parishes described in this chapter has historical precedents, such as the nineteenth-century examples described by journalist David Gibson (2003):

> Congregants in Fall River, Massachusetts stopped contributing to the parish and attending Mass over a dispute with the diocese, while in North Brookfield and other Massachusetts towns lay Catholics established their own parishes and were duly excommunicated. (p. 48)

Plummer (2004) also cites two examples of sectarian churches in the twentieth century that severed bonds with the Roman Catholic Church in an attempt to protect "the integrity of their ethnic, racial, and or cultural heritage" (p. 41), namely, the Polish National Catholic Church, founded in 1904, and the Imani Temple (also known as the African American Catholic Congregation), founded in 1989 by George Stalling, a former Roman Catholic priest.

Although underground parishes in this chapter bear some resemblance to historical schisms, their objectives are broader than autonomy or cultural preservation since they favor far-reaching reforms in theology, liturgy, and governance. These communities aim not to preserve the tradition but to reform it. They represent a more stable form of parallel organization than the communities described in the previous chapter because they have more formal structures and leadership.

---

communities describe themselves as *Catholic* (not *Roman Catholic*) to emphasize their separation from the institutional church.

[3] Chapter 8 analyzes the extent to which underground groups correspond to and deviate from the term *sect*.

ST. BRIDGET'S PARISH: THE CHURCH THAT WOULD NOT DIE

If one wanted to identify a Catholic parish with members from disadvantaged groups, a good choice would be St. Bridget's in Indianapolis, Indiana. Founded in 1879, St. Bridget's was closed by the Diocese of Indianapolis in 1994 and demolished in 2000, despite a six-year battle by parishioners to preserve their parish. Eighty of the three hundred fifty parishioners who belonged to St. Bridget's formed a parish 1994 without the sanction of the diocese. The community refers to itself as an "independent church in the Catholic tradition" (Kenny & Kenny, 2004, p. 5).

The Evolution of an African American Parish

Originally, St. Bridget's was primarily Irish, but eventually became a predominately black parish as a result of demographic shifts in the surrounding inner-city neighborhood. During its early history the parish was segregated, reflecting the policies that characterized Indianapolis at that time.[4] In spite of segregationist polices, St. Bridget's could hardly be characterized as hostile to blacks. On the contrary, in response to his vision of a black Madonna, the first pastor of the parish, Father Daniel Curran, wanted to extend educational opportunities for black children and therefore created a school (Kenny & Kenny, 2004).[5]

The parish's reputation for social justice ministry expanded in 1951 when Archbishop Paul C. Schulte asked the Oblates of Mary Immaculate of the Eastern Providence to accept responsibility for St. Bridget's.[6] Looking back on the tenure of the Oblate Fathers, parishioners remember "their kindness and community involvement" (Kenny & Kenny, 2004, p. 23). The parish thrived until 1987 when it began losing members under Father Thomas Scanlon, whose approach was "old school and rules-minded" (p. 28). St. Bridget's last pastor, Father Kenneth Taylor, an African American, claimed some success in attracting new members, admitting, "The really sad thing was that we were moving in the right direction, but it was too late" (Taylor as cited in Kenny & Kenny, p. 32).

---

[4] Given that the parish relied on income from pew rent, black parishioners were required to stand in the back of the church if they could not afford pew rent.

[5] During this historical period, on "numerous occasions" the Vatican asked bishops to "correct the unjust treatment of black Catholics" (Kenny & Kenny, p. 19).

[6] Parishioners recall Oblate pastors who accompanied juveniles to court hearings, sent food and clothes to poor families, and visited sick parishioners.

St. Bridget's Foreshadows Anticlosure Movement in Boston

The battle launched by St. Bridget's parishioners to prevent closure resembles in many respects the battles of vigiling parishes in Boston, described in chapter 7. St. Bridget's parishioners were convinced the real reason their parish had been targeted was the fact that it occupied valuable property, since St. Bridget's was located near the downtown canal where local colleges were expanding. The Council of Vigiling Parishes (CoP) in Boston also claimed that property values influenced closure decrees.[7] Just as vigilers in Boston enjoyed widespread community support, so too St. Bridget's parishioners received free legal assistance, petitions signed by more than two thousand persons, sympathetic coverage in local papers, and efforts by historical commissions to declare the church a historical landmark (Kenny & Kenny, 2004).

Unlike Boston where the vigiling movement was predominately white, St. Bridget's parishioners interpreted the reaction of the archdiocese as "disrespectful of the black community" (Kenny & Kenny, 2004, p. 37). Another dissimilarity to Boston centered on the fact that the archdiocese in Indianapolis did not claim that a fiscal crisis justified its decision to close St. Bridget's.[8]

Choosing Schism over Compliance

When St. Bridget's was officially closed on June 30, 1994, the Save Our Church Committee held services in a tent across the street from the locked church, but several months later they were offered space in the nearby St. Philip's Episcopal Church. As one might expect, many parishioners left the St. Bridget's group when they started meeting in St. Philip's, believing that attending services in a Protestant church "was a sin," (Kenney & Kenney, 2004, p. 81) which might result in excommunication.

---

[7] In addition, St. Bridget's parishioners shared the dismay of vigilers in Boston over the archdiocesan response to their appeals. They allege archdiocesan officials failed to answer most of the questions or to explain why it was necessary to close a parish that was self-supporting, that served a growing and underprivileged population whose members felt unwelcome in nearby predominately white parishes and that occupied a 121-year old building considered historically significant by local preservationists.

[8] In some respects, the St. Bridget's community was accorded less respect than the vigiling parishioners in Boston, in that they were never informed what happened to the artifacts removed from the church, and their own parish council was disbanded in favor of a transition team of parishioners "hand-picked" by the pastor.

As it happened, the pastor of St. Philip's, Richard Roos, was a former Roman Catholic priest who resigned in 1970 to marry and who had a personal history of defying his superiors. First, he refused instructions to close his own parish, St. Philip's, after consulting with his parishioners.[9] Second, Roos also rebuffed appeals from the Catholic archdiocese, which claimed St. Philip's "ministry of hospitality" was a "hindrance to ecumenism" (Kenny & Kenny, 2004, p. 81). Roos explained that the sight of St. Bridget's worshiping in a tent was "more than he could bear" (Roos as cited in Kenney & Kenny, p. 80), and that his own community unanimously agreed that "this is what God wanted us to do," particularly since the two parishes had collaborated for years on "education, liturgy and outreach" (p. 80).

The newly formed St. Bridget's community adopted a mission statement that read, "Our mission is to serve God, to share our love of God, and to grow and be strengthened in Christ. We have no boundaries. All are welcome" (Kenny and Kenny, 2004, p. 76). As an unsanctioned parish, St. Bridget's had difficulty locating priests to preside at their services, particularly since they offered a fee of only one hundred dollars a week. They ruled out diocesan priests who had refused to say Mass for them when they were resisting closure. Eventually, the community contacted the Federation of Christian Ministries (FCM),[10] which put them in touch with Adolph Dwenger, who served as pastor of St. Bridget's parish from 1990 to 1992 but had subsequently left the church.[11] Dwenger resigned as pastor of St. Bridget's for a brief period in 1999, but the community persuaded him to return when members accepted responsibility for administrative matters. Subsequently the community formalized its parish council by creating bylaws, defining duties of members, preparing a slate of candidates,

---

[9] Like St. Bridget's, St. Philip's had been targeted for closure due to its location in a declining neighborhood, but Rev. Roos consulted the congregation, which chose to remain open. Because the parish was financially independent, the Episcopal diocese could not override the decision of the parish (Kenny & Kenny, p. 80).

[10] Federation of Christian Ministries is a 600-member organization with roots in the Catholic Reform Movement that provides (a) certification for ministry for both married and single men and women; (b) support for small faith communities; (c) online religious studies programs and regional and national gatherings (www.federationofchristianministries.org).

[11] Dwenger had left the church in response to criticism from the archdiocese for serving Communion to divorced and remarried Catholics, for allowing a female associate to deliver a homily, and for refusing to accept a third ministry at a local hospital. Dwenger was fired for refusing to serve as a hospital minister in addition to his roles as pastor of St. Bridget's and chaplain at a nearby college.

and holding a town-hall-type meeting where members could voice their concerns (Kenny & Kenny, 2004, p. 85). The parish eventually adopted a model of copastors and rotating celebrants, which included Dwenger and a number of married priests in the Indianapolis area. In December 2000 Father Pat Durkin, who served as pastor from 1999 to 2001, recommended parish members Brenda and Chip Hoosier for the position of deacon. This plan reached partial fulfillment when Chip Hoosier was ordained as a deacon on March 7, 2004, in a ceremony members sanctioned and designed.[12] The ceremony included priests from St. Bridget's, the Episcopal pastor Rev. Roos, and Bishop Alfred Lankenau of the Orthodox-Catholic Church of America (Kenney & Kenney, p. 92).

Jim and Mary Kenny (2004), who joined the congregation in 2003, authored a book on the history of St. Bridget's in which they asked long-term members to reflect on their association with the parish, particularly following the decision to form an independent parish. Several members described the closing of their former parish positively, emphasizing that members could no longer remain "Sunday pew Catholics" (p. 93), but rather were empowered to run their own affairs. Parishioners also emphasized that the new St. Bridget's retained the warm, inclusive atmosphere of their former parish, but the liturgy was adapted to suit the changing nature of the community. The new parish selected its music primarily from *Lead Me, Guide Me*, a hymnal containing African American music from the Catholic tradition. The Lord's Prayer is sung by the entire congregation as parishioners hold hands and form a circle. During the sign of peace, parishioners engage in the "St. Bridget's shuffle," in which every member greets every other person in attendance until the singing of "Lamb of God" calls the congregation to resume the Mass. The liturgy includes a variety of forms of participation that match the liturgical theme, revealing that God's word can "bubble up" from the people and "trickle down" from the pope and hierarchy (Kenny & Kenny, p. 118).

Authors Mary and James Kenny (2004) cite three unique characteristics of St. Bridget's that demonstrate its moral strength and courage: their policy of open Communion, their reliance on married priests (described as "holy and committed men"), and their nonjudgmental attitude that

---

[12] Brenda Hoosier was not interested in ordination as a deacon, but recommended Mary Catherine Gibson, whose nomination was unanimously approved by the parish council. However, Gibson rejected ordination as part of a "patriarchal, ecclesial structure" and urged St. Bridget's to "go beyond" (Kenny & Kenny, p. 87) the definitions of deacon.

includes even those who have "displaced and hurt them" (p. 123). Yet, despite their strong loyalty and sense of mission, the community faces dwindling attendance and concerns about its future stability. Although the parish directory lists sixty-one active adults (whose family members would bring the total to 175–200 members), only an average of forty attend weekly services. According to the Kennys, dwindling attendance may also reflect the community's absence of a coherent vision about how to sustain and revive itself. Nonetheless, St. Bridget's community has no plans of folding, as Brenda Hoosier reported that that they are planning a twentieth anniversary celebration in 2014 (personal communication, July 8, 2008).

St. Bridget's Future Prospects

St. Bridget's survival as an independent parish for almost two decades is remarkable, particularly since it is not connected to a broader network such as the CoP in Boston, which provides a range of resources and support to parishes facing closure. Another noteworthy feature of St. Bridget's is that reform groups enabled the parish to survive by locating priests through FCM and informal networks of resigned priests in the Indianapolis area. Although the community did eventually ordain some of its members as deacons, it did not experiment with the types of priestless liturgies conducted by vigiling churches in Boston. Like the sectarian communities in chapter 8, St. Bridget's demonstrates the vulnerability and instability of sectarian communities that often do not attract a second generation to sustain the commitment and theological orientation of the founding group.

THE INCLUSIVE COMMUNITY, NUTLEY, NEW JERSEY: AN ECUMENICAL PARISH

The Inclusive Community-UCC was founded in 1986 in Passaic, New Jersey, as an innovative effort to draw on the strengths of both Protestantism and Catholicism and include members from both faiths.[13] At present, the

---

[13] Although this book focuses almost exclusively on Catholic communities, the Inclusive Community is included because it is strongly rooted in Catholicism and its members include many CORPUS priests who are active in the Reform Movement.

community meets in Nutley, New Jersey, and Anthony Padovano, ambassador for Corps of Reserve Priests United for Service (CORPUS), serves as pastor.[14] He publishes a monthly "Pastor's Message" on the community's website (www.christianbridges.com).

A Path-Breaking Community

The idea for this community was sparked by an article by William Cleary (1985) entitled "Undocumented Protestants" that describes the dilemma of Catholics attending Protestant services due to intermarriage with a Protestant spouse or to disenchantment with Catholicism, but who misses receiving the Eucharist.[15] Responding to the article by Cleary, the Reverend Anne Hess (1990), a pastor of the United Church of Christ (UCC), collaborated with two resigned Catholic priests, Robert Scharf and John Caufield, to create a combined "Protestant service of the Word with a Catholic Communion out of a shared belief in the 'oneness' of all Christians" (p. 401).[16] Following a series of Lenten discussions on the topic, the congregation voted to approve the formation of the Inclusive Community.

In its first mission statement, the Inclusive Community pledged to "preserve the spirituality of both traditions" and "embrace catholicism in its all-inclusiveness and reformation in its yearning for authenticity" (*Inclusive Community Mission,* 2007). Pastor Hess (1990) explains that both traditions enrich each other. Protestants find "worship greatly enriched by Catholic ritual and sacrament" (p. 401), and Catholics enjoy "the Protestant sense of community and reverence for the word, the ministry of ordained women," and decentralized decision making (p. 401). In its "Welcome Statement" on the community's website, Pastor Anthony Padovano (2006c) emphasizes the community's role in healing denominational division, proclaiming, "Unity is the consequence of spiritual bonding, of standing in awe together before the God who is more than the Churches."

---

[14] Padovano is a primary leader of the Reform Movement. Chapters 1 and 3 contain details of his role in it. His speeches and articles are cited frequently throughout this book.

[15] William Cleary is active in CORPUS, and his arguments urging people to abandon Roman Catholicism are cited in chapters 1 and 3.

[16] Hess (1990) explains that this move was possible because UCC is "committed to ecumenism" and authorizes the granting of ministerial status to an ordained Catholic who "meets UCC standards" (p. 401). This combined liturgy represents a milestone in ecumenical history in that the UCC "granted full ministerial standing to a married Catholic priest to serve as a Catholic pastor in the denomination" (Hess, p. 401).

Not coincidentally, the community celebrates its anniversary in October, the month that includes commemorations of St. Francis (October 4) and the start of the Reformation (October 31), reflecting that "Francis and Luther both wanted a church built on New Testament values. They stressed the spirit of Christianity rather than its structures" (Padovano, 2006c, p. 1).

Due to its unique character, the Inclusive Community has received considerable publicity in national and New Jersey publications as well as on radio and television (Padovano, 2005b). On the tenth anniversary of the Inclusive Community, the president of the UCC made a cross-country trip to attend the celebration of this "history-making initiative" (Padovano, p. 28).

An Experiment that Did Not Fail

During the community's early history, controversies surrounding the Eucharist were somewhat problematic. Several local newspaper articles on the formation of the community included statements by Roman Catholic officials challenging the legitimacy of their unconventional Eucharist celebrations. For example, the Reverend James Provost, a professor of canon law at Catholic University, stated, "We do not serve intercommunion" and priests who illegitimately perform their priestly role are "violating church law" (Provost as cited by Washburn, 1986, p. C5). Controversy over the Eucharist erupted among the congregation as well. Pastor Anne Hess (1990) acknowledged that "honest and sometimes painful feelings were shared" regarding different views on the Eucharist (p. 401). Eventually, members worked through these differences and, in Hess's words, they "finally concluded that the sacrament of communion is a mystery, and what is important is that Christ is, in some special way, present for all believers" (p. 402).

Although conflicts over theology and leadership persisted over the community's twenty-year history, members also express deep appreciation for the rewards of participating in this innovative community. Several mixed-marriage (Protestant and Catholic) couples valued liturgies that blended traditions of husband and wife, while others recall extraordinary support from the community during family crises and rewarding social justice outreach that included children (*The Inclusive Community*, 1996). Pastor Anthony Padovano (2006b) is effusive in his praise of the evening event series that features presentations by members trained in graduate theology. By the twentieth anniversary in 2006, members continued to express their gratitude for the community, but also noted tight finances and declining numbers, as well as "lack of time and energy" (Ortelli, 2006, p. 12). In an Easter sermon, Pastor Padovano (2007b) describes his preference for his community's small, intimate gatherings, affirming, "In a small room where we know the faces and names, Christ builds a community of Easter grace" (p. 3).

Challenges Ahead

In summary, the Inclusive Community represents a version of the visionary, cutting-edge theology and liturgy that appeals to what might be described as postdenominational persons, who seek a spirituality that transcends rigid denominational boundaries. Consistent with sectarian communities, this community faces difficulty attracting a second generation of members, and its current membership has dwindled to roughly fifty to sixty members.

This community also demonstrates that participation in the Reform Movement cultivates a willingness to explore unconventional forms of worship. The Catholics who joined this community included several CORPUS members who were well versed in contemporary theology and who tapped social networks of reformers to recruit new members.

GRACE CHURCH, DOVER, MASSACHUSETTS: A JOURNEY OF GRACE AND GRIT

On May 29, 2000, during the heat of the clergy abuse scandal in Boston, a column in the *Boston Globe* by Eileen McNamara (2002) boldly asserted, "The church so many disillusioned Catholics are trying so hard to envision might already exist. A carpenter built it with his wife Mary" (p. B1). Following this attention-grabbing opening line, McNamara proceeded to describe Grace Church, which occupies a small chapel in the upscale suburb of Dover and was the brainchild of Peter and Amy DiSanto. (McNamara quips: "OK, so her name is really Amy.") McNamara's column proceeds to describe a rather idyllic church that resembles Roman Catholicism (with its pews, stained glass windows, baptismal and holy water fonts, and stations of the cross, prototypical adornments of a Catholic parish). McNamara's description might lead one to believe that Grace Church represents an appealing, no-strings-attached alternative to the sterile and conformist quality of many Roman Catholic parishes, as she observes, "there is no membership book to sign, no tithe to make, no hierarchy to obey. The doors of Grace Church are open to all" (p. B1).

Grace and Grit

While McNamara's description reflects the perspective of a newcomer entering the church for the first time, who is impressed by the relaxed, welcoming, and informal atmosphere of the chapel's interior where sunlight streams through its expertly restored stained glass windows and the polished wooden pews and floors emit a satin-like glow. For their part, Peter and Amy DiSanto describe their "journey of grace" in founding this unique church as anything but effortless. Peter and Amy realized their dream of creating Grace Church after a painstaking undertaking that tapped all of their financial and personal resources. It continues to represent virtually a full-time unpaid job for each in their efforts to serve the church community and to oversee the care and financing of the property (*Journey of grace,* n.d.).

Peter devoted two-and-half years to building the chapel, which was fashioned out of a dilapidated cottage on a small lot he purchased from his neighbor for a reasonable price, though Dover is an upscale town where property commands exorbitant prices. As a professional builder, Peter constructed the chapel in his spare time, occasionally receiving a helping hand from friends and neighbors. By necessity, DiSanto was frugal in completing this project and used pews, stained glass windows, and other material salvaged from a demolished Catholic cathedral. Nonetheless, Peter confessed "the dream had become a nightmare" as he worked twelve-hour days, seven days a week (balancing his full-time job alongside this building project). He also faced mounting debt and he borrowed from friends and family to complete the project (*Journey of grace,* n.d.).

In a video about Grace Church, Peter and Amy tell their story of how they came to create an independent parish. Although Peter had abandoned his Catholic upbringing during adolescence, his interest in spirituality was ignited in Vermont when he became acquainted with Werner and Maria Von Trapp (the family made famous by the musical *The Sound of Music*). The Von Trapps introduced Peter to a community of spiritual seekers and leading thinkers from varied religious backgrounds (P. D., personal communication, January 5, 2007).

After leaving Vermont Peter, continued to pursue his interest in religion by completing courses in theology. During this time, Peter became increasingly alienated from Roman Catholicism, especially its "man-made rules that limited ordination to celibate men and denied the sacraments to the divorced" (DiSanto as cited in McNamara, B1). He and his wife Amy were eventually ordained in an independent religious group, the Community of the Crucified One, based in Pittsburgh, that claims apostolic succession. Peter maintained his interest in Catholicism and had a personal audience with Mother Teresa of Calcutta when she visited Boston in 1996 and with Pope John Paul II at the Vatican the same year.[17]

When the DiSanto family moved to Dover, Peter conducted liturgies in his home for small groups of friends, but soon the numbers grew to the point where he needed a larger meeting space. Peter completed their chapel in 1999, when he and Amy put their energy into forming a community where people could "find the strength to live out their faith amidst the pressures and complexities of modern day society" (*Grace Church, Who,* 2007). The primary goals of Grace Church are defined as (1) to offer an atmosphere of Christ-centered worship, (2) to teach the word of God, and (3) to offer the sacraments to all.

Bearing some similarity to the Inclusive Community, Grace Church identifies itself as having an ecumenical focus, particularly since Grace Church evolved from an ecumenical Christian community that attempted to "blend the powerful ministries of the Word and Worship" of Protestantism with the "rich liturgical tradition of the Catholic Church" (*Grace Church, Who,* 2007). Nonetheless, Peter characterizes the current congregation of Grace Church as 98 percent former Catholics, some of whom Peter describes as "very doctrinaire Catholics who never thought they would leave Roman Catholicism" (personal communication, January 5, 2007).

Liturgies at Grace Church

Presently, the church attracts fifty to one hundred persons to its 9:30 a.m. Sunday liturgy. The church functions much like a parish. It has a board

---

[17] When Peter met with the pope, John Paul II asked him, "My son what can I do for you?" Peter replied, "Pray for a revival of faith," and the pope responded, "Yes that's what is needed, a revival of faith." Then the pope blessed him so that he might work for this revival (*Journey of grace,* n.d.).

composed of four parishioners and two pastors, Peter (who is listed as pastor) and Amy (who is listed as associate pastor). The church sponsors a weekly prayer ministry, a Bible study, and a range of social and recreational activities, as well as religious education for children and students in middle and high school. When I attended a liturgy on June 26, 2006, sixty persons (all Caucasian) attended the liturgy dressed very casually on the hot, humid day. Worshipers represented a diverse mix of ages, including three families with children of various ages, single adults, and couples ranging from young adult to elderly.

The liturgy at Grace Church follows closely the standard prayers and format of the Catholic Mass, with no noticeable attempts at gender inclusiveness. Noteworthy features of the Grace Church liturgy include the following:

- Although Peter serves as the primary celebrant and wears a chasuble, Amy, serving as co-celebrant, wears a simple white alb-type garment[18] and serves (much like an altar server) in a secondary, helpmate role.[19]
- The liturgy includes the rite of incense that recalls the use of incense in the time of Moses and in the nativity story of Jesus; and it includes the rite of water that recalls "the deliverance of Israel as they passed unharmed through the Red Sea" (*A Guide to Our,* p. 4).
- Members of the congregation receive Communion by kneeling at a Communion rail while Peter places the host on the tongue of the recipient after dipping it in a wine goblet held by Amy.
- The music is provided by a choir composed of a dozen middle and high school students (including two DiSanto children).

The testimonials by members of Grace Church, which are posted on its website, express high praise for the role the church has played in their spiritual development. For example, Mary, who says she was in "a state of spiritual starvation" when she found Grace Church, now claims an "intimate relationship with God" (*Testimonials,* 2007). Joanne enjoys "liturgical solace" and "more importantly, the word with personal spiritual meaning," as well as "the embrace of a close-knit community" (*Testimonials*).

---

[18] An alb is a "long white garment hemmed at the ankle."
[19] Amy does serve as primary celebrant when Peter is out of town.

Reflecting on his ministry with Grace Church, Peter expresses a high degree of satisfaction, proclaiming "nothing else would give me the same satisfaction and ... contentment." Acknowledging that some people visit his church only once, he concludes, "there is no one church that can satisfy everyone." Peter refuses to characterize himself or his congregation as "liberal or conservative," insisting that he "doesn't think in those terms" (personal communication, January 6, 2007).

Future Challenges

Looking ahead, Peter stated that he is considering ordaining several members of his congregation as priests, and has already ordained five deacons.[20] Although he finds his work "interesting, exciting and awe-filled," he admits that "something has to give" (personal communication, January 6, 2007). He continues to work full time, running his construction business alongside balancing the growing demands of running his church, and admits he is "taxed to the limit." Amy juggles her responsibility as a homemaker while working virtually full time overseeing maintenance of the church property and daycare center, Little Angels Preschool, which meets in the church on weekdays. Peter admits that he would like to work full time doing "church work," which in turn would enable him to respond to the never-ending requests for advice he receives from all over the country (most recently, Texas) from groups who wanted to create their own parishes. When asked about his connections with reform groups, the only one Peter recognized was Voice of the Faithful (VOTF), since it had received massive publicity in Boston during the abuse crisis and one VOTF activist belongs to his parish. Given his harried schedule, Peter simply lacks the time to keep abreast of readings in theology or developments in Catholic reform circles.

At the end of our interview, Peter expressed confidence that "God would show him a way" to resolve his time bind and desire for full-time ministry, recalling in a calm, confident tone, "He hasn't failed me until now" (personal communication, January 6, 2007).

---

[20] Ordinations in independent dioceses do not require the same sort of formal training and extensive evaluation that characterize Roman Catholic ordination. There are networks of independent bishops who ordain deacons and priests on the basis of recommendations by priests and a brief discernment process.

Isolation: Prospects and Challenges

Grace Church resembles St. Bridget's in that both are isolated from the Reform Movement and larger networks of independent parishes. Both have ordained deacons from their own ranks, and Peter DiSanto is considering ordaining his own members as priests. Both claim vibrant communities, loyal members, and workable structures. By the same token, both groups face similar challenges in sustaining themselves, given their limited resources and volunteer staff. Due to their isolation, they lack the stimulation and opportunities for resource sharing and collaboration that might occur if they were connected to a larger network of communities. Although leaders of both communities are dedicated and resourceful, they risk burnout that might be prevented by more cooperative models of governance. Furthermore, involvement in larger networks or communities or reform groups might help them attract new members and introduce them to new models of community and liturgical innovations.

JESUS OUR SHEPHERD, NENNO, WISCONSIN: A COOPERATIVE MODEL OF MINISTRY

Jesus Our Shepherd (JOS), founded in 2001, is a unique, parish-like community of sixty members that has captured the affection of many reformers due to two distinct characteristics. First, JOS rents space for its weekly liturgies in a church in Nenno, Wisconsin, that was formerly the Roman Catholic parish St. Peter and Paul.[21] Second, in marked contrast to the priest shortage in the institutional church, JOS rotates priestly duties among four married copastors who gladly volunteer their services, welcoming an opportunity to serve a vibrant community that appreciates their pastoral gifts.

JOS defines its mission as follows: "We are a diverse and inclusive Catholic Eucharist community committed to the message of unconditional love given to us by Jesus and to our call to imitate and reflect that

---

[21] Soon after JOS was founded, the Milwaukee archdiocese threatened to shut down the community by filing a lawsuit against the owners of the church for "renting the church out as a church to serve dissident Catholics" (F. B., personal communication, August 1, 2008). The Milwaukee archbishop also sent an internal memo to parish priests asking them to dissuade parishioners from joining JOS. However, the owners of the church ignored the archdiocese and allowed JOS to remain.

love" (*About JOS*, 2008).²² JOS originally intended to become a "full service parish" and currently offers a range of ministries, including every sacrament except ordination, and a range of social get-togethers and "outreach ministries, spiritual support, healing, and faith formation" (*JOS mission statement*, 2006). By relying on a volunteer staff and renting space for liturgies, JOS operates on a small budget. Members are not charged fees or dues and there is no collection during liturgies, but members are invited to make freewill offerings at their own discretion.

A Vatican II Parish

Jesus Our Shepherd is a "Vatican II parish" whose mission statement places strong emphasis on participatory governance, social justice; and equality.²³ JOS's mission statement also emphasizes values that might be termed traditional, including "placing high value on family, especially on rural families" and "warmly welcoming children."²⁴ JOS's website includes a range of articles regarding the Catholic Reform Movement in particular and issues of peace and justice in general. In one article, JOS copastor Father Francis Baiocchi (2008) does not mince words in his critique of Pope Benedict's recent claim that obedience to the church is "the foundation of faith" (Pope Benedict as cited by Baiocchi, p. 1). Baiocchi insists that "obedience to the Gospel message of Jesus Christ, not obedience to religious authority, is the cornerstone of faith" (p. 1). He asks rhetorically if Benedict expects Catholics to obey church authority that "hides truth from people, operates behind closed doors, ... harasses abuse victims and refuses to acknowledge moral or financial accountability to the people whom it serves?" (p. 1). Remarks as bold and combative as Baiocchi's might very well evoke censure for a priest in a Roman Catholic parish, especially in the repressive climate described in chapter 6.

---

²² The mission statement goes on to state, "By diverse we mean we are genuinely enriched by each other's gifts, experience, and personality. By inclusive, we mean we welcome all, no matter where we stand on our journey, the burdens we carry or the denominational labels we wear" (*JOS Mission Statement*, 2006).

²³ The mission statement proclaims that it (1) is "committed to shared leadership and governance," (2) is "committed to justice, peace and non-violence in partnership with other faith communities," and (3) believes "in ending discrimination against women and all people regardless of their status and sexual preference" (*About JOS*, 2008).

²⁴ Although JOS does not offer formal religious education for children, they do provide parishioners with suggestions for developing "a family-style faith life" and offer a preparatory program for first communion and confirmation (F. B., personal communication, August 1, 2008).

Shared Ministry

JOS brochures explain that their four married copastors are resigned Roman Catholic priests who retain the canonical authority to confer sacraments.[25] Roman Catholic Womanpriest Kathy Vandenberg, the Reverend Robert Weiss, and the Reverend Thomas Marlier are associate pastors who "occasionally preside at Eucharist" (F. B., personal communication, August 1, 2008). Associate pastors have not gone through the process of community approval required to become copastors. Reportedly, a few female parishioners were troubled by JOS's policy of allowing women to preside at Eucharist, but they ultimately changed their minds after engaging in dialogues about the inclusivity of JOS and the role of women leaders in early church history.

JOS insists they are not in competition with neighboring churches, but rather they formed in response to an invitation from directors of A Children's Garden (the day care center that shares space with JOS), who believed that their community needed a locally based faith community. JOS does not use the term *Roman Catholic* in referring to their community, and their Liturgical Creed professed each Sunday does not include any reference to Catholicism, but rather emphasizes God's presence and the gifts of community. For example, the creed begins, "We believe that where people are gathered together in love, God is present," and "most deeply we believe that in our struggle to love, we incarnate God in this world" (*JOS: An inclusive,* n.d.).

Dilemmas of Democracy

A survey of JOS members completed by fifty-four members in 2002 revealed overwhelmingly positive evaluations of the community with fifty-three of fifty-four respondents reporting they "feel welcomed and valued" at JOS, and fifty reporting the pastors are "friendly and accessible" (*JOS parish survey,* 2002). A second membership survey conducted in 2007–2008 revealed that members wanted decisions made by the "community at large and not a parish board" (Baiocchi, 2010, p. 30), and that they favored not affiliating with another church or church group.

---

[25] JOS is listed as a Eucharistic community on Celibacy Is the Issue (CITI)'s website, and several of its priests are listed in CITI's directory of priests available for ministry.

Although the community had anticipated some growth, its membership remains stable at sixty. Pastor Baiocchi (2010) reports that the community votes on major policy decisions, but attempts to achieve consensus so as to avoid divisiveness. Baiocchi admits community feedback is "humbling at times," noting that community members "grew weary" (p. 31) of sermons about the injustices of the abuse crisis and the Vatican's exclusion of women and married priests from the priesthood. Instead, members favored homilies focused on "what today's Gospel teaches us so that we can live our own lives as Jesus directs" (p. 31). Reflecting on JOS's policy of open discussion and criticism, Baiocchi recalls that dissension was common in early Christian communities and "yet these young communities were able to grow like wildfire" (p. 31).

Carving a Path between Idealism and Realism

JOS's shared ministry provides an interesting contrast to the institutional church that suffers from a priest shortage. Although married and female priests have been rejected by the Vatican, they are lauded by JOS members. Despite its accomplishments, JOS demonstrates the always challenging struggle of reformers intent on carving a path between their idealistic goals and the preferences of new recruits. These recruits are often slow to warm up to new model of community and cutting-edge theology. To its credit, JOS pastors model patience and fairness in accepting the complaints and preferences of their members. They also have undertaken the often tedious struggle to achieve decision by consensus. By the same token, the community has not achieved the growth envisioned by its founders, perhaps reflecting the declining church attendance of American Catholics and their ambivalence regarding liberal theology. Like the Inclusive Community, JOS has discovered that creating new models of church is a demanding endeavor.[26] Although many American Catholics have expressed a desire for change in church policies, they may be hesitant about accepting new types of liturgy and community, particularly if they have no prior exposure to reform groups. Several JOS priests remain connected to the Reform Movement, which enables them to provide the

---

[26] I did not visit Jesus Our Shepherd community or the Inclusive Community and, therefore, I have no basis for evaluating the range of issues that might have influenced outreach, including recruitment, leadership, and organization.

community with a focus beyond itself and exposure to a range of new ideas and guest presiders.

SPIRITUS CHRISTI, ROCHESTER, NEW YORK: A MECCA FOR CHURCH REFORMERS

If one stepped out of a time capsule and walked into a Spiritus Christi liturgy in Rochester, New York, one might be fooled into believing that the backlash against Vatican II had never occurred and liberal Catholics had won their battle for control of the destiny of the Roman Catholic Church. True, some of the dramatic initiatives on display at Spiritus—women priests, unrestricted access to the Eucharist, blessings of gay unions—were not approved or even on the agenda for Vatican II. Still, one might assume that these reforms emerged out of the renewal process initiated at Vatican II. The lively participatory liturgy, the emphasis on lay involvement, and the extensive range of social justice ministries described below all reflect Vatican II themes. Indeed, Jim Callan (1997), associate pastor of Spiritus Christi, begins his book about Corpus Christi parish (a precursor to Spiritus Christi) by recalling Pope John XXIII's declaration that "The Church has become a museum. Let's open up the windows, get rid of the cobwebs, and get some fresh air flowing" (p. 1).

Before long, however, the time-machine visitor would discover that Spiritus Christi's revolutionary reforms were possible only because the parish had formed a schismatic parish in 1999. This decision followed a protracted battle over the fate of Corpus Christi parish, which is described in chapter 6. Following the firing of their beloved leaders (associate pastor Jim Callan and pastoral associate Mary Ramerman), a group of Corpus Christi parishioners formed the Spring Committee on August 13, 1998, to preserve Corpus Christi's inclusive spirit. After a fruitless struggle to convince their bishop to reinstate Callan and Ramerman, the committee chose to form an independent parish, named Spiritus Christi, and hired their former pastors and staff members whom the diocese had fired. This group adopted the following mission statement, which is still posted on the parish's website: "We are a Christ-centered Catholic community reaching beyond the boundaries of institutionalized church to be inclusive of all. Jesus Christ is our pastor" (*Spiritus Christi mission*, 2008). Over eleven hundred people attended the new community's first Communion services on February 13–14, 1999, and roughly half of Corpus Christi's three thousand parishioners eventually joined the newly formed Spiritus Christi parish (Callan, 2001).

Callan and Ramerman: The Dynamic Duo

One might ask why Spiritus Christi took the bold step of schism when other Vatican II parishes faced with repression and many of the vigiling churches either accepted the directives of church authorities or abandoned their lengthy struggle to preserve their parish.[27] Part of the answer lies in the unique biographies of Corpus Christi's leaders Jim Callan and Mary Ramerman, both of whom gained reputations as path-breaking agitators for church reform by boldly experimenting with liturgical innovation that violated formal church policy.

Callan (1997) candidly proclaims that during his priestly career he has been fired from every job. He was originally denied ordination due to his refusal to wear the Roman collar and his outspoken criticism of priests' privileged lifestyles. Eventually Callan was ordained, after agreeing to wear the Roman collar in certain settings. Looking back on his ordination, Callan admits to embarrassment over his prank of painting the word *help* on the back of his shoes, which were exposed as he knelt during the ordination ceremony. He also took the bold step of calling for women's ordination during the homily of his first Mass. Due to his dissident behavior, Callan was fired from his first two positions, and he was suspended briefly before being assigned to Corpus Christi, which is in a depressed downtown Rochester neighborhood.[28] Despite or perhaps in part because of his rebellious nature, Callan (2001) is reputed to be a charismatic and capable pastor, as evidenced by the transformation of Corpus Christi parish during his twenty-one year tenure as pastor, whereby a dying parish of several hundred grew into a three-thousand-member parish noted for social justice outreach.

Although Mary Ramerman does not consider herself a "feminist revolutionary" (personal communication, March 16, 2004), her influence was

---

[27] Repression of Vatican II parishes is described in chapter 6 and vigiling parishes are described in chapter 7.

[28] Callan's (1997) provocative behavior included giving homilies that contradicted those of other priests in the diocese and refusing to live in rectories he considered too lavish.

manifest in the parish's controversial and cutting-edge record of expanding roles for women in liturgy and all aspects of ministry. In fact, neither Ramerman nor Callan have the intense, caustic personalities that one might associate with provocateurs, but rather project calm and confident personas, affirming their visions for reform with humor and a generous sprinkling of biblical metaphors. For her part, Ramerman, the mother of three children, has a warm, nurturing manner; a polished speaking style; and stylish appearance accentuated by her well-groomed auburn hair and bright smile.

Yet, although Ramerman's manner and appearance may suggest conventional female virtues, there is no mistaking the bold, plucky spirit she displayed in several important milestones in her career, included marrying a Catholic and converting to Catholicism, earning a graduate degree in theology, and moving her family from balmy California to frigid Rochester, New York, to accept a position at Corpus Christi parish (where Ramerman and her husband, Jim, were offered an annual income of a mere eight thousand dollars to serve as family ministers).[29] The Ramermans were attracted to Corpus Christi's reputation for social justice and hands-on ministry that contrasted with the diocesan bureaucracy they encountered in California (Bonavoglia, 2005, p. 241). During her tenure at Corpus Christi, Mary gradually took on more prominent roles, by preaching sermons, raising a chalice during Mass in 1988 at the invitation of the presiding priest, and participating in some of the prayers previously reserved for priests (Callan, 2001, p. 69).[30] In 1993 Mary began wearing an alb and stole during liturgy;[31] it had been presented to her by parishioners in recognition of her leadership. Mary's role eventually expanded to include more priestly duties, including presiding at funerals, weddings, baptisms, and weekday Communion services. After Spiritus Christi became an independent parish, Mary was ordained by Bishop Peter Hickman of

---

[29] Eventually, Jim Ramerman returned to school and earned a graduate degree. He now works as a consultant to local businesses. The Ramermans found that they were unable to raise three children on a mere $8,000 a year (M. R., personal communication, March 16, 2004).

[30] I am referring to Mary Ramerman by her first name so as to distinguish her from her husband, Jim Ramerman.

[31] An alb refers to "a long white garment that is hemmed at the ankle." Stoles are long rectangular scarf-like ornamental apparel and are draped around the neck of the cleric presiding at liturgy. Mary Ramerman received a half stole in reflection of the fact that she was not ordained, while ordained priests wear complete stoles. Nonetheless, her decision to wear the stole was a "provocative act," given that only ordained persons are permitted to wear stoles (Bonavoglia, 2005, p. 242).

the Ecumenical Catholic Communion[32] on November 17, 2001, in an elaborate, highly publicized ceremony attended by nearly three thousand people (*History of Spiritus*, n.d.).[33]

Censure by the Diocese

On February 24, 1999, the Diocese of Rochester announced that "all those who joined the new parish had incurred automatic excommunication, and declared Spiritus Christi in schism" (*The Story of Spiritus*, n.d., p. 12). Hence, Spiritus was willing to become schismatic rather than accept what they perceived as a hostile takeover of their parish. In 2001, Bishop Matthew Clark challenged Spiritus Christi's claim that its defiance of church rules was in keeping with its emphasis on justice, stating, "This rift is not about justice, ... Spiritus Christi has chosen to leave our family" by severing its relationship with the bishop and repudiating the pope's authority (Clark as cited in Patterson, 2001, p. 11).[34]

One can speculate that for several decades after Vatican II, church officials would have negotiated a compromise with Spiritus rather than allowing a schism to occur. Chapter 6 recounts the case of Seattle Archbishop Raymond Hunthausen, who survived censure for his aberrant behavior, which involved many of the same issues of orthodoxy that surfaced at Spiritus (inadequate deference to church officials, violations of rules regarding women and homosexuals, and open access to the Eucharist). Hunthausen retained his position, thanks to the support of Vatican II bishops who retained a slide edge of control in the United States Conference of Catholic Bishops (USCCB) (Briggs, 1992).

In his role as archbishop, Hunthausen was less vulnerable than James Callan, a mere parish priest with a long record of rebellious behavior.

---

[32] The Ecumenical Catholic Communion is described later in this chapter.

[33] More than 98 percent of Spiritus Christi members voted to approve the decision to ordain Mary Ramerman as priest (Callan, 2001). A second pastoral minister at Spiritus, Denise Donato, was ordained as priest on February 22, 2003. Donato subsequently left Spiritus and established a new parish, Mary Magdalene Church in East Rochester, which describes itself as "an independent church in the Catholic tradition" (www.marymagdalenechurch.org).

[34] Additional censure was imposed on Spiritus when Father Joseph Hart, vicar general of the Rochester diocese, ordered lay and religious alike not to attend Ramerman's ordination or accept sacraments at Spiritus. Ramerman also received a letter from Bishop Clark that she described as blaming her personally for causing "scandal in the Church" and urging her to "abandon your leadership at Spiritus Christi" (Ramerman as cited by Bonavoglia, 2005, p. 251).

Nonetheless, the fate of Spiritus Christi reflects that, in the interval between the Hunthausen case in 1985 and the firing of James Callan in 1999, conservative prelates had solidified their control of the USCCB. In an ironic twist of fate, Bishop Matthew Clark, a popular Vatican II prelate, imposed the excommunication decree on Corpus Christi. We will probably never know if Bishop Clark pleaded with Cardinal Ratzinger to reconsider his stance or offer Spiritus a compromise option.

This schism at Spiritus received extensive coverage in Catholic publications, especially the liberal-leaning *National Catholic Reporter* and newsletters of reform groups. My research did not begin until 2002, and hence I was unable to interview reformers at the time the schism occurred. My conversations with reformers during 2002–2005 suggest that many reformers applauded the boldness and courage of Spiritus's leaders, but viewed this schism as an ominous development revealing the likelihood of future crackdowns on liberal Catholics.

Spiritus Christi Today

Despite or perhaps because of its censure by the archdiocese, Spiritus has become a thriving parish that claims fifteen hundred registered members and an annual budget of almost $800,000.[35] Weekly attendance ranges from nine hundred to several thousand. Spiritus also boasts small satellite communities in the neighboring towns of Elmira and Buffalo. Although Spiritus has not attained the peak of three thousand members claimed by its precursor, Corpus Christi, it has not met the doom and decay predicted by some of its critics. Callan attributes Spiritus's growth to its appeal to socially stigmatized and disadvantaged groups, including divorced Catholics who face restrictions on Communion and a cumbersome annulment process, GLBT persons and their friends and family, and many who are "Vatican II-type Catholics" (personal communication, March 15, 2004).[36] In that sense, Spiritus retains the same mission as its predecessor Corpus Christi, which Callan (1997) describes as serving

---

[35] I calculated this figure by tallying collection figures from weekly bulletins posted on the Spiritus Christi website. Spiritus priest Mary Ramerman confirmed these figures, reporting that Spiritus netted $780,000 in contributions in 2008, as well some grants and donations that support its ministry programs (personal communication, July 12, 2009).

[36] Callan noted that, contrary to his expectations, the clergy abuse crisis did not have a noticeable impact on increasing Spiritus's membership.

"those who have been injured or excluded by society and the Church" (p. 213). Spiritus also continues to sponsor numerous retreats, prayer groups, parish programs (which include four choirs, a peace group, and an environmental group), and a range of social justice ministries (which include prison ministry, a mental health clinic, and missions in Haiti and Chiapas, Mexico). In 2011 Spiritus announced plans to build a thirty-nine-unit apartment building with "a mix of market-rent and low-income units" (O'Malley, 2011).[37] Spiritus tithes 15 percent of its income to grassroots organizations involved in social justice locally and around the world (M. R., personal communication, July 10, 2009).

Although Spiritus does not own a church building, it has a cooperative arrangement with the Downtown Presbyterian Church, from whom it rents ample space for offices and parish events. While Callan is no longer invited to serve as a guest homilist at other Catholic parishes, he now receives many invitations from Protestant churches in the Rochester area and engages in ecumenical services in a variety of settings. According to Callan (2001), "If we hadn't been thrown out of Corpus Christi, we never would have connected so well with the Protestant communities" (p. 123).

Spiritus Christi has become something of a mecca for church reformers and advocates of women's ordination, who often learn about the community at conferences of Call to Action (CTA) or from other reform groups that frequently feature staff or priests from Spiritus Christi. While conducting this study, I met twenty-five people who made a "pilgrimage of sorts" to Rochester for the express purpose of visiting this renegade community.[38] All of these informants praise Spiritus's liturgies, describing them with the following adjectives: "uplifting," "upbeat," "intensely moving," and "relevant to our contemporary society."

Liturgies at Spiritus Christi

I observed four liturgies at Spiritus on the weekend of March 14–16, 2004. Listed below are the most notable and unique aspects of these services:

---

[37] This apartment building will be constructed on the site of a polling place where Susan B. Anthony was arrested for casting her ballot in the 1872 presidential election (O'Malley, 2011). The apartment building will include a café with a "Susan B. Anthony theme."
[38] These persons included three sisters, two canonical Roman Catholic priests, five women who were considering ordination by RCWP, and one man who was seeking ordination from the Ecumenical Catholic Communion.

- All masses were well attended, most notably the 9:30 a.m. Sunday service, which was held in a large, packed auditorium and featured a sign language interpreter. Each service required extensive setup and cleanup since all services were conducted in rented space. All three priests (Callan, Donato, and Ramerman) presided at the Sunday services.
- Parishioners tend to join in the singing at all the masses, especially the 9:30 a.m. service, where the band and choir produced high quality, jazzy renditions of African American spirituals and more contemporary gospel songs. The contagious beat of the music resonated throughout the auditorium, leading presider Mary Ramerman to comment that "Even the Eucharistic ministers are marching to the beat of the music" as they approached the altar. All three priests (but most obviously James Callan) moved their bodies in unison with the beat of the music.
- The prayer of peace was an occasion for vigorous hugging and handshaking among priests and parishioners.
- The 5:00 p.m. Saturday family Mass featured skits performed by children who dramatized "using your talents," reflecting the Gospel story of the fig tree from the Sunday liturgy.
- The congregation joined in the prayer of consecration that read, "When we die let us be in heaven with the saints, Mother Teresa and Martin Luther King."[39]
- Parishioners were very attentive during these liturgies, and at most a handful of persons arrived late, left early, or talked during the service.
- Guest speakers delivered the homilies. The youth minister's homily at the family Mass described the critical role a mentor played during a troubled adolescence. Gordon Webster, the minister of the Presbyterian church where Spiritus rents space, delivered the Sunday homilies, citing new understanding and appreciation of the importance of human relationships as revealed in feminist scholarship.[40] Webster's homily received a standing ovation at both services, and he joined the Eucharistic ministers in serving Communion.

---

[39] Mary Ramerman explained that Martin Luther King and Mother Teresa were often cited in Spiritus liturgies because they are persons well known to the congregation, especially children (personal communication, March 15, 2004).

[40] Rev. Webster expressed a willingness to work collaboratively with Spiritus, perhaps by creating a coffeehouse where people could share "their spiritual journeys."

- Several dozen intellectually-disabled persons from a local institution, accompanied by attendants, attended the 9:30 a.m. liturgy. Three of them joined the chorus and swayed back and forth as they sang. Other choir members watched them attentively and smiled approvingly as they participated in the singing.
- Parishioners gave a brief account of their experiences working with inmates in the prison ministry program, urging members to attend a fund-raising dinner. Presenters conveyed their stories in voices brimming with feeling, even to the point of cracking as their emotions rose to a high pitch. The last presenter, a midlife male, admitted he initially doubted the value of the program until a visit when an inmate expressed his gratitude that a "white person" would venture to visit him in prison. Each presentation received an enthusiastic round of applause.

In sum, Spiritus liturgies are not terribly dissimilar from the type of energetic, participatory, and dramatic liturgies one might encounter in a Vatican II parish—it looks, feels, and smells Catholic, but (unlike Vatican II parishes) it has the freedom to bypass restrictions it finds untenable.

Friends and Foes

I uncovered criticism of Spiritus from four Rochester-area residents whom I met during my research and in a series of letters to the editor in the *American Catholic* newspaper during 1998–1999, following Spiritus's decision to form a schismatic parish. Criticism centered on three central points. First, critics accuse the Spiritus community of disloyalty to Bishop Matthew Clark, whom they claim protected Corpus Christi parish for many years from Vatican intervention, and who suffered personally and professionally as a result of his inability to prevent a schism in his diocese. Some blame the controversy over Corpus Christi for causing Bishop Clark's heart condition. Others critics accuse Pastor Jim Callan of cultivating the "cult of personality" that contradicts the democratic, egalitarian rhetoric of Spiritus. Several claim that Spiritus misrepresents itself as a "Catholic" community and fails to explain the questionable status of its "illicit" sacraments, especially Eucharist.[41]

---

[41] As an ordained Roman Catholic priest, Jim Callan retains the authority to conduct valid sacraments, but there is controversy over the validity of sacraments performed by women priests (including Mary Ramerman and Denise Donato), who claim apostolic

The first two criticisms are rather subjective in nature and were impossible to evaluate adequately during my three-day visit to the parish. I found little evidence to support the last claim. Spiritus's literature and website consistently describe the community as an "independent" Catholic parish, and the story of its break with the Rochester diocese is included on its website and in a range of promotional material, including free paperback copies of two books authored by Jim Callan. In the Jubilee year of 2000, the parish staff of Spiritus Christi chose to address the parish's critics by writing a letter of apology to Bishop Clark. Callan (2001) explained that "in the spirit of the Jubilee's theme of forgiveness and reconciliation, we asked pardon for the polarization and damage that we had caused during and since the crisis at Corpus Christi" (p. 125). Callan explains that Spiritus chose to follow the guidance of St. Francis of Assisi who advised, "Don't protest what is bad, practice what is better" (p. 107).

Callan (2001) expressed hope that Spiritus could become a "throbbing, God centered, love-intoxicated community of diverse people ... based on the message of the Good News" (p. 106). In a similar vein, Ramerman defends her ordination by asserting, "I didn't want the people in front of me to wait 30 years for a woman priest" (Ramerman as quoted in Patterson, 2001). Following the election of Pope Benedict XVI, several activists whom I interviewed acknowledged that schismatic churches that once seemed risqué or divisive now seem "prophetic" options for keeping alive the vision of Vatican II, which seems to be fading from view. Thus, Spiritus's bold defiance of archdiocesan pronouncements and its success in forming a thriving parish made the option of schism more palatable to many Catholic reformers.

Another noteworthy feature of Spiritus Christi is the loyalty and perseverance of a solid core of faithful staff and parishioners. For example, a majority of the names listed on Spiritus's pastoral team include nine persons who were part of the original Corpus Christi parish. The fact that Spiritus has retained this loyal core of supporters through the tumultuous period of schism suggests that the parish community remains attractive and meaningful for many. Spiritus provides a vivid contrast to many Roman Catholic parishes, where so many parishioners, especially liberal ones, complain of uninspiring liturgies and the absence of a communal spirit. I interviewed two parishioners from Spiritus who raved about

---

succession but are considered ineligible for the priesthood by the Vatican on the basis of gender.

Spiritus Christi. One cited the "deep spirituality" of James Callan and Mary Ramerman and another noted the "uplifting" liturgies that attract visitors from all over the United States and beyond. Dee Carr, a long-time member of the community, considers the parish "the center of my life" and serves as an almost full-time volunteer who supports herself as a part-time nurse (personal communication, March 15, 2004).

Trendsetter or Anomaly?

In conclusion, Spiritus Christi represents the largest and probably best-known underground parish cited in this study, and some regard it as a model for independent communities. Nevertheless, a number of unique factors have influenced the creation of Spiritus Christi that may not be possible to duplicate in other settings. For starters, Rochester is a city noted for its long, bitterly cold winters, and the downtown area near Spiritus has many boarded up storefronts and abandoned buildings. Dee Carr explained that Xerox and Kodak had recently closed some of their operations in Rochester, leaving many residents unemployed (personal communication, March 15, 2004). Thus, citizens of Rochester may be more interested in church gatherings than citizens in more prosperous communities that offer competing forms of entertainment and recreation. By the same token, Spiritus's extensive range of social ministries may be particularly appealing in a community where many citizens face economic insecurity.

Another significant factor regarding Spiritus centers on its close ties to the Reform Movement, which has provided ongoing support and publicity for the community before and after its split from the Rochester diocese. The precursor parish Corpus Christi laid the groundwork for Spiritus's emergence by creating a dynamic activist community in which parishioners were exposed to liberal theology, reform group leaders, and assertive priests with a long history of challenging church teachings. Last but by no means least, Spiritus's priests and the core group of staff and parishioners who keep this parish alive have a long record as risk takers who are willing to sacrifice job security, comfortable lifestyles, and a large share of their time and resources to sustain their vision of church. Thus, it remains to be seen whether similar large-scale independent parishes will be duplicated in other settings. Prior connection to the Reform Movement may prove to be a critical variable that predicts which parishes are willing to consider schism.

An Independent Network of Parishes: Ecumenical Catholic Communion

The Ecumenical Catholic Communion (ECC) describes itself as a "community of communities" made up of "people of God baptized in Christ and professing our faith in a living Catholic tradition" (*ECC mission statement*, 2007). ECC claims nearly 3,200 members in more than thirty parishes spread over eleven U.S. states and beyond.[42] ECC operates much like some Protestant denominations in that its parishes are governed by a common constitution and governance system.

ECC did not emerge out of the Reform Movement, but is probably the best known independent Catholic network of parishes among reformers, especially since ECC has developed a collaborative relationship with CORPUS and Catholic Organizations for Renewal.[43]

Origins of Ecumenical Catholic Communion

ECC is the brainchild of Bishop Peter Hickman, and its origins trace back to his ordination as an Old Catholic priest. He began his pastoral career as a Baptist minister and became interested in Catholicism after reading Catholic theology, especially Hans Küng, and encountering many lapsed Catholics in his congregation who missed the sacramental dimension of Catholicism (personal communication, June 26, 2004). As a married father of five children, Hickman was ineligible for ordination in the Roman Catholic Church, but found an aging Old Catholic bishop who ordained him.[44] In 1995 Hickman was ordained bishop by three Old Catholic bishops. Hickman acknowledges that his liberal theology is "atypical" (Hickman as cited in Bonavoglia, 2005, p. 250) of many Old Catholics, who are often very conservative, although some Old Catholic bishops in Europe have ordained women.

---

[42] One ECC community is located in Puerto Rico and another in Canada. Many ECC affiliates are small communities that rent space from non-Roman Catholic churches or other types of buildings, like the underground communities described in chapter 8.

[43] As noted in chapter 3, CORPUS invited ECC to join its National Catholic Ministerial Alliance and the Community of John XXIII. ECC attracted the attention of many reformers when ECC bishop Peter Hickman was chosen to preside at the ordination of Mary Ramerman (described above).

[44] The Old Catholic movement began at the first Vatican Council of 1870 when a number of Catholic communities defected in protest over the issue of papal infallibility. Recent estimates indicate that the number of Old Catholics worldwide is less that 250,000 with less than 70,000 in the United States (*Old Catholics*, 2008). A noteworthy feature of the Old Catholics is that the Vatican recognizes their claim to apostolic succession.

Hickman's success in forming ECC did not come easily or quickly. In fact, the first community he built in Orange County, California, folded, but he eventually attracted three hundred families to form a parish. They meet in rented space in a shopping mall.

ECC's Appeal to the Reform Movement

Two features of ECC make it especially attractive to reformers. First, ECC spokespersons proclaim that it "seek[s] reconciliation with Rome, and pray[s] for the unity of the whole Body of Christ" (*ECC mission statement,* 2007). ECC's position statements consistently use very amicable, Gospel-like language, avoiding the angry and bitter expressions occasionally used by reformers. For example, referring to Roman Catholic hierarchs who were conducting a heresy trial against an ECC priest,[45] Hickman (2006) commented, "If only they would speak to us.... So many in the world are looking for some kind of hope that love always prevails and the gospel of Jesus really breaks down walls" (p. 20). Although reformers feel free to occasionally describe Roman Catholic hierarchs in harsh terms, they may very well take offense if someone outside the institution (like Hickman) makes derogatory statements.

The second and more distinguishing feature of ECC that impresses reformers is its elaborate constitution and governance system. Indeed, the Constitution of the Ecumenical Catholic Communion (2007) reads a bit like the reform platform of CTA and other reform groups, since all of their major hot-button issues are addressed:

- The priesthood is open to all regardless of marital status, gender, or sexual preference.
- Laypersons play a prominent role in the governance of the church, including selection of pastors and bishops.
- All baptized persons ("regardless of denomination") are welcome to receive the sacraments.
- Divorce and contraception are accepted.

---

[45] The Diocese of San Bernardino, California, found ECC priest Rev. Ned Reidy guilty of heresy and schism in a one-day closed trial on December 13, 2005. Reidy, who refused to attend the trial, was formerly ordained as a Roman Catholic priest and left by resigning from his order but not the priesthood. Reidy, who became an ECC priest and cofounded the PathFinder ECC Community of the Risen Christ in Bermuda Dunes, California, was found guilty of heresy ("rejection of fundamental matters of faith, namely the infallibility of the pope") and schism ("breaking with the church over matters of doctrine") (Rosenblatt, 2006).

- Parishes retain control of assets and are required to form finance committees.
- There are elaborate qualifications for ordination to the priesthood (including background checks and the equivalent of a master of divinity). Priests accused of sexual misconduct are immediately removed from ministry and cannot be restored if the priest is found guilty of sexual assault or homicidal threat or attempt.

According to Bishop Hickman, the constitution was modeled after the United States Constitution, with its checks and balances and clearly defined bill of rights, as well as the Association for the Rights of Catholics in the Church's (ARCC) *Proposed Constitution of the Catholic Church* (1998), with its comprehensive outline of the rights and responsibilities of clergy and laity (personal communication, June 26, 2004). Consequently, the ECC constitution establishes a House of Laity (including elected delegates from every parish), a House of Pastors (including all pastors, laypersons in formal leadership roles, and no bishops), and an Episcopal Council (including all bishops in good standing). Many positions have term limits, including the bishop, who must be elected by a two-thirds vote of the electoral college and who is limited to three four-year terms. All three of these elected bodies participate in decisions regarding finances, liturgical changes, and "intercommunion agreements with other ecclesial bodies" (p. 7). ECC's constitution also establishes a list of eleven basic rights, which flow from members' "basic human rights or their baptismal rights" (p. 16).[46]

Moveable Boundaries

Two stories I encountered in my research on ECC reflect the boundary issues faced by ECC and other independent parishes and dioceses. ECC Bishop Hickman told the first story during a workshop I attended at the CORPUS conference in 2004. Hickman describes an incident in which an ecumenical group of pastors from Orange, California (where Hickman's parish, St. Matthew's is located), met to plan an interdenominational Easter service. One of the Protestant pastors suggested that Hickman's parish should be invited to participate. In response, the Catholic priest

---

[46] These eleven rights include many rights denied to Roman Catholics, including "freedom of conscience, freedom of opinion and expression, ... the right of participation in self-governance, the right to the accountability of chosen leaders" (*Constitution*, p. 16).

responded, "Oh no, they're schismatic." When the Catholic priest left the room briefly, the Protestant clergy chuckled among themselves, commenting, "They called us schismatic once, too." In this instance, independent groups like ECC are considered schismatic, while denominations that became independent in the distant past are considered worthy of some degree of respect and collaboration.

The second story is told by ECC priest the Reverend James Lehman of the Holy Family parish in Las Cruces, New Mexico, on an ECC video (n.d) recording. Lehman's story involves three soldiers in World War II that included a Roman Catholic, a Jew, and a Protestant. The soldiers became friends and vowed to take care of one another. When one of the soldiers died, the other two soldiers asked the Roman Catholic pastor at a nearby parish to bury their friend. The pastor explained that canon law did not allow him to bury a non-Catholic in consecrated ground, so he would bury their friend just outside the fence. When the two soldiers visited the cemetery years later, they asked the pastor why they could not find their friend's grave. The pastor explained that canon law did not forbid him from moving the fence, so their friend's grave was included in an enlarged cemetery.

These two stories reveal the boundary issues that must be confronted by independent groups like ECC that hope to expand the boundaries of Roman Catholicism to include outlier communities like itself. ECC takes advantage of its location outside this shrinking Vatican-defined circle to create a form of renewed Catholicism that attracts liberal Catholics who no longer feel at home inside the formal institutional boundaries.

Another appealing feature of ECC is that it does provide some advice and guidance to groups engaged in creating independent parishes, although ECC is unable to provide financial assistance to these communities.[47] For example, the newly emerging Holy Spirit Community in Boston has received several visits from Bishop Peter Hickman when he was on the East Coast to attend reform group events (P.H., personal communication, July 19, 2008). I also interviewed Deacon Francisco A. Morales-Perez, who was attempting to build a new ECC community in Puerto Rico. He had traveled to the CORPUS convention with Bishop Hickman and was planning to spend several weeks observing the Spiritus Christi parish in Rochester, New York (A. M., personal communication, June 26, 2004).

---

[47] ECC has a policy requiring all affiliated parishes to remain financially independent and to donate an annual fee to ECC to maintain the organization.

Growing Pains

As ECC has increased rapidly in size over the past several years, it acknowledges encountering some "growing pains" over governance and finance issues. For example, ECC priest Jim Farris (2009) defended ECC's decision to create dioceses of six to twelve communities in geographical areas. Responding to charges that ECC was creating "another level of bureaucracy" (p. 3), Farris responded that dioceses would foster decentralization by allowing dioceses to function as an "autonomous unit" that would have access to a local bishop. EEC also admitted it was encountering financial problems and set up an all-volunteer committee to address fund-raising, acknowledging that "growth requires work and money" (Howard, 2009, p. 2) and both were in short supply.

A Fruitful Collaboration

ECC did not emerge out of the Reform Movement, but it has benefited from its recent collaboration with reform groups. It attracts reformers as candidates for priesthood and members of its communities. As ECC strengthens both formal and informal connections to the Reform Movement, it enhances its visibility and reputation. In turn, ECC has drawn on material from liberal Catholic theologians and reform group documents to formulate its unique and impressive structure that gives shape and substance to the vision of reformers.

One might question why the Reform Movement itself never developed a plan for institutionalizing its goals and principles.[48] One possible factor may be the fact that ECC leaders were not involved in struggles to reform the church, and so they could devote their energies to building communities and designing a workable governance structure. Another significant factor may be the fact that Bishop Hickman and many ECC priests are middle-aged, in contrast to reform group leaders who are often near or past retirement. Consequently, ECC priests, including Hickman, may have more energy to engage in the exhausting tasks of community building.

---

[48] As noted above, ARCC has drafted a *Proposed Constitution of the Catholic Church*, which delineates rights and responsibilities of clerics and laity. Although this document does propose rough outlines of a governance and judicial system, this system has never been implemented. In contrast, ECC's constitution has been in effect since 2007 and has already been amended.

ECC's success in building a network of independent worship communities provides some evidence that it may be possible to build a liberal Catholic Church outside of Vatican control. However, ECC has not escaped the debates over structure and leadership that have plagued the Reform Movement. ECC's stability and growth may be hampered if it fails to develop viable structures and leadership.

The Catholic Diocese of One Spirit: Catholic Lite and Catholic Plus

Founded in 1998 by Bishop James H. Burch, the Catholic Diocese of One Spirit describes itself as "a voluntary organization of progressive and spiritually minded persons, operating in the spiritual structure of Catholic/Christian dioceses of the early church" (*The Diocese of One*, 2010). One Spirit defines itself as a "fully Catholic, but non-Roman model of Christianity as it was practiced by the early Christians" (Burch, n.d., p. 2). One Spirit remains part of the Catholic tradition and expresses appreciation of the following characteristics (in abbreviated form):

> Theology that emphasizes we are all ... "temples of the Holy Spirit"
> The mysticism and spirituality of so many Catholics
> The Catholic liturgy, assuming it is "well done"
> The church's outreach to the poor and emphasis on social justice
> The tracing of apostolic succession ..., even though this tradition was not established by Christ (Burch, n.d.. p. 3)

While embracing many aspects of Catholicism, One Spirit does not impose any dogmas, creeds, or doctrines on members. One Spirit emphatically states that it is not an "independent" Catholic church, a term that is self-contradictory because "there is only ONE baptism" ... "ONE Body of Christ" ... and "therefore ONE Church" of which "*All* Christians are members" (Burch, n.d., p. 2). One Spirit accepts the designation "Catholic Lite," noting that "we have only shed the poundage and calories of irrelevancy" (*Another Way to Be*, 2004, p. 1). Stating their mission in more positive terms, One Spirit terms itself "Catholic Plus," noting that "we emphasize the essential principles of Catholicity" (p. 1).

Commenting on the Catholic Reform Movement, Bishop Burch explains that One Spirit respects reformers as "extremely good and dedicated people," but regards the movement as a "waste of time" (personal communication, November 12, 2006). Burch explains, "We are no longer interested in asking an entrenched hierarchy to validate what God gives us as free gifts of ministerial calling."[49]

Although One Spirit refers to itself as a diocese, in many respects it resembles Roman Catholic Womenpriests, whose primary focus is ordination. One Spirit favors egalitarian worship communities, but Bishop Burch defends ordinations as not inherently "clerical" and as a "reasonable conclusion to the movement of God's Spirit within God's people" (Burch, n.d., p. 2). As of March 2010, One Spirit's website lists short biographies for twenty-nine of the forty-one priests and deacons who have been ordained by One Spirit and who are engaged in a variety of ministries, including administration, teaching, and care for children, the physically and mentally ill, the imprisoned, and dying persons. They also preside at weddings, baptisms, and funerals (*Report of the Third*, 2007).[50]

Although One Spirit's efforts at community building have foundered, it continues to explore new forms of ministry appropriate to the current era (J. B., personal communication, July 15, 2007). One Spirit has formulated bylaws that primarily outline rights and responsibilities of its pastors and officers.

Expanding Ordination: The Priesthood of All Believers?

One Spirit serves as a type of seminary that enables a range of persons to achieve ordination, including those who would not be eligible for ordination within the Roman Catholic Church due to marital status, gender, sexual preference, age, and other factors. One Spirit provides an inexpensive route to ordination as deacon or as priest, which involves personal direction by Bishop Jim Burch and self-directed education and spiritual practice. Its priests represent a diverse range of racial, professional, and educational backgrounds.[51] Plummer's (2004) study of independent

---

[49] Despite these criticisms, Burch occasionally does attend reform gatherings and periodically contributes articles to *CORPUS Reports*, the bimonthly magazine of CORPUS. Chapter 3 cites an article by Bishop Burch in *CORPUS Reports* that defends the organization Married Priests NOW!

[50] Criteria for evaluating candidates include a range of psychological, spiritual, and educational qualifications, such as "a practice of prayer," "psychological wellness and wholeness," "a positive thinker," "education and level of knowledge commensurate with the people," and "an articulate pastoral promoter of contemporary theology" (*Report of the Third*, 2007, p. 2).

[51] Profiles of some One Spirit priests are featured on its website (www.onespiritcatholic.org).

parishes notes the attractiveness of ordination to a wide range of persons, many of whom do not expect to obtain paid positions in ministry. Hence, expanding opportunities for ministry and ordination may become a potential draw for underground communities, especially if online and community-based training programs become more visible and accessible.

A Feminist Seminary: Roman Catholic Womenpriests

Roman Catholic Womenpriests (RCWP) operates much like a seminary by sponsoring a formation program that prepares women and men for ordination as deacons and priests. Although the Vatican has imposed an excommunication decree on those who participate in RCWP ordinations, spokespersons for RCWP claim their ordinations are valid, given that their bishops were ordained by three Roman Catholic bishops who were in good standing in the church. These bishops decided to remain anonymous in order to avoid censure by the Vatican (Schaeffer, 2007).[52]

RCWP describes its mission as "to bring about full equality of women in the Roman Catholic Church," as well as "advocat[ing] a new model of priestly ministry based on union with the people with whom we minister" (*Roman Catholic Womenpriests*, n.d.). RCWP emphatically states that it does not desire a "schism." RCWP Bishop Patricia Fresen (2008) explains that "Among the womenpriests, priesthood is not part of a power structure. We see it and try to live it as a ministry of servant-leadership, not as part of a system of domination or exclusion" (p. 31).

Thus, RCWP's express aim is to effect change in the institution rather than form an independent organization, but it embraces outsider strategies to achieve its goal. After forty years of struggle by feminists to convince hierarchs to ordain women, Bishop Fresen (2006) proclaimed that it was time to experiment with "holy disobedience," citing role models such as Joan of Arc, who put loyalty to God ahead of loyalty to church authorities, and Rosa Parks, who defied segregation laws by proclaiming, "The only tired I was was tired of giving in." Fresen cites the nonviolent struggle against apartheid in her homeland of South Africa as her training ground

---

[52] The Roman Catholic bishops who performed these secret ordinations of RCWP bishops have consented to publication of their names after they die. The first priests ordained by RCWP were ordained by Bishop Romulo Braschi of Argentina, a former Roman Catholic priest who founded the Catholic Apostolic Charismatic Church of Jesus the King.

for "the present struggle for justice for women in which I have become involved" (Fresen as cited in Schaeffer, 2007, p. 15).

RCWP Challenge Excommunication

In 2002 the Vatican's Congregation for the Doctrine of the Faith (CDF) declared the first RCWP ordinations as "invalid and null," because these ordinations were a "simulation" of a sacrament and were performed by a "schismatic" priest (Johnson, 2005). In response, Dr. Ida Raming, an ordained RCWP bishop and a German theologian, insists that Canon 1024 (reserving priestly ordination to men) contradicts biblical teachings and Vatican II documents that assert the equality of women (Raming as cited in Howarth, 2002).[53] Raming further asserts that the excommunications imposed on RCWP are a "fraud," noting that many Catholics approve of RCWP ordinations, and hence the excommunications do not come from God or the entire Catholic community (Raming as cited in Oleck, 2003, p. 2).

The Appeal of Ordination by RCWP

RCWP leaders admit to being astonished at the response to their formation program, as more than fifty persons (including six men) have been ordained and more than one hundred fifty women are currently enrolled in the program, including eighty to ninety from the United States (Schaeffer, 2007). Judging by the photos of RCWP ordained priests and deacons on the RCWP website, the overwhelming majority appear to be Caucasian midlife or older women, many of whom have served as volunteers and employees in Catholic parishes and agencies. Many cite graduate degrees and extensive education in theology and ministry. Although RCWP application material does not cite specific education requirements (other than some training in theology), applicants are encouraged to earn master of divinity degrees (Taylor, n.d.). Upon acceptance in the program, applicants undergo one- to two-year training programs that

---

[53] Raming cites Gen. 1:27 that women are created in the image and likeness of God, and the teachings of Vatican II (Lumen Gentium, para 32 et al.) and Galatians 3:2:7 that state, "All baptized in Christ, you have all clothed yourself in Christ, and there are no more distinctions between Jew and Greek, slave and free, male and female, but you are all one in Christ Jesus" (Raming as cited in Howarth, 2002, p. 1).

include "study of sacramental theology and a liturgical component that calls for mentoring by a priest" (Schaeffer, 2007, p. 15).

One might ask why women and men would seek ordination in RCWP given that the process can be expensive and is not likely to result in paid employment.[54] In fact, several ordained Roman Catholic Womenpriests have faced job-related penalties because of their ordination.[55] RCWP offers two explanations to justify the decision not to seek ordinations in another denomination. First, many emphasize their strong, lifelong ties to Roman Catholicism. For example, RCWP Jane Via responds, "I can't explain it. I only know that I'm Catholic through and through" (Via as cited in Dolbee, 2006). Second, RCWP emphasizes the potential of its movement to change consciousness and mobilize pressure for women's ordination in the institutional church. RCWP Elsie Hainz McGrath reflects, "The more it happens, the more people are beginning to think things through for themselves and say— ... I'm mad as hell, and I'm not going to take it anymore" (McGrath as cited in Cooperman, 2008b, p. 3).

Many RCWPs may not be deterred by their lack of employment opportunities as ordained priests, since many are near retirement age or have jobs as teachers, therapists, nurses, retreat leaders, and chaplains (*Meet the Roman,* 2006). After ordination, Roman Catholic Womenpriests practice their ministry in many of the positions they held prior to ordination. They also serve as occasional presiders for underground Eucharistic communities and parishes and, in some cases, for Old Catholic and Protestant parishes. Several Roman Catholic Womenpriests have created successful communities, including the two communities in Massachusetts described in the vignette at the beginning of this chapter and the Mary Magdalene Apostle Catholic Community in San Diego, California, which was formed by RWCP Jane Via and claims more than one hundred members (Fields, 2006, p. B4).

---

[54] Expenses incurred by women seeking ordination by RCWP include travel expenses to RCWP events. Many women ordained by RCWP already have degrees in theology and ministry.

[55] Following her ordinations in RCWP, Bishop Fresen was "fired from a prestigious teaching post and expelled from her religious order" (Schaeffer, 2007, p. 15). As recounted in the vignette above, Jean Marchant remained undercover for one year after being ordained as a RCWP. In 2007, she had no choice but to resign as head of health care ministries for the Archdiocese of Boston after choosing to reveal her "illicit" ordination. RCWP Bridget Mary Meehan expects to lose income from the cancellation of her books from listings of her former publisher Ligori, a Catholic publishing house (Schaeffer).

Discipleship of Equals?

RCWP Bishop Patricia Fresen (2008) acknowledges that the RCWP model of ordination contradicts the teachings of prominent Catholic feminist theologians, such as Elisabeth Schüssler Fiorenza and Mary Hunt, who call for a new model of church based on a "discipleship of equals" to replace the hierarchical model of ordained clergy. Fresen (2008) defends RCWP as an intermediary step that may ultimately lead to priestless communities, but insists that women must seek ordination in the short term to "break down the sexism that is so rampant in our hierarchical structures" (p. 30). If women reject ordination altogether, Fresen argues that "we would do nothing toward claiming equal rights for women in the church and no one would take us seriously" (p. 30).

The Vatican has become increasingly punitive toward RCWP, as CDF issued a "new decree warning that women taking part in ordinations will be excommunicated" (Associated Press, 2008). Numerous reform groups, including DignityUSA, CORPUS, Women's Ordination Conference (WOC), and CTA, issued press releases challenging this excommunication decree and have circulated petitions denouncing the firing of Sister of Charity Louise Lears for attending a RCWP ordination ceremony in St. Louis on November 11, 2007 (T. Fox, 2009b). They have also sponsored petition campaigns on behalf of Maryknoll priest, the Reverend Roy Bourgeois, who was excommunicated for his participation in an RCWP ordination in Chicago on August 9, 2008 (Goodstein, 2008).[56] Given Bourgeois's stature in the peace movement, even the *National Catholic Reporter* weighed in with an editorial supportive of Bourgeois, acknowledging that his actions were "daring" (*Rome Looks Bad*, 2008, p. 28), but questioning the "or else tone" of demands that Bourgeois resign, pointing out there "is always wiggle room among Christians of good will when they wish to find it" (p. 28).

Dilemmas and Trade-offs

With the exception of VOTF, the Reform Movement has welcomed priests ordained by RCWP by featuring them as speakers at conferences and

---

[56] Bourgeois, a long-standing hero of Catholic progressives, is famous for his leadership role in founding the School of the Americas Watch. (The School of the Americas was renamed the Western Hemisphere Institute for Security Cooperation but the protest is still referred to as the School of the Americas Watch). Every year protestors gather in Fort

promoting their worship communities. Many RCWPs have roots in the Reform Movement, especially CTA and WOC. Ironically, RCWP has set itself on a contradictory path that repeats some of the failed strategies of the Reform Movement. Most notably, RCWP's strategy resembles that of VOTF, which struggles to preserve its insider status, despite the fact that it gained leverage only by resorting to outsider strategies.

No doubt RCWP is aware that prospects for women's ordinations within the Roman Catholic Church are exceedingly dim for the foreseeable future. As documented in chapter 4, Pope Benedict has taken an unequivocal stance against women's ordination. He has also followed the pattern of his predecessor, Pope John Paul II, by stacking the College of Cardinals with conservatives. Even if the Vatican somehow reversed its opposition to women's ordination, it would almost certainly not recognize priests ordained by RCWP, given its long-standing policy of penalizing those who defy its authority, especially liberal dissidents. The examples of CORPUS and Celibacy Is the Issue (CITI) priests are relevant in this regard, since they never realized their objective of returning to ministry or successfully challenged the celibacy requirement.

RCWP's claim to insider status is reflected in its assertion that it does not seek schism. This assertion is contradicted by the fact that it conducts ordinations unsanctioned by the Vatican and that some of its priests have formed independent worship communities. These acts are schismatic in nature. Furthermore, the Vatican has assigned RCWP the ultimate form of outsider status by excommunicating its priests, and even some persons who attend or participate in RCWP ordinations. Understandably, RWCP's claim to insider status reflects its desire to gain some legitimacy among Roman Catholics, for whom the term *schism* is often regarded as pejorative.[57] By the same token, one might question how much legitimacy a feminist organization like RCWP gains by claiming association with the Vatican, whose reputation has been damaged by scandals and its unwillingness to revise its authoritarian patriarchal system. Moreover, the Vatican's loss of prestige and credibility is particularly intense among

---

Benning, Georgia, where a gathering of primarily Catholics engage in highly publicized demonstrations aimed at shutting down this school. Demonstrators allege this school is a training ground for terrorists, who were responsible for the assassination of Archbishop Oscar Romero and other Catholic martyrs.

[57] In fact, Webster's dictionary even defines schismatic as "promoting or guilty of schism" (Landau, 2002, p. 653). Although Webster's dictionary is not designed exclusively for Catholics, it seems probably that Catholics are the group who associate the term *schism* with "guilt."

reformers and defecting Catholics, who represent the actual and potential audiences for RCWP ministries.

The dilemmas faced by RCWP are addressed by African American feminist poet Audre Lorde (1984) in her classic essay "The Master's Tools Will Never Dismantle the Master's House." Lorde explains,

> They [the master's tools] may allow us to temporarily beat him at his own game, but they will never enable us to bring about genuine change. And this fact is only threatening to those women who still define the master's house as their only source of support. (p. 101)

Perhaps it is hard for RCWP leaders to imagine a priestly ministry outside the "master's house," even though its priests have already begun to claim space outside the boundaries of the institutional church. I do not mean to suggest that women should never become priests within the Roman Catholic Church. One can imagine that a reformed church (which no longer constitutes the "master's house") would welcome women as priests and remove all barriers to their full participation in church governance. In contrast, existing church structures require all priests to accept the church's very constricted and clericalist concept of priesthood and to silence their objections to its oppressive policies.

Like many independent Catholic priests and many resigned Roman Catholic priests, persons ordained by RCWP can and do gain certification to perform ministry without permission or approval from the Vatican. Hence, the most credible and effective strategy for RCWP would be to acknowledge its outsider status as a parallel organization that represents a form of nonviolent resistance to discriminatory Vatican policies. As they demonstrate their gifts for ministry and leadership, RCWP priests gain recognition from members of their communities and non-Catholic clergy, which in turn strengthens public pressure for reform of Vatican policies. This outsider strategy is currently practiced by DignityUSA communities, who are excluded from operating within Roman Catholicism, but who hope that growing societal acceptance of GLBT rights will have spillover effects that create a momentum for change. RCWP might also promote the services of its priests by creating an online referral system similar to CITI's Rent-a-Priest website.

RCWP leaders already do engage in public critique of Vatican policies, even though such activity undermines their efforts to attain insider status. Most notably, RCWP issued a press release denouncing a Vatican statement that put "ordination of women in the same category as sexual abuse of priests" by denouncing both as "serious violations Roman Catholic canon law" (Meehan, 2010). RCWP called on the Vatican to "correct the damaging behaviors of patriarchy, the abuse of spiritual power." They also announced that they appealed to the United Nations to support their demands for equality within Catholicism. In this instance, RCWP challenged the legitimacy of the Vatican rather than seeking to gain legitimacy through association with it. My analysis suggests that these sectarian outsider strategies are the only viable method of reforming the institutional church.

Pros and Cons of Underground Parishes

Defenders of the underground parishes cited above describe these sect-like parishes as "something new under the sun," in that each one blends some features of traditional Catholicism with contemporary innovations tailored to the unique nature and preferences of each community. Defenders also note similarities of these communities to early Christian communities whose structures, in varying degrees, were egalitarian and inclusive. Although underground communities do retain some hierarchical distinctions, they are considerably more egalitarian than Roman Catholic communities.

Critics often describe underground parishes as schismatic, fracturing unity among Catholics, and blasphemous, daring to tinker with rituals and traditions that reflect centuries of Catholicism. In response to these critics, members of underground communities insist their communities offer a vibrant and authentic form of worship that contrasts with stale and predictable liturgies in many Roman Catholic parishes.

Although many Catholics consider *sect* a pejorative term, my analysis has demonstrated that, in contrast to ineffective insider strategies, sectarian strategies represent the only effective method of reform as long as the papacy is controlled by archconservatives who oppose any accommodation with the liberal policies of Vatican II and contemporary social trends. The trade-offs involved in the strategic choices facing reform groups and underground communities reflect the church-sect dialectic, which is examined more extensively in the conclusion that follows.

CONCLUSION

LASTING IMPACT AND FUTURE PROSPECTS OF THE REFORM MOVEMENT
"CULTURE WARS": THE GREAT DIVIDE

The struggle between the Catholic Reform Movement and Roman Catholic hierarchs represents an extremely polarized version of the "culture wars" in society as a whole. These culture wars evoke extremes of divisiveness wherever they occur, because they involve deep-seated differences between liberal and conservatives in basic values and beliefs (Hunter, 1991). This divisiveness takes an intense and extreme form within Catholicism because the last two papacies have launched an unapologetic campaign to establish conservative theological principles as the litmus test for authentic Catholicism, and have purged liberal theologians and Vatican II documents from positions of prominence. Despite a sustained and concerted effort, the liberal Reform Movement has failed to reverse these conservative trends and increasingly views insider reform strategies as futile. Consequently, many liberal Catholics are moving in a sectarian direction by breaking off from the Roman Catholic Church.

Several Catholic scholars identify the roots of this extreme polarization within Catholicism to the papacy of John Paul II, who launched a frontal assault on any trace of modernism, liberalism, and secularization within the institutional church. Margaret O'Brien Steinfels (2010), codirector of the Fordham Center on Religion and Culture, describes John Paul II's assault on the reforms of Vatican II and his appointment of conservative bishops as a catalyst for the sectarianism and polarization so evident in today's church:

> During the long years of John Paul II's pontificate, we can trace the emergence (or reemergence) of a structure and mentality that tightened boundaries and helped create slogans for those judged to be more Catholic ("orthodox") or less Catholic ("cafeteria" Catholics). Add to that the resurgence of a pre-Vatican II clerical and curial culture that served to alienate many Catholics from their bishops and led to an unprecedented level of sectarianism within the church and the sharp division we now see among American Catholics. (p. 15)

Notre Dame theologian Richard McBrien (2010c) differs somewhat from Steinfels by attributing the growing polarization almost exclusively to the conservative bishops appointed by John Paul II, as follows:

> Thus if there is any single reason why polarization exists in the Catholic Church today it is because of the type of bishops whom John Paul II appointed and promoted within the hierarchy over his 26 and a half years in office. Any other explanation ... is simply naïve.

According to McBrien (2010a), Pope Benedict XVI made some conciliatory gestures during the first five years of his papacy, but reverted to the divisive policies of John Paul II in 2009 when he lifted the excommunication of four conservative schismatic bishops, one of whom was a holocaust denier. McBrien states that a majority of bishops had asked the pope to require these schismatic bishops to express a "faithful adherence to Vatican II" before lifting their excommunication. The pope ignored this advice and, consequently, his decision to lift these excommunications evoked internal turmoil and a barrage of negative media attention.[1]

John Paul II and Benedict XVI reversed the long-standing "big tent" tradition within Catholicism that allowed a broad spectrum of Catholics on the right and left to remain faithful Catholics. The liberal Reform Movement began as a revivalist movement, which Stark and Bainbridge (1985) describe as "sect-like in nature" and designed to "protect and maintain deep attachments to the traditional religions rather than efforts to create religions" (p. 444). At this juncture, many reformers now believe that revival will not occur within institutional structures dominated by archconservatives, and, hence, are moving outside these boundaries to revive their preferred form of Catholicism.

Prospects for Progressive Reformers

Given Pope Benedict's far-reaching power and unwavering determination, one might reasonably conclude that he will achieve his goal of driving out many, perhaps most, liberals and marginalizing Vatican II policies. Yet many analysts predict success on these goals will weaken the institutional church. M. O. Steinfels (2010) claims that most Catholics welcomed the reforms of Vatican II, which also improved the church's relationship with non-Catholics. Looking to Catholicism's future, she cites Cardinal

---

[1] McBrien also asserts that Benedict had ignored warnings against his speech in 2005 at Regensburg University, which evoked the ire of Muslims, and his controversial decision to lift restrictions on the Latin Mass.

Bernardin's Common Ground Initiative, which questions whether church leaders can "confront an array of challenges with honesty and imagination and whether the church can reverse the polarization that inhibits discussion and cripples leadership" (p. 15). Although Notre Dame theologian Richard McBrien (2010b) claims that "the church is, in many ways, just fine," he describes the hierarchy as "deeply damaged from within," and that within its ranks "there is little evidence of the imagination, the creativity, the spirit, to repair or rethink the structure" (p. 28).

As Steinfels and McBrien attest, the polarizing policies of the last two popes will only further damage the declining legitimacy and stability of the American Roman Catholic Church. John Paul II's and Benedict XVI's efforts to rid the church of liberal reformers will not reverse the trend of lay Catholics, who are adopting increasingly liberal views on social issues. Harsh penalties for liberal reformers may also encourage defections by moderate Catholics who regard Vatican crackdowns as mean-spirited and high-handed.

Are Liberal Catholics Lax "Cafeteria" Catholics?

Conservatives accuse liberal reformers of being lax "cafeteria" Catholics who select only those doctrines and practices that suit them, thereby abandoning central tenets of the tradition. Liberal reformers are most likely to reject church teachings on access to Eucharist, mandatory celibacy, divorce, reproductive issues, women's ordination, and GLBT rights. Progressive Catholics defend their right to be selective regarding church doctrines by referring to the Vatican II principle of "primacy of individual conscience,"[2] whereby persons have the right to base decisions on their own conscience, even if their choice contradicts formal church dogma. Liberal Catholics also note that conservatives are also selective in their support of church policies, as many reject Vatican positions on capital punishment, the war in Iraq, and peace and justice issues.

The culture wars between liberal and conservative Catholics reflect conflicts over values and lifestyles that are present in the larger society. Just as conservatives in the wider culture favor a return to authoritarian and patriarchal structures and cultural norms of the modern or premodern era, so too Catholic conservatives favor a pre-Vatican II church that

---

[2] For a discussion of the historical development of the doctrine of individual primacy see J. L. Carroll (2007). On authority, How American ideals have changed the Catholic Church. *Boston College Magazine*, 67(2).

assigns a passive, obedient role to laypersons, strict clericalist distinctions, and a far-reaching rejection of American culture. Similarly, liberal Catholics share the preferences of liberals in the wider culture for more egalitarian, democratic societal structures and a qualified appraisal of contemporary culture.

Stereotypes of liberal reformers as lax or self-indulgent are inaccurate. On the contrary, many liberal reformers remain diligent and resilient, some might say foolhardy, despite their lack of progress on their reform agenda. Financial data of reform organizations reveal they are very low-budget operations sustained primarily by volunteers and staff with modest salaries and extensive responsibilities.

Many leaders of marginal and independent groups emphasize the considerable efforts required by their members to sustain their communities.[3] Priests involved in independent communities generally cannot rely on the stable income and range of benefits available to Roman Catholic priests, which include paid vacations and training, health insurance, sick leave, and pension. For example, Peter and Amy DiSanto perform their ministerial roles at Grace Church of Dover as unpaid, virtual full-time second jobs that they juggle alongside family and work obligations. Priests ordained by Roman Catholic Womenpriests (RCWP), Ecumenical Catholic Communion (ECC), and the Catholic Diocese of One Spirit finance their own education and often perform their ministry without pay and undertake the arduous task of building a new worship community. In the case of the independent parish Spiritus Christi in Rochester, New York, priests who serve the community earn low salaries, work long hours, and would face challenging employment prospects if their community disbanded.

Of course many who are drawn to the Reform Movement or underground communities may be merely curious or shopping for a compatible worship community, and therefore do not share the extensive commitment of its most exemplary leaders. As with any movement, supporters vary in their degree of commitment to movement groups. Nonetheless, for many the choice of moving to and beyond the margins of institutional Catholicism usually does involve rejection of some church teachings. Reformers do not regard this stance as an abandonment of one's faith but rather as a risky but necessary journey of discipleship that may impose high costs.

---

[3] Tasks involved in maintaining communities include planning and conducting liturgies, publishing bulletins, conducting retreats, organizing educational and social gatherings, maintaining websites and phone chains, and raising funds.

CONCLUSION   273

The vigorous efforts of liberal Catholics to create and sustain their reform groups and alternative communities are matched by comparable efforts on the part of conservative Catholics who maintain their own forms of parallel institutions. It seems reasonable to conclude that neither liberals nor conservatives lack devotion and loyalty to their religious convictions. Mirroring the ever-widening gulf between liberal and conservatives in society at large, conservative and liberal Catholics alike seem unwilling or unable to engage in fruitful dialogue or propose models of church that could include the full spectrum of Catholics on the right and left.

Manna in the Desert: The Rewards of Activism

The first question raised by this study focuses on how and why participants sustain their reform activities in the face of continual setbacks and stonewalling on the part of church hierarchs. Although many reformers have abandoned the movement, those who remain in it are sustained by their connections to a community of like-minded persons and a range of liturgies and educational programs that lift their spirits and enrich their spiritual search. After undertaking their exile journey, liberal reform groups have largely abandoned insider reform strategies in favor of outsider strategies that do not require approval from church hierarchs. The only exception is Voice of the Faithful (VOTF), which remains focused on insider reform but has reformulated its agenda in response to declining revenues and lack of receptivity on the part of church hierarchs.

Although the Reform Movement retains a loyal cadre of committed followers, it has also witnessed defections by members who tired of what former VOTF President James Post (2002) described as a Sisyphean struggle in which hoped-for reforms are always out of reach. Hence, the declining membership and morale evident in many reform groups fuels the willingness of reformers to abandon the movement and explore schismatic worship communities. Although many reformers retain strong ties to their Catholic roots, growing numbers insist they can practice their Catholicism as effectively, perhaps even more effectively, outside the boundaries of the institutional church.

The clergy abuse crisis that erupted in 2002 gave the movement a second wind, which energized reformers and evoked activism from a second layer of Catholics who had not responded to earlier outreach by reformers. However, the clergy abuse issue has more or less run its course in the

United States, as opinion polls show declining interest in this issue on the part of lay Catholics.

Accomplishments of the Reform Movement

Insider versus Outsider Strategies

A second focus of this study centers on the accomplishments of the Reform Movement. Progressive Catholic reform organizations have achieved only minimal, easily reversible reforms at the parish and diocesan level by relying on insider strategies. The movement can claim credit for several policy-level changes at the diocesan and national level achieved through outsider strategies (primarily lawsuits and media exposure). These reforms include policies adopted by the United States Conference of Catholic Bishops to address clergy sexual abuse and to establish tighter financial controls for dioceses, as well as the Boston archdiocese's decisions to fully disclose its annual budgets and to establish a review board, which resulted in the reversal of roughly 25 percent of planned parish closures. Several parishes outside of Boston have also successfully challenged closure decrees. Notably, these policy-level reforms focus on governance issues that do not involve doctrine.

One cannot conclude that outsider strategies would achieve concessions on doctrinal issues such as reproductive rights, a more inclusive priesthood, acceptance of homosexuality, and more democratic church structures. The current governance structure of the Roman Catholic Church is dominated by staunchly conservative clerics who believe that the reform agenda of progressive Catholics threatens core doctrines of Roman Catholicism that they are commissioned to protect. Pope Benedict XVI has repeatedly expressed preference for a "smaller, purer church" (Benedict as cited by Gibson, 2006, p. 17) that represents "the divine, unchanging and uncompromising truth" (p. 271) of the faith. In advocating doctrinal reform, reformers also face a more limited range of outsider strategies, given that legal maneuvers applied successfully in the abuse crisis do not apply to doctrinal matters, especially in the United States and other Western democratic states that have constitutional provisions regarding separation of church and state.[4] Under these circumstances,

---

[4] A case in point was legislation filed in Connecticut in 2009 that would "restructure the way Catholic parishes are organized." This legislation met with fierce opposition from

many reformers acknowledge the futility of a battle against a church hierarchy that maintains almost total control and that regards the demands of reformers as something akin to heretical.

Influence beyond the Vatican

Although church reform remains an objective of the Reform Movement, its outreach and influence is not limited to church officials. The Reform Movement, especially VOTF and Catholics for Choice, are skillful in attracting media attention, which more often than not portrays reformers in a positive light. All the liberal reform groups circulate polished press releases and have highly articulate, well-informed spokespersons who make themselves available for media interviews. While some church officials are media savvy, during the height of the abuse crisis many hierarchs came across as defensive, evasive, and sanctimonious. The Boston archdiocese publicly admitted the negative fallout from its mishandling of the vigiling movement and made a number of conciliatory gestures, including covering costs of maintaining vigiling parishes until these groups exhausted the Vatican appeals process.

Although many reform groups remain somewhat invisible, RCWP attracts massive media coverage of their ordinations.[5] The most notable activities of reform groups are widely covered by some Catholic publications and some national and international media. At least some Catholics in Europe and beyond are aware of liberal reform groups in the United States, and reform group leaders attend various types of Catholic gatherings abroad.[6] Widespread protests among American Catholics in response to the clergy abuse crisis inspired similar outbreaks of protests in response to abuse revelations in Ireland, Germany, and beyond. The activism and skillful media relations of reformers provide a model of resistance to Vatican policies for Catholics around the world and serve as a reminder that the spirit and promise of Vatican II continue to inspire liberal

---

Catholic parishioners and clerics, who decried it as "unconstitutional." In the face of this opposition, the bill was withdrawn before being considered by the Connecticut legislature (T. Roberts, 2009c).

[5] In presenting my research at conferences and in numerous conversations about my research with acquaintances, I have yet to encounter anyone who is not aware of RCWP ordinations.

[6] VOTF's only international chapter is in Ireland. This chapter has been involved the protests over abuse allegations in Ireland.

Catholics. Reformers have also lent significant support to victims of clergy abuse, primarily by supporting campaigns to extend deadlines for filing abuse claims at the state level and occasionally convincing bishops to remove abusive priests and to strengthen abuse prevention procedures in parishes. Finally, reformers provide an audience for liberal Catholic and non-Catholic theologians, whose censure by the Vatican only strengthens their appeal to reformers.[7]

A Resourceful Movement

My study is focused on a religious movement aimed at changing a church, as distinct from a social movement that aims to change the broader society. Nevertheless, some social movement theory is relevant to my study, especially resource mobilization theory as proposed by McCarthy and Zald (1977), which emphasizes the significance of resources and social networks in forming and sustaining social movements.

All the liberal reform groups in this study are low budget operations that rely primarily on volunteers and a few paid staff. Nonetheless, my study also points to organizations and communications networks, which facilitated collaboration and membership outreach by reform groups. The movement is not well funded, but it does receive generous support from its primarily middle-class, middle-aged, and elderly members, who donate considerable amounts of discretionary income and leisure time to movement groups. Although the Catholic Reform Movement has never posed a serious threat to Vatican leaders, it has endured for more than four decades, an achievement of sorts, particularly since several scholars credit movement groups with liberalizing the views of Catholic laypersons.

A Failure to Communicate

Until the outbreak of the abuse crisis, church hierarchs had grown accustomed to deferential treatment and often lacked the listening skills and openness to dialogue necessary for fruitful interaction and negotiation with reform groups. Perhaps church hierarchs were reluctant to engage in dialogue because they expected laypersons to accept their authority

---

[7] Liberal theologians favored by reformers include Tissa Balasuriya, Joan Chittister, Charles Curran, Elisabeth Schüssler Fiorenza, Matthew Fox, Mary Hunt, Hans Küng, Richard McBrien, Rosemary Ruether, and Miriam Therese Winter.

unquestionably. M. O. Steinfels (2010) supports this contention by pointing to the declining credibility of church hierarchs following Vatican II, stemming from their inability to offer well-reasoned arguments to justify church teachings.

Some reformers also occasionally exhibit poor communication skills. For example, parishioners from vigiling parishes in Massachusetts engaged in shouting matches and finger-pointing during their meeting with Archbishop O'Malley. In her study of Catholic feminists, Henold (2008) noted that feminists were often not "balanced" (p. 172) when engaging in dialogue with church hierarchs during the 1970s, as feminists placed more emphasis on being "heard than seeking the chance to listen" (p. 172).

Fault Lines within the Reform Movement

This small and declining size of the membership of reform groups reflects the apathetic response of many Catholics to reformers' outreach efforts. This response may reflect the perception that reforming the church is not a realistic goal or not worth the effort. Unlike reformers, many lay Catholics may remain in the church for sentimental reasons, but may not regard Catholicism as central to their identity, and, consequently, not worth much time or attention.

Reformers' outreach to new members also reflects reformers' tendency to engage in what might be termed "group think," as they craft their own insider lingo to describe their perspective on church politics that may be misunderstood or off-putting to potential new members. This insider lingo is apparent when reformers discuss their persistent struggle to reform an institution that, in many respects, no longer matches their beliefs and values. This issue becomes especially pertinent when one considers that many reformers have defected to liberal denominations. Some reformers cite the phrase, coined by theologian Sister Miriam Therese Winter, "defecting in place" to characterize reformers' ambivalent status, but even those who are highly educated and well-spoken often resort to phrases like "I just can't explain it" or "I'm Catholic in my bones" to justify their persistence in reform activity. The phrase "recovering Catholics" is increasingly invoked at reform gatherings, a term with apologetic undertones suggesting that Catholicism has an addictive quality that should be discarded.

The Reform Movement's unofficial in-house theologians, married priest Anthony Padovano and Benedictine Sister Joan Chittister, periodically present highly sophisticated justifications of the movement's positions and strategies, which are cited throughout this study. Yet participants rarely refer to these speakers' remarks, possibly because their ideas are not easy to summarize or because they focus on collective rather than individual perspectives. Reformers' ambivalence and apologetic tone may shed light on why the movement has difficulty attracting and retaining members, especially young persons who did not come of age during the Vatican II era, when the church was the center of family and community life. The more reformers stress the deeply entrenched flaws of the institutional church and the intransigence of its leaders, the more inactive Catholics become convinced that the struggle for reform is simply not worth the effort.

Not only do reformers sidestep questions about remaining Catholic, they also typically avoid explicit discussions of the tradeoffs involved in moving in a sect-like direction by forming independent communities.[8] Catholic Organizations for Renewal (COR) made an explicit decision to allow schismatic groups (including Spiritus Christi parish and Ecumenical Catholic Communion) to become members, because church officials excluded them for less than "essential reasons." Despite this decision, COR remains focused on church reform rather than questions of schism. Call to Action (CTA), the nucleus of liberal Catholicism, features schismatic priests as presenters at its conferences, but conference sessions are not explicitly focused on the nuts and bolts of forming independent communities or the tradeoffs involved in staying or defecting from the institutional church.[9]

Literature of reform groups and agendas for conferences seem to intentionally avoid or skirt the schism question, perhaps because it would alienate their more moderate members, or because they do not want to be identified as disloyal Catholics.[10] Although reformers acknowledge Spiritus Christi and St. Stanislaus as schismatic, they tend to describe

---

[8] Of course this question is off limits for groups like FutureChurch and VOTF, who define themselves as loyal Catholics.

[9] The question of Why stay? does come up occasionally, such as in Robert McClory's session at the CTA 2004 conference workshop described in chapter 1, but this session focused on the choices facing individual Catholics rather than the decision to form a sect or independent community.

[10] Reform groups do not use the word *sect* to describe worship communities that have severed their ties to the Vatican. My content analysis of reform group literature never uncovered use of the term *sect*. It may not have much meaning to reformers. However, even the decision to form an "independent" community is not a workshop theme.

these communities as victims of an unjust crackdown that forced them out against their will.[11] RCWP explicitly denies that they are schismatic, insisting they choose to remain Roman Catholic while urging church hierarchs to recognize the legitimacy of their ordinations. Their position is contradicted by the fact that many priests ordained by RCWP have established independent worship communities, since they have no other venue for practicing their priestly role.

Reformers hope to avoid the pejorative connotations of the word *schism*, and at least some reformers may still be uncomfortable acknowledging their defection from an institution that still shapes their identity and worldview. Regardless, one might speculate that precisely because of the momentous nature of this decision, it deserves analysis and debate about tradeoffs, planning, and long-term implications. Without this type of analysis, reformers are missing opportunities for information sharing and thoughtful deliberation. They may also damage outreach to new members who might be put off by the perception that independent parishes are somehow illicit or illegitimate.

The Emergence of Marginal and Independent Communities

Challenges and Opportunities in the Margins and Beyond

A third focus of this study centers on communities created by progressive Roman Catholics who have abandoned conventional parishes they describe as unwelcoming and uninspiring in favor of marginal or underground worship communities where they sustain their loyalty to the tradition on their own terms. These communities are distinct from the social movement organizations described in part 1. Some of these communities are members of COR and are listed in CTA's church renewal directory, but none of them are formally sponsored by reform organizations. Although leaders of these communities have ties to the Reform Movement, most are primarily focused on creating worship communities that embody their liberal values. This study examined three forms of independent worship communities:

---

[11] Although Spiritus Christi and St. Stanislaus were victims of a conservative crackdown, they also chose to become independent parishes rather than accept the conditions imposed by church hierarchs.

1. Marginal communities (including Vatican II parishes, Eucharistic Communities, religious orders of Catholic sisters, and vigiling churches) that remain Roman Catholic but risk censure by violating some church policies.
2. Underground communities that are small, grassroots organizations that do not employ canonically active priests and whose liturgies openly defy Vatican policies.[12]
3. Underground parishes that have ordained presiders and formal structures and are defined as schismatic by church hierarchs.

Although they remain Roman Catholic, marginal communities risk censure by disobeying formal church policies. The most frequent challenges to church policies include unrestricted access to the Eucharist, homilies that involve group participation or are not delivered by priests, and prayers and other practices that openly challenge church teachings on women and GLBT persons. By choosing to remain within the confines of the institutional church, these communities remain circumspect about their activities, avoiding publicity that might alert church officials and invite censure. The only exception is the vigiling movement, which represents a unique situation. Perhaps church officials have overlooked vigilers' aberrant liturgical practices (which include priestless and nonstandard liturgies) because these groups are seeking to preserve rather than avoid conventional parishes.

Due to the suppression of Vatican II parishes and lay-led liturgies, some liberal Catholics are more willing to explore underground communities and parishes or non-Catholic denominations. Underground groups are sect-like in nature because they have severed their bonds with the institutional church either by choice or because of formal excommunication decrees. They do not constitute a full-fledged sect because they have not organized into a unified structure with a consistent set of beliefs and operating principles.[13] These independent groups exemplify the advantages of their independence from the Vatican in that they have a high

---

[12] "Canonically active" refers to the status of ordained Roman Catholic priests who have not resigned or been excommunicated.

[13] The Ecumenical Catholic Communion (ECC) does have a unified structure, a well-defined constitution, and some statements of belief. However, it has never had a formal connection to the institutional church, and hence its status as a sect is less than definitive. It also includes only a small number of the schismatic communities that represent liberal Catholics.

degree of autonomy, develop decentralized and participatory governance structures, and blend contemporary and traditional features in their liturgies and educational programs that are tailored to the preferences and composition of each community. By the same token, these communities face the risks and difficulties experienced by exile communities, including instability (reflecting their small, aging memberships), challenges regarding legitimacy (reflecting the risk or reality of excommunication and other penalties), and isolation from the larger Roman Catholic community (where they may be denied sacraments or lose jobs or speaking engagements). The choice of exile may also damage relationships with family and friends who cannot accept or condone the choice to abandon the institutional church.

The Dialectics of Structure and Communitas

One might speculate that both the Roman Catholic Church and the marginal and independent communities described in this study have failed to achieved the dialectic between structure and *communitas* that anthropologist Victor Turner (1969) claims "no society can function adequately without" (p. 129). According to Turner, structure refers to a formal allocation of "positions and statuses" (p. 131), while *communitas* has a "spontaneous, immediate, concrete nature" (p. 127) and is the realm of "artists and prophets" who "enter into vital relations with other men in fact or imagination" (p. 128). Structure is essential for orderly functioning of a society while *communitas* bolsters and complements structure by forging bonds of solidarity among members and providing an outlet for expressive tendencies.

Turner points to a dialectical relationship between structure and *communitas* that resembles the dialectical relationship Goldstein (2011) identifies as characteristic of the interaction between church and sect.[14] Weber-Troeltsch's concept of church corresponds to Turner's concept of structure in that both refer to formalized and hierarchical governance

---

[14] My analysis places a stronger emphasis on Turner's model because it is a better fit for the liberal Reform Movement. Reformers' goals match Turner's concept of *communitas* with its emphasis on communal bonding and re-visioning Catholicism. In contrast, reformers do not refer to themselves as a sect and do not meet many of the characteristics of sect identified by Weber-Troeltsch. Reformers are middle class (unlike the prototypical lower-class members of sects) and they favor open-ended visionary theology, which is the polar opposite of the fundamentalism attributed to sects.

systems, while the concept of sect corresponds to the concept of *communitas,* with its emphasis on egalitarianism and revival. Hence liberal reformers point to the negative fallout from overemphasis on structure within the institutional church. They decry rigid rules, clericalist norms, and a tepid, formalistic type of worship experience. The marginal and independent worship communities created by reformers resemble sects (and the matching principle of *communitas*), as evident in their anticlericalism, intense religious expression, and strong communal bonding. As predicted by Turner and Weber-Troeltsch, both types of structures contain their own inherent contradictions. Thus, churches with their overemphasis on structure eventually lose members when they become staid and uninspiring, while sects oriented toward *communitas* lose members who tire of lack of resources and instability.

Hence, the institutional Roman Catholic Church increasingly exhibits the pitfalls of church as it prioritizes structure to the exclusion of *communitas* by creating stricter rules and regulations, by enforcing uniform dogma and rituals, and by merging many small parishes into megaparishes with fewer priests, some of whom may be assigned to multiple parishes due to the priest shortage. For their part, marginal and independent communities favor *communitas* (or sect) by creating small, close-knit communities that have minimal rules, focusing instead on inclusive, innovative liturgies and flexible, loosely designed structures reflecting the evolving nature of each community. Both types of organizations are inherently unstable, and excesses in either direction lead to oscillation to the opposite pole.

My limited data show some evidence of the oscillating trends suggested by Turner and Weber-Troeltsch. For example, as the number of Vatican II parishes decreases, some liberal Catholics have gravitated to sect-like marginal and underground communities or non-Catholic parishes known for their inclusive, welcoming spirit and imaginative, progressively oriented liturgies.[15] Alternatively, some members of marginal and underground communities have returned to conventional parishes, citing inadequate structures (i.e., the lack of religious education for members of Fatima community and Community of God's Love [CGL]). In fact, many of the marginal and independent groups in this study did not offer

---

[15] It may be that conservative Catholics are in part attracted to independent conservative communities (such as those affiliated with the Society of St. Pius X) because they offer a more communal atmosphere than is available in mainstream parishes. Since my study did not include conservative communities, I have no basis for evaluating this possibility.

religious education, which obviously undermines outreach to young families, the very age group most absent in these communities. In addition, many underground groups worship in shabby locations and lack the resources to provide live music and choral groups. Thus, underground groups exemplify the typical challenges of sects in attracting and retaining members, because they lack the services and facilities available in established churches.

Vatican II Catholics bemoan their inability to pass on their fervor and belief systems to younger generations who do not share their memories of Vatican II or their religious orientation. Some marginal and independent groups show evidence of becoming more church-like as predicted by Niebuhr (1929). For example, the Jesus Our Shepherd community has discovered that its members do not share their leaders' interest in reform issues and prefer homilies that have practical relevance to their own lives. In my conversations with attendees before and after underground worship services, I noticed that many praised these communities, using phrases like "new and different" and "warm and inviting," but did not comment on their liberalism or their dissent from Vatican policies. So, very possibly, leaders of underground groups will survive by downplaying reform issues and providing alternatives to the impersonal, uninspiring services of conventional parishes. By doing so, underground groups will adopt some church-like qualities as they translate their beliefs into a form acceptable to a mainstream audience, rather than the "true believers" who make up sects.

Drawing on both theories, one could predict that if the institutional Roman Catholic Church in the United States stays on its current path it will continue to experience a decline in membership, especially among liberal, well-educated members who favor more participatory structures and more contemporary liturgies and policies. These liberal Catholics are the type of persons who are drawn to the liberal sectarian communities described in this study. These trends contradict the typical pattern of sects, which tend to attract less educated and less affluent persons. Sectarian communities established by liberal reformers also contradict the typical tendency of sects to maintain a state of high tension with their environment (Stark & Bainbridge, 1985).

Precisely because the liberal Reform Movement differs in composition and goals from conventional sects, it logically follows that it will not resemble them. Liberal reformers are not seeking a revival of traditional Catholicism, which they regard as outmoded and tyrannical. On the contrary, they are seeking to create a new form of Catholicism that is in low tension with the dominant culture, because they accept science and many liberal social trends.[16] For the same reason, sectarian communities of liberal reformers seem eager to become church-like by appealing to a wider network of moderate and liberal Catholics. Therefore, these communities resemble sects primarily by separating themselves from their host institution. Their long-term goal is to establish a new form of Catholicism.

Stark and Bainbridge (1985) characterize churches as offering "very weak general compensators" (p. 434), because they place less emphasis on otherworldly rewards and, consequently, "offer little solace to the bereaved, to the dying, to the poor, or to those who seek to understand the enigmas of science" (p. 434). Liberal reform communities do place less emphasis on otherworldly rewards than more conservative communities. Nevertheless, one cannot necessarily conclude that they offer only "weak compensators." Liberal reformers express their religious motivation in a form and language that differs from traditional Catholicism or the fundamentalism of sects. Liberal communities point to the solace and uplift one attains from the beauty of Catholic ritual, which reminds them of their common heritage and enables them to connect with the sacred dimension of reality (which may or may not refer to an otherworldly domain). For example, at a reform gathering Tom Powers. a Roman Catholic priest, described conducting a funeral for a victim of the plane crash in Minnesota that killed Senator Paul Wellstone. He assured family members, who asked him to perform the service, that he had no difficulty conducting a funeral service for the deceased person (a former seminarian who had become an atheist). Powers explained, "Wherever there are strong emotions, the sacred is present."

Stark and Bainbridge (1985) may overemphasize the significance of otherworldly rewards, even for some sect members. Of course religions often do use the promise of an afterlife as an effective compensator for loss and as an incentive for ethical behavior. Yet critics of religion often argue that many believers do not seem particularly convinced of an afterlife, although to escape censure they may not voice doubts. It is at least possible that the type and strength of compensators in liberal communities may not differ

---

[16] Some reformers might describe themselves as in a state of high tension with the dominant society, because they reject the growing inequality of wealth and the despoiling of the environment that characterize contemporary capitalism. Nonetheless, they do not resemble typical sects because their criticisms of the status quo reflect liberal rather fundamentalist theology.

much from those of churches, whose members vary in their beliefs and motivations for religious involvement.[17]

My findings do confirm church-sect theory's emphasis on the instability of sectarian groups. Most notably, CGL, St. Bridget's, and the Inclusive Community face an uncertain future given their declining membership and resources and their lack of connection to a larger network such as ECC. Further, as ECC grows larger it requires a more elaborate structure and a more stable source of funding, trends that are viewed with suspicion by members who fear bureaucratic tendencies.

Challenges Facing Resistance Communities

While small size is conducive to the development of participatory, close-knit communities, it also has obvious limitations in terms of resources. The largest independent parish in this study, Spiritus Christi, boasts an extensive range of social justice ministries and religious education programs for all ages. Small communities could not offer such extensive programs unless they were part of a network of small communities such as ECC.[18] Notably, a number of small independent jurisdictions (which did not emerge from the Reform Movement) have signed interim or full communion agreements with ECC, which may eventually lead to their formal affiliation (Von Stamwitz, 2008).[19] This study did not investigate these jurisdictions, but it seems fair to conclude that they recognized potential benefits in forming alliances with a larger network, particularly since ECC's constitution assures them a high degree of autonomy.

Communities that remain isolated from a larger network of communities are less likely to absorb or adopt many of the movement's most

---

[17] Stark and Bainbridge (1985) predict that "faiths may lose credibility by being too inexpensive" (i.e., impose few demands on their members) (p. 436). Liberal reform communities are not necessary "inexpensive," despite the fact that they impose few demands on members. As well-educated, mature persons, reformers value their ability to make their own judgments, and they question the quality of sacrifices that are imposed by external authority rather than freely chosen. Some reformers engage in considerable risks or sacrifices in their advocacy for social justice and their efforts to create independent communities. Thus, one cannot conclude that participation in independent communities is necessarily "low cost."

[18] Some EEC parishes are clustered in various geographical areas that are now being formed into dioceses. Small ECC parishes could engage in most forms of resource sharing only if they were near other ECC parishes or some other network of parishes.

[19] The independent jurisdictions that have signed interim or full communion agreements with ECC include Apostolic Catholic Church, the Ecumenical Anglican Communion, and the American Catholic Church Diocese of California.

progressive principles. For example, the Reverend Peter DiSanto is so engaged in balancing his full-time job alongside his role as pastor of Grace Church of Dover that he has no time to engage in reading theology, to become involved in the Reform Movement, or to network with other religious leaders. His lack of connection with other independent groups robs him and his community of opportunities to join coalitions around issues of common concern and engage in a fruitful exchange of ideas for liturgy and membership outreach. Bishop Peter Hickman of ECC confessed that his ministry included scant attention to social justice ministry until he was invited to ordain Mary Ramerman of Spiritus Christi and became acquainted with the extensive social justice programs sponsored by her parish (personal communication, June 26, 2004). Thus, the isolation of marginal and independent groups may undermine the very progressive values reformers hope to promote.

Each community faces unique opportunities regarding networking, as evidenced by Jesus Our Shepherd (JOS), whose members rejected the option of affiliating with a larger network, although their liturgies have featured presiders from other communities. Nevertheless, several JOS pastors remain active in the Reform Movement and keep members abreast of new developments in an online newsletter. Since the presider role at JOS liturgies is rotated among four copastors and several associate pastors, pastors can balance their service to the community alongside other commitments.

Regarding finances, one might question whether independent communities can sustain themselves by relying so heavily on volunteers, poorly compensated staff, and free or low-cost rental space in non-Catholic churches. One might argue that independent communities were designed merely as an interim step, and, hence, need not be concerned about long-term survival. This assertion is contradicted by the fact that prospects for liberal reform in the Roman Catholic Church are dim, at least in the short term. Consequently, issues of structure and leadership succession are critical to the survival of resistance communities.

Sustaining independent communities for an extended period will require more attention to resources. Recruiting new leaders for these communities will be challenging since these roles are highly demanding and offer little compensation. The priests who currently minister to these communities include priests associated with Corps of Reserve Priests United for Service (CORPUS), Celibacy Is the Issue (CITI) and Roman Catholic Womenpriests (RCWP), who engage in ministry on a volunteer or part-time basis, and thus does not constitute their primary income.

Many of these priests were also shaped and inspired by many years of Catholic education and long-term involvement in the Reform Movement that strengthened their sense of calling. In fact, many of the women ordained by independent groups struggled with lifelong longings for a priestly career that evoked considerable personal turmoil (Henold, 2008). Despite their dedication, independent priests are in danger of burnout, as noted by the Reverend Peter DiSanto, who admitted "something has to give" as he and his wife juggle their role as pastors alongside family and work responsibilities. Members of even small Eucharistic Communities complain about the "exhausting" and "highly demanding" efforts required to sustain their communities by relying solely on volunteers.

Although even conventional Roman Catholic parishes have always relied on a range of volunteers, many studies have documented the decline in volunteerism in virtually every section of American society due to the busy lifestyles of contemporary American families, the competing attractions of mass media and an entertainment culture, and the self-absorbed orientation among younger generations (Putnam, 2000). Thus, one can reasonably question whether independent communities can be sustained primarily by volunteer labor.

One might also ask how the education of future underground priests or other types of ministry will be financed.[20] Currently the Federation of Christian Ministries sponsors an online degree program Global Ministries (www.globalministries.org) that provides degrees in ministry and theology.[21] CORPUS created the National Catholic Ministerial Alliance to provide mentoring for priests whose training and ministry takes place outside the institutional church. Despite the merits of these programs, they cannot duplicate the type of financial aid or scholarships, classroom instruction, and ongoing supervision and placements available in traditional seminaries. Many members of underground groups have been inspired by newly emerging theologies such as liberation, feminist, and environmentalist theologies. These theologies assume a basic knowledge of traditional theology and scripture and are written in a sophisticated academic style that might be inaccessible to those who lack formal training in theology.

---

[20] In his study of independent communities, Plummer (2004) pointed to the need for formal education programs and noted the emergence of online degree programs. He also recommended some sort of alliance to facilitate communication and cooperation among independent communities.

[21] Global Ministries offers degrees ranging from bachelor to doctorate, with costs for degrees ranging from $7,000 to $15,000.

This study has cited a number of sources that emphasize the advantages of marginality. CORPUS member Baute cited marginality as essential to a genuine conversion experience, and theologian Veling (1996) describes marginal communities as well suited to critical evaluation and renewal of a faith tradition. Feminist theologians have posed egalitarian communities as vibrant alternatives to the stifling and dehumanizing aspects of patriarchal structures that negate the spirit of *communitas* essential to authentic Christianity.

Indeed, the margins are home to many prophets and artists who, as Turner proclaims, play a critical role in rethinking and reimagining a faith tradition. Yet if new visions of church remain confined to the margins, they risk becoming invisible and irrelevant. Eventually underground communities will survive and thrive only by embodying their visions into a more church-like structure capable of giving form and substance to these visions.

Although reformers are united in their criticism of existing church structures as too authoritarian, patriarchal, and hierarchical, they are divided and uncertain regarding how to reform these structures. Independent worship communities do, in varying degrees, create prefigurative models, but their stability and viability remain unstable and uncertain. Many reformers are reluctant to embrace a more institutionalized model or to engage in long-term planning to bolster their prospects for survival. Some communities are caught in a catch-22 where they are so absorbed in community maintenance that they simply lack the resources to examine structural questions, a precarious situation that reinforces the validity of Turner's emphasis on structure.

Discipleship of Equals

Two types of worship communities in this study, CGL and Women Eucharist (WE) communities, are structured according to the "discipleship of equals" envisioned by Catholic feminist theologian Elisabeth Schüssler Fiorenza. They do not employ priests, and members share the tasks of organizational maintenance. These examples do not provide a ringing endorsement for the egalitarian model, because both examples are unstable, especially CGL, which is near extinction. On the other hand, WE communities describe themselves as "bridge type" networks designed to aid women in their transition away from the institutional church by creating visionary and experimental gatherings, which stretch participants' imagination and receptivity to new forms of worship. Turner's emphasis on structure is less applicable to transitional groups that may serve as a testing ground for more stable groups in the future.

Even transitional communities cannot totally ignore issues of structure, because lack of organization and insufficient resources may inhibit the formation, outreach, and short-term survival of these groups. In addition, Marjorie Procter-Smith (2010), a professor of liturgy and participant in many feminist spirituality groups, contends that many of the accomplishments of feminist spirituality groups that were prevalent in the 1970s "[are] at risk of being lost, and some [are] undoubtedly already lost because [they were] kept within women's groups, albeit often for very good reasons" (p. 230).[22] In order to preserve the tremendous outpouring of prayers, songs, and liturgical innovations generated by these groups, their leaders need to form some structure or sponsor to preserve these resources, which in turn could eventually be adopted by both underground groups and conventional parishes intent on celebrating feminist themes.

Almost all the marginal and underground communities in this study have some degree of hierarchical structure, particularly since they rely primarily on ordained clergy, most of whom wear liturgical garb, preside at liturgies, and often serve as principal spokespersons for their communities. RCWP Bishop Patricia Fresen acknowledges that the RCWP model of ordained clergy does entail some measure of hierarchical distinction, but insists it is an interim step necessary for women to gain equal status within existing church structures.

Although independent communities retain hierarchical structures in varying degrees, they are, nonetheless, considerably more democratic and egalitarian than conventional Roman Catholic parishes, especially ECC with its model constitution that has institutionalized the reform agenda of reform groups, and that allows members far-reaching control over the governance of their parishes and ECC policies.[23] Underground groups have some regard for egalitarianism, since most choose or elect their own priests or have elected or volunteer officers who consult with members

---

[22] Feminist spirituality groups were unwilling to share or expose liturgical material that might have evoked censure from church officials because it challenged the teachings and liturgical rules of church hierarchs.

[23] My research on ECC was not sufficiently in-depth to evaluate whether ECC's constitution was enforced in a consistent manner that corresponded to its democratic principles.

regarding major decisions. The priests I observed in these communities seemed eager to break down clericalist distinctions by including lay participants in many aspects of liturgies (including homilies). For example, Bishop James Burch of the Catholic Diocese of One Spirit delegates the decision on clerical garb, allowing those involved in marriage ceremonies or other rituals to decide on appropriate garments for their ceremonies (J. B., personal communication, November 12, 2006). Many independent priests also clearly enjoy socializing with community members, sharing hugs and handshakes during liturgies and social gatherings. During my visits to these communities, priests were usually called by their first name, but almost never referred to by clerical titles such as "Father" or "Reverend."

The Tyranny of Structurelessness

The fact that communities claim an egalitarian ethos or have decentralized structures does not ensure they will operate in a manner consistent with these principles. The political scientist Jo Freeman's (2009) research on feminist consciousness-raising groups indicated the pitfalls and contradictions encountered by groups that claim an egalitarian, "structureless" ethos. Her research revealed the paradox that the actual operations of these groups often violated and undermined the very principles they were designed to uphold. Although groups claimed to be leaderless, leaders did emerge but could not be held accountable because there were no formal measures of accountability. The lack of formal procedures for decision making and governance hampered rather than ensured genuine power sharing among group members.[24] Freeman's research is consistent with the theories of both Weber-Troeltsch and Turner, who emphasize that well-defined structures are essential to the long-term survival of communities.

Unlike the groups in Freeman's research, the communities I observed were not entirely without structure. They did have some rules and organizational frameworks and voted on some policy issues, and several

---

[24] Turner (1969) describes *communitas* by its very nature as "relatively undifferentiated" and as a "community of equals who submit together to the general authority of the ritual elders" (p. 96). Although he describes structure as a "differentiated and often hierarchical system of politico-legal-economic positions" (p. 96), he does not rule out the possibility of egalitarian structures. It seems fair to conclude that Turner would share the criticisms of Freeman regarding the ineffectiveness and nonsustainable nature of structureless groups.

members in each group seemed to take more responsibility than others. Since I did not attend gatherings other than liturgies, it was impossible for me to draw conclusions about the informal behind-the-scenes operations of these groups, and hence the extent of power sharing they embodied.

I raised the question of egalitarianism in formal interviews, informal conversations, and workshops that I attended at reform gatherings. Priests in independent communities expressed some degree of dismay over this question, pointing out that in their struggle to build new communities they had to offer well-organized liturgies. They could not simply say (as one priest put it), "Well let's all dream up how we want to worship—with everyone taking on an equal role" (J. M., personal communication, April 24, 2008). The group of parishioners from Corpus Christi who insisted on an egalitarian community refused to join the newly emerging Spiritus Christi, but dispersed without forming an enduring community of their own.

Finally, the experiences of the JOS community suggest that egalitarian principles may sometimes conflict with other important guiding principles. JOS's mission statement emphasizes many liberal principles, including "shared governance" and "ending discrimination" against women and other disadvantaged groups. These policies produced a contradictory outcome when one candidate who applied to be a presider withdrew from consideration after receiving critical comments from the congregation (Baiocchi, 2010). Thus, JOS's efforts to create an open and democratic process of selecting presiders undermined its egalitarian emphasis by excluding a candidate who was unable to endure a democratic form of evaluation.

Consequently, leaders of marginal and independent groups must weigh the principle of egalitarianism against other principles, including their community's viability and the needs and preferences of members. A basic principle of community organizing advises leaders to start at a point that matches the consciousness of the community and move forward in concert with the community rather than too far out in front of them.[25] This principle was cited by Roman Catholic Womanpriest Victoria Rue (2010), who for six years has performed leaderless and participatory rituals as part of a group she cofounded, A Critical Mass: Women Celebrating Eucharist.

---

[25] As noted in chapter 6, the legendary community organizer Saul Alinsky's (1972) rules for radicals include Rule 2: "Never go outside the experience of your people" (p. 172). One could argue that current church leaders are also ignoring this principle by repressing Vatican II principles, which most Catholics support.

Twelve participants began this ritual by cleaning an outdoor park in Oakland, California, and distributing food to homeless persons, followed by an outdoor Mass that "used gesture, silence, and the arts, keeping elements of the tradition and balancing it with 'something new.'" After six years of these celebrations, Rue decided that most "Catholics were not there yet," and she pursued ordination in RCWP as an "interim step" that would help Catholics "reimagine what it means to be priest by ordaining women." Rue tailored her ministry to match her audience of Catholics, who polls indicate are increasingly receptive to women's demands for equality, but apparently not ready for her dramatic reworking of the Mass.

If community leaders were to impose their preferences or demand adherence to strictly defined ideology, they would damage their outreach efforts and violate the trust and sense of belonging that are essential qualities of authentic community. The example of St. Stanislaus Parish demonstrates the extreme divisiveness that can result from highly contentious struggles over ideology and leadership, which led to a polarized community and defections by many parishioners and board members.

Exile as a Spiritual Journey Toward a New City of God

According to Veling (1996), postmodern theory interprets those drawn to the margins of their faith tradition as moving to space where they encounter their tradition in a new way and discover its relevance to contemporary challenges. Veling explains,

> It is not easy to think a new thing; harder still to live in a condition of exile. Yet sometimes that is what it takes to escape the binding of a book that no longer holds as it used to. (p. 78)

Veling advises that "when we think we are leaving we only 'get in deeper'; yet we bring with us the 'pollen of the last flowers'" that enables the book to "bloom again" (p. 79). Hence Veling insists that reexamining one's religious tradition (the book) enables us to gain new and deeper insights on the meaning of historical texts (i.e., scripture and church teachings) and their applicability to our contemporary world.

Reformers insist that they are responding to an authentic call of the Spirit and are seeking to embody their tradition's most profound truths as they pertain to the spiritual challenges of our times. Although reformers suffer personal anguish during and after their decision to loosen ties to the institutional church, they describe their choice as an act of loyalty to the highest truths and most life-giving features of Roman Catholicism, which are threatened by what some have termed the "cult-like" mentality of current church leaders.

Refusing to apologize for their exit from the church, many reformers express gratitude for the new spiritual insights they have gained by embarking on their exile journey. CORPUS leader Anthony Padovano (2007a) explains "there are no credible authorities left," so that reformers must "reach for a spirituality and ecclesiology, a vision of authority and Christology we did not know before" (p. 20). To foster their newly emerging spirituality reformers cannot rely on current church leaders, whom they regard as backward looking and intent on protecting their privileged position. Consequently, reformers are creating a new model of a church whose structure, spiritual practices, and theology are appropriate for Christians immersed in the crises and potentialities of the contemporary era. From their vantage point, they are salvaging the best of their tradition by creating a prefigurative model of a renewed church in the promised land, where the Vatican's oppressive power cannot reach.

Although reformers ardently defend the legitimacy and theological validity of their choices, many are quick to acknowledge that their understanding and interpretation of their tradition has been profoundly altered. Some admit that their "old time religion" has become something of a straightjacket or worn-out garment that no longer fits their evolving theology and liturgical preferences. For example, Jan Leary enjoys the warmth and inclusiveness of her independent Spirit of Life community in Boston, but longs for an even more innovative, cosmologically centered, and ecumenical liturgical experience. CORPUS leader Russ Ditzel (2009) confesses a growing discontent with conventional Roman Catholic liturgies, noting, "I am finding it more and more difficult to connect to the tribal, old cosmology-based theology of most of our public Catholic worship" (p. 37). Ditzel longs for a liturgy reflecting the "transcendent theological perspectives of Teilhard, O'Murchu, Morwood and Spong,"[26] which discredit

---

[26] These four authors cited by Ditzel include Father Teilhard de Chardin, a deceased paleontologist and Jesuit priest; Father Diarmuid O'Murchu, a social psychologist and priest in the Sacred Heart Missionary Congregation; Michael Morwood, a former Sacred Heart priest of twenty-eight years in Victoria Australia; and Bishop John Shelby Spong, a retired Episcopal Bishop of Newark, New Jersey. The works of these four authors focus on integrating scientific research, environmentalism, and contemporary biblical scholarship with traditional Christian theology. Their works are popular among church reformers and often cited in reform publications. Morwood and Spong have been keynote speakers at conferences sponsored by DigntyUSA and CTA.

teachings that "we are not worthy, that Jesus died to satisfy a vindictive god, that only some are god's chosen people and that only the chosen of the chosen can be leaders" (p. 37). Ditzel insists that reforms focused solely on a more inclusive ministry will only change "who can deliver a message that is at odds with the Good News of Jesus" (p. 37).

Increasingly, many reformers echo Ditzel's arguments by embracing what might be termed a post-Catholic or integralist stance that will not be satisfied with merely changing the composition of the priesthood or minor changes in liturgical language and practice.[27] Hence, those who have adopted an integralist perspective have little incentive to work for minor reforms they view as largely inconsequential (not to mention highly improbable under current leadership). They also may have little desire to return to even a Vatican II-type parish that is unwilling to risk bold new initiatives in community building and liturgy that reflect cutting-edge theology.

Many independent communities move in a direction that decreases the likelihood they could reestablish a formal connection to the institutional church. For example, after forming an independent parish, Spiritus Christi of Rochester, New York, has ordained two women priests, has affiliated with ECC, and has provided training for groups seeking to form independent parishes. Father Marek Bozek has continued the defiance he evidenced when he led the parish of St. Stanislaus in their struggle to become an independent parish. In 2008 Bozek was laicized following his decision to participate in an ordination ritual conducted by RCWP, despite a Vatican ban on participation in RCWP events.

Thus liberal reformers who have moved far outside the boundaries of the institutional church may conclude that returning to a Vatican-controlled church is no longer viable or worth the struggle. The best they could hope from the Vatican would be slight liberalization of existing policies, which would not satisfy those who have tasted the fruits of *communitas* in underground liturgies where artistic and prophetic voices are allowed free rein.

---

[27] The term *integralist* is used by the philosopher Ken Wilbur to refer to an advanced stage of human consciousness evidenced by those whose awareness "draws on all truth and perspectives," thereby "allow[ing] the integral thinker to bring new depth, clarity and compassion to every level of human endeavor—from unlocking individual potential to finding new approaches to global-scale problems" (www.integralinstitute.org). Hence, Catholic reformers can integrate the truths and practices of Catholicism with those from a vast range of other sources to create new theologies and new forms of worship communities.

Quality of Liturgies in Independent Communities

Some have questioned whether independent communities can maintain the quality and consistency of their liturgies to the same degree as Catholic parishes. My own visits to twelve independent communities revealed that the quality of liturgies is more varied than those of conventional parishes. Independent communities intentionally avoid consistency with each other or the Roman Catholic Mass, because they craft liturgies to reflect the unique interests and mission of each community.

How one evaluates liturgies is highly subjective and reflects one's aesthetic sensibilities and theological orientation. Even among liberal reformers there is considerable variation regarding the extent to which they prefer adherence to the standard liturgy for the Mass and adaptations that might include material from non-Catholic and even non-Christian sources. For example, DignityUSA liturgies are somewhat conventional, while WE liturgies are highly eclectic and innovative, and which they intentionally do not call a Mass. Spiritus Christi has dramatic and moving liturgies that incorporate many Vatican II principles and attract visitors from other states and countries outside the United States. In contrast, many conservatives favor the Latin Mass, which is increasingly available in Catholic parishes in the United States following Pope Benedict's decision in 2007 to lift restrictions on the Latin Mass.[28]

Evaluating Independent Communities

The potential of underground Catholic parishes to attract a broad network of liberal Catholics is demonstrated, to some extent, by the independent communities reformers have already created. Journalist Suzanne Strempek Shea (2008) provides liberal criteria for evaluating religious communities, based on her visits to fifty different non-Roman Christian churches throughout the United States. Reflecting her Roman Catholic background, Shea names the independent Catholic community of

---

[28] A book entitled *Priest, Where Is Thy Mass, Mass, Where Is Thy Priest?* (Kansas City, MO: Angelus Press) describes interviews with twelve Roman Catholic priests who never accepted the New Mass when it was introduced in 1969 or who came to prefer the Latin Mass postordination. These priests describe the Latin Mass as essential to their spiritual development and willingly suffered career penalties for their refusal to accept the New Mass.

St. Sebastian in Baltimore, Maryland, as one of her favorite examples, noting its acceptance of gay people and women's ordination. Shea's description of her ideal parish matches, in many respects, some of the worship communities described in this study. She describes it as

> a community that welcomed me warmly, didn't give a whit about my politics or lifestyle, gave tons of whit about the social justice needed locally and beyond,[29] contained little-to-no hierarchy,[30] ... offered a spiritual message inspired by love rather than fear, and did all of this in an art-filled place that rang with awesome music. (p. 309)

The two points in Shea's wish list where many independent parishes are most lacking include "art-filled space" and "awesome music," both of which usually require resources to fund attractive meeting places and choral directors, musical instruments, etc. A few of the more successful communities cited in this study come close to Shea's wish list, in that many DignityUSA chapters and Spiritus Christi parish have reputations for high quality music and share artfully designed space in underutilized non-Catholic churches. Grace Church of Dover and the St. Mary of Magdala community of Cape Cod have constructed their own "art-filled" chapels. However, most groups in this study are poorly funded and rely on music from a boom box or portable keyboard. They meet in inexpensive venues, including a fairground, a summer camp, community centers, and other makeshift locations.[31]

The Question of Inclusiveness—Here Comes Everybody

Some Catholic spokespersons have asked whether Pope Benedict XVI should extend to progressive dissidents on the left the same conciliatory

---

[29] Many liberal reformers would insist that, contrary to Shea's formula, one's politics reflect one's commitment to social justice. Persons committed to social justice may have different convictions regarding the meaning of this term and the most effective strategies for achieving it. Liberal reformers have uniformly voiced strong opposition to policies of some Catholic bishops who deny Communion or other sacraments to persons based on their political positions.

[30] As discussed above, almost all marginal and independent communities are somewhat hierarchical, but are much more egalitarian than conventional Catholic parishes. Many struggle to minimize hierarchical distinctions.

[31] Only one of my interview subjects complained about "shoddy" meeting space for her community (Fatima community in chapter 7). She confessed she missed the "beauty and uplifting surroundings" of her former parish, but found the Fatima community's warm and inclusive spirit to be worth the tradeoff.

overtures that he demonstrated in lifting the excommunication of the conservative Society of St. Pius X (noted for its rejection of some Vatican II principles). For example, an editorial in the British Catholic journal *The Tablet* asked, "Is dissent on the left different in kind from dissent on the right?" They note that the Vatican's highest court has ruled that "members of We are Church may be excluded from official church bodies" due to their dissent regarding church teachings, including women's ordination (*A Place for*, 2009, p. 2).[32] To date, liberal reformers have yet to challenge Pope Benedict XVI for his one-sided policies that penalize even minor infractions of liberal Catholics (for example denying Communion to divorced persons who have not received an annulment), while seeking reconciliation with conservative groups such as the Society of St. Pius X, which still refuses to accept the principles of Vatican II.

Given the vast and expanding divergence in the theologies and worldviews of conservative and liberal Catholics, it is hard to identify where they might find common ground toward designing a new model of church. A more inclusive church would include space for a broad spectrum of Catholics who could collaborate on pressing problems, such as the abuse crisis and declines in church membership, finances, and credibility. Is it possible that liberal and conservative Catholics could create a mature and spiritually inspired model of resolving the polarization and stalemate reflected in the culture wars by creating an inventive and mutually acceptable structure? In this regard, it is worth noting that Anthony Padovano (2006b) asks liberal reformers to reflect on their own sins, recalling that during Vatican II, liberals "who argued for an inclusive church may have been willing to exclude those who did not find room for us by denying them room as well" (p. 28).

Resurrecting a Big Tent Model of Catholicism

One obvious solution to the current stalemate would be a decentralized model that defines Catholicism in inclusive, nondogmatic terms and that maintains some universal principles alongside a measure of autonomy

---

[32] We are Church (described in chapter 2) is a European Catholic reform organization founded in 1996 that is "committed to the renewal of the Roman Catholic Church on the basis of the Second Vatican Council (1962–1965) and the theological spirit developed from it" (www.we-are-church.org/). Like CTA, it is loosely structured and engages primarily in outsider strategies such as press releases and petitions challenging Vatican policies.

for local units. In this model, groups with different ideologies or local cultures could, within some limits, craft their own liturgies and their own interpretation of Catholicism.[33] Although some liberals favor this model, it represents the worst nightmare of some conservatives, given that it totally contradicts their vision of Roman Catholicism as a unified, unchanging, and invulnerable institution that stands outside of and above history.

Any effort to create a structure that would return Catholicism to a big tent model would not only encounter the resistance of archconservative hierarchs but also ignite the divisive culture wars that have stymied efforts at dialogue among liberal and conservative Catholics. Stoking the flames of the culture wars may unleash the extremes of hostility and venomous rhetoric evident during the early days of VOTF, when at least one conservative priest refused to rule out violence in his efforts to thwart a "centrist" organization that accepted the teaching authority of the Catholic Church.

According to M. O. Steinfels (2010), Cardinal Bernardin's Catholic Common Ground Initiative in the 1990s failed to achieve constructive dialogue between the two sides of the Catholic culture wars. Liberals proposed that both sides "talk about their differences" (p. 16), but this suggestion "only raised conservatives' suspicions." Bernardin's attempt to find common ground between conservatives and liberals became "another source of polarization mirroring the fractured state of the church rather than healing it" (p. 16). Steinfels faults both sides for the polarization, noting that "the lack of self-criticism on the left was compared to the outsized claims of orthodoxy on the right" (p. 15).

In considering strategies aimed at inclusion, both conservatives and liberals must weigh the tradeoffs involved in any attempt at reconciliation between left and right. Mercy Sister Theresa Kane (2010)[34] offers a telling example of these tradeoffs by describing a group of sisters in the Midwest who made a conciliatory gesture toward their conservative bishop by inviting him to preside at a Mass during a conference. In response, the bishop proclaimed, "It must be in a parish church and not at the motherhouse, you must have altar boys come in to assist me, and no sister may

---

[33] This decentralized model is exemplified by the Old Catholic Church that includes a broad spectrum of conservative and liberal parishes, including the Ecumenical Catholic Communion described in chapter 9.

[34] Sister Theresa Kane is well known for her advocacy of women's ordination. As president of the Leadership Council of Women Religious in 1979, she made a televised appeal to Pope John Paul II during his visit to the United States in which she urged him to include "half of humankind" in "all the ministries of the church."

carry the cross at the beginning of the procession." Consequently, the sisters advised the bishop that their "plans had changed" and the liturgy was cancelled. Kane was disappointed that the sisters did not inform the bishop that he was "disinvited." Despite their meek response, these sisters decided the cost of inclusiveness was too high, given that the prerequisites of the bishop ran totally counter to the sisters' goal of creating an uplifting, unifying liturgy.

Each group of reformers must weigh for themselves what they would be willing to sacrifice in an effort at reconciliation with church leaders. Despite the relatively conservative theology of DignityUSA leaders, they chose exile rather than tolerate what they perceived to be hostile pronouncements regarding gays in Vatican documents. Liberal Catholics are increasingly demonstrating a willingness to abandon their ties to the institutional church as Vatican II parishes and liberal clerics are subjected to repression. Since underground groups have low visibility, one might predict that many, if not most, defecting Catholics will join other denominations or abandon organized religion. Given that these lapsed Catholics represent the persons most likely to join underground communities,[35] the future of underground communities will likely depend on their success in attracting the interest of these lapsed Catholics.

In their ongoing struggles with the Vatican, reformers must constantly assess whether their efforts are unwittingly reinforcing an anachronistic Roman-like model of governance by assuming the stance of compliant and obedient dogs begging for "a few crumbs from the master's table" (as one reformer put it). Although Vatican II laid the groundwork for more egalitarian structures, the history of the Reform Movement demonstrates the deeply entrenched nature of Vatican power that grants laypersons virtually almost no rights or meaningful voice in policy making. Church officials feel free to violate or suppress even the official church teachings of Vatican II. The seemingly irreconcilable divisions between right and left within the church and the likelihood that conservatives will control the Vatican for the foreseeable future are not favorable omens for the agenda of liberal reformers, at least in the short term. Perhaps the era conducive to a big-tent universal church has passed.

I believe that the only real option available to reformers is forming a new church. I would like to think that this progressive church would

---

[35] This conclusion is based on the fact that lapsed Catholics represented the overwhelming majority of members of all the underground communities included in my study.

return to the Roman Catholic Church when and if it reforms. After four decades of persistent outreach, reformers have found the option of dialogue and negotiation to be ineffectual and demeaning. The slogan "We are the Church" is empty rhetoric if laypersons have no meaningful voice in policy and no right to self-defense when censured. Under current circumstances, the option of rejecting Vatican control would free reformers from the ever-present threat of censure and crackdown, and would grant them the autonomy and authority to create their own vision of a renewed Catholicism. Separating themselves from the Vatican would also distance reformers from the clergy abuse and financial scandals that have besmirched the credibility of Catholicism. Successful independent communities (including Spiritus Christi, Grace Church, and St. Mary of Magdala) suggest that the option of creating a new form of church is viable. This option is a more productive use of reformers' resources than an increasingly futile battle to win the unreceptive hearts and minds of church officials.

Like Protestants, reformers might reinterpret the one, holy, universal, and apostolic catholic church as invisible and symbolic in nature and inclusive of a diverse range of communities and jurisdictions that do not require centralized control by the Vatican. In this respect, Catholicism would resemble early Christianity, which included many sects with conflicting and diverse beliefs and forms. Such a move would also be a step in the direction of reversing the Romanization of Catholicism that began in the fourth century, which many liberal and radical theologians identify as a corrupting and destructive influence, particularly since the Vatican's rigidly authoritarian and repressive structure is modeled after the Roman Empire. Reformers are fond of citing early Christian leaders who contrasted Jesus's teachings regarding justice, compassion, and servant leadership with the repressive, tyrannical, and militaristic policies of the Roman Empire. In the *Declaration of the American Catholic Council* (2010) reformers state their intent to model a renewed Catholicism on the principles of early Christian communities:

> The disciples of Christ became a New Testament community of churches, democratic in believing the Spirit was given to all. These communities were never perfect. St. Paul tells us there was factionalism as well as harmony and confusion as well as clarity. Nonetheless, these communities proved themselves reliable and became the embodiment of the living Christ. They selected their leaders and held them accountable. They recognized a wide diversity of charisms and ministers, validated not by one person or office, but by the community at large.

Thus, the American Catholic Council explicitly aims to reverse the Romanization of Catholicism in favor of a decentralized, democratic model that grants some measure of autonomy for the American Catholic Church.[36] They invite the participation of all Catholics who share the goals of the liberal Reform Movement:

> We take as our norm the Gospel and the life-giving elements of our Tradition, especially the earliest history of the Church and the renaissance promised by the Second Vatican Council. We are guided, furthermore, by the wisdom gained from the decades of intensive reform and renewal efforts in the post-Vatican II Church in the United States. (*Declaration of the*, December 16, 2010)

The declaration identifies the goal of the Council as "reform of the governing structures in our church" to ensure that "all the baptized have an effective voice in decision-making and a ministry worthy of their calling."

INSIDE, OUTSIDE, ALONGSIDE

Although Roman Catholics are often stereotyped as sheep and "pay, pray, and obey" types, my study has documented that the resistance strategies adopted by Catholic reformers encompass the full range of nonviolent strategies in Sharp's (1973, 2005) model, including protest and persuasion, noncooperation, and parallel institutions. One criticism of the Reform Movement is that "you can only change things from the inside." My conclusion challenges this cliché by asserting that under the conservative policies of John Paul II and Benedict XVI, change, to the extent that it occurred at all, was evoked primarily by outsider strategies that did not depend on the cooperation or approval of Vatican officials. Paradoxically, although outsider strategies trumped insider ones, it was insider Catholics with a deep and abiding commitment to their Roman Catholic roots who resorted to outsider strategies essentially as a last resort after all attempts at insider reform had failed.

Progressive Roman Catholics occupy a broad range of positions along the insider-outside divide, and the divide itself is a constantly moving and disputed boundary whose permutations are difficult to identify

---

[36] Journalist Robert Blair Kaiser (2006), an endorser of the Council, has proposed that American Catholics form an autochthonous church that retains allegiance to the Vatican but has a large measure of local autonomy.

and define. In the parable of the graveyard in chapter 9, the priest managed to extend the boundaries of consecrated ground by moving the fence to a location that included the grave of the non-Catholic soldier who had initially been buried outside the fence. So too, the range of the reformers outlined in this book are pushing from various vantage points to enlarge the circle of Roman Catholicism to include those who are currently marginalized, while the Vatican struggles to shrink the circle to include only those willing to pledge fidelity to its code of behavior and beliefs.

Reformers' idealism notwithstanding, liberal Catholics are caught in a church-sect dialectic. Goldstein (2011) identifies this pattern in religious conflicts in the culture wars between conservatives and liberals within denominations and among social and religious movements within the larger society. These dialectical patterns of interactions move in a progressive direction rather than a cyclical one, such that each movement and countermovement arrives at a new point rather than returning to the starting point. These trends also reflect underlying differences correlating with denominational differences in class, education, region, race, and ethnicity.

This dialectic between church and sect is evident in the pattern of movement and countermovement between the Roman Catholic Church and the liberal Reform Movement. The Reform Movement emerged in response to the rollback of Vatican II policies by Pope John Paul II. The Reform Movement, in turn, evoked a hostile response from church hierarchs, who responded to liberal demands by imposing increasingly punitive policies on outspoken reformers and by institutionalizing their conservative principles in formal church documents. This repression of liberals by church hierarchs pushed reformers in the direction of sectarian strategies. At this juncture, a movement toward a more church-like model is emerging in some sectarian communities, who are seeking to gain stability and attract members from outside the Reform Movement. Conversely, one might predict that, if the Vatican continues to be led by archconservatives, it may eventually become sect-like by barricading itself from the contemporary world and rejecting any accommodation with liberals. Vatican II scholar Hans Küng predicted such a development in a video-taped interview with Anthony Padovano broadcast at the first conference of the American Catholic Council on June 10, 2011. Küng (2011) predicted that to avoid being "left behind completely and becom[ing] a big sect, the Vatican must be willing to move forward" rather than resist the modern world. Already the Vatican's views are increasingly out of step with the views of many Catholics across the globe, especially well-educated persons who are accustomed to democratic governance and liberal social reforms. Thus, we see a series of moves and countermoves in the interaction between both church officials and reformers that create pressures toward being more church-like or sect-like in both groups.

My research also supports Goldstein's (2011) conclusion that the church-sect dialectic moves in a progressive direction. If there is one point that conservative and liberal Catholics would agree on, it would be that the relationship between the Roman Catholic Church and its members has undergone a dramatic transformation since Vatican II. The Vatican has moved to the right under the last two popes, while a majority of Catholic laity has moved to the left by adopting many liberal values and critically evaluating their adherence to the church (as evidenced by declining church attendance and dissent regarding church teachings). These historical conflicts do represent a trend of lay Catholics toward increased secularization as predicted by Goldstein. My study has also supported Goldstein's contention that the polarization of religious liberals and conservatives reflects variables of education, social class, and race, given that the Reform Movement is composed of primarily Caucasian, highly educated, and middle class Catholics from the Midwest and Northeast. This finding is consistent with Wuthnow (1988), who found religious liberals tend to have higher levels of education than conservatives.

Both the Reform Movement and the institutional church face challenges characteristic of their position on the continuum between church and sect. Reformers could develop a model of church more flexible, egalitarian, and democratic than Vatican structures, but its future seems dim if it remains clustered in small, breakaway, sect-like communities with no overarching structure to ensure resources and ongoing leadership. In contrast, church leaders face the opposite dilemma, as they appear to be choking on the church's institutional excesses and dismantling the strong community orientation and big tent model that have long been regarded as hallmarks of Catholicism.

The Prophetic Imagination

As a Protestant Old Testament scholar, Walter Brueggemann (2001) may seem a strange source to cite in concluding this study. Yet his voice speaks most eloquently and clearly to the dilemmas and opportunities facing liberal Catholic reformers, who remain intent on resurrecting the legacy of

Vatican II and on preserving Catholicism's ability to guide and enlighten future generations.

Brueggemann notes that in the Judeo-Christian tradition "our history always begins with the barren, with Sarah (Gen 11:30), with Rebekah (Gen 25:21), with Rachel (Gen 29:31), with Hannah (1 Sam 1:2), and with Elizabeth (Luke 1:7)" (p. 75). Brueggemann interprets biblical stories of births to formerly barren women as symbolic events that mark the emergence of new life and hope within communities sunk in despair and lacking a vision of the future.

Thus the Reform Movement and the institutionalized church are experiencing a type of barrenness as younger generations show little interest in a tradition that they describe as lifeless and spiritless. Brueggemann contends that despair and listlessness are inevitable when one is enslaved by indoctrination in what he refers as "the royal consciousness" of the powerful, who silence and oppress their subjects.[37] Only prophetic voices can expose the false claims of empire and ignite the fire of hope and renewal that is latent in those willing to struggle for a new order in church and society. Brueggemann explains,

> And when the prophet returns, with the community, to those deep symbols, they will discern that hope is not a late, tacked-on hypothesis to serve a crisis but rather the primal dimension of every memory of this community. The memory of this community begins in God's promissory address to the darkness of chaos, to barren Sarah, and to oppressed Egyptian slaves. The speech of God is first about an alternative future. (p. 64)

Thus reformers face this epic choice of succumbing to the despair that Brueggemann describes as the root of empire, or becoming prophetic by boldly proclaiming and creating an alternative to the barrenness of Vatican empire.

---

[37] Brueggemann notes that "perhaps it must be concluded that the vision emerging from Moses is viable only in an intentional community whose passion for faith is knowingly linked to survival in the face of a dominant, hostile culture. That is, such a radical vision is most appropriate to a sectarian mood, which is marginal in the community. Such situations of risk do seem to call forth such a radicalness. Conversely situations of cultural acceptance breed accommodating complacency" (p. 22).

APPENDICES

APPENDIX A

COMPARATIVE DATA ON VATICAN II REFORM ORGANIZATIONS

Name of Group	Year Founded	Annual Income	Membership
Call to Action USA (CTA)	1977	$1,327,429 (2009)	25,000
Catholics for Choice (CFC)	1973	$3,000,000 (2010)	Not applicable
Catholic Organizations for Renewal (COR)	1991	Not available	24 organizations
Corps of Reserve Priests United for Service (CORPUS)	1974	$82,051 (2009)	800
DignityUSA	1969	$372,729 (2009)	3,848
FutureChurch	1990	$271,768 (2009)	5,000
Voice of the Faithful (VOTF)	2002	Not available	30,000
Women's Alliance for Theology, Ethics and Ritual (WATER)	1983	Not available	Not applicable
Women-Church Convergence (W-CC)	1984	Not available	27 member organizations
Women's Ordination Conference (WOC)	1975	$247,212 (2008)	2,000
Women's Ordination Worldwide (WOW)	1996	Not available	14 member organizations

APPENDIX A

Organization	Goals and Objectives
Call to Action (CTA)	CTA is an organization of progressive Catholics that advocates equal rights for women and homosexuals in the Roman Catholic Church, an end to mandatory celibacy, and a greater role for laity in decision making.
Catholic Organizations for Renewal (COR)	COR is a coalition of twenty-four reform organizations that meets three times per year. The organization is primarily a forum for discussion, but occasionally engages in joint activity such as letter campaigns or newspaper ads around issues of common concern.
Corps of Reserve Priests United for Service (CORPUS)	CORPUS is composed primarily of resigned Roman Catholic priests who promote an end to mandatory celibacy and a more inclusive priesthood. Currently this organization is primarily focused on mentoring non canonical priests.
DignityUSA	Dignity advocates the inherent dignity of gay, lesbian, bisexual and transgender Catholics. The organization has a network of local chapters that include worship communities oriented to the needs of GLBT Catholics. The organization also challenges and critiques statements by the Vatican and American Catholic bishops that are discriminatory toward their membership.
FutureChurch	FutureChurch is a coalition of parish-based Catholics that works to preserve the Eucharist by advocating a priesthood that is open to all the baptized. It relies primarily on insider strategies and its priorities include women's issues and preserving parishes.
Voice of the Faithful (VOTF)	VOTF is a national organization whose members are concentrated in the Northeast. It was created in response to the clergy sexual abuse crisis that erupted in Boston in 2002. VOTF describes itself as a centrist organization that accepts the teaching authority of the Roman Catholic Church. Its goals include supporting abuse victims and priests of integrity and achieving structural reform to grant the laity a greater role in decision making.

Cont.

Organization	Goals and Objectives
Women's Alliance for Theology, Ethics and Ritual (WATER)	WATER is a think-tank organization that provides a range of services and policy papers supporting the efforts of Catholic feminists to advocate for equality within the Roman Catholic Church and to create feminist worship communities.
Women-Church Convergence (W-CC)	W-CC is a coalition of Catholic women's organizations that advocate a democratic, egalitarian transformation of the Roman Catholic Church and society.
Women's Ordination Conference (WOC)	WOC is an advocacy organization that includes a range of activities designed to promote more equal roles for women in the Roman Catholic Church, including the right to ordination.
Women's Ordination Worldwide (WOW)	WOW is an international coalition of fourteen women's groups that favor women's ordination in the Roman Catholic Church. WOW holds periodic conferences and engages in networking.

APPENDIX B

FIELD RESEARCH

Academic Conferences

Going beyond the Blame Game, conference on clergy abuse crisis. Regis College, Weston, MA. October 15, 2002.
Women, Church, Society: Challenges and Possibilities. Regis College, Weston, MA. October 19–20, 2003.
Pastoral Summit. Marriott Hotel, Boston, MA. October 7, 2003.
The Church Women Want. Boston College, April 16–17, 2004.
Why Women Stay. Boston College, September 15, 2005.
Symposium on VOTF. Boston College, October 23, 2005.
Creating the Church Women Want. Boston College, July 15, 2006.

Catholic Reform Groups

Call to Action (CTA) Conferences
CTA New England Regional Conference, "Priestly People, Spirit Led." Best Western Royal Plaza Hotel, Marlboro, MA. April 26, 2003.
CTA Pre-Conference Session, "What Are They Saying about Jesus?" Midwest Conference Center. Milwaukee, WI. November 7, 2003.
CTA National Conference, "Called to Be Peacemakers." Midwest Convention Center. Milwaukee, WI. November 7–9, 2003.
CTA Regional New England Conference. "Justice and Action in the Church and in the World." Worcester Centrum. Worcester, MA. April 24, 2004.
CTA New England. Lecture by Michael Morwood, private residence. Natick, MA. May 14, 2005.
CTA Pre-Conference Session, "Bridging the Gap, Gender Equality, Sex and Ordination." Midwest Conference Center. Milwaukee, WI. November 3, 2006.
CTA National Conference, "I AM, Rise Up People of God." Midwest Conference Center, Milwaukee, WI. November 3–5, 2006.
CTA National Conference, "From Racism to Reconciliation: Church beyond Power and Privilege." Midwest Conference Center, Milwaukee, WI. November 2–4, 2007.

Catholic Organizations for Renewal (COR) Meetings

COR Biannual Meeting. Sheraton Hotel, Milwaukee, WI. November 6–7, 2003. (observer status).

COR Biannual Meeting, Sheraton Hotel, Milwaukee, WI. November 2–3, 2006. (observer status).

COR Biannual Meeting. Sheraton Hotel, Milwaukee, WI. November 2–3, 2007. (observer status).

Celibacy Is the Issue (CITI) Events

CITI Board Meeting, "Chartering the Institute of Faith Communities." Duncan Retreat Center, Delray Beach, FL. February 17–20, 2005.

CITI Forum, "Catholics Yesterday, Today and Tomorrow." Holiday Inn, Brookline, MA. October 16, 2005.

Outdoor Mass, celebrated by CITI priests. Natick, MA. March 27, 2006.

CITI Forum, "Catholics Yesterday, Today and Tomorrow." Miami Lakes Congregational Church, Miami Beach, FL. February, 18, 2006.

CITI Forum, "Catholics Yesterday, Today and Tomorrow." Hilton Hotel, Gaithersburg, MD. February 16, 2006.

Corps of Reserve Priests United for Service (CORPUS) Conference

CORPUS 30th Anniversary Conference, National Conference Center. Landsdowne, VA. June 25–27, 2004.

Council of Vigiling Parishes (CoP) Meetings

COP Steering Committee Meeting. St. James the Great Parish. Wellesley, MA. June 5, 2005.

COP Steering Committee Meeting. St. James the Great Parish. Wellesley, MA. January 5, 2006.

COP Steering Committee Meeting. St. James the Great Parish. Wellesley, MA. July 24, 2006.

COP Steering Committee Meeting, St. James the Great Parish. Wellesley, MA. September 1, 2006.

Dignity/Boston Events

Dignity/Boston liturgy. St. John the Evangelist Episcopal Church, Boston, MA. March 2, 2004.

Dignity/Boston meeting on same-sex marriage ruling by Massachusetts Supreme Court, St. John the Evangelist Episcopal Church, Boston, MA. March 2, 2004.

Dignity/Boston liturgy. St. John the Evangelist Episcopal Church, Boston, MA. November 12, 2006.

Joint Conference
Conference cosponsored by Federation of Christian Ministries (FCM), Women's Ordination Conference (WOC), Roman Catholic Womenpriests (RCWP), and Corps of Reserve Priests United for Service (CORPUS). "Ministry and Renewal in a Complex Age." Boston, MA. July 18–20, 2008.

VOTF Conferences
VOTF Convention, "Response of the Faithful." John Hynes Auditorium, Boston, MA. July 20, 2003.
VOTF Conference, "Being Catholic in the 21st Century." Fordham University, NY. October 25, 2003.
VOTF planning meeting for VOTF Boston Area Conference. Our Lady Help of Christians Parish, Newton, MA. June 4, 2003.
VOTF Boston-area Conference. Trinity Catholic High School, Our Lady Help of Christians Parish, Newton, MA. June 7, 2003.
VOTF New England Conference. "It's Time for Renewal." Worcester Centrum, Worcester, MA. November 13, 2004.
VOTF New Jersey Chapter, "Forum on Imagining New Ways of Being Catholic." Birchwood Manor, Whippany, NJ. October 28, 2006.

VOTF Events
VOTF Organizing Meeting. St. John the Evangelist Church, Wellesley, MA. May 14, 2003.
VOTF Organizing Meeting. St. John the Evangelist Church, Wellesley, MA. June 20, 2003.
Fireside Chat. Wellesley Middle School, Wellesley, MA. January 25, 2003.
Lecture by Walter Cuenin. Paulist Center, Boston, MA. September 23, 2003.
Lecture by Richard McBrien. Stonehill College, Easton, MA. August 20, 2004.
Winchester Area VOTF, Forum on Intentional Communities. St. Eulalia's Parish, Winchester, MA. May 23, 2005.
VOTF protest of firing Rev. Walter Cuenin. Our Lady Help of Christians Parish, Newton, MA. September 29, 2005.

Women's Alliance for Theology, Ethics and Ritual (WATER) Conference
WATER 20th Anniversary Conference. Trinity College, Washington, DC. September 26, 2003.

Women-Church Convergence (W-CC) Meeting
W-CC board meeting. Trinity College, Washington, DC. September 26, 2003.

Marginal Communities
Liturgy by CITI priests. Framingham Unitarian Church, Framingham, MA. August. 26, 2003.
Anonymous. MA. July 11, 2004.
Anonymous. MA. September 11, 2005.
Anonymous. MA. January 25, 2005; January 8, 2006; March 30, 2007; July 11, 2007; April 11, 2009.
Anonymous. MA. July 12, 2004.
Joint liturgy of two communities. Arlington, MA. July 20, 2006.
Anonymous. MA. February 11, 2007.
Anonymous. MA. April 18, 2008.
Anonymous. MA. October 19, 2008.
Anonymous. MA. November 16, 2008.

Massachusetts Women-Church Events
Massachusetts Women-Church, steering committee meetings. August 16, 2006, and August 22, 2007.
Massachusetts Women-Church, presentation by Angela Bonavoglia, author of *Good Catholic girls: How women are leading the fight to change the church*. Randolph, MA. May 12, 2005.

Underground Communities
Community of God's Love, liturgy. Chelmsford, MA. September 16, 2004
Spiritus Christi Parish, five separate liturgies. Rochester, NY. March 16–18, 2004.
Anonymous. MA. February 26, 2005.
St. Patrick's Catholic Church, liturgy. Cranston, RI. January 22, 2006.
Grace Church of Dover, liturgy. Dover, MA. June 26, 2006, and January 5, 2007.
Evensong by the Sea, liturgy. St. Mary Magdala Chapel. August 19, 2007.
Spirit of Life, liturgy. Congregational Church of Wayland, Wayland, MA. December 31, 2007.

Holy Spirit Catholic Community, liturgy. Wellesley Library, Wellesley, MA. February 17, 2008.
Anonymous, liturgy. MA. May 16, 2008.
Anonymous, liturgy. MA. June 7, 2009.

Visits to Vigiling Churches
St. Albert's the Great, Weymouth, MA. November 21, 2004.
St. Anselm's Parish, Sudbury, MA. July 10, 2005.
St. James the Great, Wellesley, MA. December 24, 2005.

Other Events
Good Friday Vigil by reform groups. Cathedral of the Holy Cross, Boston, MA. March 30, 2002.
Retreat cosponsored by Massachusetts Women-Church and CORPUS, Boston, MA. Glastonbury Abbey, Hingham, MA. May 2003.
St. Luke's Parish meeting, "Where Do We Go from Here?" Westborough, MA. October 16, 2005.
St. Luke's Parish, liturgy. Westborough, MA. October 7, 2005.
Deliver Us from Evil. Video premier. Boston, MA. May 2007.
Demonstration outside installment ceremonies of Cardinal Sean O'Malley. Cathedral of The Holy Cross, Boston, MA. March 24, 2006.
Ordination ceremony of Roman Catholic Womenpriests. Church of the Covenant, Boston, MA. July 20, 2010.

BIBLIOGRAPHY

About Jesus Our Shepherd. (2003, March 6). Retrieved May 13, 2008, from http://www.jesusourshepherd.org/jos.asp

About us, The Quixote Center. (n.d.). Retrieved July 5, 2005, from http://quixote.org/about

About us, Woven Word Press. (n.d.). Retrieved June 13, 2008, from http://www.wovenword.press.com

A call for reform in the Catholic Church: A pastoral letter from Catholics concerned about fundamental renewal of our church. (1990, February 28). P. A17. First printed by Call to Action in *The New York Times*, p. B4. Reprinted in *Called to be peacemakers: Prophetic leadership for world and church* [2003 CTA Conference Brochure], p. 36.

After Detroit, 1977. (n.d.) [Call to Action Brochure]. Chicago, IL: Author.

Alinsky, S. (1972). *Rules for radicals: A pragmatic primer for realistic radicals.* New York, NY: Vintage.

Allen, E. (2009, March 29). Rebel will lead flock in exile. *Courier Mail*, p. 8.

Allen, J. L., Jr. (2004). *All the pope's men: The inside story of how the Vatican really thinks.* New York, NY: Doubleday.

———. (2005). *The rise of Benedict XVI: The inside story of how the pope was elected and where he will take the Catholic Church.* New York, NY: Doubleday.

———. (2007a, August 17). The feminization of the church. *National Catholic Reporter*, pp. 13, 17.

———. (2007b, November 23). U.S. bishops project "air of unity." *National Catholic Reporter*, p. 7.

———. (2008a, May 2). Pope in U.S. wins friends on first US trip. *National Catholic Reporter*, p. 8.

———. (2008b, November 21). "Poped out" Wills seeks broader horizons. *National Catholic Reporter*, p. 1.

———. (2010a, August 16). Why Rome scorns resignations: And a great week for wonks. Message posted to http://ncronline.org/blogs/all-things-catholic/why-rome-scorns-resignations-and-great-week-wonks.

———. (2010b, December 24). Tobin urges "strategy of reconciliation." *Catholic Reporter*, p. 5.

A Mouse that Roared Turns 25: An interview with CFCC President Frances Kissling. (1998, May). Retrieved June 7, 2005, from http://www.catholicsforchoice.org

Another way to be Catholic. (n.d.). Retrieved July 28, 2004, from http://www.onespiritcatholic.org/anothercatholicway.html

Anson, P. F. (2006). *Bishops at large.* Berkeley, CA: Apocryphile Press.

A place for dissent. (2009, June 6). [Editorial]. *The Tablet*, p. 2.

Arbuckle, G. (2004). *Violence, society and the church: A cultural approach.* Collegeville, MN: Liturgical Press.

Associated Press. (2004, April 6). Polish church defies Burke's authority. Retrieved April 10, 2004, from http://news.google.com/newspapers?nid+1683&dat+20050110&id

———. (2005, October 3). Mass churches campaign against gay marriage. Retrieved December 14, 2009, from http://www.foxnews.com/printer_friendly_story/0,3566,171088.00html

———. (2008, May 30). Vatican: Excommunication for female priests: Catholic Church says it's following tradition. Retrieved July 1, 2008, from http://www.msnbc.msn.com/id/24894993

Association for the Rights of Catholics in the Church. (1998, September 19). *Proposed constitution of the Catholic Church.* Retrieved June 14, 2006, from http://arcc-catholic-rights.net/

Baiocchi, F. (2008, July 27). Pope Benedict XVI asserts authority over his "flock." *News for the week of July 27, 2008* [Newsletter]. Retrieved September 4, 2008, from http://www.jesusourshepherd
———. (2010, July/August). Jesus Our Shepherd: An inclusive Eucharistic community. *CORPUS Reports, 36*(4), 26–32.
Banished priest gets a hero's welcome. (2005, December 16). *The Los Angeles Times*. Retrieved January 23, 2006, from http://www.articles.latimes.com/2005;dec/26/nation/na-priest26-
Bannan, P. R. (n.d.). Impact of Catholic feminist dissent. Retrieved July 7, 2005, from http://www.womensordination.org/pages/art_impact_html
Barnes, J. (2005a, Spring). WOW responds to papal transition. *New Women, New Church* [Newsletter], *28*(1), 1.
———. (2005b, Summer). Embracing diversity at 2nd WOW conference in Ottawa. *New Women, New Church* [Newsletter], *28*(2), 1, 4.
Bartley, D. (2008, May 30). A 'year end' VOTF resolution. Message posted to VOTF on behalf of Voice of the Faithful electronic mailing list.
Baute, P. (1994, January). On the value of being marginal. *CORPUS News* [Newsletter], *2*(1), 1–2.
Belleville priests call for Bishop Braxton to resign. (2008, April 4). *National Catholic Reporter*, p. 3.
Belluck, P. (2004, May 26). Archdiocese in Boston plans to close 65 Catholic parishes by end of the year. *The New York Times*, p. 14.
———. (2007, June 24). Catholic lay group tests a strategy change. *The New York Times*, p. A16.
Berggen, K. (2008, June 13). Lay ministries: Minnesota parishes tussle with impending ban on lay preaching. *National Catholic Reporter*, p. G1.
Berry, J. (2009, January 14). A tale of two archdioceses [Editorial]. *The Boston Globe*, p. A13.
Black, D. E. (2006, February 1). Cuenin breaks his silence. *The Newton Tab*. Retrieved August 28, 2006, from http://www.ourladysfriends.org/newsNewtonTab_20060201.htm
Bodengraven, B. R. (2004, May 14). Women call for transformed church. *National Catholic Reporter*, pp. 7–8.
Bole, W. (2005, Fall). Sound check: Scholars find faith but little range in survey data on Voice of the Faithful. *Boston College Magazine 65*(4), 44–45. Retrieved December 12, 2005, from http://www.bc.edu/publications/bcm/fall_2005/c21_votf.html
Bonavoglia, A. (2005). *Good Catholic girls: How women are leading the fight to change the church*. New York, NY: HarperCollins.
Bonnike, F. (2005, January/February). A homily. *CORPUS Reports, 31*(1), 22–23.
Bono, A. (2005, January. 16). Survey: Catholics worried that sex abuse costs curtail church work. *Catholic News Service*. Retrieved January 7, 2009, from http://www.jknirp.com/bono3.htm.
Boorstein, M. (2010, March 18). Dissent among Catholics seen as nuns' groups back health bill. *The Washington Post*. Retrieved June 14, 2010, from http://www.washintonpost.com/wp-dyn/content/article/2010/03/18AR2010031802456.htlm
Boulcin, M. (2008). Call to ministry: Binding the wounds of clergy abuse. In E. H. McGrath; B. M. Meehan, & I. Raming (Eds.), *Women find a way: The movement and stories of Roman Catholic Womenpriests* (pp. 47–54). College Station, TX: Virtualbookworm.com
Boulding, E. (1976). *The underside of history: A view of women through time*. Boulder, CO: Westview Press.
Boyd, M. (Ed.). (1969). *The underground church*. Baltimore, MD: Penguin.
Breslin, J. (2004, September/October). Excerpt from The church that forgot Christ. *CORPUS Reports, 30*(5), 7.
Brief history and description of Catholic Organizations for Renewal. (n.d.). Retrieved August 9, 2007, from http://www.cta-usa.org/COR.html
Briggs, K. A. (1992). *Holy siege: The year that shook America*. New York, NY: HarperCollins.
———. (2006). *Double crossed: Uncovering the Catholic Church's betrayal of American nuns*. New York, NY: Doubleday.

Bruce, T. C. (2011). *Faithful revolution: How Voice of the Faithful is changing the church*. New York, NY: Oxford.
Brueggemann, W. (2001). *The prophetic imagination* (2nd ed.). Minneapolis, MN: Augsburg Fortress.
Burch, J. (n.d.). *The pastoral church at the dawn of the new Christian era* [Brochure]. Clifton, VA: Author.
———. (2007, March/April). Archbishop Milingo energizes the married priest debate. *CORPUS Reports, 33*(2), 15–17.
Burke, D. (2007, January 18). Five years on, Catholic group tries to hold the center. *National Catholic Reporter*, pp. 6–7.
Burns, G. (1992). *The frontiers of Catholicism: The politics of ideology in a liberal world*. Berkeley: University of California Press.
Call to Action. (n.d). *Call to Action mission statement*. Retrieved May 24, 2008, from http://www.cta-usaa.or/about/mission
———. (n.d.). *Our history*. Retrieved June 28, 2009, from http://www.cta-usa.org/about/history
Cachia. E. (2006, April). Father Edward Cachia's response to Bishop Nicola De Angelis' statement regarding his excommunication, issued the first week of April, 2006. Message posted to news://www.womensordination.org/content/view/231/
Call to Action (1997, March).Vatican reinstates Balasuriya. *CTA ChurchWatch* [Newsletter], 1.
———. (2001, October). 25 years of spirituality and justice. *Call to Action News Anniversary Edition* [Newsletter].
———. (2005, February/March). Culture of Conversation hosts national parley. *CTA ChurchWatch* [Newsletter], 2.
———. (2006a, May/June). People's action rescues historic New Orleans parish. *CTA ChurchWatch* [Newsletter], 1.
———. (2006b, November). *I am: Rise up people of God* [Conference Brochure]. Chicago, IL: Author.
———. (2006c, December 8). *Catholics will appeal excommunication* [Press Release]. Retrieved June 6, 2007, from http://www.cta-usa.org
———. (2007). *Call to Action annual report* [Brochure]. Chicago, IL: Author.
———. (2010, February). Conference attendees support women religious. *CTA News* [Newsletter], 6.
———. Local CTAers press bishops for disclosure. (2003, October). *CTA ChurchWatch* [Newsletter], 7.
Callahan, P. (2008, January/February). Gone from priesthood ... gone from the church: Why so many resigned priests leave the church. *CORPUS Reports, 34*(1), 15–18.
Callan, J. B. (1997). *Can't hold back the spring*. Rochester, NY: Corpus Christi Publications.
———. (2001). *The Studentbaker Corporation: A vehicle for renewal in the Catholic Church*. Rochester, NY: Spiritus Publications.
Calling all Catholics to transform our Church. (2008, April 8). Voice of the Faithful full-page ad in *The New York Times*, B4. Retrieved May 4, 2008, from http://votf.org/pope/ad.html
Carroll, J. L. (2007, Spring). On authority: How Americans ideals have changed the Catholic Church. *Boston College Magazine 67*(2). Retrieved December 12, 2007, from http://www.bcom.bc.edu
Casey, B., & Bartley, D. (2009, July 13). VOTF in urgent need of funds. Message posted to VOTF on behalf of Voice of the Faithful mailing list.
Caspary, A. M. (2003). *Witness to integrity: The crisis of Immaculate Heart Community of California*. Collegeville, MN: Liturgical Press.
Catholic Culture. (2009, February 26). News briefs: Number of US Catholics declines by 398,000. Retrieved July 6, 2009, from http://www.catholicculture.org/news/headlines/index.cfm?storyid=2115
Catholics for Choice. (n.d.). *About us*. Retrieved June 15, 2009, from http://www.catholicsforchoice.org

Catholics for Choice. (2011). *Support Catholics for Choice*. Retrieved January 6, 2011, from http://www.catholicsforchoice.org

Catholic women's ordination group protest lack of women's voices in conclave [Press Release]. (2005, April 12). Retrieved July 24, 2006, from http://women'sordination.org/content/view;123/42/

Celibacy Is The Issue. (n.d.). *What Catholics should know* [Brochure]. Framingham, MA: Author.

Chittister, J. (2006, November 3). Rise up, people of God: Spirituality for beginning again. Keynote address, CTA 2006 National Conference, Milwaukee, WI. *CTA Spirituality and Justice reprint* [Newsletter]. (2007, January-February), 1–6.

Church history, St. Stanislaus Kostka. (n.d.). Retrieved June 15, 2005, from http://www.ststanislauskostka.com

Cleary, W. (1985, August 14). Undocumented Protestants. *Christian Century 102*, 736–739.

———. (2004, November/December). [Review of the book *The Church that forgot Christ*] *CORPUS Reports, 30*(6), 46.

———. (2005, March/April). What made me Unitarian. *Corpus Reports, 31*(2), 20–22.

Clements, G. (2007, May/June). Some things to think about before you come to Providence. *CORPUS Reports, 33*(1), 35–37.

Coday, D. (2006, May 12). Extreme makeover: The diocese: new bishop quickly discards programs, people. *National Catholic Reporter*, pp. 6–10.

Colbert, C. (2006a, February 3). Priest recounts forced resignation. *National Catholic Reporter*, p. 9.

———. (2006b, November 10). Archdiocese sells former grade school to community. *National Catholic Reporter*, p. 8.

———. (2007, November 2). Reformers meet, reports of abuse in R.I. released. *National Catholic Reporter*, p. 9.

Coleman, J. A. (1968). Church-sect typology and organizational precariousness. *Sociological Analysis. 29*(2), 55–66.

Coleman, N. (2008, March 4). Free republic parishioners "walkout" & "underground church" (Minneapolis Archdiocese cracks down on liturgy). Message posted to http://157.64.200/focus/f-religion/1980281/posts

Collins, P. (2002). *The modern inquisition: Seven prominent Catholics and their struggles with the Vatican*. New York, NY: Overlook Press.

Community of God's Love. (n.d.). *Community of God's Love summer liturgy packet* [Brochure]. Lowell, MA. Author.

Community of God's Love. (n.d.). *Welcome packet* [Brochure]. Lowell, MA: Author.

Congregation for Catholic Education. (2005, November). *Instruction concerning the criteria for discernment of vocations with regard to persons with homosexual tendencies in view of their admission to seminary and hold orders*. Retrieved May 18, 2007, from http://www.vatican.va/.../rc_con_ccatheduc_doc_20051104_istruzione_en.html

Congregation for the Doctrine of the Faith. (2005, July 13). *Considerations regarding proposals to give legal recognition to unions between homosexual persons*. Retrieved June 25, 2008, from http://vatican.va/roman_curia/congregations/cfaith/documents/rc_con_cfaith_doc20

Constitution of the Ecumenical Catholic Communion. (2007, October 26). Retrieved December 6, 2007, from http://www.ecumenical-catholic-communion.org

Cooperman, J. (2008a, February 22). In a face-off with authority, Polish priest stands to be defrocked. *National Catholic Reporter*, pp. 5–7.

———. (2008b, May). A conversation with Elsie Hainz McGrath. *St. Louis Magazine*. Retrieved June 24, 2008, from http://www.stlmag.com/media/St.Louis-Magazine/May-2008/A-conversation-withElsieHainzMcGrath

CORPUS position statement on Married Priest Now. (2007, March/April). *CORPUS Reports, 33*(2), 27.

Crosby, M. (2005, May/June). Developing a spirituality of exile. *CORPUS Reports, 31*(3), 4–12.
Cuneo, M. (1997). *The smoke of Satan*. Baltimore, MD: Johns Hopkins University Press.
D'Antonio, W., & Pogorelc, A. (2007). *Voices of the Faithful: Loyal Catholics striving for change*. New York, NY: Crossroads.
Declaration of the American Catholic Council. (n.d). Retrieved July 6, 2008, from http://www.americancatholiccouncil.org
Demerath, N. J., III, & Thiessen, V. (1966). On spitting against the wind: Organizational precariousness and American irreligion. *American Journal of Sociology 71*(6), 674–687.
Devine, M. (2007, May). Two years later: Surprises in Pontificate of Benedict XVI: Summary of lecture by Father McBrien. *The American Catholic*, pp. 8, 16.
Dialogue with the diocese: The Chicago drama. (2007, November 13). *In the Vineyard* [Newsletter], *6*(12). Retrieved November 11, 2008, from http://www.votf.org/vineyard/Nov. 8_2007/dialogue.html
Dierks, S. D. (n.d.). *About the author*. Retrieved July 16, 2008, from http://www.wovenword.com
———. (1997). *WomenEucharist*. Boulder, CO: Woven Word Press.
———., & Meehan, B. M. (2008a). *Eucharist prayers for inclusive communities: Volume II, possibilities for the liturgical year*. Boulder, CO: Woven Word Press.
———. (2008b. May/June).When grandmothers get ordained. *CORPUS Reports, 34*(3), 19–21.
Dignity/Boston (n.d.). *Liturgy at Dignity/Boston*. Retrieved June 16, 2009, from http://www.dignityboston.org
———. (2003, December). *Order of liturgy* [Brochure]. Boston, MA: Author.
DignityUSA statement of position and purpose: Who are we? (n.d.). Retrieved June 14, 2008, from http://www.dignityusa.org
DignityUSA vision statement. (n.d.). Retrieved May 13, 2008, from http://www.dignityusa.org
DignityUSA. (1987, July 23). *Declaration of non-reception of the letter on pastoral care of homosexual persons* [Press Release]. Retrieved November 13, 2007, from http://www.dignityusa.org
———. (2005a, March 1). *DignityUSA calls for apology from Bishop of San Diego* [Press Release]. Retrieved June 5, 2006, from http://www.dignityusa.org/node/756
———. (2005b, April 19). *DignityUSA sees challenge ahead in new papacy* [Press Release]. Retrieved July 13, 2005, from http://www.dignityusa.org/node/761
———. (2007, May). DignityUSA revenue and expense summary 1 Oct 2006 to 31 Mar 2007. *Dateline Monthly News Bulletin* [Newsletter], *16*(5), 5.
———. (2008, December). Operating statement of revenue and expense for the period 1 October 2007–30 September 2008. *Dateline Monthly News Bulletin* [Newsletter], *17*(12), 14.
Dillon, M. (1999). *Catholic identity: Balancing reason, faith, and power*. Cambridge, United Kingdom: Cambridge University Press.
———. (2007). Bringing doctrine back into action: The Catholicity of VOTF Catholics and its imperative. In W. D'Antonio & A. Pogorelc, *Voices of the Faithful: Loyal Catholics striving for change* (pp. 105–120). New York, NY: Crossroads.
Distinctives. Ecumenical Catholic Communion. (n.d.). Retrieved July 21, 2007, from http://www.ecumenical-catholic-communion.org/html/distinctives.html
Ditzel, R. (2003a, January/February). Adsum: Renewing our church. *CORPUS Reports, 29*(1), 22–23.
———. (2003b, August 22). Letter to Bishop Wilton Gregory. Retrieved October 30, 2003, from http://www.corpus.org
———. (2005, March/April). Renewing our outreach. *CORPUS Reports, 31*(2), 19.
———. (2009, January/February). Adsum: Mama LaCorte. *CORPUS Reports, 35*(1), 36–37.

Dolbee, S. (2006, August). Ordination puts women, Backers at odds with the Catholic Church. *The San Diego Union-Tribune.* Retrieved September 23, 2007, from http://signonsandiego.com/uniontrib/.../news-1cO5woman.html

Donato, D. (2005, Fall). A letter from Denise Donato [Letter to editor]. *New Women, New Church* [Newsletter], *28*(3), 6.

Doucette, D. B. (2008, February 26). Letter to Voice of the Faithful. Retrieved February 28, 2008, from http://www.votf.org

Doyle, T. P. (2008, January). VOTF and reform of governmental structures of the Catholic Church. Retrieved February 15, 2008, from http://www.votf.org

Doyle, T. P., Sipe, A. W. R., & Wall, P. J. (2006). *Sex, priests and secret codes: The Catholic Church's 2000-year paper trail of sexual abuse.* Los Angeles, CA: Volt Press.

Dujardin, R. C. (2007, October 20). Allowing priests to marry may be group's next goal. *The Providence Journal.* Retrieved October 31, 2007, from http://www.projo.com/news/content/faithful_meet20_10-20-2007_K87IDVL.3275835.html

Eckstrom, K. (2010, March 19). Health care pits Catholic against Catholic. *Religious News Service.* Retrieved June 4, 2010, from http://www.religionnews.com/index.php?/rnstext/health_care_fight_pits_catholic_against

Ecumenical Catholic Communion. (n.d.). *ECC video.* Orange, CA: Author. Available from: http://www.ecumenicalcatholic-communion.org

———. (2007). *The constitution of the Ecumenical Catholic Communion.* Orange, CA: Author.

Ecumenical Catholic Communion mission statement. (n.d.). Retrieved July 31, 2007, from http://www.ecumenical-catholic-communion.org/html/distinctives.html

Edman, P. (2009, March 8). Maverick Australian priest sacked. *National Catholic Reporter,* p. 14.

English, B. (2004, Aug. 17). Man in the middle: Pastor directs closing of his church while supporting the fight to keep it open. *The Boston Globe,* p. D1. Retrieved August 25, 2004, from http://www.boston.com/news/globe/living/articles/2004/08/12/man_in_the_middle/

Farrell, S. A. (2005, Spring). Reframing social justice: Feminism and abortion. *Conscience, 26* (1). Retrieved June 4, 2005, from http://www.catholicsforchoice.org/pubs/ctc.archives/articles/AbortionArchives/asp

Farris, J. (2009, December). Growing pains. *ECC News* [Newsletter], *4*(2), 3.

Feeney, M. (2003, April 8). Globe wins Pulitzer gold medal for coverage of clergy abuse crisis. *The Boston Globe.* Retrieved November 2, 2009, from http://www.boston.com/globe/spotlight/abuse/extras/pulitzers.htm

Feuerherd, J. (2007, March 9). Kissling leaves, with barbs for the left. *National Catholic Reporter,* p. 19.

Feuerherd, P. (2006a, May 19). Priests offer mediation for bishops, laity. *National Catholic Reporter,* pp. 7–8.

———. (2006b, December 29). Villanova study of embezzlement in dioceses. *National Catholic Reporter,* p. 18.

Fiedler, M. (2005, Spring). Some observations out of Rome. *New Women, New Church* [Newsletter], *28*(1), 3.

Fields, R. (2006, August 14). In San Diego, Jane Via leads a Mass by herself: She is facing possible excommunication. *The Los Angeles Times.* p. B4.

Filteau, J. (2011, March 18). Parishioners' appeals see partial victories: Vatican ruling on closed US churches called landmark. *National Catholic Reporter,* p. 12.

Fiorenza, E. S. (2005, July 22). We are church—A kindom of priests. Paper presented at the Women's Ordination Conference Worldwide, Ontario, Canada. Retrieved November 18, 2006, from http://www.womensordination.org

Fisher, M., & Leen, J. (1997, November 24). Stymied in U.S., Moon's church sounds a retreat. *Washington Post,* p. A1.

Five years later: Many Catholics lack awareness of steps taken by the church to deal with and prevent abuse. A study conducted by the Center for Applied Research in the

Apostolate. (2007). Retrieved August 6, 2008, from http://www.cara.georgetown.eduPR51507.pdf

Fowler, J. W. (1981). *Stages of faith: The psychology of human development and the search for meaning.* New York, NY: HarperCollins.

Fox, M. (1983). *Original blessing: A primer in creation spirituality, presented in four paths, twenty six themes and two questions.* Rochester, VT: Inner Traditions.

Fox, M. (2006). *A new reformation: Creation spirituality and the transformation of Christianity.* Rochester, VT: Inner Traditions.

Fox, T. (2003, November 21). Need hope? Join Call to Action ranks. *National Catholic Reporter,* p. 7.

———. (2009a, April 21). Vatican investigates U.S. women religious leadership. *National Catholic Reporter.* Retrieved June 28, 2009, from http://ncronline.org/women/vatican-investigates-us-women-religious-leadership

———. (2009b, July 2). Community supports ousted St. Louis nun. *National Catholic Reporter.* Retrieved July 5, 2009, from http://www.ncronline.orgn/print/1330

———. (2009c, September 29). Mercy Sister Theresa Kane criticizes church hierarchy. *National Catholic Reporter.* Message posted to http://ncronline.org/news/mercy-sister-Kane-criticizes-church-hierarchy

———. (2009d, December 11). Women religious not complying with study. *National Catholic Reporter,* p. 1.

France, D. (2004). *Our fathers: The secret life of the Catholic Church in an age of scandal.* New York, NY: Broadway Books.

Freeman, J. (n.d.) Tyranny of structurelessness. Retrieved April 11, 2009, from http://www.jofreeman.com

———. (1999). Introduction. In J. Freeman & V. Johnson (Eds.), *Waves of protest, social movements since the sixties* (pp. 1–6). Lanham, MD: Rowman & Littlefield.

Fresen, P. (2006). Long walk to freedom. Paper presented at 2006 Call to Action National Convention, Milwaukee, WI [Cassette]. Sophia's Market Online Store at http://cta-usa.org/

———. (2008). A new understanding of priestly ministry: Looking at a church in crisis. In E. H. McGrath, B. M. Meehan, & I. Raming (Eds.), *Women find a way: The Movement and stories of Roman Catholic Womenpriests* (pp. 28–35). College Station, TX: Virtualbookworm.com

Fujimori, S. (2006, December 7). Renegade bishop set to rattle Rome. Retrieved January 12, 2007. Message posted to http://religonnewsblog.com/.../renegade-bishop-set-to-rattle-rome

FutureChurch. (n.d.). *About us.* Retrieved April 12, 2004, from http://www.futurechurch.org/about/htm

———. (n.d.). *FutureChurch separating fact from fiction.* Retrieved on June 2, 2010, from http://futurechurch.org/fact-faction.hmtl

———. (2005, April 19). *Crisis kit for parishes* [Brochure]. Lakewood, OH. Author.

———. (2006, October 25). *Catholic groups call for "best practices" in time of fewer priests* [Petition]. Retrieved June 2, 2009, from http://www.futurechurch.org/press/102506.htm

———. (2008, September 8). *Women and the word: Historic outcome of synod work, put women back in the biblical picture* [Press Release]. Retrieved June 2, 2009, from http://www.futurechurch.org.press/090808.htm

———. (2010a, July 12). *Catholics organize 300 worldwide celebrations of early women leaders on St. Mary of Magdala feast* [Press Release]. Retrieved July 24, 2010, from http://www.futurechurch.org/CatholicsOrganize300WorldwideCelebrations.htm

———. (2010b, Fall). Some parishes win, others reorganize. *FOCUS on FutureChurch* 7(3), 5.

Gautier, M. L. (2005, September 30). Lay Catholics firmly committed to parish life. *National Catholic Reporter,* pp. 20–21.

Gay clergy issue letter on Vatican policy. (2005, December 16). *TriCity Herald*. Retrieved January 30, 2006, from http://www.freerepublic.com/focus/religion/2540879/posts

Geranios, N. (2006, February 17). Spokane parishes oppose settlement offer. *The Seattle Times*. Retrieved February 24, 2006, from http://www.seattletimes.nwsource.com/html/localnews/2008118 79_webspokanesteelement17.http

Gibson, D. (2003). *The coming Catholic Church: How the faithful are shaping a new American Catholicism*. San Francisco, CA: HarperSanFrancisco.

———. (2006). *The Rule of Benedict: Pope Benedict XVI and his battle with the modern world*. San Francisco, CA: HarperCollins.

Glock, C. Y., & Stark, R. (1965). *Religion and society in tension*. Chicago, IL: Rand McNally.

Goldstein, W. (2011, March). The dialectics of religious conflict: Church-sect, denomination and the culture wars. *Culture and Religion, 12*(1), 77–99.

Goodstein, L. (2005, September 23). Gay men ponder impact of proposal by Vatican. *The New York Times*, p. A10. Retrieved December 5, 2009, from http://www.nytimes.com/2005/09/23/.../23priests.html

———. (2008, November 14). Catholic priest faces excommunication. *The New York Times*, p. A19. Retrieved July 5, 2009, from www.nytimes.com/2008/11/14/us/14priest.html?_l&em+&pagewante=print

Grace Church of Dover. (n.d.). *A guide to our worship* [Brochure]. Dover, MA. Author.

———. (n.d.). *A journey of grace* [Videocassette]. Dover, MA. Author.

———. (n.d.). *Grace Church of Dover*. [Brochure]. Dover, MA. Author.

———. *Who are we?* (n.d.). Retrieved April 1, 2007, from www.gracechurchofdover.com

Gray, M. M., & Perl, P. M. (2006, April). Catholic reactions to the news of sexual abuse cases involving Catholic clergy: A publication of the Center for Applied Research in the Apostolate. Retrieved August 8, 2009, from http://www.cara,georgetwon.edu.pubs/CARA%20Working%20Paper%208.pfd

Groome, T. H. (2003).*What makes us Catholic? Eight gifts for life*. New York, NY: HarperCollins.

Grosswirth, R. (2004, July/August). Ray's musings. *CORPUS Reports, 30*(4), 24.

———. (2005, May/June). How would Jesus rate our cardinals and bishops? *CORPUS Reports, 3*(3), 39–40.

Guntzel, J. S. (2005, August 26). Digging in to stay and pray. At some parishes they defy O'Malley's plan. *National Catholic Reporter*, pp. 13–16.

Haggett, L. (2005) *Bingo, mandatory celibacy and clergy sexual abuse*. Freeport, ME: Center for the Study of Religious Issues.

Hemmer, C. J. (2005, January./February). Where is CORPUS going? *CORPUS Reports, 31*(1), 26–30.

Henold, M. J. (2008). *Catholic and feminist: The surprising history of the American Catholic feminist movement*. Chapel Hill: The University of North Carolina Press.

Hess, A. L. (1990, April 18). Catholics and Protestants in a UCC Church. *The Christian Century, 107*(13), 401–402.

Hickman, P. (2006, March 31). Heresy Trial [Letter to the Editor] *National Catholic Reporter*, p. 20.

Hines, M. (2007). Voice of the Faithful survey: An ecclesiological reflection. In W. D'Antonio & A. Pogorelc, *Voices of the Faithful: Loyal Catholics striving for change* (pp. 121–134). New York, NY: Crossroads.

Hirschman, A. (1970). *Exit, voice and loyalty: Responses to declines in firms, organizations, and states*. Cambridge, MA: Harvard University Press.

History of Solidarity Sunday. (n.d.). Retrieved May 14, 2007, from http://dignityusa.org/content/history-solidarity-Sunday

History of Spiritus Christi Church. (n.d.) [Brochure]. Rochester, NY: Spiritus Christi Parish.

Hitchcock, H. H. (2000, September/October). Helpful changes: New liturgy rules precede missal. *Adoremus bulletin. 6*(6). Retrieved July 15, 2008, from http://www.adoremus.org/NewLiturgy9102K.htlm

Hoge, D. R., & Wenger, J. E. (2003). *Evolving visions of the priesthood: Changes from Vatican II to the turn of the century*. Collegeville, MN: Liturgical Press.
Homan, M. (1998). *Rules of the game: Lessons from community change*. Florence, KY: Cengage Learning.
Howard, C. (2009, April). National meeting on finance. *ECC News* [Newsletter], *4*(1), 2.
Howarth, R. (2002). Witness to herstory: Austrian and German women ordained priests. *Speaking Out: The Newsletter of Catholics Speak Out* [Newsletter], 1–3. Retrieved April 17, 2003, from http://www.quixote.org/cso/HerStoryWitness%20to20%herStory.htlm
Humphreys, L. (1970). *Tearoom trade: Impersonal sex in public places*. New York, NY: Aldine de Gruyter.
Hunt, M. (2003, Spring). Twenty years of Water: What differences does it make? *Waterwheel* [Newsletter], *16*(1), 1–3.
———. (2004, May 15). Women, religion and justice: A new equation for troubled times. Paper presented at Women-Church Convergence Conference. Cincinnati, OH. Retrieved July 7, 2006, from http://www.womenchurchconvergence.org/conclatve/articles/articles5.hmtl
———. (2006, Spring). Catholic pride ... and prejudice: The story behind the hierarchy's obsession with sexuality. *Conscience, 26*(3). Retrieved from http://www.catholicsforchoice.org/conscience/archives/c2006spring_catholicpride.asp
———. (2008, October 27). Catholic voters no longer beholden to bishops and abortion. *RD Magazine*. Retrieved July 5, 2010, from http://religiondispatches.org/archive/sexandgender/650/catholic_voters_no_long_be
———. (2010, Winter/Spring). Father does not know best: How to fix the Catholic Church. *New Women, New Church* [Newsletter], *33*(1), 3, 14.
Hunter, J. D. (1991). *Culture Wars: The struggle to define America; Making sense of the battle over the family, art, education, law and politics*. New York, NY: Basic Books.
The Inclusive Community: Celebrating our tenth anniversary, 1986–1996. (1996) [Brochure]. Nutley, NJ: The Inclusive Community.
The Inclusive Community mission statement. (n.d.). Retrieved March 15, 2007, from http://www.christianbridges.com/index.html
Investigative staff of the Boston Globe. (2002). *Betrayal: The crisis in the Catholic Church*. Boston, MA: The Boston Globe.
Jesus Our Shepherd. (n.d.). *Jesus Our Shepherd Church: An inclusive faith community* [Brochure]. Nenno, WI: Author
Jesus Our Shepherd Mission Statement. (n.d.). Retrieved September 14, 2006. from http://www.jesusourshepherd.org
Jesus Our Shepherd Parish Survey. (2002). Nenno, WI: Jesus Our Shepherd.
Johnson, J. (2004). Ordinations on the St. Lawrence. Retrieved May 2005, from http://www.womensordination.org/pages/art_2005Ord
Jones, J. (2005, November 28). Priest hangs up collar for change: Questioning traditions has led to the Rev. Stier's exile from Freemont church. Associated Press. Retrieved January 12, 2006, from http://catholicforum.fisheaters.com/index.php?topic+772716;wap2
Johnson, S. (2005). Will U.S. Catholics keep giving? Retrieved on June 18, 2006 from http://msnbc.com/id/.../will-is-catholics-keep-giving/-
Kaintz, B. (2006, Jan. 12). Into the light. *In the Vineyard* [Newsletter], *5*(1), 1. Retrieved January 19, 2006, from http://www.votf.org/vineyard/Ja12_06/kaitz/html
Kaiser, R. B. (2006). *The church in search of itself: Benedict XVI and the battle for the future*. New York, NY: Knopf.
Kane, T. (2010, August 9). St. Theresa Kane speaks on effective liturgy at Celebration Conference in Chicago. Message posted to http://ncronline.org/news/sr-thresa-kane-speaks-effective-liturgy-celebration-coference-c
Kennedy, E. C. (2005, October 21). Bishops and the beached whale. *National Catholic Reporter*, pp. 11–13.
———. (2010, June 3). The all American culture team. Message posted to http://ncronline.org/blogs/bulletins-human-side/all-american-clerical-cultural-team

Kenny, J. (2010, August 24). St. Louis parish rejects archdiocesan proposal. *National Catholic Reporter*. Retrieved on September 30, 2010, from http://ncronline/org/news/faith-parish/st-louis-parish-rejects-archdioceses-proposal

Kenny, J., & Kenny, M. (2004). *The church that refused to die*. Indianapolis, IN: The Bridgetine Press.

Kissling, F. (2000, Summer). Abortion: Articulating a moral view. *Conscience, 20*(3). Retrieved June 9, 2005, from http://www.catholicsforchoice.org

———. (2004/5, Winter). Is there life after Roe? *Conscience, 26*(4). Retrieved July 7, 2005, from http://www.catholicsforchoice.org/.../c2004win_lifeafterroe.asp

Kuenstler, K. (2007, Spring). Counterpoint on the riverboat rituals of ordination. *New Women, New Church* [Newsletter], *30*(2), 10.

Küng, H. (1981, November 7). The Church from above and the church from below. Paper presented at fifth anniversary celebration of Chicago Call to Action. Chicago, IL. Retrieved June 6, 2006, from http://www.cta-usa.org/foundationdocs

———. (2003) *My struggle for freedom: Memoirs*. Grand Rapids, MI: Eerdmans.

Landau, S. I. (Ed.). (2002). *The new international Webster's collegiate dictionary of the English language*. Naples, Florida: Trident Press International.

Lavoie, D. (2010, May 17). Vatican rejects closed Mass. churches' appeal. Associated Press. Retrieved July 7, from dailytrib.com/index.php?...vatican-rejects-closed

Lavoie, D., & Lindsay, J. (2011, February 15). 3 Mass churches should reopen, Vatican rules. Associated Press. Retrieved on February 20, 2011, from http://news.yahoo.com/s/ap/20110216/ap_on.../us-church-closing_8

Lee, B. J., with Elizando, V., & D'Antonio, W. (2000). *The Catholic experience of small Christian communities*. New York, NY: Paulist Press.

Lee, B. J., & Cowan, M. (2003). *Gathered and sent*. New York, NY: Paulist Press.

Letter to Cardinal George asking for openness. (2009, July 24). *In the Vineyard* [Newsletter], *8*(14), 1.

Levenson, M. (2005, September 30). Westborough priest pulled from the altar: Bulletin raps call for gay union ban. *The Boston Globe*, p. B4. Retrieved November 4, 2005, from http://www.boston.com/news/local/.../westborough_priest-pulled-from-the-altar

Lewis, H. M., & Appleby, M. (2003). *Mountain sisters*. Lexington: The University Press of Kentucky.

Lorde, A. (1984). The master's tools will never dismantle the master's house. In A. Lorde. *Sister outsider: Essays and speeches by Audre Lorde* (pp. 110–113). Berkeley, CA: The Crossing Press.

Lytton, T. (2008). *Holding bishops accountable: How lawsuits helped the Catholic Church confront sexual abuse*. Cambridge, MA: Harvard University Press.

Macisse, C. (2003, November). Violence in the church. *The Tablet, 22*, 9.

Manseau, P. (2005). *Vows: The story of a priest and a nun and their son*. New York, NY: The Free Press.

Manseau, W. J. (2005, March/April). A national ministerial alliance. *CORPUS Reports, 31*(2), 28–29, 44.

———. (2007, January/February). Interview with Archbishop Milingo. *CORPUS Reports, 33*(1), 35–39, 41.

———. (2009, May/June). From the president's desk. *CORPUS Reports, 35*(3), 11–13.

Markey, E. (2008, April 4). Unruly Americans vie for attention. *National Catholic Reporter*. Retrieved June 9, 2009, from http://ncronline.org/node.568

McArron, P. (2003, Autumn). Our voice is louder than ever and yet not quite loud enough. *The Dignity Journal* [Newsletter], *35*(4), 14–15.

———. (2005, March 21). *Dignity/San Diego and DignityUSA express gratitude for Bishop Brom's apology* [Press Release]. Retrieved July 13, 2005, from http://www.dignityusa.org/node/757

McBrien, R. (2005a, April). The stalemate over abortion. *The American Catholic*, p. 10.

———. (2005b, May). When the pope speaks. *The American Catholic*, p. 10.

———. (2008, September 19). Debate over the role of 'bishop' in apostolic succession is church-divide issue. Message posted to http://ncronline.org/node/1862
———. (2010a, May 17). Pope Benedict XVI: After five years—part 2. Message posted to http://ncronline.org/print/18336
———. (2010b, July 8). A hierarchy deeply damaged from within [Editorial]. *Catholic Reporter*, p. 28.
———. (2010c, October 19). John Paul II: The real reason for church polarization. Message posted to http://ncronline.org/print/20826
McCabe, K. (2007, July 23). Churches mark 1,000 days in vigil: Organizers seek their reopening. *Boston Globe*, pp. B1, B2.
McCarthy, J. D. (2007). Fundamental strategic tasks for leaders organizing grassroots insurgencies, with particular reference to VOTF. In W. D'Antonio & A. Pogorelc, *Voices of the Faithful: Loyal Catholics striving for change* (pp. 156–169). New York, NY: Crossroads.
McCarthy, J. D., & Zald, M. N. (1977). Resource mobilization and social movements: A partial theory. *American Journal of Sociology, 82*(6), pp. 1212–1239.
McClory, R. (2002). *Faithful dissidents: Stories of men and women who loved and changed the church*. Maryknoll, NY: Orbis Books.
———. (2003, September). Taking the pulse of Call to Action: What does the future hold? An interview with Dan and Sheila Daley. *Call to Action News* [Newsletter], *25*(2), 4.
———. (2005a, February/March). CTA helps Oregon CTA cope with the bishop's loyalty oath. *CTA ChurchWatch* [Newsletter], 3.
———. (2005b, March/April). Why do I stay in this church? Humor helps. Speech at 2004 CTA National Convention. *CTA News* [Newsletter], *26*(1), 2.
———. (2006, January 13). Bishop shuts us out, says priests: Belleville's Braxton, one of John Paul's last picks, said to be 'imperial.' *National Catholic Reporter*, p. 5.
———. (2007a, August). Battle fatigue: Five years into the sex abuse crisis, some Catholics are growing weary, while others are cautiously optimistic. *U.S. Catholic 72*(8), 18–23. Retrieved April 14, 2008, from http://www.uscatholic.org
———. (2007b, December 14). The Dutch plan: Will innovation save this church? Amsterdam and other cities in Holland. *National Catholic Reporter*. Retrieved February 16, 2008, from http://natcath.org/NCR_Online/archives2/2007d/121407d/121407/121407a.htm
———. (2008a, May 2). Calls for bishop's removal step up. *National Catholic Reporter*. Retrieved December 12, 2008, from http://ncronline.org/print/799
———. (2008b, August/September). An interview with Dan and Sheila Daley: The legacy will live. *Call to Action News* [Newsletter], *30*(3), 3.
McCool, J. R. (2004. January/February). Personal authority: Catholic adulthood. *CORPUS Reports, 30*(1), 32–34.
McDermott, A. (2005, September 15). Keynote Address at Boston College Forum *Why women choose to stay* sponsored by the Council for Women of Boston College and the Church in the 21st Century. Chestnut Hill, MA. Retrieved April 22, 2007, from http://www.bc.edu/church21/
McGrath, E. H., Meehan, B. M., & Raming, I. (Eds.). (2008). *Women find a way: The movement and stories of Roman Catholic Womenpriests*. College Station, TX: Virtualbookworm.com
McGrory, B. (2005, September 27). Smear tactics. *The Boston Globe*, p. B1. Retrieved November 2, 2005, from http://www.boston.com/news/local/articles/2005/09/27/smear_tactics
McNamara, E. (2002, May 29). A Catholic alternative. *The Boston Globe*, p. B1.
McNeill, B. (2007, March). *History in the United States, Australia, and England*. Retrieved December 12, 2009, from http://www.rainbowsashallianceusa.org/history_htm.html
Meehan, B. M. (2010, July 15). Vatican: Ordination of women a grave crime—Roman Catholic Womenpriests respond with demands for justice for women in the church. Retrieved on August 20, 2010, from www.romancatholicwomenpriests.org

Meet the Roman Catholic Womenpriests. (n.d.). Retrieved December 28, 2006, from http://www.rcwp.org/

Mehren, E. (2005, July 8). Fathers, husbands and rebels. *The Los Angeles Times*, p. A1. November 13, 2005, from http://newsyahoo.com/s/latimest/s/fathershusbandsandrebels

Michalek, J. C. (2008, February). Panel "voices the need for renewed, reflective faith." *Boston College Heights* [Boston College student newspaper]. Retrieved March 7, 2008, from http://bcheights.com/home;index/cfm?event+displayArticlePrint

Miles, D., & Miles, C. (2008, August/September). Write on column [Letters to the editor]. *Call to Action News* [Newsletter], *30*(2), 3.

Moore, A. (2007, May/June). Conference news. *CORPUS Reports, 33*(3), 24.

Morris, A. (1984). *The origins of the civil rights movement.* New York, NY: The Free Press.

Most, W. G. (1990). The Magisterium or teaching authority of the Church. Retrieved June 24, 2008, from http://www.ewtn.com/faith/teachings/chura4.htm

Moynihan, J. J. (2006, April). Has Call to Action been called to action? *The American Catholic*, pp. 12–13.

Muller, J., & Kenney, C. (2004). *Keep the faith, change the Church.* New York, NY: Rodale.

National parish inventory. (2000, October). Special Report, Center for Applied Research in the Apostolate. Retrieved August 1, 2009, from http://www.carageorgetown.edu/index/npi/index.htm

NCR staff. (2010, May 5). Zogby poll: U.S. Catholics say pope should not resign. *National Catholic Reporter.* Retrieved May 31, 2010, from http://ncronline.org/news/zogby-poll-us.catholics-say-pope-should-not-resign

Neu, D. L. (1995). Women-Church on the road to change. In M. T. Winter, A. Lummis, & A. Stokes, *Defecting in place, Women claiming responsibility for their own spiritual lives* (pp. 241–247). New York, NY: Crossroads.

Niebuhr, H. R. (1929). *The social sources of denominationalism.* New York, NY: Henry Holt.

No rationale for upheaval in Kansas [Editorial]. (2006, May 12). *National Catholic Reporter,* p. 24.

O'Brien, J. (2006, December 11). Memo to CFFC supporters. Message posted on an electronic mailing list to *Conscience* subscribers.

———. (2007a, Spring). How Catholics for a Free Choice saved civilization. *Conscience, 38*(1), 17–21.

———. (2007b, May). President's message. You don't need a weatherman to know which way the wind blows. Retrieved August 5, 2007, from www.catholicsforchoice.org/about/message/MessagefromJonObrienMay2007.asp

Old Catholics: An introduction and historical sketch. (n.d.). Retrieved January 15, 2008, from http://www.oldcatholicchurch.org/Old_Catholic_History.html.

Oleck, J. (2004, July 22). Catholic presses women's claim on priesthood. *WE News.* Retrieved July 22, 2004, from http://www.womensnews.org

O'Malley, M. (2010, August 15). Parishioners, priest from closed St. Peter Catholic Church defy bishop, celebrate Mass in new home. Message posted to http://blog.cleveland.com/metro/2010/08/parishioners_from_closed_catholic.html

———. (2011, April 3). Breakaway Catholic flock flourishing in New York. *The Plain Dealer.* Retrieved April 7, 2011, from http://www.cleveland.com/religion/index.ssf/2011/04/breakaway_catholic_flock_flour.html

O'Murchu, D. (2010). *Adult Faith, Growing in Wisdom and Understanding.* New York: Orbis.

Orso, J. (2006, November 4). While some bishops want to change Catholic attitudes, bishops are united in their support of marriage amendment. *LaCrosse Tribune.* Retrieved December 28, 2006, from http://www.lacrossetribune.com

Ortelli, W. (2006, September/October). Wayne Ortelli writes. *The Point* [Newsletter], 12.

Owens, A. M. (2006, April 22). Women's rites: How an Ontario priest's 'heresy' reignited the debate over female ordination in the Roman Catholic Church. *National Post* (Canada), p. A1.

Padovano, A. (n.d.). *The Inclusive Community-UCC: A new vision of Christianity since 1986* Retrieved October 3, 2006, from http://www.christianbridges.com
———. (n.d.). *Welcome statement: The Inclusive Community.* Retrieved March 27, 2006, from http://www.christianbridges.com/
———. (1994, January). Is CORPUS Catholic? *CORPUS News, 2*(1) [Newsletter], 9.
———. (2005a, May/June). A community for the twenty first century. *CORPUS Reports, 31*(1) 32–37.
———. (2005b, May/June). The Inclusive Community-UCC. *CORPUS Reports, 32*(3), 28–29.
———. (2005c, July/August). Reforming the church, electing a pope. *CORPUS Reports, 31*(2), 36–40.
———. (2006a, September 24). *The history making Inclusive Community celebrates 20 years* [Press Release].
———. (2006b, September/October). To what have we been committed? *CORPUS Reports, 33*(3), 21–30.
———. (2006c, September/October). Testimony. *The Point* [Newsletter], 1.
———. (2007a, January/February). Boundaries. *CORPUS Reports, 33*(1), 13–20.
———. (2007b, April 15). Peace and forgiveness: Reflections on John 20 and doubting Thomas, pp. 1–3. Retrieved July 26, 2007, from http://www.christianbridges.com/index.html
———. (2010, September/October). Encounters with freedom. *CORPUS Reports, 36*(5), 14–23.
Pagels, E. (1981). *The gnostic gospels.* New York, NY: Vintage Books.
Patterson, M. (2001, Dec. 7). Breakaway parish ordains woman priest: Bishop says ceremony seals schism between congregation, Catholic Church. *National Catholic Reporter,* p. 11.
Paulson, M. (2002, December 10). Fifty-eight priests send a letter urging Cardinal to resign. *The Boston Globe,* p. A34.
———. (2004, November 14). Anguished O'Malley explains fiscal crisis. *The Boston Globe,* p. A1. Retrieved November 30, 2004, from www.boston.com/new/local/artuckes/2004/11/14/anguished_omalley_explains_fiscal_crisis/
———. (2005a, March 26). Closed parish sent priest, O'Malley averts unsanctioned Mass. *The Boston Globe,* pp. B1, B6.
———. (2005b, June 10). Catholic school lockout angers parents. *The Boston Globe,* pp. B1, B4.
———. (2005c, June 19). O'Malley intensifies actions on closings: Eager for new issues, Focus. *The Boston Globe,* A1. Retrieved June 30, 2005, from http://www.boston.com/news/local/.../articles/.../omalley_move_follows_crisis/
———. (2005d, August 11). Vatican stops diocese in taking parish assets. Millions at stake as O'Malley must get OK of pastors. *The Boston Globe,* p. A1.
———. (2005e, October 2). Dislocation, scrutiny of priests raise fears: Archdiocese denies politics behind move. *The Boston Globe,* p. A1.
———. (2006a, April 20). Church tackles $46 m gap: Financial disclosures win praise. *The Boston Globe,* pp., Al, A21.
———. (2006b, June 11). Ousted Newton priest cheered at gay pride service. *The Boston Globe,* p. B1.
———. (2006c, July 28). Making a stand for women priests, archdiocesan official quits, saying she was ordained. *The Boston Globe,* p. B1.
———. (2008a, January 18). Big tab still rises at shut churches. *The Boston Globe,* p. A30.
———. (2008b, February 26). US religious identity is rapidly changing, study finds. *The Boston Globe,* pp. A1, A11.
———. (2008c, June 3). Diocese offers Indian Catholics use of parish it closed. *The Boston Globe,* pp. B1, B4.

———. (2008d, June 11). Vatican tribunal hands loss to 8 local groups on closing. *The Boston Globe*, pp. B1, B4.

———. (2008e, December 28). A interview with the Rev. Richard P. McBrien: Life as a theologian, commentator—and lightening rod. *The Boston Globe*, p. A10.

Petition from a people in exile [Advertisement] (2005, November 11). *National Catholic Reporter*, p. 11.

Pierce, C. P. (November 12, 2003). The crusaders: A powerful faction of religious and political conservatives is waging a latter-day counterreformation, ... *Boston Globe Magazine*, pp. 10–14, 17–18.

Pinto, L. (2009, May/June). CORPUS board meeting, 2.13.09, Convent Station, N.J. *CORPUS Reports*, 35(3), 14–17.

———. (2011, January/February). Giving voice to your vision. *CORPUS Reports*, 37(1), 6.

Plummer, J. (2004). *The many paths of the independent sacramental movement*. Dallas, TX: Newt Books.

Podles, L. J. (2008). *Sacrilege: Sexual abuse in the Catholic Church*. Baltimore, MD: Crossland Press.

Pope John Paul II. (1994). *Apostolic letter* Ordinatio Sacerdotalis *of John Paul II to the bishops of the Catholic Church on reserving priestly ordination to men alone*. Retrieved October 4, 2006, from http://www.vatican/va/.../hf_ip_ii_apl_22051994_ordinatio-sacerdotalis_en.html

Post, J. E. (2002, July 20). Voice of the Faithful: The road ahead. Presentation delivered to the first international convention of Voice of the Faithful, Boston, MA. [Cassette]. Resurrection Tapes, Minneapolis, Minnesota.

———. (2004, November 13). It's time for renewal. President's address at VOTF New England Conference, Worcester, MA.

———. (2005, October 3). Letter from the Voice of the Faithful's president. Retrieved November 23, 2005, from http://www.votf.org

———. (2006a, January 26). On our watch: VOTF president on VOTF's Campaign 2006, *In the Vineyard* [Newsletter], 5(2), 1.

———. (2006b, February). Making lemonade. *In the Vineyard* [Newsletter], 5(3), 1. Retrieved February 9, 2006, from http://www.votf.org/vineyardFeb9_2006/post.html

Powers, W. F. (1992). *Free Priests: The movement for ministerial reform in the American Catholic Church*. Chicago, IL: Loyola University Press.

Press release signed by the undersigned members of Catholic Organization for Renewal. (2006, November 12). Retrieved November 30, 2006, from http://www.dignityusa.org/node/805

Priestly membership. (n.d.). Retrieved November 30, 2007, from http://onespiritcatholic.org/My_homepage_Files/Page8.html

Priests for Equality. (n.d.) *Cycle C inclusive lectionary Readings* [Brochure]. Hyattsville, MD: Author.

Price, D. (2005, May 23). Gay Catholics fight for church acceptance. *The Detroit News*. Retrieved July 13, 2005, from http://www.dignityusa.org/media

Proctor-Smith, M. (2010). "The ones who've gone before us": The future of feminist artistic and liturgical life. In M. Hunt & D. L. Neu (Eds.), *New feminist Christianity: Many voices, many views* (pp. 222–231).Woodstock, VT: Skylight Paths.

Pullella, P. (2010, November 20). Pope puts stamp on church future with new cardinals. Retrieved January 5, 2011, from http://www.msnbc.msn.com/id/40270553/ns/world_news/

Putnam, R.D. (2000). *Bowling alone: The collapse and revival of American community*. (New York, NY: Simon & Schuster.

Putnam, R.D. & Campbell, D.E, *American Grace: How religion divides and unites us*. New York, NY: Simon & Schuster.

Raminez, M. (2008, June 1). Catholic activists mark end of an era. *Chicago Tribune*, p. 1. Retrieved June 11, 2008, from http://www.chicagotribune.com/news/local/chi-call-to-action_bd01jun01,0,2045666story

Rather, J. (2003, August 2). The battle is joined over Murphy. *The New York Times*. Retrieved June 30, 2010, from www.nytimes.com>...>ROCKVILLE CENTER

Reeves, B. (2006, April 25). Diocese in national spotlight. *Lincoln Journal Star*. Retrieved April 30, 2006, from http://www.journalstar.com/articles/2006/04/25/values/doc444d 572efb8981944197.txt

Report of the third annual convocation: Diocese of One Spirit. (July 8, 2007). Retrieved August 12, 2007, from http://www.onespiritcatholic.org/

Roberts, K. A. (2004). *Religion in sociological perspective.* (4th ed.) Belmont, CA: Wadsworth/ Thompson.

Roberts, T. (2008a, July 11). Contentious prelate leaving St. Louis for Rome appointment. *National Catholic Reporter*, p. G1.

———. (2008b, May 30). Retiring reformers note new goals, younger members' resistance prompt changes, Daley says. *National Catholic Reporter*, p. 12.

———. (2009a, March 20). Proposed bill on parishes gets strong reaction. *National Catholic Reporter*, p. G1.

———. (2009b, June 8). Carving out a spiritual home. Message posted to http://ncronline/ news/faith/carving-out-spiritual-home

———. (2009c, July 16, 2009). A map to the future. *National Catholic Reporter*. Message posted to http://ncronline.org/print/14073

———. (2010, October 11). The "had it" Catholics. *The National Catholic Reporter*. Message posted to http://ncronline.org/print/20673

Roman Catholic Womenpriests, USA and Canada. (n.d.) [One-page flyer distributed at Call to Action 2007 National Conference, Milwaukee, WI].

Rome looks bad in bout with Bourgeois [Editorial]. (2008, November). *National Catholic Reporter*, p. 28.

Rosenblatt, S. (2006, January 21). The diocese of San Bernardino has formally excommunicated a former Coachella Valley priest for heresy. *The Los Angeles Times*. Retrieved April 12, 2007, from http://www.articleslatimes.com/keywork/excommunication

Rue, V. (n.d.). *My journey to priesthood*. Retrieved June 12, 2010, from http://www .victoriarue.com

Ruether, R. R. (1985). *Women-Church: Theology and practice of feminist liturgical communities.* New York, NY: Harper & Row.

———. (1995). Defecting in place: Reflections on women's spiritual quest and new support groups. In M. T. Winter, A. Lummis, & A. Stokes (Eds.), *Defecting in place: Women claiming responsibility for their own spiritual lives* (pp. 248–353). New York, NY: Crossroads.

———. (2006). *The Church women want: The challenges of being Catholic in 2006* [Excerpt from speech at Conference sponsored by Boston College Church in the 21st Century]. Retrieved June 22, 2007, from http://bcm.bc.edu/issues/fall_2006/c21_notes/quotable .html

Save our parish community. (n.d.) [Brochure]. Retrieved June 15, 2010, from http://www .futurechurch.org/sopc/parishionerwebistes.htm

Schaeffer, P. (1997a, May 30). Dueling Catholics enliven Lincoln. *National Catholic Reporter*, p. 5.

———. (1997b, August 1). Tissa outser not canonically legal, lawyers say. *Catholic Reporter*. Retrieved July 20, 2009, from http://natcath.org/NCR_Online/archives2/1997c/080197/ 080197g.htm

———. (2007, December 7). Though church bans women priests, more and more women are saying: "Why wait?" *National Catholic Reporter*, pp. 15–17.

Scaine, R. (2007, July/August). Community of John XXIII. *CORPUS Reports, 33*(4), 30.

Schenk, C. (2010, Fall). Cardinal Newman on consulting the faithful. FutureChurch celebrates 20 years of doing just that. *Focus on Future Church* [Newsletter], *7*(3), 1.

Schilling, T. P. (2003, September 12). When bishops disagree. *Commonweal, 30*(15), 15–22.

Schismatic St. Louis parish loses appeal to Vatican. (2008, May 29). Retrieved July 4, 2008, from http://www.cbcpnews.com/?q=node/2942

See Change Campaign. Retrieved June 19, 2007, from http://www.seechange.org/bluebottom5c.htm

Sharp, G. (1973). *The politics of nonviolent action.* Boston, MA: Porter Sargent.

———. (2005). *Waging nonviolent struggle, 20th century practice and 21st century potential.* Manchester, NH: Extending Horizons Books.

Shea, S. S. (2008). *Sundays in America: A yearlong road trip in search of Christian faith.* Boston, MA: Beacon Press.

The shock fades in Lincoln. (2006, June 16). *National Catholic Reporter* [Editorial], p. 24.

Sinnett, S. (2007, July). President's address, Dignity convention speech. Retrieved July 23, 2007, from http://www.dignityusa.org/convention07/sinnett-cov07html

Sneak preview of WOC membership. (2007, Summer). *New Women, New Church* [Newsletter], *30*(3), 7.

Solidarity Sunday. (2005, October 9). Retrieved July 7, 2006, from http://www.dignityusa.org/solidarity

Sotelo, N. (2009, July 9). Education is a dangerous thing. *National Catholic Reporter.* Retrieved August 12, 2010, from http://ncronline.org/print/13966

Special Report: Catholic Bishops and sex abuse archives. (n.d.). *Dallas Morning News.* Retrieved June 15, 2009, from http://www.dallasnews.com/cig-bin/dallas/2002priests.cgi?bishop=12&diocese

Spiritus Christi. (n.d.). *The Story of Spiritus Christi* [Brochure]. Rochester, NY: Spiritus Christi Parish.

Spiritus Christi mission statement. (n.d.). Retrieved March 11, 2008, from http://www.spirituschristi.org/About_Us.html

Spitz, J. (2007, June 6). Vigils continue at closed churches, groups meet in Wellesley to weigh its next steps. *The Metrowest Daily News,* A1, A8.

Stanton, H. (Ed.). (1997). *Mary and human liberation.* Harrisburg, PA: Trinity Press International.

Stark, R., & Bainbridge, W. S. (1985). *The future of religion, secularization, revival, and cult formation.* Berkeley: University of California Press.

Steinfels, M. O. (2010, December 3). Defenders of the faith! A personal reflection on recent history. *Commonweal, 137*(21), 11–16.

Steinfels, P. (2003). *A people adrift: The crisis in the Roman Catholic Church in America.* New York, NY: Simon & Schuster.

Stone, J. (2003, Autumn). National convention features membership meeting for the first time. *Dignity USA Journal* [Newsletter], *(35)*4, 18.

Strout, V. (1998, Autumn). Where do we go from here: What *Ad Tuendam Fidem* means for progressive Catholics. *Conscience, 19*(4). Retrieved May 9, 2005, from http://www.cathollicsforchoice.org

Szaniszlo, M. (2005, September 29). Priest one of 20 critics of law. *Boston Herald,* p. 22.

Taylor, A.S. (2007, Spring). Largest World Day of Prayer for women's ordination ever. *New Women, New Church* [Newsletter], *30*(2),1, 8.

———. (n.d.) Frequently asked questions. In *Where the spirit moves us: Reflections for women considering ordination* [Brochure]. Boston, MA: National Catholic Ministerial Alliance.

Testimonials. (n.d.) Grace Church of Dover. Retrieved June 3, 2007, from http://www.gracechurchofdover/testimonials

Thompson, B. (Ed.). (2001, October). *Call to Action: 25 years of Spirituality and Justice, CTA Anniversary Edition* [Newsletter].

Time for a few creative decisions [Editorial]. (2005, January, 7). *National Catholic Reporter,* p. 2.

Tolfree, D. (2004, August 20). VOTF holds Mass in response to church closings. Retrieved November 30, 2004, from http://pilotcatholicnews.com/article2.asp?ID=1525.

Townsend, T. (2008, October, 11). Two more face excommunication at St. Stan's. *St. Louis Post Dispatch.* Retrieved September 2, 2008, from http://www.stltoday.com/news/stories.nsf/religion/story/09

Townsend, T. (2009, December 12). Bozek's authority: The Reformed Catholic Church dissolves. *St. Louis Post Dispatch*. Retrieved February 5, 2010, from www.stltoday.com/.../ article_25de3728-7a9b-5b40-a6ec-4e069de024d4.html.
Troeltsch, E. (1931). *The social teachings of Christian churches*. New York, NY: Macmillian.
Trounson, R. (2008, May 25). Parishes help pay sex abuse tab. *Los Angeles Times*. Retrieved June 11, 2008, from http://articles.latimes.com/2008/may/25/local/me-churches25? pg+3
Turner, V. (1969). *The ritual process: Structure and anti-structure*. New York, NY: Aldine De Gruyter.
Tussle at Brighton school [Editorial]. (2005, June 10). *The Boston Globe*, p. A18.
Van Biema, D. (2008, May 3). Is liberal Catholicism dead? *Time Online Edition*. Retrieved June 29, 2007, from http://www.nytimes.com/2007/06/24/us/24voice.html?_r+2&oref +slogin&oref+slogin
Vatican tribunal won't consider excommunication appeal. (2007, February 21). *Omaha World-Herald*. Retrieved June 16, 2008, from http://www.bishop-accountability.org/ news/2007/01/02/2997_02_21_OmahaWorldHerald
Veling, T. (1996). *Living in the margins: Intentional communities and the art of interpretation*. Eugene, OR: Wipf & Stock.
Vennochi, J. (2005, October 6). Reality sets in—Rome rules Boston. *The Boston Globe*, p. D11.
Viser, M. (2005b, October 3). More than 1,000 attend ex-pastor's farewell service. *The Boston Globe*, p. B1.
Voice of the Faithful. (2005, July). *The VOTF national working group presents: What do we do next? A project workbook* [Brochure]. Boston, MA: Author.
———. (2006a, March 16). *Voice of the Faithful calls for bishops to step down from U.S.S.C.B* [Press Release]. Retrieved July14, 2008, from http://www.voiceofthefaithful.org/Press/ pressrelease/031606.html
———. (2008, June 12). *Voice of the Faithful petitions pope to hold bishops accountable*. Retrieved May 24, 2009 from http://www.votf.org;pressrelease/press-release-for -immediate-release/17
———. (2007, June 16). *Voice of the Faithful calls for Vatican to review mandatory celibacy* [Press Release]. Retrieved June 16, 2007, from http://www.voiceofthefaithful.org/Press/ pressrelease/070207.html
———. (2008a). *Voice of the Faithful accountability NOW campaign summary report, convocation implementation team* (CIT) 2005–2008. Retrieved May 31, 2008, from http://www .votf.org/Focus/020708.html
———. (2008c, August 19). *Unfit to lead: Deposition provides concrete evidence, VOTF to Cardinal: "Step down"* [Press Release]. (2008, August 19). Retrieved November 22, 2008, from http://www.votf.org/press-release-for-immediate-release/760
———. (2009a). *Voice of the Faithful strategic plan 2009–2011* [Brochure]. Retrieved June 15, 2009, from http://votf.org
———. (2009b, July 21). *VOTF gratified by generous response of donors* [Press Release]. Retrieved December 18, 2010, from http://www.votf.org/pressrelease/press-release -for-immediate-release/7492
———. (2009c, January 7). *Voice of the Faithful names bishops who should resign* [Press Release]. Retrieved July 6, 2009, from http://www.votf.org/Press/pressrelease/01709 .html
———. (2010). *Ten steps toward reforming the Catholic Church*. Retrieved August 18, 2010, from http://www.votf.org/featured/tensteps
Voice of the Faithful mission statement. (n.d.). Retrieved May 14, 2004, from http://www .votf.org/who-we-are/100
Voice of the Faithful project workbook. (n.d.). Retrieved June 23, 2004, from http://www.votf .org
Von Lehmen, J. D. (1996, September). Real presence in the Eucharist. *American Catholic*. Retrieved December 3, 2010, from http://www.americancatholic.org

Von Stamwitz, G. (2008, December). Update on ECC relationships with other jurisdictions. *ECC News* [Newsletter], *3*(3), 3.
Wangsness, L. (2011, January 6). Ex-parishioners still hope to reverse parish closings. *The Boston Globe,* p. B3.
Washburn, L. (1986, March 11). Diverse congregations share a communion of faith. *The Record,* C-5.
Watanabe, T. (2002, October, 21). Young priests hold old values: Their views are often at odds with liberal reform of Vatican II in 1960s. *Los Angeles Times,* A1.
Welch, B. (2007). Celebrating Relationships. *Quarterly Voice of DignityUSA* [Newsletter], *6*(1), 1–7.
Who we are, Grace Church of Dover. (n.d.) Retrieved June 3, 2007, from http://www.gracechurchofdover/whoweare
Why we wear the rainbow sash. (n.d.). Retrieved June 11, 2009, from http://rainbowsashmovement.com/Articles/Why_Wear_The_Rainbow>Sash.html
Wilkes, P. (2001). *Excellent Catholic parishes: The guide to best places and practices.* Mahwah, NJ: Paulist Press.
Wink, W. (1998). *The third way: Reclaiming Jesus' nonviolent alternative.* Alkmaar, The Netherlands: International Fellowship of Reconciliation.
Winter, M. T. (2005). *Eucharist with a small "e."* New York, NY: Orbis Books.
Winter, M. T., Lummis, A., & Stokes, A. (Eds.). (1995). *Defecting in place: Women claiming responsibility for their own spiritual lives.* New York, NY: Crossroads.
Wittenauer, Cheryl. (2008, June 28). First American named to head Vatican high court. Wtopnews.com.RetrievedJuly4,2006,http://www.wtopnews.com/?nid=104&sid=1430498
Women-Church Convergence. (n.d.) *Women-Church Convergence: Common commitments.* Retrieved April 16, 2008, from http://www.women-churchconvergence.org
———. (n.d.) *Women-Church Convergence: Working for recognition and empowerment of women in church and society* [Brochure]. Chicago, IL: Author.
Women's Ordination Conference. (n.d.) *About us.* Retrieved May 23, 2009. from http://www.womensordination.org.content/view/655
———. (n.d.) *History, the WOC story.* Retrieved July 7, 2005, from http://womensordination.org/content/view/8/59/
———. (2008, October 15). *Vatican police stop and apprehend passports of Catholic representatives delivering petition* [Press Release]. Retrieved November 12, 2008, from http://www.womensordination.org/content/view/282/42/
Women's Ordination Conference Budget Report. (2005, Spring). *New Women, New Church* [Newsletter], *28*(1), 2.
Wooden, C. (2009, June 2). Congregations can more easily laicize priests. *National Catholic Reporter.* Retrieved July 9, 2009, from http://ncronline.org/news/vatican/congregation-can-more-easily-laicize-priests
WOW Speaker's calls for the rejection of Papacy of Benedict XVI [Press Release]. (2005, July 8). Retrieved July 8, 2006, from http://www.womensordination.org
Wuthnow, R. (1988). *The restructuring of American religion.* Princeton, NJ: Princeton University Press.
Young, J. (2006, January 27). 'Celibate gay priest' resigns as university chaplain. *National Catholic Reporter,* p. 6.
Zagano, P. (2006, May). Pope could show charity to women. *The American Catholic,* p. 6.
———. (2007, May). Ordaining women as deacons in the Catholic Church. *The American Catholic,* p. 3.
———. (2010, December 24). Rome's checkbook strategy on women religious. *National Catholic Reporter,* p. 24.
Zaiger, A. S. (2005, January 10). Mo. parish rejects church takeover. *Boston Globe,* p. A3.

INDEX

Accountability Now Campaign (VOTF) 78–79
abortion 50, 163, 166
A Critical Mass, Women Celebrating Eucharist 122
advocacy groups 29, 291
African American Catholic Congregation 51, 227
alb (liturgical garment) 238, 246
Alinsky, Saul 162
Allen, E. 158
Allen Jr., John 53, 68, 79, 93, 128, 133, 139, 151, 182
alternative worship communities 4, 6, 9, 36, 167, 170, 211
America (magazine) 119
American bishops 49, 74, 81, 88, 93, 106, 125, 151
American Catholic Church 69, 144, 186, 197
American Catholic Church Diocese of California 285
American Catholic Council 83, 144, 301, 302
American Catholic laity xv, 50, 51, 275
American Civil Rights Movement 23
American contributions to the Vatican 197
Anson, Peter F. 14
Anthony, Susan B. 249
anticlosure movement 79, 184–196
anti-Semitism 28
Apostles' Creed 202
Apostolic Catholic Church 285
Apostolic Signatura 47, 166, 194
apostolic succession 203–207
Appleby, Monica 220
Appleby, R. Scott 71
Arbuckle, Gerald A. 27–28
ARCC Proposed Constitution of the Catholic Church 256, 258
Archdiocese of Boston 214, 262, 275
Archdiocese of Indianapolis 229
Archdiocese of Los Angeles 178
Arinze, Francis (Cardinal) 89
Arlington Street Church (Unitarian) 215
Ashe, Arthur 63
Association for the Rights of Catholics in the Church xvii, 130, 256

Baier, Paul 60
Baiocchi, Francis (Father) 241–243
Balasuriya, Tissa (Father) 51, 276
Bannan, Regina 132
Baptist minister 254
Barnes, Joy 120, 136
Barr, Walter (Father) 100
Bartley, Dan 75
base ecclesiastical communities 172
Basile Ryan (consultants) 95
Bathersby, John (Archbishop) 157
Baute, Pascal 108, 288
Belleville diocese 164–165
Belluck, P. 71, 74, 189
Benedict XVI (Pope) ix, 2, 10–11, 30, 68, 69, 72, 81, 129, 132–133, 137–139, 152, 166, 194, 197, 241, 252, 264, 270–271, 274, 295–296
Berger, Peter xii
Berggen, K. 156
Bernardin, Joseph (Cardinal) 50, 271, 298
Berrigan, Daniel 49
Berry, Jason 189
Betrayal, the Crisis in the Catholic Church (*Globe* staff) 80
bill of rights for lay Catholics 6
Bingo Report (The) (Haggett) 169
Binkowski, Peter 41
Bishops' Committee on Women in the Church 117
black Catholics 228
Black, D.E. 149, 158
black Madonna 228
Blaine, Barbara 63
blessing of same-sex unions 94
blue states 9
Bole, W. 66
Bonavoglia, Angela 12, 62, 114, 127, 128, 130, 246, 254
Bonnike, Frank 100
Bono, A. 72
Boorstein, M. 182
Borre, Peter 187
Boston Archdiocese 5, 81, 193, 274
Boston College 35, 82, 186
Boston College Church in the 21st Century 66, 123, 131, 219
Boston Dignity Chapter 212–216
Boston Globe 62, 81, 226, 235

Boston, Massachusetts 35
Bouclin, Marie (RCWP) 157
Boulding, Elise 31
Bourgeois, Ray 264
Boyd, Malcolm 31
Bozek, Marek (Father) 162
Brandeis University 149
Braschi, Romulo (Bishop) 261
Braxton, Edward K. (Bishop) 164–166
Breslin, Jimmy 103
Briggs, Kenneth A. 153, 181–182
Bodgraven, B.R. 131
Brom, Robert H. (Bishop) 90, 91
Bruce, Tricia Colleen 12
Brueggemann, Walter 303–304
Bruskewitz, Fabian (Bishop) 47, 81, 163
Burch, James H. (Bishop) 105, 259–261, 290
Burke, D. 74
Burke, Raymond L. (Archbishop) 161–163, 166, 175
Burns, G. 117
Bush, George W. (President) 16

Cachia, Edward (Father) 147
Caesar 170
cafeteria Catholics 269
Callahan, Patrick 115, 117
Callan, James (Father) 158, 159, 244
Call to Action (CTA) xvii, 6, 41–54, 64, 83, 91, 99, 101, 106, 130, 135, 163, 175, 249, 255, 278–279, 293
   achievements 48–52
   comparison to VOTF 81–82
   conferences 25, 44, 48–49, 141, 182, 209
   criticisms 52–53
   local chapters 52
   membership 7–10, 25, 44,
   website 34
Call to Action communities 171, 173, 264
Call to Action: Liberty and Justice for All (USCCB Conference) 42–43
compassion fatigue 71
canonically active priests 93
canon law 91, 117
   Code of Canon Law (1983 revision) 77
   Canon Law # 27 169
   Canon Law# 290 43, 89
   Canon Law #1024 262
capital punishment 271
Carlson, Robert J. (Archbishop) 162
Carr, Dee 253
Carroll, J.L. 271
Casey, Bill 75
Caspary, A.M 221

Catacombs 201
Catherine of Sienna 137
Catholic and Feminist (Henold) 12
Catholic Apostolic Charismatic Church of Christ the King 297
Catholic bishops 43, 59, 67, 69, 75, 78, 102, 104, 194, 195
Catholic Charities (Boston) 60
Catholic colleges 21, 24,
Catholic dioceses 2
Catholic feminist movement 111–134, 183, 201
Catholic feminists 86, 111–146, 132, 137, 223
Catholic feminist theologians 112
Catholic Identity (Dillon) 13
Catholic League for Religious and Civil Rights 127
Catholic Organizations for Renewal xvii, 42, 51, 86, 89, 91, 100, 105–107, 125, 278–279
Catholic sisters 178–181, 249
Catholic social teachings 149
Catholic tradition 2
Catholic University 234
Catholic Worker Movement 6, 217
Catholics for Choice (CFC) 47, 112, 124–128, 133, 136, 139, 144, 275
Caufield, John (Reverend) 233
Celibacy Is the Issue (CITI) 150, 169, 178–179, 178–180, 187–189, 242, 265–266, 286
Center for Applied Research on the Apostolate 73–74, 133
Center for Critical Research on Religion ix
Chardin, Teilhard de 293
Charter for the Protection of Children and Young People (USCCB)
Children's Garden (A)
Chittister, Joan 16, 28, 49, 118–119, 131, 141, 276–267
Christian Formation Center 208
Christian socialism 6
Christ the King Eucharistic community 157
church (definition) 14, 202
church-sect typology 17
Church Women Want Conference series (The) 131
CITI xvii
CITI communities 178–180, 242
CITI priests 178–180, 187, 242
Clark, Matthew (Bishop) 160, 251
Cleary, William 54, 103, 233
Clements, George 26, 145

INDEX

clergy abuse crisis 1, 2, 17, 79, 248, 273, 274
clergy abuse litigation 1, 69, 72
clericalism 68, 139
Clinton, Bill (President) 95
Clohessy, David 63
Coalition of American Nuns 106
Coalition of Concerned Catholics 83
Coday, D. 164
Colbert, C 74, 149, 193
Coleman, John A 17, 18
Coleman, N. 157
College of Cardinals 265
College of St. Rose 135
Collins, Paul 10
Common Ground Initiative 271
Communion 88, 152, 177, 246, 248
communitas (term) 19, 130, 281–282, 288, 290
Community of God's Love 207–211, 282, 285, 288
Community of John XXIII 102, 222, 254
Community of the Crucified One 237
Community of the Risen Christ 246
Companions in Hope 83
Condoms4Life Campaign 129
Conference for Catholic Lesbians 113
Congregationalists 115, 226
Congregation for Catholic Education 159
Congregation for the Clergy 194
Congregation for the Doctrine of the Faith 69, 92, 119, 161, 213
Conscience (magazine) 145
conservative bishops 8, 10, 17, 53, 62, 78, 87, 151–152, 166, 188, 196, 274
conservative Catholic groups 30, 86
conservative Catholics 8–9, 56, 61, 64, 83, 86, 87, 191, 271, 282
conservative pastors 87
Constitution of the Ecumenical Catholic Communion 255–246
contraception 1, 6, 9, 15, 204, 255, 271
Cooke, Bernard 45
Cooperman, J. 161, 263
Corps of Reserve Priests United for Service (CORPUS) 2, 7, 26, 34, 42, 86, 87, 89, 98–105, 106, 114, 115, 126, 136, 140, 142, 145, 169, 222, 232–233, 235, 254–257, 260, 264, 286–288, 293
Corpus Christi Parish (Freemont) 158
Corpus Christi Parish (Rochester) 159–160, 196, 244–246, 251, 253, 265, 291
CORPUS Reports (magazine) 99, 101, 260
Council of Vigiling Parishes 35, 79, 154, 186–195, 229

countermovement 16–17
Coyne, Ron (Father) 185
creation spirituality communities 208
Crisis Magazine 72
Critical Mass: Women Celebrating Eucharist (A) 122
Crosby, Michael H. 88
Crusades 28
CTA Nebraska Chapter 47, 163
CTA Oregon Chapter 163
CTA NextGeneration program 44, 45
Cuenin, Walter (Father) 149, 153–154, 158, 167
cult 16, 20, 141
Culture of Conversation Project 50
culture wars 271
culture wars within Catholicism 8–10, 152, 167, 298
culture wars within religious denominations 22
Cuneo, Michael W. 30
Curran, Daniel (Father) 228, 276
Cycle C lectionary readings (Priests for Equality) 210

Daley, Dan 41, 44, 50
Daley, Sheila 41, 50
Dallas Charter for the Protection of Children 94
Dallas Morning News 69
D'Antonio, William 12, 32, 66, 172
David and Goliath (myth) 113–114
David, Jim 225
David, Marie 225
deacons 138
DeAngelis, Nicola (Bishop) 157
Dear, John (Father) 45
Deardon, John (Cardinal) 100
Declaration of the American Catholic Council 144, 300–301
defecting in place (term) 113, 116, 277
Degollado, Marcial Maciel (Father) 137
Delacerate, Frank 61
Demerath III, N.J. 17
denial of sacraments 16
Devine, M. 137
DeWayne, Frank (Bishop) 166
Deysher, Cynthia 187
dialectical of religious conflict 16
dialectical tension between structure and anti-structure (Turner) 19, 288–289
dialogue-homily 174
Diaspora of Resigned Sisters and Priests 220

Dierks, Sheila Durkin 94, 115, 201, 216–219, 223
Dignity/Boston 212–214
DignityUSA xvii, 7–10, 30, 42, 85, 88, 89, 90–98, 106, 107, 113, 122, 126, 130, 136, 139, 152, 207, 264, 266, 293, 296, 299
DignityUSA communities 211–216
Dillon, Michelle 13, 67, 92, 119, 126, 212
Diocese of Indianapolis 228
Diocese of One Spirit 226, 259–261, 272, 290
Diocese of Rochester 247
Diocese of San Bernardino 255
Diocese of San Diego 90
DiSanato, Amy (Reverend) 235, 272
DiSanto, Peter (Reverend) 235, 272, 285
Ditzel, Russ 102, 136, 293–294
divorced Catholics 15, 152, 248, 255
Dolbee, S. 263
Donato, Denise (Reverend) 120
Donilon, Terrence C 194
Doucette, Donna 82
Dowling, Kevin (Bishop) 129
Downtown Presbyterian Church (Rochester) 249
Doyle, Anne Barrett 75
Doyle, Sipe & Wall 69, 78
Doyle, Tom (Father) 59, 67
Dujardin, R.C. 74
Durkin, Pat (Father) 231
Dutch Dominicans 31
Dwenger, Adolph 230

early Christian communities 13, 15, 207, 243
Eastern Rite Catholic Community 191
ECC Community of the Risen Christ 255
ECC communities 195, 223
ecclesiology from below 82
Eckstrom, Kevin 182
Ecumenical Anglican Community 285
Ecumenical Catholic Communion (ECC) xvii, 102, 106, 141, 201, 226, 246, 249, 254–259, 272, 278, 285–286, 289
Edman, P 158
egalitarianism 290–291
English, B. 185
environmentalist theology 20, 287
Episcopal Church 96, 115
Episcopal Council (ECC) 256
Erie Benedictine Community 118
Estes, Clarissa Pinkola 49
Eucharist xi, 48, 137, 175, 176, 179, 187, 203–207, 226, 232, 247, 271, 280

Eucharistic Centered Community (ECC) 170–178
Eucharistic community 6, 34, 155, 242, 285
Eucharistic ministers 88, 177, 213
Eucharist Prayers (Dierks) 202
Eucharist with a small "e" (Winter) 204–206, 219
Evensong by the Sea Retreat and Spirituality Center 225
Excellent Catholic Parishes (Wilkes) 78
excommunication 16, 27, 31, 46, 47, 48, 87, 145, 152, 161, 163,196, 265, 270

factionalism 21
Faithful Dissidents (McClory) 163
Faithful Revolution (Bruce) 12
Faithful Voice 61
Farrell, Susan 127
Farris, Jim (Reverend) 258
Federation of Christian Ministries (FCM) 101, 230, 232, 287
Federation of Communities in Service (FOCIS) 207, 221–222
Feeney, M. 80
Fellowship of Reconciliation (FOR) 45
Fellowship of Southern Illinois Laity (FOSIL) 34
feminists 4, 7, 87, 277
feminist reform groups 9
feminist spirituality groups 289
feminist theology 6, 20, 117, 183, 287, 288
Ferraro, Geraldine 127
Feuerherd, J. 130
Feuerherd, P. 2, 65–66, 69
Fiedler, Maureen (Sister) 137
Fields, R. 263
Filteau, J. 194
financial accountability 1, 2, 43, 65
Finn, Gerry 112
Finn, Robert (Bishop) 164
Fiorenza, Elisabeth Schüssler 93, 114, 119–120, 222, 276, 288
Fischer, Mark 77
Fisher, & Leen 104
Fitzgerald, Jim 54
Fitzpatrick, Jim & Mary 167
Flynn, Harry (Archbishop) 156, 213
Fowler, James 108
Fox, Matthew 28, 45, 47, 119, 208, 264, 276
Fox, Thomas 26, 48, 182
France, David 80
Fraser, Scott 10
Freeman, Jo 18, 24, 290
Freie Gemeinde sect 17

INDEX

Fresen, Patricia (RCWP Bishop) 261–265, 289
Fujimori, S. 104
FutureChurch xvii, 7–8, 12, 42, 101, 106, 142–144, 184–187, 193–194, 278

Gallup poll (1992) 51
Gateley, Edwina 176
Gautier, M.L 116
Gay and Lesbian Alliance 95
gay liberation movement 7, 90
gays and lesbians 4, 9, 30, 90, 92
George, Francis (Cardinal) 68, 71, 83
Georgetown University's Woodstock Theological Center 73
Geranios, N 72
Gibson, David 6, 11, 61, 77, 132, 227, 274
Gibson, Mary Catherine 231
Gil Foundation 96
Gilligan, Carol 218
GLBT Catholics 91, 92, 93, 95, 96, 97, 107, 113, 142, 211, 212, 223
GLBT persons 9, 14, 88, 95, 97, 98, 138, 142, 152, 248
GLBT rights 256, 271
Glenmary Sisters 208, 220–222
Glennon, Sean Patrick 188
Global Ministries 287
Glock and Stark 15
Gnostics 206
Goedert, Raymond (Bishop) 83
Gold Star Families for Peace 45
Goldstein, Warren ix, xvi, 16, 281, 302–303
Good Catholic Girls (Bonavoglia) 12, 130
Goodstein, Laurie 159, 264
Gore, Al (Vice-President) 95
Grace Church of Dover 226, 235–240, 272, 296, 300
Gramick, Jeannine (Sister) 213
Gray & Perl 73
Greeley, Father Andrew 49
Gregory, Wilton (Bishop) 102, 164
Groome, Thomas 186, 190
Grosswirth, Ray 104, 105, 107
group think (term) 277
Guntzel, J.S. 184, 186, 190

Haffner, Debra 62
Haggett, Louise 169, 188
Haight, Roger (Father) 102
Harrington, Sharon 193
Harris, Kim and Reggi 49
Hart, Joseph (Father) 247
Haugen, Marty 210

Hehir, Bryan (Father) 192
Hemmer, Carl 101
Henold, Mary 12, 127, 277, 287
heresy 255
Herr, Mary 221
Hess, Anne 233–234
Hickman, Peter (Bishop) 104, 201, 246, 254–257, 286
Hildegard of Bingen 137
Hindelang, Ron (Reverend) 225
Hines, Mary 67, 82
Hirschman, Albert 25
Hitchcock, H.H. 174
Hoge, D.R. & Wenger, J.E 150–151
Holocaust, 270
Holy Family Parish (New Mexico) 257
Holy See 128
Holy Spirit Catholic Community (Boston) 167, 195, 257
Holy Trinity Church 41
Homan, M. 61
homophobic 92
homosexuality 90, 97, 106, 163, 213, 274
homosexuals 6, 15, 90, 92, 96, 161
homosexual unions 87, 94
Hoosier, Brenda 231–231
Hoosier, Chip 231
house churches 171
House of Laity (ECC) 256
House of Pastors (ECC) 256
Howard, C. 258
Howarth, R. 262
Hudson, Deal W. 62
Hughes, Alfred (Archbishop) 189
Humanae Vitae 21
Humphreys, L. 90
Hunt, Mary 5, 112, 113, 114, 123, 127, 276
Hunter, James Davison 8, 22, 207, 269
Hunthausen, Raymond (Archbishop) 152–153, 247–248
Hurley, Susan 189
Hussein, Saddam 187

Iliff School of Theology 202
Imani Temple 227
Imbelli, Robert P. 66
Immaculate Conception Parish (Springfield) 194
Immaculate Heart Sisters 221
Inclusive Community-UCC (The) 226, 232–235, 237, 285
independent dioceses 14
independent ordinations 9, 239

independent priests and bishops 180–181, 239, 256–266
independent sacramental movement 13
independent seminaries 226
independent worship communities ix, 3, 5, 13–15, 34, 98, 138–139, 166, 188, 272, 279, 286, 292 (*also see underground communities*)
Inquisition 10
insider strategies 4, 35, 42, 51, 55, 71, 76–78, 83, 98, 101, 131, 139, 142, 179, 197
Interfaith Voices radio show 37
integralist philosophy 294
International Physicians for the Prevention of Nuclear War 55
International Synod of the Word 142
Iron Curtain in Eastern Europe 31
Isasi-Diaz, Ada Maria 131

Jesuit Urban Center (Boston) 173
Jesus 14, 27, 53–54, 91, 105, 107, 111, 170, 175, 203–206, 219, 241, 244, 294, 300
Jesus Our Shepherd Community 178, 240–244, 286, 291
Joan of Arc 261
John XXIII (Pope) 132
John Paul II (Pope) ix, 10–11, 16, 55, 67, 104, 113, 132, 136, 137, 152, 172, 181, 265, 269–271, 301
Johnson, A. 262
Johnson, Elizabeth (Sister) 131
Johnson, Steve 197
Jones, J. 158
Jubilee! Community (North Carolina) 209

Kaintz, B. 161
Kaiser, R.B. 180, 301
Kane, Theresa (Sister) 26, 298–299
Kansas City-St. Joseph diocese 164, 201
Kautzer, Kathleen ix, xi, xiii
Keep the Faith, Change the Church, (Muller & Kenney) 55, 64
Kelley, Kathy 45
Kennedy, Eugene Cullen 145, 166
Kennedy, Joe 135
Kennedy, Peter (Father) 157–158
Kennedy, Sheila Rauch 135
Kenney, Charles 10, 12
Kenny, Jim & Mary 228–232
Kenny, Joseph 162–163
Kerry, John (Senator) 166
King, Martin Luther (Reverend) 187
Kissling, Fran 114, 125–129
Knowles, Alice 107

Kodak 253
Krueger, Steve 60
Kuenstler, Kate (Sister) 120
Küng, Hans 28, 48, 132, 137, 254, 276, 302

Ladner, Frank S. 165
Landau, S. 265
Lange, George (Father) 156
laicization 99
Lankenau, Alfred (Bishop) 231
Larkin, Bill (Father) 173
Last Supper 206
Latin Mass 10, 164, 270, 295
Lavoie, D. & Lindsay, J. 194
Law, Bernard (Cardinal) 55, 60, 81, 149, 151–154, 165, 173, 193
Law resignation petition 149–154, 185
Lawson, James 49
lawsuits by abuse victims 1, 4
lay Catholics 56, 72
lay ecclesial ministers 133
lay synods 51
Leadership Conference of Women Religious 181–183
Lears, Louise (Sister) 166, 264
Leary, Jan 135, 293
Lee, Bernard (Father) 171–173
Lee & Cowan 171
Legionnaires of Christ 137
Lehman, James (Reverend) 257
Leibig, Anne 221
Lennon, Richard (Bishop) 89, 195
Levada, William Joseph (Cardinal) 182
Levenson, M. 156
Lewis, Helen M. 220
liberal Catholics 3, 6, 8–10, 56, 61, 64, 72, 83, 167, 196–197, 204, 206, 257, 269, 271, 273, 294–295
liberal Catholic reform groups 9, 25, 223, 231, 274, 282, 283
liberal theologians 10, 24, 27, 276
liberation theology 6, 20, 287
Light of Christ community 201, 223
Little Angels Preschool 239
liturgies 48, 173, 231, 238, 156, 295–296
Long Island Voice of the Ordained 70
Lorde, Audre 266
Lord's Prayer 231
Los Angeles Archdiocese 178
Los Angeles Times poll 151
Loverde, Paul (Bishop) 51
Luckmann, Thomas xii
Luther, Martin 187
Lytton, T. 78

Macisse, Camilo 26–29
Magisterium 7–8, 61
Maguire, Daniel C. 114
Mahoney, Robert (Cardinal) 68, 74, 154
Mahoney, Tom (Father) 154
Malia, Charles 74
Mananzan, Mary John (Sister) 180
mandatory celibacy 9, 98, 169, 271
Manseau, Bill (Reverend) 85, 89, 101, 104
Manseau, Mary 85
Manseau, Peter 85, 89
Marchant, Jean Marie 225, 263
marginal communities 25, 34, 159, 170–197, 272, 279, 260, 291
Markey, Eileen 139
Marlier, Thomas (Reverend) 242
Mananzan, Mary John (Sister) 180
married priests 4, 15, 60, 87, 187, 204
Married Priests NOW! 104, 105, 162, 260
Marrone, Bob (Father) 195
Mary and Human Liberation (Stanton) 51
Mary Magdalene Apostle Community (San Diego) 263
Mary Magdalene Church (Rochester) 247
Mary of Magdala community (Harwichport) 178, 225, 296
Mashburn, Linda 222
Mass 45, 94, 188, 214, 218, 230, 238, 245, 295, 298
Massachusetts Council of Churches and Temples 79
Massachusetts Supreme Court ruling on same-sex marriage 94, 214
Massachusetts Women-Church 61, 69, 111
mass attendance 37
McArron, P. 91, 94, 216
McBrien, Richard (Father) 74, 126, 137, 151, 164, 293, 270–271, 276
McCabe, K. 186
McCarthy, J.D. 23, 67
McCarthy, John (Bishop) 95
McCarthy & Zald 276
McClory, Robert 31, 41, 53–54, 69, 163–164, 278
McCloskey, John, (Reverend) 62
McCool, Joe (Reverend) 108
McCormack, John B. (Bishop) 68
McCusker 90
McDermott, Alice 113
McGrath, Elsie Hainz (RCWP) 263
McGrory, Brian 153
McIntyre, James Francis (Cardinal) 221
McMahon, Pat 125
McManus, Robert J. (Bishop) 156

McNamara, Eileen 235–237
McNeill, John (Father) 95, 213
McNulty, Frank (Father) 100
McQuillan, Patricia 126
McSorley, Patrick 215
media attention 1, 4, 69, 80
Medical Mission Sisters 217
Meehan, B.M. (RCWP) 267
Mehren, E. 174
Mendez, Dom Luis Castillo (Patriarch) 104
Menino, Tom (Mayor) 192
methodology of study 34–35
Midwest 303
Miles, John & Carol 41
Milingo, Emmanuel (Archbishop) 104
Milwaukee Archdiocese
moderate Catholics 56, 191
Montalvo, Gabriel (Monsignor) 164
Moon, Sun Myung (Reverend) 104, 162
Moore, Allen 34
Morales-Perez, Francisco A. (Deacon) 257
Morris, Aldon 23
Morwood, Michael (Reverend) 293
Most, W. G 7, 61
Mother Mary Catherine 220
Mother Teresa of Calcutta 128, 137
Mountain Sisters (Lewis & Appleby) 220–222
Moynihan, John 52, 75
Mullarney, Lenore (Sister) 220
Muller, James 10, 12, 55, 58, 59
Muller & Kenney 55, 60–65, 68, 76, 81
Murphy, Thomas J. (Bishop) 153
Murphy, William F (Bishop) 69, 71, 112

National Catholic Ministerial Alliance 101, 104, 142, 254, 287
National Catholic Reporter 42, 48, 68, 88, 116, 130, 139, 164–165, 192, 264
National Coalition of American Nuns 122
National Coming Out Day 95
National Leadership Roundtable on Church Management 79
National Review Board (NSCCB) 78
Network of Intentional Eucharistic Communities 170
Neu, Diann L. 121, 123
Newman, John Henry (Cardinal) 12
New Testament values 234
New Ways Ministry 213
New York Dignity chapter 91
New York Times 159
New York Times ad ('90) 43
New York Times ad ('08) 68

342   INDEX

New York Times ad (1984) 126
New York Times (article on VOTF) 74
Niebuhr, Helmut Richard 15, 17, 283
Nienstedt, John (Archbishop) 157
Nobel Peace Prize (Muller) 55
noncooperation 36, 170
nonviolent theory 37
Normandin, Jeannette (Sister) 173
North American Alliance for a Renewed Catholic Priesthood 104
Northeast 65, 303
Nugent, Roger (Father) 213
nun (definition of term) 182

Obama, Barak (President) 182
Oblates of Mary Immaculate of the Eastern Province 228
O'Brien, J. 125, 128, 129
O'Brien, Stu 100
O'Brien, Tom 193
O'Connor, John (Cardinal) 127
O'Dea, Thomas 14, 202
Old Catholic bishops 254
Old Catholic Church 203, 254, 263, 298
Old Catholic priest 254
Old Testament prophets 114
Oleck, J. 262
Olmstead, Thomas (Bishop) 166
O'Malley, M 162, 195, 249
O'Malley, Sean (Cardinal) 26, 79, 81, 89, 131, 184–191, 277
O'Murchu, Diarmuid xv–xvi, 222, 293
Opus Dei 164
Ordinatio Sacerdotalis 113
O'Reilly, Thomas P. (Attorney General) 69
Original Blessing (Fox) 45
Ortelli, W. 235
Orthodox-Catholic Church of America 231
Orthodox schism 227
Our Lady Help of Christians (Newton) 149, 167
Our Lady of Presentation School (Brighton) 192–193
outsider strategies 4, 35, 51, 78–81, 83, 98, 120, 122, 142, 196

Padovano, Anthony (Pastor) 2, 11–12, 16, 99, 107, 109, 128, 137, 140–141, 146, 277, 293, 297, 302
Pagels, Elaine 206
Paprika, Thomas (Bishop) 166
parallel organizations 29, 36, 227
parish finance councils (PFC) 156
Parish of St. Peter and Paul 240

parish pastoral councils (PPC) 64, 76, 166, 230
Parks, Rosa 260
Passover celebration 205
Pathfinder Community of the Risen Christ 255
Patterson, M. 160, 247, 252
Paulist Center (Boston) 173
Paulson, Michael 79, 82, 89, 149, 151, 154, 188, 189–192, 226
Pax Christi 6, 164
Pax Christi Community 76
Pension Advocacy Campaign 83
Pentecost Sunday 95
Perl, P.M. 73
Pew Forum poll (2008) 82
Philadelphia archdiocese 81
Physicians for the Prevention of Nuclear War 55
Pierce, Charles 62
Pierson, Robert (Father) 159
Pilarczyk, Daniel (Archbishop) 68
Pilgrim People (The) 167
Pinto, Linda 101–102
Plummer, John P. 13–14, 227, 287
Podles, Leon J. 69, 78
Pogorelc, Anthony 12, 32, 66
Polish National Catholic Church 227
Post, James E. 55, 59, 61, 63, 65, 67, 79, 153, 273
postmodern theory 292
Power, Tom, (Pastor) Massachusetts 55
Powers, Tom (Father) Minnesota 78, 284
Powers, W.F. 114, 115, 117
Presentation School (Brighton) 192
Pre-Vatican II Church 10, 107, 145, 269, 271
Pre-Vatican II theology 15
Price, D. 107
priestless liturgies 180–181, 280
Priests for Equality 210
primacy of individual conscience 108, 271
prior conversion experience 14–15, 202
Procter-Smith, Marjorie 289
progressive, Catholics 45, 46, 170, 227, 259, 274, 301
prophetic 130, 252, 304
Proposed Constitution of the Catholic Church (ARCC) 256
protest and persuasion 35
Protestant communities 229, 249, 263
Protestant denominations 213
Protestantism 222, 232, 237
Protestant Reformation 227, 234
Protestant service of the Word 233

INDEX 343

Provost, James (Reverend) 234
Pulitizer Prize (Globe coverage) 80
Pullella, P. 132
Putnam, R. 287
Putnam & Campbell 116

Quixote Center 210

Rainbow Sash Movement 95
Ramerman, Jim 246
Ramerman, Mary 244, 286
Raming, Ida (RCWP Bishop) 262
Rather J. 70
Ratzinger, Joseph (Cardinal) 92, 119, 132, 137, 160, 172, 248
Rausch, John 221
real presence of Jesus in the Eucharist 203–207
recovering Catholic (term) 277
red states 9
Reese, Thomas (Father) 73, 119
Reeves, B. 47, 163
Reformed Catholic Church 162
Reform Movement ix, xi, xiii, 3, 14, 31, 52, 85, 88, 91, 98, 107, 135, 138–139, 142, 145, 145, 161, 186, 197, 202–204, 235, 241, 243, 253, 258, 265, 269–270, 272–273, 302–304
  achievements 1, 9–10, 274
  criticisms 2, 130, 259, 301
  demographics 7, 15, 23, 25, 32
  first wave 7
  future of 2, 3
  history 6–8, 15
  influence of Vatican II 2
  invisible nature of xiii, 31
  precariousness 4, 87
  religious movement 22–23
  revivalist movement 20–21
  sect-like characteristics 5, 15, 17
  theology 22
  second wave 7, 17, 273
  view of science 20–21
reformist movement 6
Regensburg University 270
regional synods 52
Regis College xi, 35
Reidy, Ned (Reverend) 206, 255
Religious Coalition for Reproductive Choice 125
religious movement 42, 276
Renahan, Susan 58
Rent-A-Priest website 155
reproductive rights 43, 124–129, 133
resigned nuns and sisters 7, 220

resigned priests, (*See also married priests*) 7, 36, 94, 100, 152, 213, 220, 266
resistance communities 171
resource mobilization theory 23, 276
revivalist movement 20, 42, 87
revolutionary movement 5, 20
Rigali, Justin (Archbishop) 161
Roberts, Keith A. 16, 141
Roberts, Tom 41–42, 50, 143, 166–167, 172, 275
Robinson, Gene, (Bishop) 96
Roe vs. Wade Supreme Court decision 126
Rogers, Jon 194
Roman Catholic Church 5, 87, 97, 98, 106, 108, 207, 226–227
  as church par excellence 16
  declining membership in U.S. 4, 37
  financial accountability 1–2, 76
Roman Catholic Church doctrine 203, 226
Roman Catholic Church hierarchs 2, 3, 4, 21, 30, 55, 59, 85, 88, 89, 92, 141, 206, 269, 275
Roman Catholic laity 2, 75
Roman Catholic parishes 34, 87, 207, 211, 252
Roman Catholics priests 249, 272
Roman Catholic theology 127
Roman Catholic Womenpriests xi, xvii, 47, 103, 120, 141, 162, 166, 203, 225–226, 242, 249, 261–267, 272, 279, 286, 289, 291–292
Roman Curia 26
Roman Empire 31
Roman Rota 135
Roos, Richard (Reverend) 230
Rosenblatt, S. 255
Rue, Victoria (RCWP) 291
Ruether, Rosemary Radford 88, 117, 119, 122, 131, 139, 216, 276

Sacred Heart Cathedral (Rochester) 160
Sacred Heart Parish (Natick) 192
Sacrilege (Podles) 78
San Martin de Porres Mission (Dayton) 194
Save Our Church Committee 229
Save Our Parish Community Project 185
Save Our Sacrament (SOS) 34
Scaine, Richard 222
Scanlon, Mary 68
Scanlon, Thomas (Father) 228
Schaeffer, P. 262–263
Scharf, Robert (Reverend) 233
Schenk, Christine (Sister) 12, 143

344   INDEX

Schilling, T.P. 152
schism 15, 97, 162–163, 165, 183, 194–196, 227, 245, 255, 261, 267, 278–279
schismatic bishops 270
schismatic Catholics 5
schismatic communities 28
schismatic parishes 160–161, 167, 226–267
School of the Americas Watch 264
Schulte, Paul C. (Archbishop) 228
Second Coming 22
Second Vatican Council. (*See Vatican II*)
second wave of reform movement 7, 17
sect 4, 16–19, 202, 226, 270, 280–283
sect (definition) 14, 87, 202, 219, 223, 226, 278
sectarian parish 158
sectarianism 21, 269
sectarian organization 99, 102, 235
secularization 16, 21
See Change Campaign 128
sensus fidelium 92
Sharp, Gene 5, 24–26, 170, 183, 186, 301
Shea, Suzanne Strempek 295
Sheehan, Cindy 45
Sheehan, John 77
Sheehan, Marie 111
Sherman, Kathy 210
Shutte, Dan 210
Sinnett, Sam 85, 96
Sinsinawa Dominican Women's Network 122
Sipe, Richard 46
sister (definition of term) 182
Sisyphean struggle 273
sixties era 7, 45
Skylsad, William (Bishop) 72
small Christian communities 170–172
small "e" eucharist 204–207
social movement 22–23, 276
Society of Pius X 19, 282, 297
Solidarity Sunday 94
Solidarity Walk for victims 73
Sotelo, Nicole 44, 133
Spirit of Life Community 135, 226, 293
spiritual journey 32
spiritual suicide 145
spiritual violence 26
Spiritus Christi Parish 47, 106, 158, 160, 165, 244–253, 257, 272, 278–279, 286, 295, 296, 300
Spitz, J. 194
Spong, John Shelby (Bishop) 293
Spotlight Team of the *Boston Globe* 80
St. Albert the Great Parish (Weymouth) 185-6, 191
Stalling, George 227
Stanton, H. 51
St. Anselm's Parish (Sudbury) 189
Stark, Rodney ix, 15, 20, 285
Stark & Bainbridge 14, 20, 270, 283, 284
St. Augustine parishioners, (New Orleans) 51
St. Bernard Parish (Newton) 187
St. Bridget's Parish (Indianapolis) 195, 228–232, 239, 285
St. Catherine of Siena Parish (Charlestown) 187
Steinfels, Margaret O'Brien 21, 37, 269–271, 277, 298
Steinfels, Peter 151
stem cell research 9
Stevens, Ed xi–xiv
St. Frances X. Cabrini Parish (Scituate) 195
St. Francis of Assisi 234, 252
Stier, Tom (Reverend) 158
St. James the Great Parish (Wellesley) 189, 191
St. Jeremiah's Parish (Framingham) 191
St. John the Evangelist Episcopal Church (Boston) 212
St. John the Evangelist Parish (Wellesley) 56
St. John University (Collegeville) 159
St. Louis archdiocese 161
St. Luke's Parish (Westborough) 156
St. Mary of Magdala Chapel (Harwich Port) 225, 300
St. Mary's Parish (Brisbane) 157–158
St. Matthew's ECC Parish (Orange, CA) 256
St. Nicholas's Parish (Evanston, IL) 5
Stone, J 96
St. Patrick's Cathedral (New York) 92
St. Paul 300
St. Peter 11, 53
St. Peter's Parish (Cleveland) 194–195
St. Philip's Episcopal Church (Indianapolis) 229
Stroud, Valerie 114
structural reform 2, 3, 51, 77, 80, 281
St. Sebastian's (Baltimore) 296
St. Stanislaus Kostka Parish (St. Louis) 160–163, 165, 196, 278–279, 292
St. Stephen's Parish (Minneapolis) 157
St. Theresa of Avila 137

Survivors' Network of those Abused by
    Priests 26, 83, 139
Sweatt, Michael 74
Swett, Marty 209–210
Szaniszlo, M. 154

Tamberg, Tod 178
Taylor, A 121, 262
Taylor, Kenneth (Father) 228
Teresa, Mother 111, 137
Tertullian 206
The Bingo Report (Haggett) 169
The Church that Forgot Christ (Breslin) 103
theological conservatism 30, 90
theological liberalism 30
The Sound of Music (musical) 236
The Story of a Priest, Nun, and Their Son 85
The Story of Dorothy Day (play) 49
The Tablet (British journal)
The Underground Church
    (Kautzer) ix, 30–31
Thiessen, Victor 17
Thompson, Bill 42–44
Tilley, Terrence 49–50
Time Magazine 49
Tobin, Joseph (Archbishop) 182–183
Tolfree, David 79
Townsend, T. 162
Troeltsch, Ernest ix, 14, 202
Transubstantiation 203
Trounson, R. 74
Turner, Victor 18–20, 130, 281–282,
    288–289, 290
tyranny of structurelessness 18–19

Underground Church (Kautzer)
    (title) 29–30
underground church (term) 202
underground parish 223, 225–267, 263, 280
underground worship communities 2, 7,
    30, 34, 90, 159, 172, 202–267, 280, 287, 289
Unitarian 115, 167
United Church of Christ (UCC) 234
United Nations 127, 129, 267
United Nations Conference on
    Women 129
United States Conference of Catholic
    Bishops (USCCB) 35, 70, 76, 117, 138, 153,
    173, 177, 182, 212, 247, 274
    audit of child abuse policies 5
    Conference (1976) 6, 41–44, 82, 177
    finance policies 79
    Office of Child and Youth Protection 47
    Social Ministry Gathering 50

United States Constitution 256
United States Presidential Election 8
University of Creation Spirituality 208
USA Today 165

Van Biema, David 2, 49, 73,
Vandenberg, Kathy (RCWP) 242
Vasa, Robert (Bishop) 163–164
Vatican 77, 81, 87, 90, 92, 96, 97, 125,
    128 –129, 132, 134, 138, 144, 162, 166,
    167, 169, 176, 179, 181–184, 197, 206,
    213, 265, 301
    allegations of violence 26–29
    fundamentalist-leaning theology 15
    invincibility of 3–5, 136
    policies on resignation of
        bishops 68–69
    resistance to Vatican II
    response to reform movement 1, 47, 51,
        53, 89, 118, 193
Vatican appeals process 275
Vatican Congregation for the Clergy 194
Vatican Council I 254
Vatican Council II ix, 81, 141, 162, 166, 167,
    244, 247, 267, 270, 271, 275, 278, 299, 301,
    303–304
    influence on reform movement xi, 2, 7,
        42, 99, 107
    response of conservative papacies ix, 16
    resurrection of 1
Vatican Council II bishops 151, 247
Vatican Council II Catholics xv, 54, 140,
    248, 283
Vatican Council II documents 10–11, 269
Vatican Council II liturgy 160
Vatican II parish 150, 159, 241, 244–246,
    280, 294
Vatican II priests 149–167
Vatican II reformers 1, 87, 89, 135, 138, 145
Vatican II reforms xii, 1
Vatican courts 184, 194, 297
Vatican decrees xv
Vatican Empire iii, ix, 304
Vatican investigation of religious
    sisters 26, 196
Vatican Rota 135
Vatican Supreme Court 189
Vatican Synod on the Eucharist ('05) 12
Vatican Synod on the Word ('08) 143
Veling, Terry 25, 288, 292
Vennochi, Joan 153
Via, Jane (RCWP) 263
vigiling parishes 34, 36, 184–196, 229, 275,
    277, 280

INDEX

Villanova University study ('06) 65, 79
violence (definition) 27
Violence, Society and the Church
 (Arbuckle) 27
Virgil's Aeneas 140
Viser, M. 149
Vladimiroff, Christine (Sister) 118
Voice of the Faithful xv, xvii, 12, 51–52,
 55–83, 86, 91, 130, 135, 139, 149, 175, 179,
 193, 239, 273, 278
 achievements 65, 76–81
 calls for resignations 68, 69–70
 centrist policies 7, 29, 33, 61, 136
 comparison to CTA 81–82
 conferences 59, 61, 63–64
 conservative attacks 30
 criticisms of 66–67
 decline of 74–76
 demographics 7–10,
 media relations 78–79, 275
 membership 32–33
 mission statement 58
Voices of the Faithful
 (D'Antonio & Pogorelc) 12, 66
Voices in the Wilderness 45
Voices of the Ordained 70
Von Lehman, Jeffrey D 203
Von Stamwitz, G. 285
Von Trapp, Maria & Werner 236
VOTF Boston-area conference ('02) 64
VOTF Boston College Forum ('05) 66–67
VOTF Convention ('02) 59–61
VOTF Fordham University
 Conference ('03) 64
VOTF New York Chapter 69
VOTF Winchester, MA Chapter 177
Vows (P. Manseau) 85

Wangsness, L. 194
Washburn, M. 234
Washington Theological Union 123
Watanabe, T. 151
We are Church 60, 297
Weber, Max 14
 concept of *disenchantment* 21
 rationalization of religion 21
 transition from *other worldly to this
  worldly* goals, 21
Weber-Troeltsch church-sect typology 14,
 17–19, 170, 202–203, 281–285, 290
 as measure of precariousness 17, 19
Webster, Gordon (Reverend) 250

Weigel, George 61
Weisenbeck, Marlene (Sister) 182
Weiss, Robert (Reverend) 242
Welch, B. 94
Wellstone, Paul (Senator) 284
Weston Congregational Church 226
Weston School of Theology 115
Wilbur, Ken 294
Wilkes, Paul 78
Wills, Gary 53
Winchester VOTF Chapter 177
Wink, Walter 25
Winter, Lummis & Stokes 115–116
Winter, Miriam Therese 45, 204–207, 219,
 276, 277
witch hunts 28
Wittenauer, Cheryl 161
Women-Church Convergence xvii,
 30, 86, 88, 112, 121–123, 135, 136, 144,
 201, 216, 217
WomenEucharist (Dierks) 201
WomenEucharist communities 207,
 216–219, 288
Women in the Word Campaign 143–144
Women's Alliance for Theology, Ethics and
 Ritual xvii, 86, 112, 123, 144
women's ordination 87, 102, 116, 121, 123,
 245, 271
Women's Ordination Conference xvii, 7
 33, 42, 86, 101, 112, 116–118, 122, 123, 130,
 133, 136, 142, 144, 201, 264
Women's Ordination Worldwide xvii, 86,
 93, 112, 118–121
Wooden, C. 99
Worcester, Massachusetts diocese 156
World Day of Prayer for Women's
 Ordination 118, 121, 142,
Worship communities of Catholic
 sisters 179–183
Wuerl, Donald (Cardinal) 132
Wuthnow, Robert 8, 22, 207, 303

Xerox 253

young Catholics 2, 42, 44, 81
Young, J. 159

Zagano, Phyllis 137, 183
Zaiger, A.S 161.
Zald, Mayer N. 23
Zogby poof U.S. Catholics ('10) 69
Zogby poll of U.S. Catholics ('05) 72

www.ingramcontent.com/pod-product-compliance
Lightning Source LLC
Chambersburg PA
CBHW071147070526
44584CB00019B/2689